the ultimate
HOME DESIGN
sourcebook

the ultimate HOME DESIGN sourcebook

ANOOP PARIKH, DEBORA ROBERTSON, THOMAS LANE, ELIZABETH HILLIARD, MELANIE PAINE

conran
OCTOPUS

First published as THE CONRAN OCTOPUS DECORATING BOOK in 1996
By Conran Octopus Limited
a part of Octopus Publishing Group
2–4 Heron Quays, London E14 4JP

Reprinted 1998 (twice) 2000

COMMISSIONING EDITOR Denny Hemming
SENIOR EDITOR Catriona Woodburn
ART EDITOR Tony Seddon
PICTURE RESEARCHER Rachel Davies
PRODUCTION CONTROLLER Mano Mylvaganam
COPY EDITORS Sarah Sears, Margot Richardson, Sally Harding,
     Jackie Matthews, Alison Bolus
PROOF READER Annie Lee
INDEXER Hilary Bird
DESIGNERS Isabel de Cordova, Amanda Lerwill
ARTWORK VISUALIZER Jean Morley
ILLUSTRATOR Clare Melinsky

PUBLISHER'S ACKNOWLEDGEMENTS
The publisher would like to thank the following for their invaluable assistance with
this book: Tessa Clayton, Lesley Craig, Helen Dore, Mollie Gillard, Helen Green,
Clare Hill, Karen Howes, Lesley Levene, Felicity Quant

British Library Cataloguing in Publication Data.
A catalogue record for this book is available from the British Library.

ISBN 1 84091 157 3

Colour separation by Chroma Graphics Singapore
Printed and bound in Spain by Bookprint, S.L, Barcelona

CONTENTS

▽

FLOORS
122–195

WINDOWS & DOORS
196–269

FURNITURE & FURNISHINGS
270–339

DESIGN &
DETAILING

The greatest thing about decorating your own home is that it allows you to say 'I made that' or 'I did it myself'. In an age when so much daily activity seems pre-programmed or conducted via a computer keyboard without regard to physical distances or borders, there is something inherently precious about this. From the moment when you hit on an idea, through the stages of planning out your changes, gathering tools and materials, preparing the ground, doing the job and finally standing back to admire your handiwork, decorating requires you to make the decisions, be they budgetary, aesthetic or just plain practical. The essence of its appeal is that it allows you to take control.

As we all know, however, being decisive is not always easy. In decorating, as in life, issues can become confused by the sheer range of options that seems to be available, fear of what the neighbours might think and a lack of confidence in your own abilities. It often seems easier to put a room together by

buying bits and pieces in a piecemeal and rather half-hearted fashion or to opt for the safest, most familiar solutions. Unfortunately, the former approach can make a room seem unpleasantly 'bitty', and the latter all too often results in bland and depressing spaces, devoid of any sign that they might be lived in by real people.

Creating a home with personality, therefore, begins with the question: 'What do I really want?' You will find this easier to answer if you look closely at rooms that appeal in some way and identify those aspects or details that you like most. It might be the way the colour of the furniture contrasts with that of the walls or something as minor as a cute curtain trim. Try also to describe the atmosphere in these rooms. Is it lively or serene? Airy or claustrophobic? Does the decor make you feel calm or jumpy? Identifying the qualities that appeal, as well as those that repel, enables you to focus on how you would like your home to look and feel.

You do not have to limit yourself to looking at other houses for ideas. It may be that a place that features in childhood memories, a favourite item of clothing or a holiday postcard are equally evocative. Whatever they happen to be, the next step is to collect all your sources together. Spread them out on a flat surface or paste them onto a board and see whether some kind of story begins to emerge. It may be that the colours in front of you form a kind of family or that similar styles of furniture appear in several of the photographs.

These themes provide the perfect starting point, as they can be used as reference material to suggest paint colours, for example, or to guide your choice of furnishings. Use them as a springboard for ideas. A preponderance of coarse, natural textures, for example, might suggest slubby linen and hessian for upholstery and window treatments. You will probably reject some of these ideas further down the line and modify others to suit your budget or as a compromise with loved ones, but no matter. The important thing is that you are no longer stuck at square one.

You will probably also notice that your tastes are more eclectic than you thought. Modern furnishings put in a guest appearance alongside your favourite traditional interiors, or vice versa, and some elements are there just for fun. These should not be discarded when it comes to turning inspiration into reality, quite the opposite, in fact. The most stylish and welcoming interiors are always those which contain intriguing contrasts or one or two surprises.

This chapter aims to provide you with all the information you need to put a basic decorative scheme together. It begins by looking at colour, texture and pattern – the basic building blocks of any decorative scheme – and explains how to interpret a decorative style so that it fits comfortably into your surroundings. The chapter then goes on to tell you everything you need to know about working with architectural detail, lighting and storage – the three elements of a scheme that pretty much determine how a room is both used and enjoyed.

◄◄ *Simple decor and furnishings allow distinctive architectural character to shine through. Here, attention is drawn towards the beamed ceiling and double-sided fireplace by picking them out in a contrasting colour, while the seating blends with the pale floor and walls.*

◄ *Small rooms benefit just as much as their larger equivalents from a bold and consistent decorative approach. Areas of strong colour and pattern give this compact bedroom instant character, but it is important that relative proportions are finely judged, so that no one element of the scheme overwhelms the others.*

Colour, pattern and texture

Colour and, to a lesser extent, pattern and
texture elicit powerful and sometimes
unpredictable responses in each of us. When we
flick through a paint chart or gather swatches of
fabric, spiritual traditions, gender conditioning,
fashion and much else come into play. And you
can be sure that no two people will describe a
colour's qualities or create a co-ordinated set of
patterns in exactly the same way.

Colour in particular is so much a part of our lives that we often take it for granted – until such time as we are deprived of it. Not so long ago, visitors to the former Soviet Union invariably remarked on how colourless the cities there seemed, thanks to the absence of any street advertising. And in the earth's deserts and at its ice caps it is not just the extremes of temperature which inspire awe but also the seemingly monochrome barrenness of those landscapes.

There is no doubt that using colour and ornament is a basic form of creative self-expression. Even those cultures with the most limited resources manage to find ways of decorating their surroundings and possessions, and they do it in ways that are often exuberant and joyful. Yet in the developed world today only children seem to enjoy colour and pattern for their own sakes. As we grow older we become self-conscious about using them, perhaps out of fear of ridicule or in conforming to the outdated and inaccurate notion that modern means white and plain.

Although it is not always easy to ignore all those so-called rules for using colour and pattern, such as blue always being chilly and mixing no more than three patterns in one room, do try. Be guided by your likes and dislikes, and think about how you and others will be using the room. If it is to be used for relaxing in, and as a foil for your favourite objects, a harmonious colour scheme and a relatively plain backdrop are probably in order. On the other hand, a room that is likely to bustle with activity all day, such as a family kitchen, needs to be bright and welcoming, but not so full of decorative distractions that it becomes tiring.

Take note also of the room's position relative to the sun. Rooms that receive sunlight for long periods have a tendency to overheat in the warmer months, so you may want to include a touch of cool colour, such as a minty green or ultramarine blue, in your scheme. Those rooms that get very little natural light will need brightening up; white is the most commonly used colour, but pale grey-blues and greens work just as well. And don't forget you have other weapons in your dec-

orative armoury; a cheerful rug and strategically placed mirrors will also help to brighten a dingy room.

There is no mystery to mixing colours, patterns and textures in a decorative scheme; it is all about creating contrasts of scale and proportion. Most co-ordinated fabric and wallpaper ranges are based on mixing large-scale patterns with small all-over motifs and plain colours, and these work best when one design plays the starring role and the rest are used in smaller quantities. The same applies when creating colour combinations. While a small amount of contrasting colour can liven up a scheme, living with large areas of competing colour soon becomes uncomfortable.

◀◀ A seemingly simple and uninspiring-sounding arrangement of brown objects against a yellow wall looks anything but dull when it includes pleasing textural contrasts, such as that of the old wood cabinet against the smooth wall, and whimsical found objects that introduce a touch of pattern.

◀ Shiny materials, such as stainless steel, not only contrast well with rough textures, such as stone and brick; they also take on and reflect the colours of objects nearby. This is a useful way of softening the cold and hard character of metallic surfaces. It also makes a small amount of intense colour go further.

In general, decorative schemes that are composed of different tones of the same colour are the most harmonious and calming, while room schemes that contain contrasting colours tend to be livelier. If you bear this in mind, there is absolutely no reason at all why a room filled with both pattern and texture shouldn't be relaxing and easy to live with, or why a room containing just a few carefully chosen objects shouldn't be lively and inspiring. The secret is to experiment and not to be afraid to change your mind as you go along. You may not get exactly the effect you want immediately, but decorating would be no fun if it wasn't a little bit unpredictable.

Talking about colour

While our perception of colours is entirely subjective, it is useful to have some idea of how colours behave with one another, both in theory and in practice, and to know how to describe their qualities or characters. This makes life easier whether you plan to mix colours yourself or to order special paints to match a favourite object or fabric.

Colour spectrum

Modern colour theory is based on the spectrum – the series of colours that we see when white light passes through a prism or when sunlight passes through airborne droplets of water to create a rainbow. Although each colour blends almost imperceptibly into its neighbour, for convenience we tend to depict the spectrum as six distinct bands of colour: namely red, orange, yellow, green, blue and violet.

The ends of the spectrum can be brought round to form a circle, to create what is known as a colour wheel. This shows the relationship of each colour to the others more clearly, and it becomes easier to see that there are three pure or primary colours, blue, red and yellow, and three secondary colours, green, orange and violet, each created by mixing two primary colours. Mixing equal parts of a primary colour with an adjacent secondary colour gives rise to a tertiary colour: green and yellow, for example, produce lime green, blue and green create turquoise, while violet and red make a bluish red known as crimson.

Descriptive terms

Colours that stand opposite each other on the wheel, and which are therefore as unlike one another as possible, are known as complementary colours. They create the strongest contrasts, and therefore the liveliest colour schemes. Adjacent colours, particularly those that sit between two primary colours, for example turquoise, blue and green, are harmonious, as the eye can travel easily from one to another. Strong, pure colours may be described as saturated. And a colour that is said to have been 'knocked back' or 'dirtied' has had its intensity deliberately weakened. This is a device often employed by professional designers to add a touch of drab colour to a bright or pastel scheme to make the main colours seem even fresher in comparison.

The qualities that we most often ascribe to colours are warmth and coolness. The warm colours – reds, yellows and oranges – seem to come towards you, and this is what makes rooms decorated in these colours seem cosy and welcoming. They also seem to make a room look smaller. In contrast, cool colours – violets, blues, greens and black – seem to recede and appear to create a sense of space. As with everything there are plenty of exceptions, however. The colour of faded denim, for example, is a ubiquitous and much-loved warm blue, while nature provides more such examples in cornflowers and forget-me-nots. Red – supposedly the hottest colour of all – is anything but when it appears as a sugary pink or in crimson pigment.

Tone

A colour's tone describes its darkness or light-ness. Darker tones – also known as shades – are created by adding black to a saturated colour, while light tones – sometimes called tints – are created by adding white. Two of the easiest ways to create a harmonious scheme are to put together colours that are similar in tone or to combine several tones of a single colour.

A colour scheme based on combining more than one tone of a single hue is often called monochromatic, and when it is based on a neutral colour, such as beige, the shades blend to create a muted and subtle backdrop. Sometimes, though, the different tones vary so much that it is hard to believe they are all derived from one colour. An example would be a scheme based on an orangy red, which might deepen to chocolate brown and lighten to a rosy pink.

Contrasting colour

We tend to think of single-colour schemes as being the easiest to live with but they can look flat and uninspiring until small amounts of subtly contrasting colour are added. Living with strongly coloured surroundings is easier than you might think. Painting one wall of a room in a deeper colour creates an instant focal point and if the colour is a warm red or a yellow it will provide a wonderful backdrop for wooden furniture.

A designer I know paints each wall of a room with a different colour; one might be inky blue, another terracotta, the third oxblood, and so on. The scheme works because all the shades have a similar tonal value and are more or less as strong as each other. Instead of being knocked out by ▷

◀ *When using more than one strong colour in a room, give each one the same amount of space. Alternatively, use colours of similar intensity. It is worth remembering that when light bounces off a wall, it transfers the colour of that wall to objects nearby. This is easy to see when deep or saturated shades are used, as here.*

▲ *In a nineteenth-century Parisian apartment, details such as door panels and skirtings have been played down by the blanket application of deep colours, in order to focus attention on the custom-designed furniture and the plaster ceiling decoration. This is a good quick fix when walls and woodwork are in less than perfect condition.*

This all sounds rather academic, but is useful to bear in mind when you are working around an existing feature in a nondescript colour, such as a fireplace or carpet. A dull, reddish-brown carpet, for example, will spring into life if it is teamed with walls painted in aquamarine, an intriguing colour that hovers between blue and green, and perhaps one or two accessories in a yellowy green such as lime.

Acquiring colour sense

Hardly anyone is born with great colour sense so when it comes to choosing colours it is natural to hesitate. As an understanding of how colour works is gained only through familiarity and practice, there is nothing wrong with settling for a neutral background at first then adding colour to it by degrees. You might, for example, begin with off-white walls and wooden furniture, then add some decorative interest in the form of colourful pictures and add more colour, if you feel that the room needs it, in the form of cushions and displays. Try to create specific areas of interest, which will give coherence and greater impact to displays, rather than just scattering objects at random around a room.

Colour and light

Unless you only ever use a room at night, it is a good idea to check that your colour scheme works in both natural and artificial light. As daylight in a room is usually directional, it highlights those objects nearest the window, leaving the rest in progressively deeper shadow as you move away from the window. If the room is not too deep and contains only one window, the wall facing it will be brighter than the side and window walls. At night, however, the room is likely to be more evenly lit, with several light sources ensuring that all the surfaces, and hence the colours and textures, are seen more clearly.

You may have noticed that colours change in artificial light. Halogen and low-voltage halogen bulbs emit a bright white light, which renders colours more true, while common household or incandescent bulbs

the colour when you enter the room, you feel welcomed and cosseted. Because your eyes are not constantly straining to distinguish between lighter and darker shades, the overall feeling is relaxed.

That is not to say that strong tonal contrasts are a bad thing. The classic black-and-white tiled floor laid in a chequerboard pattern gives hallways, and any other area where you don't spend much time, a graphic and efficient appeal. When one of the colours predominates, however, the result is more subdued and easier on the eye, without being any less smart or crisp.

Mixing lighter and darker tones also helps to balance complementary colours, such as orange and blue. You might, for example, place bright orange glass vases on a pale blue shelf or window sill.

Subtler contrasts can be created by putting together a split-complementary scheme. Here, a colour is teamed with those that sit on either side of its complementary colour on the colour wheel. Orange, for example, may be combined with green and violet – the shades that are found on either side of blue – or with turquoise and violet blue, which are more closely related to blue.

◀ An apartment's industrial origins are revealed by picking out structural elements such as the steel beams in scarlet and black. Later additions to the space, such as the kitchen, are made to blend in by painting them in similarly strong shades. The pressed metal ceiling panels help tu direct the light downwards.

emit a yellowish light, which makes most colours warmer. The latter isn't always the blessing it seems, as pale yellows tend to disappear, terracotta becomes orange, and reddish-purples turn brown. But there is something reassuring about the familiar glow. It is worth remembering that a coloured lampshade will also tint the light shining through it.

The texture of a surface also affects how we see a colour. In general, matt or rough surfaces, which absorb light, look darker than glossy or shiny ones, which reflect it. It is especially important to bear this in mind when choosing fabrics, as there is a great deal of difference between how a colour will appear say, on brushed cotton and on silk satin. Extremely shiny surfaces, such as those made from chrome, seem to have no colour of their own, as they reflect those around them. Even the texture of a paint finish affects the colours we see. Many of the latest natural paints are formulated without light-reflecting plastics, which has the effect of making the colours appear softer and chalkier than those of synthetic paint finishes.

▲ The colour and surface variation found in natural building materials may be all the 'decoration' you need. However, it is important to get the details right. The planking used on the floor and ceiling runs in the same direction, and at right angles to that used on the walls and the floor in the hall, so that each area remains clearly defined.

Choosing and using pattern

Pattern can be bought off the shelf as fabric or wallpaper or it may be created when a decorative element is repeated several times, as in the slats of a blind, or a row of candlesticks on a mantelpiece. It can be something that you apply by hand, by using a stencil or a simple printing block perhaps. Our nineteenth-century forebears loved pattern and layered it over every available surface but few of us today would feel comfortable with such an approach. Instead, we tend to use it as a focal point, in the form of a row of pictures perhaps or as the decorative equivalent of cake icing, to make a plain interior feel more homely and special.

Scale

However you choose to use pattern, the most important factors to consider are scale and colour. Large-scale patterns are like warm colours (see pages 14–15) in that they appear to come towards you. They create a lively and stimulating atmosphere and they can make a large space seem cosier. In small spaces, however, they need to be handled with care. Unless they are used as a focal point, in the form of a rug perhaps, they can easily swamp a scheme and make walls and other surfaces appear to close in.

Like cool colours (see pages 14–15), small-scale patterns appear to recede, making small spaces seem bigger. They can be used as an effective form of camouflage – awkward angles and corners will be played down if you use a subtle, non-directional wallpaper pattern. Unfortunately, small-scale patterns applied over a large area can be bland, unless vibrant colours are used, and when viewed from a distance they may 'read' as a single colour and so blur into insignificance.

For this reason, it is often a good idea to match the scale of the pattern to that of the area over which it is to be used. A large sofa will obviously display a grandiloquently patterned damask better than would a simple dining chair with an upholstered seat. Similarly, a small spriggy stencil looks charming when used to define the edges of a tabletop, but would simply look lost on an expanse of wall or ceiling. This is a far from hard and fast rule, however, and sometimes

a small-scale pattern is used as a backdrop instead of a plain colour. Patchwork effects are actually enriched by the use of both large- and small-scale pattern fragments.

When you are applying pattern to a three-dimensional object, such as a table or a sofa, consider using designs that enhance the form in some way. A boxy chair, for example, can be made to look even more rectilinear by covering it in a geometric pattern or it can be softened by using a rambling floral. Creating a sense of balance and symmetry also matters. When using a boldly patterned fabric to cover a sofa or chair, make sure that you have enough material to centre the design on the chair back and seat. If the pattern has a clear direction, such as a stripe, it

should also follow through over the back, seat and front, and the arms should mirror one another as far as possible.

Mixing pattern

As you gain confidence in your own tastes, try experimenting with simple pattern mixes. Many types of geometric pattern have a natural affinity for one another. Stripes, for example, look good not only with checks but also with spots and stars. Mixing geometric and non-geometric designs also works well. A traditional *toile de Jouy* pattern, for example, looks more modern when teamed with a check or stripe in a toning colourway.

Mixing patterns is easier when they have one or more colour in common and there are contrasts or harmonies of scale and

design. Thus a leafy print might be mixed with a check that picks up a colour in the motif, or the zig-zag pattern of a tribal fabric could be echoed by a subtle patterned weave.

Mixing patterns becomes even more satisfying when you include your own designs. This is not as difficult as it sounds. You could, for example, use patterned wallpaper below a dado rail and paint a stripe that is based on one or two of the colours in the paper above. Or you could create a simple co-ordinating stencil by tracing a suitable motif from a print that you plan to use in the same room. An image can be turned into a pattern by experimenting with a photocopier (see pages 98–99). In time, it will no doubt be possible to create customized and highly sophisticated patterns using computer-aided design.

▲▲ *A scheme based on a single colour is far from monotonous when it includes touches of pattern in harmonious shades. In this living room, patterned soft furnishings and accessories in cool reds provide visual relief from the expanses of warm pink, yet remain in keeping with the room's cosy and feminine character.*

▲ *A paper frieze of Matisse-inspired figures and a chequered tile floor add the personal touch to a functional kitchen. At first sight the frieze appears to consist of random flowing shapes, but it is in fact made up of repeated panels for easy application. Space has been left around the frieze to make it easier to see.*

Surface effects and textures

▶ *The highlights and shadows on partitions made from woven metal strips are an intriguing source of pattern, and complement the graphic use of wood and colour in the room that they enclose. A space divider such as this would have to be custom-built, but it has the advantage of taking up less floor space than a conventional wall.*

Textures do not always register as strongly as colours and patterns do. A red sofa or a green wall, for example, are just what they appear to be to most people until they look more closely and see that in fact the sofa is velvet or the wall has been distempered. Nevertheless, textures play a central role in any decorative scheme. If you visualize the walls of a room painted in a flat colour, for instance, then imagine them treated with a paint effect based on the same colours, you will 'see' the difference. Certain textures also give greater depth to patterns. A print that looks crisply detailed on smooth cotton will be softly blurred on nubbly chenille.

Smooth and coarse textures

As with colour and pattern, it is convenient for the purpose of definition to divide textures into two camps. The first consists of shiny or smooth surfaces and includes many metals, glass, gloss paint and silky fabrics. These reflect light and can, therefore, be used to brighten a room or make it seem larger. Like warm colours and bold patterns, they also stimulate the senses, which makes them a useful addition to work spaces and other activity areas. However, a room with too many shiny surfaces can be chilly and will work on your nerves after a while.

In contrast, coarse textures such as natural floor-coverings, hessian, rough-hewn wood and wool tweed absorb light so they seem duller, but with more subtle variations in colour. Natural materials also have the advantage of ageing better than synthetics. Rough or soft textures create a feeling of intimacy and absorb sound, which makes them perfect for living spaces and bedrooms. The tactile pleasure they provide can more than make up for any absence of colour or pattern. Too much softness, however, in the form of fussy curtains or soft furnishings perhaps, can make a room seem overdecorated and stifling.

A material's texture also suggests its suitability for a particular purpose or environment. For example, smooth, polished wood and laminates are usually chosen for kitchen work surfaces, because they are considered to be easy to clean. Damasks, however, are usually reserved for formal or grand rooms, partly because they look expensive and delicate but also because they catch the light in interesting ways and so lend sparkle to rooms that are mainly used in the evenings.

Decorative use

Using texture as a decorative tool is all about creating pleasing contrasts. For example, the spartan feel of a featureless room can be tempered by hanging curtains that fall into deep folds by the windows. Or an expanse of polished wood floor could be broken up with rag rugs or dhurries. An eclectic

approach to furnishing also helps. You might mix a cotton-covered sofa with wooden chairs upholstered with criss-cross webbing or place battered leather chairs around a pristine glass table.

Textural mixes can be theatrical as well as subtle and nowhere is this easier, or more appropriate, than at the dining table. Rather than setting smooth porcelain and glass directly onto the table, try placing them on folksy, crocheted mats. Or mix rustic earthenware with a psychedelic fabric print. As well as creating a sense of occasion, this approach allows you to experiment with decorative effects without having to commit yourself to living with the results for any length of time.

Ringing the changes

It makes a great deal of sense to be able to change the look of a room to suit your mood or the occasion, not least because most rooms need to serve more than one purpose. It is also pleasing to be able to reflect the changing seasons. Few of us have the means to

◀ Naturally-striped beech veneer creates a pleasingly irregular pattern on the fronts of fitted kitchen cupboards and on the sides of the breakfast bar. The asymmetric vertical stripes help to soften the overall geometric feel of the kitchen by providing a contrast to the grid-like patterns of the slate-tiled floor and bottle rack.

◀◀ A feeling of opulence is conveyed by basing the scheme on a patinated oak herringbone parquet floor. Its colour is echoed in the walls and mouldings, which have been painted with layers of tinted glaze. The walls and floor are able to play a more important role as distracting clutter has been kept to a minimum.

completely redo a room at whim but well chosen finishing touches, such as armfuls of fresh flowers or adding a new accent colour in the form of accessories or soft furnishings, can make a surprisingly large difference.

Ringing the changes will be even easier if some of the latest developments in textile technology become more widely available. Fabrics that change colour with temperature already exist, so, in theory, it should become possible to buy fabric that changes from a warm colour in winter to a cooling tint during the summer months.

Some textiles can even be used as building materials. Tensile roofing structures made from glass-fibre cloth keep the wind and rain out as effectively as a conventionally built roof, but they let in light and can be rolled back at the touch of a button. Such innovations are currently found mainly on top of

large buildings, such as sports stadia and factories, but are beginning to be used on a smaller scale.

Perhaps more importantly, textile designers are creating useful, and in some cases highly sophisticated, materials from rubbish. In Britain, PET plastic soft drink bottles and other household containers are now recycled on a commercial basis to make a strong and colourful sheet material that can be used in much the same way as man-made boards; while a Japanese company has developed yarns with quick-drying and solar heat converting properties, with obvious implications for energy consumption in the home.

No one can be sure when developments such as these will become widely available but certainly the potential uses of contemporary textiles in interiors are limited only by our imagination.

Interpreting a style

▶ *A cool colour palette and simple yet punchy patterns are combined to create a particularly sophisticated country style. Loose covers and a layered window treatment provide softness and a sense of welcome in what might otherwise have been a rather austere room scheme, and the use of natural and washed-out greens as accent colours helps to refresh the eye without upsetting the calm and muted feel of the room.*

▶▶ *A sample board allows you to preview and make adjustments to a scheme before it is completed, so helping to avoid unnecessary heartache and expense.*

The whole point of decorating is to create more pleasant surroundings for yourself and your loved ones, perhaps even, and we could be talking heresy here, to have some fun. It is not about being slavishly faithful to a historical period or imitating a look in a photograph down to the last detail, both of which are impossible. Rather it is about gathering and interpreting information to suit your budget, your surroundings and, not least, your lifestyle.

The easiest way to do this is to take your colour scheme from a source of inspiration. For a period look, you may be able to locate the right paint shades in one of the many 'historical' ranges. Alternatively, look for colours that are evocative of the time:

in mid-eighteenth-century England, for example, subtle pastel colours were in vogue. Trying to match a colour to a magazine picture is rarely straightforward, as the way the room was lit to take the photograph greatly affects the colours shown. However, it can be done by laying paint samples next to details of a room.

Materials can be highly evocative of period or ethnic themes but it is often more appropriate to adapt an idea rather than copy it exactly. For example, if you love stone floors, but laying one in your apartment is not an option, try incorporating the material in the form of decorative accessories, or perhaps by choosing a soft flooring in a similarly neutral colour; alternatively you could

lay plywood squares and paint them in imitation of flagstones (see pages 144–145).

Careful choice of seemingly minor elements, such as light switches and door handles, will add character and period flavour, making the difference between a room that feels stylishly pulled together and one with a vaguely half-hearted feel.

Once you have a look that you like, you can use elements of it throughout your home. You might, for example, use colours with similar tonal values in each room or include a favourite material. This establishes connections between different parts of the house and gives you the chance to enjoy it as a whole rather than treating it as a set of unrelated boxes.

This is not to say that each room should look the same. Homes are divided into rooms beçause human beings have a need for both private and communal space and the demands we make on our surroundings vary according to whether we are alone or in company, even according to the time of day or year. That some rooms will get more sun than others, for instance, must be taken into account. Your decorative vocabulary also needs to be able to express changes in mood as you move through your home and reflect the fact that each space has different uses.

Making a sample board

The first step towards converting a collection of samples and colour references into a three-dimensional room is to fix them onto a sufficiently large piece of paper or board, known as a sample board.

Think of it as a miniature version of the room and try to keep samples in proportion. If, for example, the colour of the flooring is to provide a neutral backdrop, try to get hold of a sample that is large enough to allow you to place fabric and paint swatches on top of it. If you plan to use a certain fabric for decorative piping only, place only a fragment next to the upholstery or cushion fabrics. Use the board to check that paint and fabric colours match, if that is what you intended.

Look at the assembled board in the room that you are planning to change over several days to get an idea of how the scheme will alter on sunny and overcast days as well as at night. Ask yourself whether you would be happy to wake up in such a room or to walk into it at the end of a long and tiring day. Look at the scheme as a whole and at individual contrasts of colour, pattern and texture, and use your reactions as a guide to where changes might need to be made.

Sample boards do not stop being useful once the room is decorated and furnished. Any stylistic references that you have collected may suggest ideas for finishing touches such as display arrangements. When you are decorating more than one room in the house, it is a good idea to look at all the sample boards together to see how and where themes can be carried through.

Architectural details

The term architectural detail encompasses
all the fixed features that you might
find in a building. In the home, this includes
decorative mouldings such as ceiling roses,
skirting boards, dado and picture rails, cornices
or their humbler cousins covings, fireplaces,
door and window architraves. Similarly,
stair balusters and hand rails can also be
termed as fixed architectural details.

Ornamental plasterwork

While wood has been fashioned into architectural details for centuries, the use of ornamental plasterwork is relatively recent. It first became common in the mid-eighteenth century, when it would have been moulded on site by craftsmen. Increased demand led to the development of mass-produced ornaments made from cast plaster, papier mâché, and even cast iron, and the patenting of fibrous plaster in the 1850s made it easier to produce large and complex designs in one piece. By the end of the nineteenth century plasterwork had come to be regarded as just another building trade and the end of the First World War marked the beginning of a long and gradual decline in its popularity.

Architectural mouldings

Anyone who lives in an old building where the original architectural details have been lost knows that they have a much greater impact than the word 'detail' implies. Their main practical purpose is to neaten the joins where two surfaces meet. Cornices and skirtings, for example, help to conceal the cracks and rough edges that invariably occur where walls respectively meet the ceiling and floor. In addition, they create a visual link or 'bridge' between the two surfaces, to make it easier for the eye to travel from one to another.

Mouldings also help to add a sense of scale, and improve proportions. Architraves make doors and windows, in particular, seem more imposing while dado and picture rails help to break up expanses of wall.

If you are lucky enough to live in a house or apartment that retains its original features, you only have to decide on a suitable decorative approach and the extent to which you wish to highlight them. In rooms where you are likely to notice a decorative ceiling, such as bedrooms and bathrooms, it can be fun to draw attention to mouldings by picking them out in a contrasting colour. This has the added advantage of making the ceiling seem lower. Elsewhere you may want to blend them into the background, so that the effect is that of a relief pattern.

Restoration

Replacing broken or missing details is a straightforward matter, unless you plan to install a fire surround. If you are starting from scratch, there are plenty of books that will tell you which styles are appropriate to the age and scale of your home.

Reproduction mouldings, which are available in a wide range of styles and materials, are easy to install. Those made from synthetic

▲ An open staircase creates a dramatic focal point in any hall or circulation area, and as it is partly transparent, it can help to make a small space seem bigger. It should, however, be good to look at from every angle, so it is not necessarily the cheapest option, and any items stored under the stairs will need to be attractively organized.

◄ You don't have to live in a castle or château to indulge a taste for panelled walls: a relief grid pattern made from timber strips looks good in any moderately high-ceilinged room. Painting them the same colour as the walls, as in this instance, allows attention to be focused on both the fireplace and the furnishings.

materials, such as polythene, are virtually indistinguishable from the real thing once they are fixed and painted, but do check that they exactly match any existing mouldings in profile and scale. If the range at your local store looks a bit basic, you can combine simple mouldings and rails to imitate grander effects. A skirting board, for example, can be made deeper by topping it with a profiled moulding. Alternatively, it may be possible to cast replacements from broken examples or from items that have survived in the home of a friendly neighbour.

Modern style

In modern buildings, that is anything built after the 1920s, architectural details need to be added with great sensitivity. Houses in a self-consciously modern style were designed to be free of mouldings and ornament, because this was thought to reduce the places where dirt could collect, and it is perhaps best to keep them that way.

However, such single-mindedness seems inappropriate for a modern house that apes traditional building styles, or one with a smattering of 'period' features. In such cases, perhaps the safest option is to forget historical accuracy, and only add ornament where it serves a practical purpose. You might make a narrow room seem wider by dividing the walls with dado and picture rails, or install a fireplace in a room to provide a focal point. If the fireplace works, and you can comfortably arrange seating around it, it is much less likely to look out of place. Similarly, hanging paintings from the picture rail will make it look like a planned decision rather than an afterthought.

Whatever the age or style of your home, it is vital to use details that correspond in scale. Their size should reflect the height of the room, or the ceiling area in the case of roses and cornicing. It can be fun to exaggerate their proportions slightly when creating a themed or theatrical scheme. For example, you might widen the door and window architraves in a modern house so that they 'go' better with period furnishings, but they should not be so large that they become visually distracting.

Cornices and covings

Cornices and covings are fixed at the point where the walls meet the ceiling. A cornice is a projecting ornamental moulding while a coving is a plain moulding with a concave profile. Both are manufactured as long lengths that can be cut to size. Fibrous plaster is the most popular material for these and other mouldings.

Like all plasterwork, they do not last for ever. In converted houses, sections were often hacked away to make space for partition walls; intricate cast detail can be submerged under layers of paint or chipped; and if your building has ever suffered from severe damp, the bond between the moulding and the wall may have come loose. However, they are easy to replace or repair (see pages 96–97). Walls and ceilings should be dry and free of dust before starting work, and wallpapers and any linings should be removed.

▲ Like any other work of art, an intricately patterned ceiling deserves to be properly framed. Here, the job is carried out by a cornice that echoes the stepped profile of the plasterwork. Cornicing is ideal for breaking up a large expanse of wall and most rooms will benefit from this prominence of detail.

▶ A coving with curved edges typically requires special casting in order that it matches the curvature of the walls. Creating a step between the straight and curved sections of the walls, as shown here, makes it a great deal easier to conceal imperfect joints. Notice that coving gives an unadorned ceiling and wall a sense of interest.

Architraves and ceiling roses

Architraves

The moulded or carved part of the frame surrounding a door or window opening is known as an architrave. As well as making the opening more imposing, it serves to hide the join between the structural part of the frame and the walls. It can be made from profiled softwood, man-made boards such as medium-density fibreboard (MDF) or fibrous plaster.

Most modern architraves are relatively plain, although historical designs are also available. To draw attention to mouldings in good condition, or a fine example, try painting it in a colour that contrasts with, or complements, that of the door.

Ceiling roses

A ceiling rose is an ornamental motif, usually circular or oval in shape, with a pattern that radiates from the centre. It creates a focal point for the ceiling plane and acts as a suitably impressive foil for a pendant light fitting or chandelier hung from its centre. It can be fixed against a plain background or it can form the centrepiece of a richly patterned surface. A wide variety of sizes and patterns, ranging from Adam-style to late nineteenth-century stylized florals, can still be found.

Reproduction rose designs are manufactured from fibrous plaster, fibreglass, CFC-free resin and polythene with a resin core in a variety of sizes, commonly ranging from 15cm (6in) to 90cm (36in). Look out for casts with crisp details and neatly finished edges.

Ceiling roses are easy to install. If a light fitting is to be fixed in the centre of the rose, make sure there is a pre-formed hole for the flex or that it will be easy to create one.

▲ *A standard-sized door opening is given a touch of grandeur by fitting an architrave with a small pediment on top. Here, this consists of a plain inner moulding that has been cut to shape and painted to match the walls, surrounded by a more detailed design in a contrasting colour.*

▶ *Even where a ceiling rose no longer serves its original purpose, which was to draw attention to a chandelier, it is well worth retaining as a purely decorative feature. This is especially true of rooms where you spend any time seated or lying down, as the ceiling occupies a large part of your field of vision.*

Picture rails, dado rails and skirting boards

As they are commonly made from low grade softwoods, plastic or plaster, picture rails, dado rails and skirting boards are relatively cheap to buy, and can be found in a variety of patterns. To fit picture rails, dado rails and skirting, see pages 120–121.

Picture rails

Situated a short way from the top of the wall and immediately below a frieze, picture rails were originally used, as the name suggests, for hanging pictures. A groove or channel was formed along the top edge of the moulding to hold picture hooks securely; if this was made deep enough, it could also be used to display plates. Like dado rails (below), picture rails can make a large difference to the way we perceive space. By dividing the wall into smaller areas, they help to establish a visual rhythm which the eye reads as an improvement in the proportions of the room.

Dado rails

Dado rails are usually placed about one third of the way up the wall. Their original function was to prevent chair backs from being pushed up against the wall and damaging it. They were also used to signal the division between a hard-wearing finish or panelling used on the lower part of the wall, known as the dado, and the finer finish used on the upper part. Late eighteenth-century examples would have been decorated with neo-classical motifs made from gesso or carved wood, and those in grand Victorian hallways were sometimes made from ceramic tiles. Modern examples tend to be made from humbler materials, such as softwood, or are replaced by wallpaper borders.

Skirting boards

Although the line created by a skirting board is regularly broken by doorways and fireplaces or obscured by furniture, it nevertheless plays an important decorative role. It draws attention to the floor by framing it and when used in conjunction with a dado and a picture rail it can be used to create bands of colour and texture on the walls. Usually between 10cm (4in) and 30cm (12in) high, the taller examples are often fashioned from two or more mouldings joined together. Skirting boards are often absent in minimal or rustic interiors and are perhaps replaced by a band of painted colour or flawless plastering. Although architraves are not, strictly speaking, wall mouldings at all, because they are fixed to the outer rim of the door frame, it is usual for the architrave and skirting patterns to match, although the width of the architrave is slightly narrower.

▶ Mouldings in a room need not all be painted the same colour. Here, a white cornice helps to brighten up a dark background of teal green, while a gold painted picture rail provides a decorative theme and, like the coachlines painted onto the sides of expensive cars, conveys a sense of luxury.

Plaques, columns, corbels and friezes

lends itself well to being coloured or decorated. Traditionally, this took the form of gilding or painting, but it can also be tinted with pigments before casting. The latter is surprisingly easy to do yourself and worth considering as paint effects never achieve quite the same depth of colour.

Friezes

The band of decoration along the upper part of a wall and immediately below a cornice is known as a frieze. In recent years, this area seems to have been reserved for stencilling or embossed wallpapers, if it is decorated at all, but in the late eighteenth century it would have consisted of interlocking pieces of plasterwork covered in a mixture of classical patterns. The inaccessibility of the mouldings made them an obvious dust trap, so it is perhaps not surprising that they are no longer popular. But the idea is worth considering in boxy rooms, as a frieze would visually expand the ceiling and make the room seem bigger.

Plaster mouldings

Larger eighteenth- and nineteenth-century houses were often embellished with a variety of plaster ornaments, including plaques, columns and corbels. Plaques were placed like pictures on the wall, while columns and corbels provided support for arches, beams and cornices. (For fixing, see pages 96–97.) Plaster was also moulded, and later cast, into wall alcoves and emblems such as anthemions (a stylized honeysuckle leaf shape), lion heads, urns and acanthus leaves. Ornamental plaster has enjoyed something of a revival in recent years, thanks to its cool yet matt finish when left bare. This time around, however, castings play a purely decorative role. They may be hung on the wall, propped on a shelf or made into accessories such as vases, lamp bases, and picture frames. The material also

Staircases

▶ *While it is often desirable to make a feature out of a staircase, a bold decorative treatment is not always the answer, as it can seem out of character. Here, a limed wood effect and subtle distressing soften the appearance of a traditional wooden staircase, and echo the subtle pink tint of the surrounding walls.*

▼ *In a double height living space, a galleried walkway allows the full height of the walls to be used for storing books, and gives the seating area a more human and intimate scale. The perforated metal staircase is not set at an angle purely for dramatic effect – it also maximizes the amount of clear living space.*

A staircase is almost always the largest item of joinery or cast detail in a house and usually dominates the space in which it is contained. Yours may not have the sweeping curves of those found in the grandest houses but it is unlikely to be an eyesore either so it makes sense to play up its features. In older houses, these may well include ornately turned balusters (the upright posts that join the handrail to the beam that supports the outer edge of the stairs, known as a string) and newel posts (the thicker post found at each end of a run of stairs). These are mostly made of wood, so lend themselves well to painting and staining.

The stairs themselves are almost always made from cheap wood or concrete – they were seldom meant to be left on show. Wood treads and risers that are in good condition can be stained or decorated with painted patterns, but avoid polishing or covering them in gloss paint, as this makes them slippery and dangerous.

Carpet or matting is the most popular choice, as it dampens noise. Look out for densely woven materials with a short pile as these are less likely to permanently trap dirt and dust. Seagrass is perhaps the most suitable of the natural mattings currently available, while carpet aficionados should search out wool-nylon and polypropylene examples with a pile that runs in one direction, often known as twists, or corded textures. Cotton rugs have the advantage of being cheap and machine washable, but they do get rather squashed with time.

Hallways in modern buildings often consist of a double-height space in which the staircase makes an attractively sculptural shape, or it may simply be placed in a large living area. To prevent the staircase from overwhelming its surroundings, it is often made with materials that help to create a feeling of transparency, such as barely-there metal handrails, open-tread stairs and wire balustrading. Here too, however, safety is paramount. The stair treads should be covered in, or made from, a material with a suitable texture, such as perforated metal and rubber. And it should not be possible for children to slip through the balustrading.

Fireplaces

▲ *The ideal fireplace would look wonderful and serve a useful purpose, whatever the weather or time of year. This fine example approaches perfection by acting as a support for the staircase that runs immediately behind it and also by offering a variety of levels and surfaces on which to sit or display favourite possessions.*

Almost all fireplaces consist of a grate where the fuel is burnt, a surround, usually made from marble, stone or wood, and a hearth which protects the floor from ash.

The surround can do much to animate a room and provide a focal point but all too often a fireplace has a rather forlorn and unloved look. It may be too large or too small, or finished in an unsympathetic material. The grate may have been removed or boarded up. However, there may well be redeeming features. The fireplace may have a pleasing shape or finish, or an attractive detail hidden behind paint or boarding. A

fine wood or cast-iron surround can be cleaned and polished, while poor quality wood can be customized with paint effects or applied decoration. Cosmetic repairs, such as removing scratches in wood, are easy enough to do yourself, but larger repairs, such as replacing a broken section of a marble fireplace, should be left to experts.

An inappropriate fire surround can be replaced. The replacement must suit the scale of the room: in particular, make sure the distance between the ceiling and mantelpiece is neither too small nor too large. And bear the overall character of the room

in mind, as well as your property. If your budget won't stretch far enough for a ready-made surround, you could consider making one from MDF or lengths of architrave and moulding.

It may be that the surround is let down by the fire that sits inside it. Old gas and electric fires can usually be replaced with more up to date models but if you want to burn solid fuel again, it may be necessary to have the cavity and flue lining rebuilt. Missing or ugly grates are easy to replace.

If the entire fireplace is a total eyesore, the surrounding firebricks can be pulled out along with the surround, to create a deep recess, which is then lined with a heat-proof material such as bricks, slate or tiles, and the same material can be used for the hearth. The recess can then have a grate, stove, or perhaps a gas log-effect fire installed.

▲ *Fireplaces for small rooms are often delicately shrunken affairs. If this doesn't appeal, a custom-built surround with a chunkier outline may be the answer. This one is made from rough-hewn sections of tree trunk arranged in a way that evokes the order and symmetry of neo-classical architecture.*

Lighting

As lighting determines how you use your home and feel about it at night or when it is dull outside, it is difficult to overestimate its importance. The subject is sometimes made needlessly complex, with much bandying-about of technical terms such as lumens and kelvins, but fortunately it is easy to distinguish between good and bad lighting. Good lighting relaxes and warms you, blending into the background and leaving you free to enjoy spaces and the people within them. Bad lighting competes for your attention, making you jumpy and tense.

The right lighting can reveal space that was formerly hidden. It can make rooms look bigger and turn awkward or unused areas into intimate corners. It can enhance architectural details and decorative fixtures, reducing the need for additional furnishings and clutter. It can even alter colours and textures.

Lighting needs to be considered from the earliest stages of planning a room. In fact, the position of the major light sources should be determined at the same time as the furniture layout. A scale plan of the room and the main items of furniture is invaluable as it allows you to work out the best positions for built-in sources, such as recessed downlighters. And it suggests where you might safely and usefully locate plug-in fittings, such as reading lamps and floor-standing uplighters. As many rooms are multi-purpose, a key requirement of any lighting system is that it should be flexible.

Most lighting needs can be met by a mix of three different types of light. Ambient or background light, from uplighters or wall-washers perhaps, helps you to move around a room and creates a little extra brightness on dull days. Task lights, such as desk lamps, bump up the brightness level in those areas where you work, read or pursue hobbies. You may also need display lighting to draw attention to favourite objects. Light fittings that are more beautiful than useful, such as chandeliers and candelabra, are sometimes referred to as decorative lighting.

It also helps to vary the direction and intensity of light fittings. A desk lamp with a pivoting head, for example, can be used as a small uplighter or wall-washer when it is not required for task lighting. Dimmer switches are ideal for changing the mood of a room from bright and business-like to softly relaxing and most designers regard them as essential.

There are plenty of ways to improve the quality of existing lighting without having to endure the mess and upheaval caused by chasing cables into walls or running them above ceilings. If your current arrangements consist simply of a central pendant fitting, try replacing the existing flex with a longer piece, so that the fitting can be moved to where it will be most useful, perhaps over a dining or display table. Alternatively, for greater flexibility, replace it with spotlights on a track system.

The range of plug-in fittings includes picture lights, clip-on spots and wall-washers as well as floor and table lamps. Of course, the flex is usually exposed but some modern designs turn it into a feature. In many cases it may be possible to play down the flex by running it along a skirting board, around a corner or behind furniture. There should never be any danger of someone tripping over it, however, and if there are no power sockets nearby, compromises may have to be made.

If there are several light sources in a room, but you are still unhappy with the effect, check the bulbs. They may simply be too bright, or dim, for their surroundings, or glare could be reduced by replacing a standard bulb with a crown-silvered one.

Changing shades also makes a big difference. Dark colours glow softly when the light is turned on, while translucent materials allow more light into a room and thereby help to make the space seem brighter. Those with a spreading shape cast a wider pool of light than upright examples. Repositioning a shade in relation to the bulb can help: the closer the bulb to the bottom edge of the shade, the larger the pool of light .

If adding extra power sockets or re-routing cables and conduits is inevitable or if you think the wiring system in your home might need to be updated, call in a qualified electrician. The installation of electrical systems and the use of fittings near water are governed by safety regulations. You may also be prevented from using certain types of fitting in very old buildings if the heat they emit cannot be sufficiently well isolated from the surroundings.

◄◄ *When several examples of a simple light fitting are grouped together, they create an attractive rhythmic pattern. The light produced is less tiring – the pool of light from each bulb overlaps with the others, so the contrast between bright and shaded areas decreases, and your eyes no longer need to adjust.*

◄ *Candles and night-lights are a highly evocative, if sadly inefficient, source of light, and well worth considering for situations where creating the right atmosphere matters more than providing safe levels of illumination. A chandelier such as this makes a stunning focal point, as long as it can be lowered for easy lighting.*

Designing with light

▲ *Timeless and relatively inexpensive, paper lampshades look good whether or not they are lit. The range of shapes, sizes and colours of paper shades is now enormous, but they all have one thing in common: none should be fitted with a bulb that exceeds the manufacturer's recommended wattage.*

As well as working out which types of light fitting would best suit your needs, it is vital to ensure that they are correctly positioned. If you adhere to the principle that good lighting is efficient yet unobtrusive, it follows that fittings should be placed where they can do their job without casting unwanted shadows or creating glare.

Indirect lighting

One way to do this is to shine light indirectly into a room by using an uplighter to bounce it off the walls and ceiling. To do this effectively, the light source needs to be far enough away from the ceiling to create a broad glow yet high enough to be above the eye level of anyone standing in the room. Most floor-standing models are tall enough to satisfy these requirements but the more elongated designs can look awkward in low-ceilinged rooms. If you plan to use wall-mounted fittings, try holding them about 170cm (67in) from the floor to begin with and adjust the height from there.

Glare-free lighting

Local pools of glare-free light can also be produced by fittings that encase the bulb in a translucent material, such as frosted

▶ *There is seldom room for a whimsical approach when lighting a kitchen. Sources should be placed so that work surfaces remain shadow-free, and where they illuminate the contents of open cupboards. It is also extremely helpful if they can be recessed out of dirt's way, or at the very least be encased in easy-to-clean fittings.*

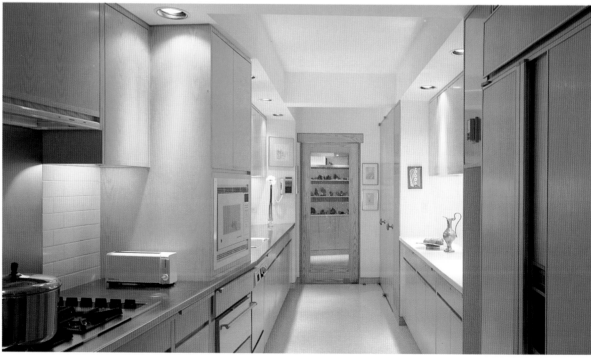

◄ *If you plan to use a room for more than one purpose, several types of fitting will be necessary. These need not match; instead choose fittings that do their job properly. Pendant lamps fixed close to the ceiling are fine for background illumination, but task lights should be placed so that they keep work or display areas free of shadow.*

glass or paper, or by traditionally shaded lamps. These are best used in places where you can get away with low levels of background light, such as bedrooms or dining rooms. They are not really suitable for lighting your path through a space or for use as task lighting.

When used on its own, however, indirect lighting can make a room look flat and uninteresting. Visible sources of light, such as ceiling spots, some pendant fittings and even candles add sparkle and life; perhaps they remind us of man's original light sources, the sun and fire. But they need to be carefully controlled to avoid glare, which can be done in a number of ways: by reducing the size of the fitting's opening, as in an eyeball fitting; by using reflective material around or inside the bulb; or by making them appear less bright, by using low-wattage bulbs and dimmers.

Direct lighting

Special care needs to be taken with task and display lamps, as the bulb is more than likely to be exposed. When a table or floor lamp is being used as a task light, the bottom edge of the shade should be positioned high enough to allow light to fall on your work area or lap, but not so high that the bright inner surface of the shade can be seen.

Light distribution

The distribution of light around a room matters too. The areas where you are likely to sit and relax or work should obviously be brighter than the background, so that you are drawn into a pool of light. And displays need to be highlighted, but not to the same extent that they become distracting. In general, it is best to avoid over-dramatic contrasts of light and shade, especially if you are reading or working in a space, as this causes eye strain.

Of course, compromises will have to be made, especially if you are furnishing on a tight budget or find your options severely limited by a tenancy agreement. If the only source of light is a centrally-placed bulb on a flex, consider replacing it with a surface-mounted track or 'bare wire' system positioned close to one of the walls – this allows you to use several smaller light sources to wash the wall, and perhaps highlight an item of furniture such as a dining table. You will need to run a longer piece of flex from the centre of the ceiling to your new fitting, but this can be concealed in a channel painted to match the background.

Make the most of plug-in fittings too. Look out for designs that will take tungsten or halogen bulbs, as they can be used with dimmer switches. Consider also whether you can improve on existing or inherited lamps; replacing lined fabric lampshades with examples made from a light-diffusing material, such as paper, does much to brighten up a gloomy room, and don't forget that a simple change of bulb – from pearl to crown-silvered, for example – can do wonders for the efficiency and attractiveness of a fitting.

Selecting fittings

Finally, consider the style of the fittings. Choosing all the fittings from a single range or made in the same material can help give a co-ordinated look to a room scheme. But there is absolutely no reason at all why you shouldn't select the fittings on an individual basis, especially if they are attractive objects in their own right. However, bear in mind the overall look and feel of a room as well as the uses to which the fittings will be put. While a table lamp with a pleated silk shade may look cosy and elegant in a living room, it will seem incongruous, to say the least, in a busy, steam-filled kitchen.

Directory of lighting

Task lights

Task lighting is a must in any area where you plan to read or do close work. It can be provided by a desk lamp, a floor-standing lamp with an adjustable head, an industrial-style lamp that clamps to a desk or shelf or a rise-and-fall pendant fitting. Whichever design you choose, position it so that your work area is kept free of shadow, without exposing the bulb to the extent that it causes glare. Lamps with a long reach are useful where the light source needs to be moved closer for detailed work, such as over a craft bench or if you simply like to read while sitting in the middle of your sofa. **2**

Display lighting

As well as drawing attention to objects and pictures, display lighting subtly adds sparkle to interiors. Picture lights and cabinet fittings are two of the fixed or built-in options but a plug-in mini-spot or clip-on lamp often work just as well if you do not want to go to the trouble and expense of permanent fittings. To light a picture, the lamp should be angled towards the image to minimize awkward reflections and glare. Decorative objects are best lit from above or the front to accentuate their shape and texture. Large areas of displayed books or CDs should be evenly lit, so that their covers can be read easily.

Pendant fittings

As they are often to be found hanging from a single central point on a ceiling, pendant fittings echo the old-fashioned practice of lighting rooms with chandeliers. Unfortunately, a single overhead fitting produces a directional light that is both difficult to adjust and unflattering to faces and should not, therefore, be relied upon as the main source of light in a room. Instead, fit it with low-wattage bulbs so that it merely glows decoratively

1

and add extra background light with wall lights or free-standing fittings. Simple pendant lamps and lanterns look best when they are grouped in some way. Try hanging two or three in a row over a kitchen counter, desk or dining table. **3**

Downlights

Compact and unobtrusive, downlights can be fixed directly onto the ceiling or partly or totally recessed. If they are fixed to a track, they can be removed or repositioned, which is an advantage in areas where the furniture is regularly moved around. A row of downlights may be used to provide a wash of background light while individual lamps can be turned into display lights with the help of lenses and cowls. It is easy to recess downlights into a ceiling, as fittings are supplied with a template for cutting the hole and the wiring is the same as for a pendant lamp. Apartment dwellers may not be allowed to install these types of fittings, however. **1**

2

3

Table lamps

Modernists may well sneer, but old-fashioned table lamps are among the most versatile fittings available. They are portable, need little room, provide a useful mixture of task and ambient lighting as well as elegantly underpin the style of your decor. The shade is the business end of the lamp, as the material from which it is made diffuses and colours the light, and its shape dictates how much light is cast below it: those with a spreading shape cast wider pools of light. When combining shades and bases, aim for a well-proportioned and balanced look.

Candlestick-style bases suit shades with a small diameter, while solid bases go better with wide-angle examples. **5**

Wall lights

Wall lights have obvious advantages in areas where floor space is limited and need not involve chasing cables into the wall if the flex is attractive. The output of wall lights is usually directed up at the walls and ceiling, making them a good source of ambient light. As they are on display, their visual impact can be significant. A sconce can be used to give a bare patch of wall a sense of purpose while a row of lamps in a hallway adds rhythmic pattern. **4**

Floor lamps

As much of the furniture in a room tends to have a strongly horizontal feel, the vertical lines of floor lamps often add a welcome contrast. They vary enormously in style and function, and range from traditional standard lamps which provide both ambient and task lighting, through spindly uplighters, to tough and powerful studio lights. Floor lamps are easy to move, some are even mounted on wheels, but for safety try to avoid having trailing flexes across thorough-fares and do not place the lamps in a position where there is a risk of causing an obstruction.

Organized living

Due to the ever-increasing cost of land and
building materials, homes are getting smaller yet
the list of goods and gadgets found within them
grows ever larger. And few of us care to call a place
home until it contains what the architect
Christopher Alexander, in his book *A Pattern
Language*, calls 'things from your life', items such as
family snapshots and collections which have
sentimental rather than practical value.

Organizing your home so that possessions and people can co-exist in harmony is vital for most of us know how time-consuming and exhausting it can be to live amidst chaos and muddle. And as Sir Terence Conran says in his *The Essential House Book*: 'Your basic approach – whether you like to leave everything out on view or to banish all your belongings to cupboards and closets – will determine the basic character of your home more surely than any palette of paint colours or soft furnishing style.'

Cramming your home with cupboards is not the answer, however, and the most effective long-term solutions are arrived at by looking closely at how you use your home as a whole. Look particularly at how activity tends to be concentrated in certain areas. This might include the living room and the kitchen, a shared children's room, or a bedroom that doubles as a study. If both you and your possessions are fighting for space in these places, one solution is to try to spread the load a little. It may be possible, for example, to turn a box-room into a shared study thereby keeping the rest of the house relatively free of homework and office clutter. Or, as is often the case in older houses, there may be circulation areas, such as landings and hallways, that can be fitted out with storage or shelving.

With a little creative thinking, even areas that are usually written off as wasted space can be put to good use. In Japanese homes, the space under the floor is often fitted with shallow boxes that are accessed by lifting trap-doors in the floor. Or it may be possible to fit shallow overhead storage in a bed alcove.

Of course, organizing your home is also about being able to find things with the minimum of fuss and being able to put them away easily when you have finished with them. The first step is to get rid of those items that you no longer want or need but have simply got used to having around. Next, sort the remainder of your possessions according to frequency of use. Those that are used constantly, such as the bread bin in the kitchen or clothes for work, should obviously be the most accessible while those that are used on a seasonal basis or only once in a while can be stored in more out of the ▷

◀ Look beyond the idiosyncratic appearance of this kitchen, and it becomes clear that a great deal of thought has gone into the selection and siting of each item of storage. Wire baskets and the like allow air to circulate, and no shelf is so deep that it would be difficult to reach items stored at the back.

▲ Storing items close to where they are needed is the most important thing to consider when planning any kind of storage. That is why it makes sense to hang clean clothes near where you wash and bathe. However, leaving them on show may not be such a good idea if you are less rigorous than this in your choice of colours.

▶ *There is no reason why the inside of a cupboard shouldn't be as good to look at as the outside – and a glimpse of brilliant colour whenever you open a kitchen cabinet door may be just what you need to momentarily forget about daily grind.*

▶▶ *Although they can be expensive, built-in cupboards are often the most efficient option when space is needed for a large number of different sized items. Cheaper versions often lack character, but they can be perked up by customizing the baseboard or plinth, or by choosing unusual door pulls and handles.*

such as kitchen condiments, it is better to arrange them in single rows on several narrow shelves than on a single deep shelf.

Personal taste, finances and the size of the available area are other factors to bear in mind. In small rooms, wall-mounted cabinets or shelves can help to increase the feeling of space, as they allow the floor to be kept clear. Also, the visual impact of different styles of storage varies greatly. Imagine an alcove filled with glass shelves, then with built-in cupboards that match the surrounding walls and finally with an ornate piece of furniture. Each storage style is more prominent than the last and affects to a greater extent how you perceive the space around it.

A common dilemma is not knowing how much storage is necessary. Interior designers often say it is twice as much as you think. Certainly, it is always advisable to err on the generous side. If nothing else, it allows you to find room for future acquisitions. It is also a good idea to build more strength into a storage system than you need, not only to make it last longer but also to allow for changes in use at a later date.

▲ *Fabric wardrobes and hanging shelves are cheap, light and pack flat, which makes them ideal for anyone who moves home regularly, and for use in infrequently used spaces such as guest rooms. Cheerful designs such as this also help to personalize a space when permanent decorative changes are out of the question.*

way places. It does not take long to pack winter coats and sweaters away in an attic or high cupboard at the onset of summer, and doing so will not only make it easier to find those clothes that you do want to wear, but also keep them in better condition.

Remember, though, that some items do have specific storage requirements. Large suitcases, for example, are bulky and therefore difficult to manoeuvre in and out of tight spaces, while medicines and household chemicals should be kept away from children and extreme temperatures.

Now you can begin to devise solutions for individual rooms or areas. Decide which parts of the room are to be given over to storage while taking into account factors such as whether this is likely to impede movement around the room or will block your view of focal points such as windows.

Large cabinets are focal points in themselves and if they are attractive they should be placed where they can be appreciated.

On the whole, it is better to collect storage together in one part of the room, in the form of a row of built-in cupboards or shelves perhaps, or a freestanding cabinet that is also used as a room divider, rather than scattering it. However, avoid placing it in front of electrical sockets, switches, taps and other services.

Knowing which type of storage to buy is not easy, as the choice of styles is enormous and it is not always clear why some cost much more than others. To a certain extent you should be guided by the objects that are to be stored. A row of books weighs more than a few wooden ornaments so the shelf supporting them should be correspondingly stronger. If you are trying to store a lot of small items,

Storage and shelving

Although storage systems come in all shapes and sizes, they can all be regarded as some form of variation on the idea of a shelf, a hook, or a box or, of course, a combination of the three. A chest of drawers, for example, is a series of boxes placed on top of one another and many modular storage units allow you to combine boxes, in the form of drawers and cupboards, with open shelving. And a peg rail is simply a row of hooks joined together.

The inside of a unit should be tailored to suit the items that you plan to store. Good storage is governed by the 'divide and rule' principle, which states that items are easier to see and much likelier to remain tidy when stored in groups that are as small as possible. Short runs of shelving, baskets on a shelf and a wall of cupboards, each one sub-divided by adjustable partitions, are just some of the options that make this possible. Smaller items are usually stored in drawers but they

can also be arranged in lidded jars, hung from pegs or sorted into files or trays. It is all a question of scale. The smaller the item, the more compact its home needs to be. The only exceptions to this rule occur when small objects are massed together for visual effect as when a collection is displayed in a glazed cabinet.

Some items need special treatment if they are to be stored efficiently. A television, for example, may have to be fixed to a hydraulic-lift mechanism or a shelf on gliders so that it can be pulled out of storage and retracted as necessary. Fresh fruit and vegetables need air to circulate around them and so are best stored in pull-out wire trays or baskets.

Putting a face on storage, in the form of doors and drawers, protects the contents from dust and prying eyes, as well as making it look neater. It can also, of course, add decorative interest and character to a room. In small spaces it may be necessary to use sliding or

folding doors as they take up less space. Glazed or wire-mesh doors will give a unit a sense of lightness and the right handles and hinges could well turn a bland or beaten-up piece of furniture into something rather special.

Shelving

Open shelving is often regarded as the cheap and cheerful answer to every storage need and there are plenty of times when it cannot be improved upon, especially if you want to be able to display objects, or have them instantly to hand. It can be much the best solution if you are on a tight budget, but it needs to be designed as carefully as any other form of storage.

It is also a good choice when you want your storage to be as unobtrusive as possible. Slim glass shelves or solid shelves that are

▲ In an open-plan apartment, it is essential to keep clutter under control, and create private areas without carving space up insensitively. Well-planned storage can help to do all this and a great deal more; here, steps double as drawers, and bookcases act as a screen to section off a raised sleeping space.

◀ *Storage was traditionally made from solid wood, but as this is no longer cost-effective, a good alternative is to make it from manufactured boards such as medium-density fibreboard (MDF). Here, the drawers are fashioned from plain MDF, while the cupboard front and door consist of sheets that have been routed to resemble tongue-and-groove boards.*

◀◀ *Buying fitted cupboards is not always the answer to kitchen storage problems. If you prefer leaving crockery and utensils on view, and are sure that they will be used often enough to keep them dust free, a mix of shelving and baskets is both practical and charming.*

The thickness of your shelving material and the distance between the supports, or span, determine its load-bearing capacity. If you plan to use your shelves to store anything heavier than lightweight ornaments or glass-ware, they should obviously be able to take the strain.

Making the most of storage

- High shelves should be narrow so that you can see what is on them from below. If they are deep, use them to store light and infrequently used large items, such as spare blankets and towels.
- When storing large numbers of objects on a shelf, arrange them in rows, with taller items at the back.
- Try to store heavy items at waist height to avoid bending and stretching with them.
- Items stored at ground level with a shelf or some other obstruction above are easier to reach if they are stored in boxes on wheels or with grab handles.
- Use the insides of doors to store small items, such as saucepan lids in the kitchen and ties or scarves in a wardrobe.
- If storage units are large or deep, consider fitting a built-in light.
- Decorate the insides of open storage units to show off the contents to their best advantage. Multi-coloured displays, such as books, look good against neutral backgrounds while shiny or clear objects, such as glass, could be set against deep colours or lustrous textures.

coloured to match their surroundings focus your attention on the displayed objects. A freestanding shelving unit makes a great room divider as it helps to enclose a space while offering you glimpses of what lies beyond.

Open wall shelving can be fixed by a number of methods: fixed brackets, which are available in a wide range of styles and materials; adjustable brackets that slot into tracks screwed to the wall; and cantilever strips which hold the shelf along its entire back edge in a U-shaped channel. It is often recommended that brackets are placed some way in from the ends of the shelf, to distribute the load more evenly, and that the front of the shelf should project no more than 2.5cm (1in) beyond the end of the bracket.

Alcove and cupboard shelves are almost always fixed at the sides. The simplest method is to support them on wood or angled metal battens screwed into place. An adjustable system, in which the shelves rest on small pegs or studs pushed or slotted into holes made at regular intervals in each side, is fairly easy to install. Alternatively, the pegs may be hooked into a continuous metal strip, often called bookcase strip. Two supports are usually required for each side.

Whichever method you decide to use, it is essential to attach the supports with fixings that are appropriate to the construction of your wall. General-purpose plastic plugs are fine for solid walls made from brick or concrete but stud partition walls (made from a wooden framework covered with plasterboard) and cavity walls (consisting of hollow bricks or blocks) require special anchors or toggles.

Storage and shelving guide

▶ *In this cottage, built-in cupboards and shelves ensure that the space in boxed-in corners and partitions does not go to waste. Restricting their size – the top rail of the cupboards is just below head height – ensures that they never seem overwhelmingly tall, something that is likely in a room where you spend much of the time seated or lying down.*

▲ *With its exaggerated height, this tallboy almost becomes part of the architecture of the room – one can imagine it serving much the same purpose as a chimney breast or column. In the room beyond, another wooden column, this time of Shaker boxes, provides more convenient access to smaller items.*

Built-in storage

Built-in furniture makes good use of limited space and can be tailored to meet every need and whim. But it is there for good and the fancier it gets, the more expensive it becomes. Built-in furniture is often thought of as a modern idea, but it has been a feature of houses since at least the early sixteenth century when cupboards in recesses and fixed benches with under-seat storage were used for the safe-keeping of clothes and valuables. It is much the best option in awkwardly shaped areas, such as those under the roof and stairs.

Freestanding storage

The most traditional storage options take the form of freestanding furniture pieces, such as bookcases, chests of drawers, sideboards and wardrobes. They are often larger and more decorative than other forms of storage and so lend themselves well to being used as focal points. They can also be taken with you when you move house. However, they do waste space and the bulky appearance of older examples can be overwhelming in smaller rooms, although they can be improved by using paint to give them a lighter feel (see pages 274–275).

Modular storage

A modular storage system can be built out of something as simple as a row of pigeonholes or lockers or it can be a sophisticated mix of cupboards, shelves and drawers. Mass-produced systems can be added to over time and are often sold as self-assembly units, which makes them ideal for anyone furnishing on a budget. Some are stacked on the floor like building bricks while others can be fixed to the wall. A surprisingly large number are too shallow to accommodate items such as large books, so choose a system that is suitable for your possessions.

Storage containers, boxes and baskets

Although they are often overlooked in the search for whole-room solutions, boxes, baskets and other containers play a vital role. They can impose order on chaotic open storage and allow you to shift possessions easily from one place to another. If they are sturdy enough they can simply be stacked on a surface to create temporary structures. However, non-transparent containers should always be labelled so that you can tell at a glance what is inside. There is nothing organized, or amusing, about unpacking several boxes to find one elusive item.

Hooks

A hook may be all you need to turn dead space into useful storage. Screwing one or two into the back of a wardrobe door allows you to use the space to store belts and other accessories, while bicycles and cumbersome sports equipment can be kept out of the way by hanging them from the wall or ceiling high above your head. A use can be found for hooks wherever objects need to be kept to hand, yet off the floor and other surfaces. Used in quantity, in the form of a row of knobs, perhaps, or to store a variety of items on a peg board, they add a touch of pattern to a scheme.

Freestanding shelving

Rough-and-ready answers to many a storage problem can be provided by freestanding shelving. At its cheapest and most basic, it consists simply of lengths of board that are stacked on top of one another, with spacing provided by bricks or boxes. If this seems a little too radical, most home improvement stores sell systems that allow you to create units from uprights and shelves with cross-braces added for stability. Look for one with a high degree of adjustability. Screw units to the wall if there are children around.

Open-wall shelving

The term open-wall shelving covers any situation where the sides of a wall-mounted shelf are open to the room. Shelves that are placed in this way can be approached from several angles, so they need to be fixed securely to their supports. Small shelves are often decorative as well as functional; the brackets or supports are attractive objects in their own right and the shelf itself may be given an unusual profile or fashioned from a distinctive material.

Alcove shelving

Alcove shelving is extremely space efficient and it is cheap to install if it is supported on fixed battens. It is also very versatile. It can be painted so as to blend into its surroundings. Attaching a chunky trim or lipping to the front edges will give it an architectural feel. Combining alcove shelving with a low-level cupboard will turn it into a piece of built-in furniture. If you possess basic woodworking skills, this type of shelving can also be vastly improved by the simple addition of vertical dividers. These create convenient partitions and prevent wide shelves from sagging but they should be used over the entire height of the shelving so that the weight can be transferred to the floor.

◀ *A modular system of glazed and closed cabinets provides a flexible mix of storage and display space, and it can be a welcome source of pattern in a simple scheme, as here. The light-reflecting properties of glass, and the right choice of colour, will also help to brighten a dull room.*

▶ *You know a shelving system works when it draws attention to your possessions rather than itself. Inexpensive slotted metal uprights and laminated chipboard shelves can look perfectly at home in a smart living room, as long as they are spaced at useful intervals and securely fixed to the wall.*

Display principles

Creating displays is a bit like putting on make-up. Whilst not strictly necessary, it can make a room look wonderful and it is often the easiest way to create a new look. As with cosmetics, we use displays to make a dramatic visual statement, perhaps by placing a picture where it creates a focal point, and to make the most of a room's good points, for example by drawing attention to a mantelpiece arrangement above a fireplace.

In fact, it is hard to see how you might stamp your personality on a space without resorting to some kind of display, and few rooms are so perfectly conceived that there is no need for a picture or some other point of focus to break up an expanse of wall. Personal possessions provide evidence of human activity and a room that lacks this is regarded by most people as alienating and uncomfortable.

Some of the most satisfying displays are created simply by storing useful objects efficiently, such as a wall of books on sturdy, well-spaced shelves or shiny saucepans hung on hooks above a cooker. However, most of us also collect 'stuff' that serves no practical purpose whatsoever which can probably also be attractively and effectively displayed.

Much of the skill in displaying objects lies in making them look as though they belong where they have been placed rather than as though they have been left lying around. Giving them due prominence, perhaps by keeping the surrounding area clear or by picking their features out with accent lighting, subliminally reinforces this message.

Displays are seen as part of a larger whole. The size and colour of a display surface, as well of any items nearby, will greatly influence how an exhibit is seen. Most of us have held a picture up to a wall only to find that it was too large or too small. You may also have seen how repainting a wall or the interior of a display cabinet can suddenly bring the objects on show to life.

The simple act of grouping similar or related objects also increases their impact. As any child knows, the most unprepossessing items can be turned into great collections as long as they are amassed with commitment and passion. As grown-ups are quick to point out, however, they are seldom seen at their best when scattered over the floor or piled up in a drawer. Each item needs to be clearly seen. A stockpile of beer cans from around the world will look much more impressive if

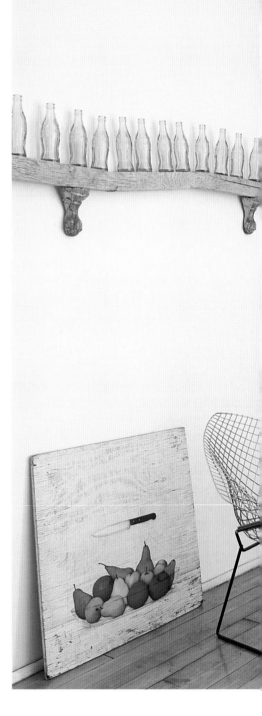

◀ Here, a formally arranged group of prints adds a welcome sense of order to a casually furnished and rustic hallway. Placing a mass of plants and other objects directly in front of the pictures links them visually to the rest of the room, and helps to make them appear less out of place.

it is ranged over several closely spaced, narrow shelves rather than on a single, deeper surface.

Not everyone has a passion for collecting, and displays often need to be created out of rather muddled groups of objects. A set of pictures in different shapes and sizes, for example, can be lent a sense of unity by hanging them as a group on one wall. If they still look lost and out of place, you could try hanging them above a piece of low furniture. If the pictures are linked by colour, it can be fun to emphasize this with matching frames, although you do run the risk of making the framing more important than the images.

Rather than lining objects up like soldiers, try forming them into groups that display strong contrasts of scale, form and material. Curvy or spherical objects will seem even more rounded if they are mixed with a rectangular item, such as a propped-up tray or an empty frame. Try combining transparent objects, such as those made from glass or wire, with solid stone or earthenware pieces,

and natural materials with synthetic or man-made ones. It does not matter if a grouping looks a little unbalanced or strange. Better that than a 'perfect' arrangement that merely looks lifeless and contrived.

There are occasions when a more three-dimensional approach is called for, as when a table or a shelving unit is used as a space divider. In such cases, it makes sense to display things that can be viewed from all sides. Leave plenty of space between objects, so that you can see through an arrangement to the other side.

In many ways, the hardest part of creating displays is knowing when to stop. The line that divides collections and clutter is a fine one. You can be fairly certain that a display has grown too large if it begins to spill over into living space by colonizing surfaces that are used for eating or working or if you find yourself placing objects where they could easily be damaged. When this happens, the time has come to rethink a display or do some serious weeding out.

◀ With their delicate construction and graphic outlines, model boats are tailor-made for displaying, especially when they are seen in a flotilla, as here. Matching the background colour to the sails ensures that the boats blend in with the rest of the scheme, and the most fragile examples are placed high on the wall, to keep them safe.

▲ In this room, convention is turned completely on its head by casually propping works of art on the floor and windowsill, while formerly commonplace items, including a collection of empty drinks bottles, are prominently displayed in ways that force us to look at them afresh.

WALLS

Walls almost always dominate the look of a room, so they are one of the most important aspects of decorating your home.

As we move away from the more showy and 'decorated' interiors of the 1980s and into a more organic, evolved and understated look, it is important to find a look that suits you perfectly. If this sounds like a difficult task, bear in mind that it is also immensely liberating. Quite literally, anything goes. If you wish to combine a Mediterranean sense of colour with your favourite primitive oil paintings and a collection of Chinese ceramics, you can. It is simply a question of balance.

But how do you choose a style when the choice of wall-coverings is simply so dazzling in its breadth and variety? Deciding on the final scheme is a source of enormous anguish to most home decorators. How many of us have considered fantastically colourful swatches of paint, paper and fabric for months, only in the end – out of fear, confusion and terror of blowing our budget – to plump for magnolia in a cowardly fashion? But choosing a colour scheme does not have to be such an ordeal or fraught with difficulties. Colour is the most wonderful tool; it literally transforms everything it touches. Whether you wish to create a sense of peace in a bedroom, or a sense of drama in a dining room, the colour of the walls will have a profound effect on the finished product. Start thinking of colour as your ally, rather than as a source of anxiety, and you are on your way to a wonderful decorating adventure.

Before you start, gather together lots of samples of wallpaper and paint. If possible, get into the habit of carrying around Polaroids, fabric and colour swatches so that, wherever you are, you can match things up.

If you are keen to use specialist paint techniques, try them out on sheets of lining paper first, in order both to perfect the technique and to get a realistic sense of the colour and effect you are going to achieve. You can also make up the paint, wallpaper, tile and fabric swatches you have collected into colour boards, just as a professional interior decorator would.

Ideally, you should pin these up in the room where you intend to use them and then live with them for as long as you can. You will be amazed to see how that terracotta can look cosy and warm in one room and yet can appear a cheap and nasty orange in another. This exercise also allows you to get a sense of how the different elements work together, and gives you some idea of the effect daylight has on colour. This exercise may initially require time and patience, but it is worth the wait and the effort as it means that you are more likely to avoid expensive mistakes and also – ultimately – to create a scheme you are happy to live with for a long time.

Old houses present particular challenges. Often, the desire to be historically correct can be overwhelming but today the trend is against the slavish imitation of historical styles. Houses should reflect the lives, passions and preoccupations of their owners, rather than recreating an uncomfortable museum or quaint period drama. It is a

▲ The wall treatment invariably dominates the overall look of a room. In this instance, a fabulous mosaic inspired by the planets and stars demonstrates that, in a small space, a bold scheme allows you to keep the rest of the interior furnishing details simple.

question of reaching a successful compromise between sensitivity to the quality of your surroundings and your desire for a workable, modern scheme. And remember, the use of colour in old houses was often much more vivid than fading interiors, pictures and samples of fabric now would lead us to believe.

Practically speaking, several factors determine what kind of wall treatment is right for your home: budget; decorative style; your own level of skill and/or willingness to experiment with new techniques; and finally, practicality.

Of all the materials available to you, paint is probably the most versatile. Certainly, it is ideal for the budget decorator. Its versatility and dramatic potential has endeared it to many people working within strict financial constraints.

Wallpaper is available in myriad styles and patterns. Whether you are after floral abundance or formal restraint, there is something for you. For those people who are hesitant about attempting paint techniques such as dragging or sponging, there are wallpapers which imitate these effects quite realistically. Papers can be combined with borders and friezes for additional dramatic effect. And if wallpapering frightens you, because you think it takes a high level of skill, developments in recent years should take away any residue of anxiety. For example, self-adhesive papers can be hung straight from the roll and, more to the point, repositioned instantly if you make a mistake.

There are several other options if you are feeling courageous and would like to try something a little more unusual, or something a little less conventional than paint and paper. Fabric makes a fantastic wallcovering, and wood or metal cladding on interior walls has been through something of a revival in recent years.

The key to success is to spend some time evaluating the options open to you before you start to make any major decisions. You must work out exactly what is going to look right for your space. After that, be bold, be brave, be prepared to experiment – and follow the correct techniques to get it right!

◀ *The wall treatment you choose should be in keeping with the room's other decorative and practical elements. Here, a rough plaster wall distressed in warm ochre perfectly complements the simple units and collection of rustic kitchen accessories.*

▲ *A sense of harmony is created in this peaceful bathroom by using simple, blue-stained timber on walls, floors and window. The staining, when teamed with a classic white suite and a Matisse-inspired motif, creates a chic rather than a rustic look.*

Paint

Paint has often been called the decorator's best friend. Quite justifiably so, for not only is it the most versatile and the least expensive wall treatment available, it can also be used to create an enormous range of effects. Even a novice can produce some dazzling wall treatments in a relatively short period of time. It is also an enormously liberating material to work with, because even if your experiments go disastrously wrong, it is a relatively inexpensive and quick exercise to paint over them.

Whether you are inclined towards a bold modern look, or a delicate, subdued scheme, you can create any effect with paint; practically anything is possible. Your best guide will undoubtedly be the room itself.

There are, of course, some things that you probably cannot change – short of a complete remodelling job. The room's proportions, and the size and position of windows and architectural details, are probable starting points when you are deciding how to tackle the space. If you have a small room, for example, a pale colour will give you a brighter, more airy look. But equally, you might like to go in the opposite direction and use dark colours to enhance or create a cosy or 'clubby' feeling.

However, there is little point in setting yourself an impossible task. You can only work against a room's natural inclination to a certain point – further than that, and it proves to be a frustrating, fruitless and expensive exercise. For instance, a dark, north-facing room can rarely be made to look bright and cheerful, whatever its proportions. Indeed, a chilly light on bright, jolly colours can even make them look harsh, dreary and depressing. It is always best – as with other aspects of decorating – to work with what you have, enhancing and developing it. It is probably better to choose dark colours such as terracotta, mossy green or midnight blue for a north-facing room and then enjoy the challenge of creating a rich, opulent scheme.

In a badly proportioned room, using the same colour throughout, on walls, ceiling, and even on the floor, will blur the confines of the space. But remember that you can also combine paint colours and finishes to great effect. So, in a small room, gloss paint will reflect the light and give a more spacious feel. And if a room seems too high for its dimensions, a dark, matt paint on the ceiling will 'lower' it, or alternatively, you could add a dado rail and paint the area beneath it in a darker colour than the rest of the walls. If your room has low ceilings, you can create a more lofty appearance by painting the walls with vertical stripes (see pages 70–71), or by making the ceiling either matt white or a paler colour than the rest of the walls.

Of course, there are many different paint effects you can use to disguise the room's less attractive features; but equally, they can be used simply to create a dramatic effect. *Trompe l'oeil* effects, for instance, can also be used to create architectural interest where once there was none – and at a fraction of the cost of the real thing.

These days, we have moved away from some of the showier effects of the 1980s, when many a decorative crime was committed in the name of sponging and marbling. The look now is more subtle; the colours are more subdued; and, ultimately, final appearances are more sophisticated. If you are a decorating novice, this trend actually works to your advantage, because if you are working with two different shades of cream, terracotta or grey, mistakes and irregularities will be less glaringly obvious than if your colours had been more strident, and your overall schemes altogether less subtle. The fact that more relaxed, distressed interiors are increasingly popular probably also works in your favour.

As well as the enormous variety of paint colours available, the kind of paint you choose will have a huge bearing on the look you eventually achieve. Some purists would never use anything except matt emulsion finish on the walls and eggshell on the woodwork, but gloss finishes have gone through something of a revival recently. Vinyl silk and gloss finishes are wonderful in areas such as halls, bathrooms and kitchens which receive a lot of wear, as scuff marks can simply be washed off. Remember not to ignore the possibilities of textured paint either, because this does not have to mean full-blown Artex: manufacturers have recently developed a new range of paints, designed to cover minor cracks and imperfections in walls and ceilings, while appearing only slightly more textured than traditional vinyl matt emulsion – useful and unobtrusively interesting.

Paint's possibilities are almost endless. Practically speaking, it is simply a question of finding a product that suits the surface you are decorating and creates the look you want.

◄ In a small room where solid terracotta walls could be rather oppressive, the decorator has used a clever, if simple, technique. The walls are painted off-white and small pieces of masking tape are stuck in a random pattern on the wall. The walls are then colour-washed and the tape peeled off to reveal white space beneath.

▲ Paint is the simplest and least expensive way of making a decorating statement. In this instance, a monochrome scheme is given an injection of humour with one wall coated in blackboard paint. It's such a good idea, there is no need to restrict it to the nursery.

Directory of paint
Standard paints

Eggshell

Oil-based eggshell has a smooth, hard-wearing surface and a slight sheen. A more elegant finish for woodwork than gloss, it can also be used on furniture and interior walls and ceilings as it provides a resilient surface and wears beautifully. It is therefore good for heavy-duty areas such as halls, bathrooms and kitchens. Can also be used for paint effects. Drying time: 12–16 hours. Look out for quick-drying water-based eggshell; this gives the same effect but lives up to its name and dries in 2–4 hours. **1**

Enamel

Use on metalwork for best effect, including radiators.

Gloss

Shiny gloss paints are mostly oil-based, but water-based varieties are now available. Available in semi-gloss, gloss and high-gloss finishes. High-gloss paint shows every bump and surface flaw. Durable, chip-resistant, and easy to wipe clean, gloss paint can be used on woodwork, metalwork and walls; it can also be used on plastic without an undercoat. It is perfect for heavy-use areas: hallways, door and window frames, children's rooms, kitchens and exterior woodwork. Liquid gloss must be used over proprietary undercoat, whereas non-drip and self-undercoating versions do not need undercoats. Drying time: 12–16 hours. **3**

Kitchen/bathroom emulsion

A water-based paint containing fungicide, for areas that may become damp.

Limewash

See Whitewash (below).

Oil-based mid-sheen paint

Also known as semi-sheen or satin finish. Similar to eggshell but with a

less attractive finish, this paint has been adapted for faster application; some varieties need no undercoat, require only one coat, and are drip-resistant. Can be used on woodwork, window and door frames. Drying time: 2 hours.

Primer

Specially designed to seal bare surfaces and available in water- or oil-based versions, special primers should be used for wood, plaster and metal.

Quick-drying eggshell

See Eggshell, water-based (above).

Soft distemper

See Whitewash (below).

Solid emulsion

See also Vinyl matt and Vinyl silk emulsions (below). A thick type of paint that comes ready to use in its own tray. Its heavy consistency reduces the risk of drips and splatters and is therefore appropriate for use on walls and ceilings. Do not use on new plaster without primer.

Textured paint

A water-based paint that adds texture to plaster surfaces. Usually used on walls and ceilings, it is particularly useful for covering up minor imperfections and rough surfaces. Difficult to clean. Be warned too: it is extremely difficult to remove if you change your mind.

Undercoat

A thick, opaque paint that fills in small cracks and irregularities in the surface being painted. Matt, slightly chalky texture. Available in either oil-based or water-based versions. Easy to apply and though it comes in few colours, it can be easily tinted. Use on primed surfaces. Do not use on plastic or stainless steel. Not intended as a finish but sometimes used as such. In heavy-use areas, where it is likely to get scuffed, use a matt varnish to protect it. Drying time: 8–12 hours.

Vinyl matt emulsion

A water-based paint with a flat finish. Easy to apply, vinyl matt emulsion gives good coverage, and is quick to use – and cheap. It should be used on walls and ceilings, and can be used for paint effects – thinned to create a wash, it provides a good base for stencilling; thickened with whiting, it has a textured effect. Can be used on new plaster (once thoroughly dried) or on rough, porous surfaces such as interior stone or brickwork. Not easy to wash clean. Drying time: approx. 4 hours.

Vinyl silk emulsion

A water-based paint similar to vinyl matt emulsion, this silk emulsion has a slight sheen finish and is more durable. Best suited to walls, it is also a good base for decorative finishes, mixing well with stainers, powder colours and water-based artist's tube colours. Drying time: 2–4 hours.

Special paints

Buttermilk

One of the earliest domestic paints, buttermilk was used widely in early American interiors and is still good for creating an authentic country feel. Made from soaked, dry pigment, buttermilk and a small quantity of fungicide to prevent mould, it has a matt appearance. As inconsistencies in mixing show up more markedly in dark colours, it lends itself better to paler shades.   **4**

Flat oil paint

A smart, flat paint which is a great favourite with decorators as a finish, or thinned as a glaze. Obtainable only through specialist paint suppliers. Drying time: 6–12 hours.

Historic colours

Enjoying a huge revival, these paints are sometimes mixed by eye – even today – using traditional materials, recipes and techniques. They do provide a wonderful depth of colour and the range of colours available is surprisingly wide. As a concession to modernity, these paint ranges are often available in a variety of finishes: matt emulsion, flat oil, eggshell, gloss, exterior paint, distemper, floor paint.

Use a brush, rather than a roller or pad, for a truly authentic effect.

Metallic paints

Using metallic paints in interiors is becoming increasingly popular. Basic metallic paints are cheaper than gold leaf where cost is a factor, although the finish is not as lustrous. Hammer-finish paints provide a variegated texture. Metallic paints usually require proprietary primers and thinners; they give a better finish if sprayed rather than applied with a brush, although on smaller areas such as radiators they can be brushed on if preferred.   **5**

Whitewash

Inexpensive matt paint with a soft, powdery finish. It is easy to make, using a combination of calcium carbonate powder, rabbit-skin glue (or PVA) and water.

Distemper (limewash) is the same, but the whitewash is mixed with powder pigment to tint it to the colour required. Experiment until you get the right consistency and colour. Because it cannot be cleaned, it may be short-lived; it can even be rubbed off with time. Remove before applying oil-based or emulsion paint.   **2**

Preparing the surface for painting

Preparing to paint

▲ *Paint is truly the simplest – and cheapest – way of making a decorating statement. Here, walls in blue and orange pick out colours from the stained glass window to stunning effect and require no further adornment. These colours are further reflected in the floor and interior furnishing.*

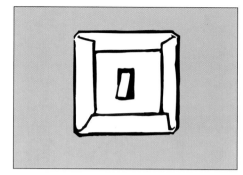

1 *Protect light switches, electrical sockets and woodwork with strips of masking tape before you start.*

2 *Wash down the walls with a sponge and a solution of detergent.*

3 *Use a squeegee mop and a solution of detergent to wash the ceiling.*

4 *Before painting, prepare the surface, using a wide-bladed scraper to remove flaking paint.*

The quality of a paint finish is almost entirely dependent on thorough preparation. It is worth spending as much time as you can on this stage, in order to get it absolutely right.

A clean, smooth starting surface is essential to a smart finish. A good preparation will also make the application of paint easier, unless you want to achieve a 'distressed' effect (see pages 62–65). Invest in good-quality equipment – buy the best you can afford because it will last longer than cheaper alternatives.

Estimating quantities

The amount of paint you will need will depend upon the kind you are intending to use and the colour of the existing walls. For example, if you are painting dark green walls white, you will need more coats than if you were painting white walls dark green. If a wall has been replastered, bear in mind that new plaster will absorb more paint than old. The instructions on your tin of paint will give the amount of coverage you can expect from 1 litre (1¾pt) if you use it undiluted. This is sometimes called the 'spreading rate'. It is easy to work out how many square metres (yards) you have to cover. For the ceiling area, measure the length and width of the floor and multiply one measurement by the other. Calculate each wall separately: multiply the height by the width. Then add the wall areas together.

To calculate the amount of paint you will need, take the total area you are going to paint and divide it by the figure specified as the spreading area for 1sq m (1sq yd) on the tin. The result of this sum will be the number of litres (pints) of paint that you will need.

Preparing to paint

Before starting to paint, remove as much furniture as possible. Cover the remainder with dust sheets and the floor with plastic sheeting. Protect window frames with masking

Filling cracks

1 *Use a filling knife or scraper to remove any debris from larger cracks.*

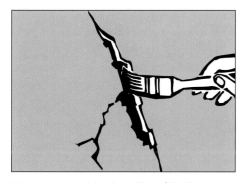

2 *Remove any remaining dust with a soft-bristled paintbrush, or you could use a vacuum cleaner hose.*

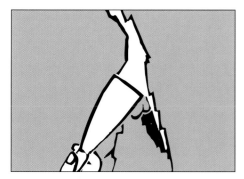

3 *Fill the crack with a filling knife. Fill deep cracks in layers, allowing 24 hours' drying time between each.*

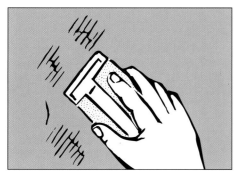

4 *When the filler is dry, gently smooth the crack with a sheet of sandpaper wrapped around a sanding block.*

tape. Cover anything you do not wish to paint, such as a radiator, with plastic sheeting, sticking it down with masking tape. Mask areas such as a ceiling with wide tape, if you are painting the walls, and vice versa. Assemble all the equipment you will need before you start and ensure that the room is ventilated. Wear overalls, but avoid woollens as fibres may stick to the paintwork.

Preparing the surface

Before painting a wall, you need to ensure that the plasterwork is in good condition; if it is not, it is essential that the old plasterwork is professionally removed and replaced before you begin. New plaster generally needs about four to five weeks to dry properly, so be sure to allow for this in your decorating schedule. It will then need a coat of plaster primer or thinned emulsion before being painted. New plasterboard walls require a coat of plasterboard primer-sealer or diluted PVA.

A previously painted wall should be thoroughly cleaned with strong detergent diluted in warm water. With walls, work from the bottom to the top, and pay particular attention to the areas around light switches where fingermarks accumulate. Wash ceilings using a clean squeegee floor mop. Rinse all surfaces with clean water. Allow to dry thoroughly before repairing minor defects in the walls. Remove flaking paint with a wide-bladed scraper. Then rub down walls with fine sandpaper to ensure a smooth finish, and dust off.

Treat any water stains or mould growth with proprietary stain blocks before you start.

Filling cracks

Any cracks should be filled with an interior filler. Using a scraper, first clean out the crack, removing any loose plaster or dust. Then, with an old paintbrush and clean water, dampen the crack and the surrounding area, so that it will bond well with the filler. Overfill the crack with all-purpose filler. Large holes can be built up in layers, but you will need to allow plenty of drying time between each one. Allow the filler to dry thoroughly and finally sand it smooth and level with the surrounding wall surface.

Tools and equipment

Have all the equipment you are likely to need to hand before you start, in order to minimize the time you spend preparing the wall or other surface to be painted. It is a good idea to put together a basic decorator's kit, rather as you would a family first-aid kit. This means that you are always equipped to tackle modest painting jobs, and only need add to it for more specialized tasks.

- **Sandpaper:** fine-grade glasspaper, wet-and-dry and coarser varieties, to key woodwork or smooth over repaired cracks.
- **Sanding blocks:** made of wood or cork, to wrap the sandpaper around.
- **Lint-free rags:** to wipe up spillages.
- **White spirit (or turpentine):** solvent for oil-based paints.
- **Masking tape:** narrow tape to protect light switches, sockets, window panes etc, from paint; wide tape to mask off large areas such as edges of ceilings or walls.

- **Dust sheets:** either plastic or fabric.
- **Old spoon:** handle to be used to open pots of paint.
- **Scraper:** wide-bladed, to remove patches of flaking paint.
- **Filling knife:** to press filler into holes and cracks.
- **Wooden dowel:** to mix paint.
- **Sugar soap or household detergent:** to clean down walls prior to painting.
- **Interior or all-purpose filler:** to fill cracks or holes in walls.
- **Large decorator's sponges:** to wash down walls.
- **Clean glass jars:** to soak brushes, store small quantities of paint and numerous other uses.
- **Face mask, eye protection and disposable gloves:** essential when working with solvents and other harsh decorating materials.
- **Painting platform:** for reaching high ceilings and painting in hallways.

Using brushes, rollers and pads

▶ *Walls painted in contrasting solid blocks of colour have immense visual impact. When using solid colour, however, the finish needs to be immaculate, making it imperative that the surface preparation is thorough. Large expanses of wall without obstacles to paint around perfectly suit use of a roller and paint tray.*

Brushes, rollers and pads

Make sure that you have the correct equipment for both the material you are using and the surface being painted in order to minimize the time the task will take. Never use brushes, rollers and pads that are past their best; the end product will not reflect the amount of time you have invested.

Good brushes have a decent length of bristle; they should not be stubby. Rollers can be more messy than brushes, as the paint is more likely to splatter, but they are a good choice for large areas such as walls and ceilings because they speed up the application.

Rollers produce a slightly more mottled surface than brushes. Indeed, if you want a super-smooth surface, do not use a foam roller, because the air trapped in the foam will produce an 'orange-peel' effect. And this texture will survive subsequent paint layers.

Paint pads are similar to rollers; using a paint pad is an excellent and speedy way of covering large surfaces. Made from mohair bonded onto a foam backing, they are available in several sizes. There are special edging pads for precision painting and small pads to use on mouldings and glazing bars. Best used with water-based paint, paint pads produce a smooth finish, but they do apply less paint per coat than rollers, so you may need an extra coat for the same density of finish.

Buy enough of the appropriate paintbrushes, rollers and paint pads for the task, but it is probably not worth buying heavy-duty industrial equipment unless you are renovating a whole house from top to bottom. If you require any expensive or specialized tools, consider hiring them instead.

First steps to painting walls

Before you start, dust the rim of the paint can with a dry brush or damp cloth to remove any dust or grit which could fall into the paint and contaminate it. Work your way around the tin with the spoon handle, levering gently until the lid flips off. Stir the paint thoroughly in a figure-of-eight movement with a clean piece of dowel.

Pour a quantity of the paint into a clean paint kettle, tray or plastic bucket because, when you are moving up and down ladders, this is easier to handle than a full tin.

Using a brush

Before using a new brush, get rid of loose bristles by working it vigorously backwards and forwards across the palm of your hand.

To begin painting, dip the brush into the kettle until one third to half of the bristles is covered. Remove the excess by dabbing the brush against the inside of the kettle, not by scraping the brush against the rim of the tin. Scraping it pulls the bristles out of the brush, contaminates the paint with stray bristles, and can make a mess of the outside of the tin. Alternatively, you could tie a piece of string taut across the top of the kettle and clean the brush against that. Do not be tempted to overload the brush as it will be much more difficult to manoeuvre and it will almost certainly result in drips that will show on the finished paint surface. It is also essential not to apply the paint too thickly and that you leave enough drying time between coats; consult the directions.

If you are using emulsion paint, you need to work fast because the rapid drying time of the paint can lead to shading. Using a 10–15cm (4–6in) brush, work across the room in areas approximately 70cm (28in) square. Use criss-cross brush-strokes to cover the area evenly and finish on a light, upward stroke. This is called 'laying off'. Move swiftly and methodically as you paint across the wall.

Handling the tools

1 *When completing an area of painting, and before reloading a brush, finish with a light upward stroke.*

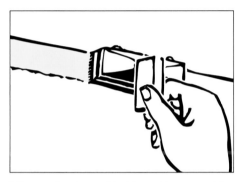

2 *Use a small pad or special edging pad to go around the edges of the wall before you tackle the central area.*

3 *Apply the paint in overlapping criss-cross strokes working on an area of 1 sq m (1 sq yd) at a time.*

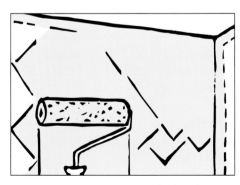

4 *With a roller, apply the paint in overlapping criss-crosses followed by solid strokes.*

Oil-based paint requires a different approach. It dries more slowly than emulsion and thus allows a little more flexibility. Use a smaller, 2.5–5cm (1–2in) brush, held between thumb and forefinger, like a pen, and begin to make parallel vertical lines of paint across an area measuring approx. 30 cm (12 in) square. When you have used up most of the paint on the brush, work swiftly across the vertical lines, blending them together into a solid layer of paint. Finish the area off with light, vertical strokes and move on quickly to the adjoining area.

Using a paint pad

Pour some well-mixed paint into a paint tray; you can use either a standard roller tray or one specially designed for use with pads. Load the paint by running the pad backwards and forwards over the ridged area of the paint tray, or over the loading roller in a paint-pad tray, to ensure an even application. Work on the edges of the wall first using a small pad or a special edging pad. Then, using a larger pad (approx. 20cm [8in] long is usually best), apply the paint in overlapping criss-cross strokes, working on an area of 1sq m (1sq yd) at a time. If you are painting ceilings or high walls, fitting the pad to an extension pole will speed up the process considerably.

Using a roller

Select a suitable sleeve for the wall surface and slide it onto the roller cage until it clicks shut. Pour some well-mixed paint into a roller tray and run the roller down the sloping part of the tray into the paint. Roll it up and down along the ridged slope to remove excess paint.

After cutting in (see pages 60–61) with a paintbrush at the edges of the room, apply the paint in side-to-side, up-and-down strokes, spreading the paint evenly over areas approx. 60cm (24in) wide. Lay off on a light upward stroke before reloading for the next area, taking care to blend the edges of the two areas together. If you are working on a ceiling or on high walls, you may wish to add an extension pole to the roller.

For advice on patterned rollers and use of rollers with textured paint, see pages 70–71.

Tools and equipment

- **Containers:** for paintbrushes, use metal or plastic buckets; for rollers, plastic trays.
- **Decorating brushes:**
  10–12.5cm (4–5in) brushes for walls.
  2.5–5cm (1–2in) brushes for details.
  5–7.5cm (2–3in) brushes for 'cutting in' around the tops of walls.
  2.5cm (1in) brushes or angled-headed brushes for window frames.
  a selection of artist's brushes for details.
  5–10cm (2–4in) oval-headed brushes for applying varnish.
- **Roller cage:** can hold a variety of sleeves.
- **Roller sleeves:**
  short-pile mohair for applying silk emulsion.
  medium-pile sheepskin for matt emulsion.
  medium-long pile for textured surfaces.
  patterned foam rollers for dramatic effects.
- **Extension pole:** for pads and rollers, when painting high areas such as ceilings.
- **Radiator roller:** small roller on a long handle for reaching into the awkward space behind radiators.
- **Paint pads:** often have hollow handles so they can be used with an extension pole.
- **Mahl stick:** to steady your hand for details.
- **Stepladder or ladders:** to create a painting platform.
- **For decorative paint effects:**
  pieces of natural sponge.
  flogger: for dragging.
  dusting brush or specialist graining brush.
  selection of stencilling brushes.
  large stippling brush.
  softener brush: to soften brush marks.
  fitch brushes: for spattering and stippling.
  specialist rollers, rockers and combs.
  lint-free rags: for rag rolling.

Equipment to hire

- **Spray guns:** to cover large areas very quickly. Always wear a face mask.
- **Battery-powered paintbrushes and rollers:** the paint is pumped from an attached reservoir along a plastic tube.
- **Scaffold tower:** a safe platform if painting a very high room.

Applying paint

Sequence of painting a room

Professional decorators always paint a room in a particular order. They start with the ceiling. The walls are next; then the woodwork around doors and windows; then cornices and skirting board; and finally, the floor. This ensures that paint spattering down from the ceiling does not ruin newly painted walls. Cleaning off any paint that drips onto woodwork immediately is another tip. It is easier to remove when it is still wet.

Applying paint

Before covering the walls in swathes of colour, you need to give some attention to the smaller details to ensure a professional finish. It is very important to create a precise finish around doors, windows and light fittings, as well as ensuring a neat line between ceiling and wall, as these are junctions which you will notice every time you enter or leave the room, or open or shut a window. You

Order of painting

1 Professional painters paint a room in a particular order. Follow this order for a professional finish.

2 Paint walls and ceilings in strips – top to bottom for walls; for ceilings, in alternating directions.

need to use a technique called 'cutting in'. Using a small brush, 2.5–5cm (1–2in), pressed firmly against the wall surface so that the bristles are slightly splayed, paint a band of paint approx. 2.5cm (1in) wide into the internal corners, wall and ceiling angles and above the skirting board.

You will need to make a similar band around doors and windows. You can do this in the same way or use a slightly different technique which ensures a neater finish. Paint a series of small, horizontal strokes at right angles to the door or window frame. Join together with a steady, firm vertical stroke of the brush, easing the bristles of the brush tight against the wooden frame.

Paint the ceiling using a roller attached to an extension pole. Paint sections in strips, working from one side of the room to the other and back again, so that the direction of application alters with each strip. In order to give solid paint coverage, within each strip apply the paint as when using a roller on a wall: starting with overlapping criss-crosses and finishing with straight strokes. When painting walls, paint in strips from the top of the wall to the bottom, starting from the side of the wall closest to any natural light source. Having painted the walls and ceiling, you should turn your attention to the precision painting areas: the doors and window frames.

Painting plaster mouldings

Next item in the sequence is the plasterwork: mouldings such as cornices and ceiling roses.

Because of the porous nature of plaster, mouldings are particularly susceptible to staining caused by damp, mould, mineral salts and nicotine. You must ensure that these have been adequately dealt with, the surface made good and primed before you start repainting. Ask at your hardware store for suitable products to tackle specific problems.

Mouldings should be painted with small paintbrushes or artist's brushes, depending on their size and the amount of detail they entail. Start by using a 2.5cm (1in) brush to apply the base colour, ensuring that the bristles are gently splayed to create a neat outer edge. When this colour has dried, you may wish to pick out some of the detail in a

Applying paint

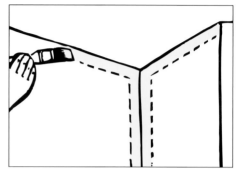

1 Before painting the wall, 'cut in' around the edges with a 2.5–5cm (1–2in) brush, with bristles slightly splayed.

2 Next, begin applying paint with a roller – in criss-cross followed by vertical strokes.

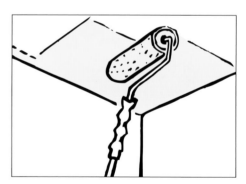

3 Paint the ceiling with a roller attached to an extension pole, working in alternating strips across the ceiling.

contrasting colour using a smaller artist's brush. If you are trying to paint a straight line or particularly fine detail, steady your hand by resting it against a mahl stick.

Painting metal pipes and radiators

Before you paint pipes or radiators, ensure that heating or hot-water appliances have been switched off. Check that the metal fixtures have had time to cool down. Ensure previously painted surfaces are free of dust by washing them down with a solution of household detergent. Key a high-gloss surface by rubbing down the paint with fine wet-and-dry paper. Rinse and ensure it is completely dry before starting to paint.

The longest-lasting finish for metal is created by using a proprietary metal or radiator paint or enamel. On radiators, use a 5cm (2in) brush and apply the paint as thinly as possible, working quickly with long, light strokes. Be very careful to avoid getting paint on or near the valves, as dried paint will cause them to stick. Use a small piece of card to prevent flicking paint onto the wall surface when you paint the edges of the radiator.

Pipes should be painted with the same paint as the radiator with a 2.5cm (1in) brush, working vertically from top to bottom.

Painting tiles

Applying paint to ceramic tiles is usually a short-term solution because, no matter how careful you are with preparation and application, paint will eventually chip or peel away from the glazed surface.

However, if you have a run of ugly tiles, giving them a quick coat of paint can act as a good facelift. Prepare the tiles for painting by washing them down with household detergent and a damp cloth.

It is now possible to purchase a proprietary tile primer which may prolong the life of a coat of paint. After this primer you should use two coats of gloss or enamel paint if you want a durable, waterproof finish.

◄ *When painting details in contrasting colours, such as here on the wooden panelling and moulding, precision is essential. Use low-tack masking tape to define the areas to be painted. When painting on wood, first apply a primer and then an undercoat to ensure that a smooth, problem-free finish is achieved.*

Painting other areas

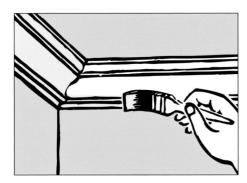

1 When painting details in contrasting colours, precision is essential. Use tape to mark off the areas to be painted.

2 Use a 2.5–5cm brush (1–2in) to paint radiators. Work quickly, applying the paint in a thin coat.

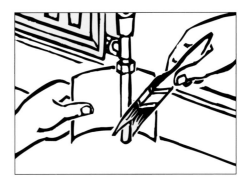

3 When painting pipes, use a piece of cardboard to prevent flicking paint onto the wall or skirting.

Paint effects guide

▲ *Oil glazes are a simple way to give walls a sophisticated sheen, however it is worth bearing in mind when you are deciding on what colour and how much to tint the glaze that the colour will become noticeable quite quickly once on the walls. Here, a preliminary coat of pale yellow eggshell has been given greater depth and texture with a grey-tinted glaze.*

Before embarking on painting a whole wall with a special technique, try out your chosen effect, either on a piece of board or on an inconspicuous corner of the wall. This will give you a chance to perfect the finish you require, and an opportunity to see how the colours work together. Cover your practice area with a coat of paint, allow to dry and only then start work on the rest of the wall.

Glazes and washes

Glazes

Transparent, oil-based glaze can be bought ready-coloured, but you can tint proprietary oil glaze to match a colour exactly. To make a basic tinted glaze, mix 1 part glaze with 3–4 parts white spirit and 25ml (1tbsp) white eggshell per 500ml (approx. 1pt) of glaze, using universal stainers to add colour.

A glaze must be applied over non-porous paint, such as eggshell. Depending on the composition, it may take up to two days to dry hard, which gives you plenty of time to correct and rework if you get it wrong first time. For this reason, glaze is easier to handle as an amateur than a wash (see below).

If you are preparing your own glaze rather than using a ready-made one, it is essential to mix up enough for the whole project before you start, because it is almost impossible to duplicate a colour exactly later.

Using glazes

Possibly the simplest material for the amateur to master, a tinted oil glaze applied on a base coat will add a subtle layer of colour, softening it and giving it greater depth.

Walls need to be carefully prepared (see pages 56–57) and then coated with one or two layers of eggshell paint. Sometimes, it is possible to use emulsion and a water-thinned wash as an alternative to glaze. However, the finished effect is seldom as elegant as that produced by an oil-based finish.

You can prolong the life of the effect – whether oil or water-based – by applying a coat of matt varnish when it is thoroughly dry. This is very important if you have painted a heavy-traffic area such as a hallway, or if it is likely to need frequent sponging.

To apply, paint the glaze onto the wall with a medium-sized decorating brush, covering 1sq m (1sq yd) at a time, using quick, random strokes. Soften brushmarks with a wide, short-bristled brush, and continue until the surface is evened out, and until you have created a thin film of near-transparent colour.

Washes

Washes are made from water-based paint. They provide a soft finish but they are less flexible and less easy than glazes for the beginner because they dry quickly.

Washes are best applied over a matt emulsion base. For effects such as rag rolling, the wash needs to comprise 1 part emulsion to 3–5 parts water. For colourwashing, it needs to be thinner: 1 part paint should be mixed with as much as 8 parts water.

Colourwashing

Colourwashing imitates the appearance of old-fashioned, distemper-painted walls and, as such, is particularly appropriate today, when natural, texture-rich interiors are popular. Some specialist paint suppliers continue to stock distemper, but it is relatively simple to recreate the same rough, slightly chalky look with thinned emulsion.

Because of the essentially uneven appearance of a colourwashed finish, it is a simple technique to master and looks particularly good on walls with a slightly irregular surface.

Because this is a very wet wash, ensure that you have covered everything that is not to be painted before you start.

Apply a coat of emulsion to the wall and allow it to dry thoroughly. Create the colourwash by thinning emulsion paint: 1 part paint to 4–8 parts water and then experiment on a small area until you find a mixture that is both easy to work with and which creates the soft gradations of colour you require. Using a large decorating brush, apply the wash in random, bold, criss-cross strokes over an area of approx. 1sq m (1sq yd); do not attempt to cover the whole wall. Then, take a slightly damp paintbrush and go over the wash to soften the brushmarks and wipe up any drips.

Do not worry if the walls look very messy and unattractive at this stage. Leave this coat to dry overnight, or for at least 12 hours, and it will improve with the wait.

Repeat the wash technique, again working on 1sq m (1sq yd) at a time. This time apply criss-cross strokes to the areas you missed the first time. If you are working in a heavy-use or humid area such as a hallway or bathroom, it is possible that the finished effect would benefit from a protective coat of matt polyurethane varnish.

Dry brushing

Dry brushing creates a rougher, more intensely dramatic effect than both glazing and colourwashing. First of all you need to apply a base coat of matt emulsion, and then pour some emulsion in your chosen top-coat colour into a paint tray.

Dip a wide, hard-bristled decorating brush into the paint and scrape off the excess against the tray's ridges or on a wooden board. Then, with cross-hatching strokes (as with colourwashing), apply the top coat. It is very important for this effect – as the name suggests – that you make sure that you keep the brush very dry and that you apply the paint in light strokes using the tip of the brush rather than its flat surface. Allow some of the base colour to show through to evoke a slightly misty effect.

For a greater depth of colour and more intensity, repeat the process, having first allowed the paint to dry thoroughly overnight, or for at least 12 hours anyway. And once again, you may wish to finish the effect with a coat of matt varnish.   ▷

▲ *Although a simple technique to master, two-colour colourwashing in the right colour combination can bring grandeur to a plain wall. Here, the layers of wash have been built up deliberately in some areas more than others, so that the varying degree to which the base colour shows through creates a sense of texture.*

▶ *Dry brushing is a great technique to use with strong colours, the dramatic texture of the cross-hatched brushstrokes enhancing vibrant shades; here green and yellow zing off each other. Equally, if you find solid colour boring, dry brushing can create a slightly distressed look: dry brush a lighter emulsion over a darker tone, say.*

Dragging

If you are looking for an elegant, softly striped effect which can enhance doors and wood panelling as well as walls, dragging is the technique you need to master. The background colour shows through the top coat as a series of fine, uneven stripes of colour.

Dragging requires a steady hand and is more tricky than washing or glazing, because of keeping the brushstrokes even along a run of wall. For beginners, it might be a good idea to start on a small area such as the panels of a door. If you are going to use this effect on walls, it is imperative that the surface is smooth and free of bumps (see pages 56–57).

Either an oil-based glaze or a diluted emulsion top coat can be used for dragging, although the oil-based version looks considerably more grand. Remember that emulsion dries faster than oil-based paint, so it may be easier for a beginner to start with an oil-based glaze: it will give you more time to work on the finish and even allows you to wipe the whole thing off and start again.

Apply two coats of eggshell paint to the wall and leave them to dry thoroughly. Next, apply a coat of oil-based glaze, working from top to bottom, and painting an area that is small enough to work on easily: a vertical strip 60cm (2ft) wide is usually practical.

Before the glaze or paint begins to dry, quickly drag a long-haired, dry flogger from the top of the wall to the bottom in a long, even stroke. It is important to move on to the next area before the edge dries. Clean excess glaze from the brush with a lint-free rag before starting each stroke.

If you use emulsion, use a mid-sheen paint as a base and be careful not to add too much water to the wash at once. Once the oil or water-based glaze has dried, protect the finish with a coat of matt varnish – or, for an even better result, several coats.

Rag rolling

A quick and easy technique suitable for a beginner, rag rolling is also an excellent way of disguising less-than-perfect walls. The more virulent colour combinations of the 1980s have been replaced by more stylish combinations where the colour of the base coat is similar to that of the top coat: try pale pastels over creamy white for a smart effect.

Oil-based paint is more suitable for rag rolling than water-based paint because of the quick drying time of the latter. However, you can use a mid-sheen emulsion if you so wish; the technique is the same.

Paint the surface with two coats of eggshell or mid-sheen emulsion and leave to dry. Prepare the tinted oil- or water-based glaze and dip a lint-free rag or chamois leather into the mixture, ensuring that the cloth is evenly soaked to avoid blotches on the wall. Squeeze out and roll it up into a loose sausage. Roll the cloth gently over the wall's surface in a random motion.

For a gentler effect, try rag rolling off. Having painted the dried base coat with a top coat of oil- or water-based glaze, roll a clean rag across the glaze to expose the colour beneath. For an even softer look, go over the surface with a softening brush about half an hour after rolling off.

Sponging on

One of the speediest techniques, sponging on is one of the easiest to master. Again, it looks better if the two colours you choose are similar in tone and intensity. You can achieve a richer look by sponging two different shades over the base coat.

Apply two even coats of eggshell or emulsion. Mix the glaze or wash and pour it into a paint tray. Soak a natural sponge in water for the emulsion wash, or in white spirit for an oil-based glaze; wring it out carefully.

Dip the sponge into the paint and rub off any excess against the ridges of the paint tray. Gently dab the sponge on the wall; wring it out frequently to prevent the paint building

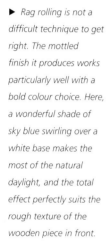

▶ *Rag rolling is not a difficult technique to get right. The mottled finish it produces works particularly well with a bold colour choice. Here, a wonderful shade of sky blue swirling over a white base makes the most of the natural daylight, and the total effect perfectly suits the rough texture of the wooden piece in front.*

Paint effects

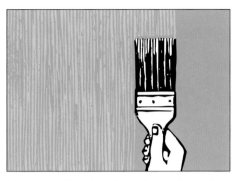

1 For colourwashing, apply the paint in bold, criss-cross strokes across an area of approximately 1sq m (1sq yd).

1 For a smart effect, drag a long-haired, dry flogger from the top of the wall to the bottom in a long, even stroke.

1 Randomly roll a chamois or lint-free cloth soaked in your second shade of paint over the wall's surface.

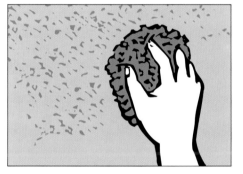

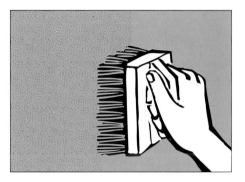

1 Gently dab a sponge coated in your second colour over the wall. Wring out frequently to prevent ugly splodges.

1 Load a large brush with paint and knock the metal part against a ruler. Stand back to check for bare patches.

1 Load a stippling brush with paint and remove excess with newspaper. Work slowly down the wall.

---

up into clumps. If you are using a second colour, wait until the first coat is thoroughly dry before applying it.

Sponging off

Sponging off – like rag rolling off – creates a slightly more subtle, cloudy effect than its technical counterpart.

Brush a coat of tinted oil glaze with the consistency of thick cream over the dried base coat using a wide decorating brush. Working on 1sq m (1sq yd) at a time to avoid the glaze drying out, wring out a sponge in white spirit and dab it swiftly on the wet glaze, lifting some away from the surface.

Bagging is adapted from these techniques. Using a small cloth in a scrunched-up plastic bag, dab the wall in the same way as you did with the sponge to create lively patterns. To prevent blotches of colour, wipe excess paint from the bag from time to time.

Ideally, sponged and bagged walls which could be easily damaged should be sealed with a protective coat of matt varnish.

Spattering

A dramatic and relatively simple process to master, spattering is messy, so before you begin, ensure that the floor is covered with plastic and that you are wearing a mask and eye protection. The effect is cumulative, built up by spattering tiny dots of one or more colours against a base coat; two or even three spattering colours will add to the depth and richness of the effect.

Using a piece of newspaper as your practice wall, load a large decorating brush with paint or glaze and knock the metal part of it against a stick to flick off excess paint until you achieve the size of dots you want. Then, hold the brush parallel to the wall and knock it in the same way against a stick or piece of batten. Continue until the wall is covered in a fine spray of dots; stand back to check for any slightly bare patches and go over it again until the coating is even.

If you are using a second colour, allow the first dots to dry, before repeating the process with a second colour.

Stippling

This effect is best suited to walls in reasonable condition and needs a base of oil-based, non-porous paint in order for it to 'take' evenly. Glazing liquid, eggshell thinned with white spirit or mid-sheen emulsion thinned with water can all be used.

Coat the base colour with a thin film of glaze using a wide decorator's brush, working on 1sq m (1sq yd) at a time. Using a specialist stippling brush, jab the bristles against the wall in sharp, rhythmic strokes, creating an elegantly mottled surface. (Purpose-made stippling brushes can be prohibitively expensive. Although you will not get the same super-sophisticated effect as with a professional brush, it is worth experimenting with any large, firm-bristled brush – a new household broom can be quite a good substitute.) Work swiftly across the area, blending sections together; take care to avoid sliding the brush across the surface as this will create smears. Wipe the stippling bush periodically with a lint-free cloth to remove excess glaze.

Faux finishes

▲ *Walls that imitate materials such as terracotta or plaster are a wonderful foil for relaxed interiors. They look particularly good as a backdrop for wood or sumptuous textiles. Picking out the colour and, as here, the texture of the wall in the furnishings of a room brings cohesion to a scheme that may in fact contain many disparate elements.*

the kind of effect you want to recreate and practise on a piece of paper or board before you embark on your panelling or walls.

Use a soft cloth to rub some transparent oil glaze onto a base of two coats of eggshell. Dip a fine artist's brush into a glaze of the required colour; quickly and gently flick some veins across the paint surface. Do not worry about a few breaks and blobs in the paint; this will add to the finished effect. Using the tip of a softening brush, softly stroke the veins to blur them. Dip a fine artist's brush into white spirit and gently go over the glazed surface, roughly following the lines of some of the veins. Soften the surface again, this time in one direction only. And finally, take a clean softener brush and go lightly over the surface to eliminate any brush marks, and creating the desired cloudy finish.

Faux bois

Elaborate wood-graining effects that are designed to imitate rich and desirable marks and patterns – those found in burr walnut,

Once you have mastered some basic paint techniques, you may wish to try something a little more adventurous. *Faux* finishes allow you to imitate the effect of wood, stone, fabric and other unusual materials at a fraction of the cost. The key to success is to use a light touch – and to know when to stop. Never be tempted to splash on too much paint; rather, build up the effect in layers.

Draw inspiration from a wide variety of sources. Begin by looking at the real thing – marble, wood grain and stone – then at postcards, books, paintings, even films.

Antiquing

Few people are fortunate enough to live with genuine, original old plaster walls. 'Ageing' a surface is a relatively simple process,

however, and fun to do too. Dry brushing (see pages 62–63) is an effective way of re-creating the effect of an old wall, or you may wish to use layers of paint in slightly different tones. Start with the brightest shade and gradually 'age' the surface with layers of wash, working with the original shade and darkening it by degrees with a little raw umber. Smear on the paint roughly with a brush or cloth and when it is dry, rub gently at the paint surface with some sandpaper or wire wool, revealing glimpses of the original colour and even touches of plaster.

Marbling

There are many different kinds of marble and, consequently, many different kinds of marbling. Study the real thing to decide on for instance – will take some time to perfect, but even a decorating novice can achieve good basic graining effects.

Choose a suitable base colour – deep red is a good base for a mahogany effect while a pale golden cream creates realistic oak grain – and apply two coats of eggshell. Mix up the graining colour by thinning some transparent oil glaze with white spirit and colouring it with a little artist's oil paint: a dark purplish brown or even black creates a realistic glaze for mahogany, while a little burnt umber can replicate oak. Apply the glaze in an even, dense coat on top of the eggshell.

Take a dusting brush and drag it along the length of the surface in a light sweep. Repeat this sweeping brush-stroke to blur any hard lines. With a clean softener or dusting brush, quickly and gently work across the grain.

Imitation terracotta

Warm 'terracotta' walls are the perfect backdrop for today's ethnically inspired interiors, and a convincing effect is simple to achieve.

Paint the wall with a base coat of matt emulsion in a creamy gold colour. Dilute terracotta-coloured emulsion – equal parts of paint to water – and coat the wall with a wide decorating brush, brushing backwards and forwards over the painted surface, continuing even when the wash begins to dry.

Allow the paint to dry out completely and then take a clean decorating brush dipped in water to dampen down the surface, working on the usual 1sq m (1sq yd) at a time. Dilute some cream-coloured emulsion: mix 1 part paint to 2 parts water. Using a 2.5cm (1in) decorating brush, make a rough pattern of lines across the damp piece of wall. Using a

▲ *The key to successful marbling is subtlety. Here soft creams and greys applied with a very light touch look as appropriate with the wooden floor as they do with the more contemporary chrome table.*

◀ *There are really no limits to the kind of effects you can achieve on your walls. These walls have been given the soft, coppery bloom of verdigris. As with all* faux *techniques, it is essential that you study the real thing before you start, to ensure that you get the detail right.*

slightly dampened natural sponge, dab at the paint surface to blur and smudge the lines. Keep gently sponging the area until you have achieved the soft, cloudy bloom of terracotta. Use this technique with different colours to imitate lead or unfinished plaster.

Verdigris

To recreate on walls the wonderful blue-green patina of weathered copper, brass or bronze, start with a dark brown coat of matt emulsion. When it has dried, stipple a light covering of bright turquoise green over the entire surface, allowing a trace of the base colour to show through. Repeat the process in some areas, making the turquoise deeper.

Then look at a real piece of verdigris to get an exact colour match for the kind of effect you want and choose a bright shade of green. Go over parts of the turquoise green with a stipple brush. And finally, with a very light hand and an almost dry brush, stipple some of the wall once more – with faint traces of dark gold or bronze paint.

Finally apply a coat of matt varnish; you might perhaps like to mix a little white paint into it to dull the finish slightly.

Faux leather

A leather effect in deep oxblood, bottle green or dark brown can look very smart, particularly when used to add richness to a small space. Using a small to medium-sized decorating brush, stipple the wall thickly with a paler-coloured matt emulsion than the finished effect you are looking for. Allow to dry for at least 24 hours.

Repeat the process with a darker shade of emulsion, this time splaying and twisting the brush as you work to create texture. Allow this layer to dry, again for at least 24 hours.

Mix some artist's oil paint – one part raw umber to one part burnt sienna – into a transparent oil glaze and rub this over the surface of the wall with a cloth; take another soft cloth and gently but thoroughly rub off the excess glaze, allowing the texture of the emulsion to show through. In places, rub the surface with fine sandpaper to reveal some of the emulsion, but ultimately protect the surface with a semi-matt varnish.

Trompe l'oeil

Paint is a truly versatile material which, provided you have time and patience on your side, allows you to create a huge range of decorative effects for relatively little cost.

Trompe l'oeil painting has a lineage almost as long as the history of painting. Although it tends to bring to mind the grandiose ceilings of Italian palazzi or mural schemes in the great country houses, this is nothing more than a great misconception. The term means 'an accomplished visual trick' – and whether you want to reproduce a vista on a wall, or a grisaille frieze, or an eighteenth-century 'book door', or the effect of tiles or marble, sandstone or granite, *trompe l'oeil* is the name of the game. It is merely a question of playing a witty visual trick on the passer by.

Painting a mural

Whilst not necessarily possessing the creative or technical abilities of Mantegna, Tiepolo or Veronese, you should not be frightened of trying to create a grand pictorial effect for yourself in your own home. You could add a sumptuous garden view to a windowless room, or create a fantastic landscape mural on an entire wall, or you could complement a simple period scheme with painted architectural detailing: just consider which seems most appropriate to the scale and function of the room. What is more, *trompe l'oeil* painting is ideal for having fun; exaggeration and weird perspective may result in a surreal effect, but that may be just what you want – a visual diversion and a talking point!

Perhaps you have been inspired by an illustration in a book or magazine; in a way this would be an easier course to pursue than working from scratch if your artistic skills are limited because all the basic techniques of copying an image from a book are relatively easy to master. Someone else has done the difficult bit, making all the elements of the image work together; all you need to do is scale up the image to fit the chosen site.

The first thing to do is to trace the design onto tracing paper using pen or pencil and then draw a grid over it, numbering each square. Next, draw a grid directly onto the wall, with the same number of squares, numbered to correspond with your original grid.

▲ *Successful* trompe l'oeil *painting requires a substantial level of skill, but the finished result is worth the work. You can expand a small space or contract a large one, you can even create an Aegean view in the middle of a city, with views of islands across the bay – the stuff of daydreams, the perfect setting for a cosy armchair and a good book.*

Squaring up

1 Copy the desired image onto tracing paper, simplifying it for clarity, and then draw a grid of squares over it.

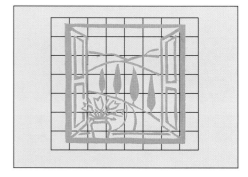

2 Draw another grid on the wall, and sketch in the main lines of the design as a painting guide, square by square.

Fake tiles

1 Create a wall of 'tiles' with a small roller. Work in horiz-ontal rows; uneven edges add to the handmade effect.

2 Vertical bands of diamond-shaped tiles are equally quick and simple; use a small roller held diagonally.

It is worth remembering to prepare your wall with a base coat of paint before you transfer your design. Then copy the traced design closely onto the wall in pen or soft pencil, using the grid to guide you. Work square by square; it may help to look at each square as a series of abstract lines, rather than as part of the whole scheme; you can always soften up the junctions between the squares once you have copied all of them. It may help also to fix the traced design onto the wall using masking tape as a constant refer-ence; you should always stand back and take stock as you work. Do not pay too much attention to detail at this stage as you only want a sketched guide. If you define every-thing too rigidly, you will find it very difficult to paint freely and this will most likely result in a stiff, lifeless design. Once your sketch exists, start painting and be bold!

If you are not confident about your tech-nique with a paintbrush, do not struggle with an ambitious project in the vain hope of pro-ducing a masterpiece. Try decoupage to recreate decorative plasterwork rather than trying to reproduce a Renaissance frieze free-hand. If you have access to a photocopier and your desired motif is reasonably small-scale, it is obviously very easy to enlarge or shrink a design mechanically, and to repeat a motif for a border. Or mock up panels using stone-effect paper, antiquing it with a tinted glaze.

In a kitchen or bathroom, it might be more appropriate to think simple, and to use a small radiator roller to create a quick and effective tile effect. Load the roller evenly and paint rows of tiles – either horizontally or as diamonds – leaving a 'grout' space between each 'tile' for a more realistic look.

◄ *Trompe l'oeil can be as elaborate as the sea view (left) or as simple as a couple of runs of tiles, here. It is important that you match your aspirations to your level of skill, but almost anyone could have a stab at this effect.*

Stripes, checks and patterns

▲ *Paint allows you to get the effect of hand-blocked wallpaper at a fraction of the cost. This sophisticated looking lattice was created by painting a red top coat over the undercoat which had been covered in criss-crossed masking tape.*

Making stripes

Stripes and checks comprise a decorating trend that never goes out of fashion; they have a striking, graphic quality, and a fresh, well-ordered, clean-cut appearance, whether or not their edges are sharp, making them suitable for practically any situation – in combination with areas of plain colour or with each other. Hugely versatile, stripes and checks are equally varied in their effect; wide stripes will be bolder than narrower ones, or you can create a more sophisticated rhythm, following one wide with three narrow stripes, for instance, and then repeating it.

Think too about the effect of colour on your chosen stripes; you could create a stunningly dramatic study using dark paint and wide stripes, provided that you could then light it efficiently, but that combination would not work in a kitchen or dining room, where a fresher and lighter effect would be better. All you need is a little patience, a plumb line, your paint and tools.

The quickest, simplest method of creating stripes is to paint the wall in your chosen base colour and then use a roller to create stripes in a contrasting shade using a plumb line to guide you. If you wish to create broader stripes than it is possible to paint with a roller, mark out the area to be painted with masking tape before you start, again using a plumb line to establish a true vertical. If you like stripes but are wary of the crisp, bandbox look, roughly and lightly paint in your stripes and then immediately go over the wet paint with a dry roller to create a

Making stripes

1 Use a plumb line to mark out vertical stripes. Use a soft pencil and a very light touch.

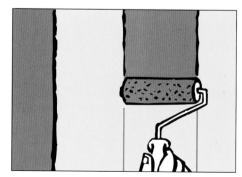

2 With the pencil marks to guide you, carefully paint the stripes with a wide roller.

slightly distressed effect. A smaller, 'pin-stripe' effect can be created by cutting a foam roller into narrow stripes, using tape to keep each part of the roller separate.

You could use this stripe both vertically and horizontally, and in more than one colour, to create a chequered effect.

Using patterned rollers

Patterned rollers have been used to decorate walls for several centuries. They are enjoying a popular revival today because they are easy to use and create interesting effects cheaply – either with colour or with textured paint. You can make your own, or specialist suppliers stock rollers and rockers for more difficult effects – from wood graining to damask.

Using textured paint

Apart from the practical aspects of textured paint, and it is very useful for covering less than perfect surfaces, its aesthetic potential is much under-rated. You can buy a range of patterned roller sleeves specifically for textured paint and with a little time, effort and imagination, it is possible to achieve sophisticated, sculpted effects for relatively little.

▶ *Few paint effects are simpler to achieve or more dramatic in appearance than stripes. In this country-style bedroom, all four walls have been painted with wide stripes. Marked out using masking tape and a plumb line and then roughly painted in deep red, they are bold and yet far from brash, producing an all-American look.*

3 If you are worried about creating precise edges, use masking tape to mark off the lines.

4 To create narrow stripes, divide the roller in two with an elastic band.

5 To create checks, use the roller to go across the vertical lines in a horizontal band.

Stamping, stencilling and gilding

▶ *Stamping is the ideal paint technique if you're short of time – or skill. A repeat design, such as this simple pattern of hearts stamped onto a colourwashed wall, gives a dramatic effect, but takes only a matter of hours to carry out.*

design onto an acetate sheet and cut out with a sharp knife. Attach to the wall with masking tape or spray adhesive.

Next, apply the colour. Whether you are using a stencil brush or a spray can, the secret is a light touch. With a spray can, waft it quickly and gently over the surface, gradually building up the colour in subtle layers. If using a stencil brush, rub it on a piece of paper towel until almost all the paint has been removed from the head of the brush, then stipple or swirl it over the stencil. Remove the stencil, reposition and repeat the process.

Gilding

Few decorating projects are more satisfying than working with gold leaf. However, the expense of the material puts it far outside the pocket of most amateur decorators. There is no reason, though, why you should deprive yourself of using lustrous metallic materials in small quantities, perhaps on a motif against

Stamping

Compared to other paint effects, stamping really can be, quite literally, child's play. Make your own stamps from medium to high-density foam in the same way as a child makes potato-cut stamps, drawing on a design and then cutting away the excess foam with a scalpel. Stick the sponge onto a piece of wood and attach a small door knob to the back of it to make application easier. If, however, you would rather buy a stamp, there are many outlets that now stock a wide range of designs made from rubber or foam, thus making them very hard-wearing.

Apply the paint either with a roller or by dipping the stamp into a plate containing a small amount of paint. Ensure an even coating and then set to work, taking your design across the whole wall.

Stencilling

This is one of the cheapest ways to provide a decorative finish. Use stencils to create a dramatic pictorial effect or use a motif to create a border or all-over pattern at a fraction of the cost of wallpaper. Choose from the enormous selection of pre-cut stencils available or make your own. Draw your

Stamping

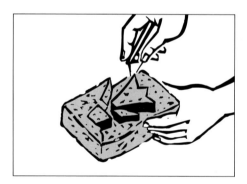

1 First draw the outline of your design onto the sponge. Cut away the surrounding areas using a scalpel.

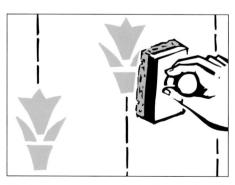

2 For large-scale patterns, chalk guidelines onto the wall. Coat the sponge evenly with paint and dab on firmly.

Stencilling

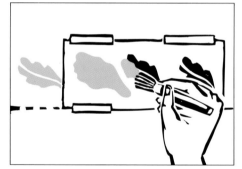

1 Remove excess paint from the brush with a paper towel before swirling or stippling it lightly over the stencil.

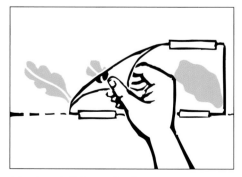

2 Gently peel off the stencil, taking care not to smudge the paint, and reposition it.

a wall painted in a deep rich colour such as lacquer red, midnight blue or forest green. Dutch metal leaf or aluminium leaf are less expensive alternatives to the real thing. Aluminium leaf can be made to gleam like gold with one or two coats of orange shellac. These, and the substances mentioned below, are available from specialist decorating outlets.

First, give the wall to be gilded a coat of flat or mid-sheen oil-based paint. Decide on your design or motif and either draw it free-hand on the wall or use a stencil as a guide. Paint the areas to be gilded with ready-made red gesso for Dutch metal, or cobalt blue casein for silver or aluminium leaf. When this is dry, paint on a thin layer of goldsize, following the manufacturer's instructions. When the goldsize is only slightly tacky, gently press on a sheet of leaf, leaf-side down, on the sized area. Carefully peel away the leaf's wax backing and lay down the next sheet so that it slightly overlaps with the first. Continue until you have built up your pattern. Leave for several hours to dry and rub off the loose leaf with a soft cloth; the rest of the leaf should remain in the sized area of your motif.

Finish off by varnishing the whole surface with a clear, semi-gloss oil-based varnish.

For those who long for glitter, it is also worth checking out the wide range of metallic paints, powders, creams and pens on the market. These can be put to a wide range of decorating uses, from painting a whole wall to picking out moulding detail.

Gilding

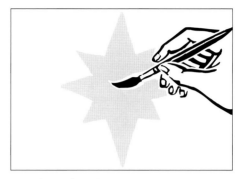

1 *Paint the motif in red gesso or cobalt blue casein. When dry, paint a layer of goldsize over the top.*

2 *When the goldsize is only slightly tacky, press on the sheet, leaf-side down.*

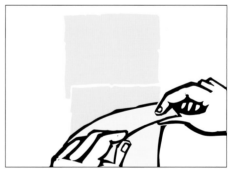

3 *Carefully peel away the wax backing and apply the next sheet, overlapping the first slightly. Let dry overnight.*

4 *Rub off the excess leaf with a soft cloth, leaving the original motif intact.*

▲ *Given the costs involved, it makes sense to restrict the use of gilding to small areas. This random design of horizontal and vertical gold blocks is restrained but nonetheless extremely effective, giving interest to plain white walls and mirroring the angular patterns of the parquet flooring.*

Problems with paintwork

Most flaws in paint surfaces can be avoided if you are scrupulous in your preparation and always use the correct materials. Even with the utmost care, however, some problems may occur, but these can usually be salvaged and sometimes do not entail too much extra work.

Blistering
This is caused by moisture or air trapped beneath a coat of oil-based paint. The answer is to strip off the paint, carefully fill any holes and then repaint. With wood, it may be necessary to prime, undercoat and then repaint.

Flaking
When the new surface reacts badly to what is underneath it, flaking occurs. Emulsion paint, for example, can flake when painted over a high-gloss finish or distemper. Unfortunately if this occurs there is no alternative but to strip the flaking surface, get back to the base, prepare it again properly and paint the area again.

Wrinkling
If you apply a second coat of oil-based paint, such as eggshell, before the first coat has dried thoroughly, the surface may wrinkle. Strip the paint and reapply it.

Runs and drips
Possibly the most common problem, runs and drips are caused by loading too much paint onto the brush. Let the paint dry, rub the proud blobs gently with fine-grade sandpaper, remove the dust created by the sandpaper and touch up with fresh paint.

Paint faults

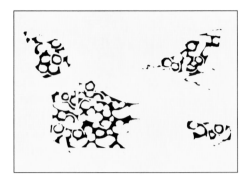

1 Blistering is caused by air trapped beneath a coat of paint. It has to be stripped off and the surface repainted.

1 The only solution to an area that is flaking is to strip the area back to the original surface and begin again.

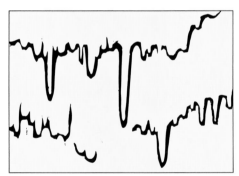

1 Drips can be corrected by rubbing them flat with sandpaper, cleaning off the dust and repainting.

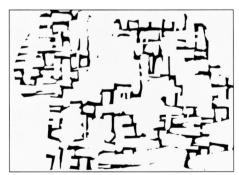

1 Crazing occurs when the top coat of paint reacts badly with the surface beneath. Strip off and repaint.

▲ *Strong blocks of contrasting solid colour can work wonderfully if walls are in good condition and prepared thoroughly. When using strong colours, however, it is wise to create some kind of continuity. Here, the midnight blue dining room has a terracotta picture rail and yellow stained chairs to continue the scheme from the living room.*

◀ *Cloudy colourwashing, rubbed on with a cloth rather than applied with a brush, is a wonderfully speedy technique perfectly suited to the style of this country interior. Paint treatments that have the effect, visually, of texturizing the surface are suited to walls that may have minor imperfections such as slightly uneven plastering.*

Cleaning equipment

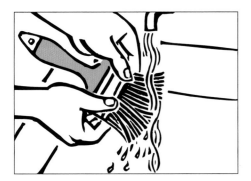

1 Clean off excess paint under running cold water. Then wash in a weak solution of warm water and detergent.

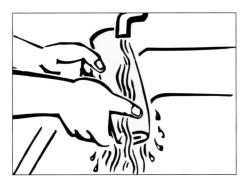

2 Prolong the life of a roller by rinsing out emulsion paint under a cold running tap until the water turns clear.

Crazing

This occurs when a layer of new paint reacts badly with a painted surface underneath, or if layers of paint have different drying times. The only option is to repaint, removing all the layers of paint and preparing the surface again from scratch.

Grit, dust or insects in the paint

If this occurs, wait until the paint dries, then sand the area gently with fine sandpaper and wipe off the dust. If you sand lightly enough, you may not need to touch up the paint.

Stains in paintwork

Stains occur when insufficient preparation is done before the emulsion is applied. Mineral salts, moulds and other residues and impurities can react badly with the water in emulsion and will seep through the surface. Get back to the original surface and coat it with a proprietary primer-sealer and when that has dried, repaint.

Poor coverage

This is most likely to show when you are applying a light colour over a dark base.

Streaky flashes of the base colour will appear under the top coat. Apply further coats of paint, until you have a solid top colour.

Cleaning equipment

Cleaning your equipment after you have finished painting will significantly prolong its life. Brushes, rollers and pads that have been used with emulsion or other water-based paints should be rinsed with cold water to remove excess paint, paying particular attention to the base of the bristles, and then washed in a weak solution of warm water and detergent to remove the residue.

Equipment used for oil-based paint or varnish should be cleaned with turpentine, white spirit or a proprietary cleaner, ensuring that it is worked well into the bristles or pile. When all the paint has been removed, all equipment should be rinsed thoroughly in warm water and shaken vigorously to remove the excess.

To keep their shape, brushes can be wrapped in clean paper towels fixed with masking tape. Hang up brushes and rollers, and place pads face-up to maintain the pile, and your equipment should last you for years.

Paper and fabric

Many home decorators are hesitant about
hanging wallpaper themselves because they
imagine that it will be terribly difficult to
achieve a professional finish. However, if
the task is approached in a methodical way
and the chosen paper is not too difficult to
handle and match, you may be surprised
how easy and satisfying it is to put up
your own paper.

After many years in the decorative wilderness, wallpapers seem to be enjoying something of a revival. The enormous selection of designs available, and the ability of paper to disguise everything from cracked walls to clumsy proportions, make them a great resource for the decorator.

Whether you want to recreate the look of a Palladian villa, a Victorian boudoir or a 1950s diner, you will find that there are papers on the market to make your task easier. And once you have chosen your main paper, you can turn your attention to the many co-ordinating borders and friezes that will create a more 'finished' job. They can be used in combination with wallpaper, by themselves to pep up painted walls, or to create architectural interest where it is lacking. Indeed, such combinations seem to tap into the mood of the moment, for they tend to allow the feeling of an easy layering of pattern and texture to predominate.

Basic principles

Having decided to be brave and work with wallpaper, there are several basic principles to follow to get maximum mileage from the wallpaper you choose.

Wallpaper is a great ally when you want to play optical tricks with a space. Use it to expand or contract the space in which you are working, or to draw the eye away from ugly but immovable features. Turning to the detail of the matter, dark colours and heavy patterns will generally make a room seem smaller, while pale, loosely patterned ones – and large trellised papers too – will make the room seem larger, and vertical stripes on the walls tend to make low ceilings appear higher.

In general, rooms that are used a lot prefer plainer papers because heavy patterns can be wearing on the eye, and are therefore tiring to live with. They are also more difficult to mix with other furnishings, particularly if you do not have the well-experienced decorator's touch.

One of the aspects governing the revival of interest in wallpaper is technology. Wallpapers are now easier to hang than ever before, not least because of the ready-pasted

varieties, and can be used with ease on a far greater variety of surfaces than they used to be. So, while in the past wallpapering was seen as a daunting prospect for almost all but the most experienced of decorators, nowadays that dubious reputation is beginning to be dispelled as myth. And justifiably

▲ Walls don't have to be covered with wallpaper – there are many different techniques that could be used to achieve an interesting effect. Here, the walls have been covered in brown packaging paper to provide a cheap but extremely effective covering. Other sorts of paper can also be used. Try sticking up sheets of music, photocopies of old prints or even pictures cut out from magazines.

◄ Wallpaper can be used in any part of the house, even the bathroom. Papers are available in different weights and for different uses. Here a vinyl-coated wallpaper has been used to combat potential problems from heat, damp and humidity.

so, for with the correct equipment and a methodical approach, wallpapering is a relatively straightforward task to get right – on most of the walls in a home.

At its most basic, wallpapering with plain lining paper is a way of covering less-than-perfect walls in preparation for painting or papering with a decorative paper. Even a beginner can tackle this, as it does not require the matching of difficult patterns and repeats.

Lining paper can be purchased in several thicknesses, and it is definitely easier to work with the heavier ones because they are less likely to stretch or tear as you work. If you are daunted by the prospect of papering but it is really the only option for the room you are decorating, give yourself some confidence by tackling a small job like lining a room and then move on to a more ambitious project with a patterned paper.

If your skills have not been tested, or you consider yourself unskilled, there are several basic guidelines you can follow to make your life easier: buy ready-pasted wallpaper; be cautious about using strong patterns as they are harder to measure up for and more difficult to hang; and avoid cheaper papers as they have a tendency to tear. (It is a false economy to think that you should buy cheaper paper in order not to waste money if everything goes wrong, because the reality is that it is far more likely to go wrong if you do. Be bold and buy good-quality paper in the first place and you are more likely both to do a good job and to achieve a good finish.)

Whatever your level of skill, buy all the wallpaper you need for a job in one go in order to avoid variations in colour, and always buy one more roll than you have calculated as being needed just in case your calculations are slightly inaccurate. And the best tip comes from the professionals: always, always clear up as you go along. Although getting rid of damp scraps of paper and wiping up paste smears as they occur may seem enormously time-consuming, it is this kind of attention to detail that can make all the difference between a shoddy job and one that looks enviably professional.

Directory of wallpaper and vinyl

There is a massive range of wallpapers available, in every kind of finish – from traditional patterns to imitation paint effects. Decoratively, the possibilities are endless. Practically, some papers are more suitable for some tasks than others.

Cheap papers tend to be thin and are therefore tricky to handle and consequently more difficult to hang. They are also more liable to show wear and tear. Sturdier – and therefore more expensive – papers are usually a better investment.

Most rolls come in standard sizes: 10m (33ft) long and 52cm (20½in) wide. Fabric papers are generally exorbitantly expensive – so much so that they are sometimes sold like fabric, by the metre.

Most papers are treated to repel moisture to different degrees: spongeable papers can be wiped clean; washable papers can be washed with water. Vinyls, which are coated with a tough plastic, can be scrubbed clean.

Textured papers are very good for covering small cracks and other minor imperfections in the wall surface. Lending a variety to the texture of surfaces in a room is a good alternative to using a variety of colours or tones.

1

2

4

Woodchip

A tough, durable paper designed to cover small imperfections in wall and ceiling surfaces. It is inexpensive and is supplied in an off-white colour, to be painted to match the room's colour scheme. It is extremely difficult to remove once it is in place and has rather fallen out of favour recently. If your walls are imperfect, go for a more interesting relief paper such as anaglypta, or for a distressed paint finish for a more dramatic effect. 1

Lining

Heavy-duty off-white paper which is applied to walls after any levelling out of the plaster but before any painting and papering. It is used to achieve a smooth, professional finish, and can be bought in five different thicknesses.

Vinyl

Possibly the most widely available species of wallpaper, vinyl is now obtainable in a massive variety of designs, many with co-ordinating borders or friezes. A paper backing is covered with a layer of waterproof vinyl, thus making the surface extremely durable as it can be sponged down without risk of spoiling the finish. Easy to hang and remove, vinyl is available with an unglued or ready-pasted backing. If you intend to use an unpasted paper, it is advisable to use a fungicidal adhesive to prevent mould from growing underneath.

Embossed

Available in a wide selection of relief patterns, from floral designs to patterns imitating wood panelling, ready to be finished with gloss or emulsion paint. Their hard-wearing finish makes them popular for the area below the dado in hallways and for any walls with a less-than-perfect finish; once painted, their tough surface is washable.

Lincrusta has a texture that can resemble anything from tiles to wood grain. A solid paper backing is coated with a pliable filler and linseed oil. This is pressed into a pattern while soft, and once hard gives a tough, scrubbable wall-covering, particularly when coated with eggshell or a high-gloss oil-based paint, as many manufacturers recommend, especially if it is being used in a heavy traffic area.

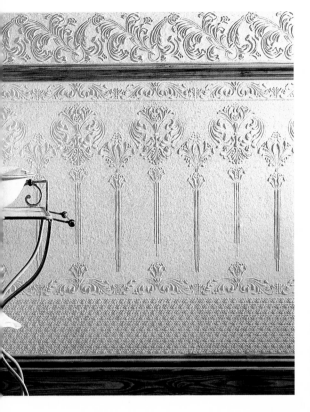

Anaglypta is a lighter, more flexible paper than lincrusta, but its finish is also extremely durable. It is made from two layers of paper, pressed together and embossed with a huge variety of relief patterns.   **2**

Hand-block-printed

These papers come in a huge variety of designs and their quality and depth of colour cannot be surpassed. They are, however, expensive to buy. To defray the costs and make a little paper go a long way you could consider hanging them as panels edged by narrow wooden moulding, or using them above or below the dado in combination with a less expensive paper or paint. They are bought unpasted and hanging them requires great diligence.   **4**

Machine-printed

The most widely available kind of wallpaper, machine-printed papers come in a huge variety of designs and finishes and are less expensive than hand-blocked paper. They can sometimes be dressed up with a coat of matt polyurethane varnish.   **5**

Foamed polyethylene

A soft, lightweight paper, also called Novamura. Comes in a wide range of designs and is relatively easy to hang.

Friezes and borders

Wallpaper ranges now nearly always include a series of co-ordinating borders or friezes, which means that making a decision about detailing and finishing can be completely straightforward. However, you should feel free to create different effects, using more original combinations, and picking up on painted finishes too. Borders and friezes are sold in rolls and are roughly 7.5–30cm (3–12in) wide. And although friezes are usually hung horizontally at the level of the skirting board, dado rail or picture rail, borders can also be used to create 'panels', by making up squares or rectangles.   **3**

Preparing the surface for wallpapering

▶ *Wallpapers come in a dazzling selection of finishes and styles, from rustic to romantic, from delicate hand-blocked to tough vinyl. This country-style paper is strikingly pretty but has a washable surface – invaluable in a kitchen.*

As with painting, the quality of the finish you will achieve with wallpaper is dependent upon thorough preparation. A new wallpaper will transform the look of a room but it will not necessarily hide the basic defects of the wall beneath. Some textured papers, such as woodchip or anaglypta, will successfully cover minor imperfections, but smooth-finish papers can be extremely unforgiving.

Prepare for wallpapering in the same way as you would for painting (see pages 56–57) by moving as much furniture as you can out of the room and pushing the rest into the centre where you can cover it with dust sheets. You will need to cover the floor in plastic sheeting which should then be covered by a fabric dust sheet, to prevent you slipping on the wet plastic. Stripping old wallpaper is an extremely damp process, so it is also vital that you pay attention to your own safety while you do it. Because of the amount of water you are using, you may wish to turn off the power temporarily at the mains while you strip the paper near light switches, electrical sockets and other fittings.

Preparation

It is very important to remove old wallpaper properly and then rectify any damage to the wall beneath before starting to paper. Left untreated, damp patches will eventually seep through, and impurities in the plaster could eventually spoil the paper. It is essential to investigate any problems at this stage and have them dealt with before wasting money on decorating what may then have to be redone.

Stripping old wallpaper

Vinyl papers are generally the simplest to remove. In fact, many of them are specifically designed so that you can simply peel them off the wall. Gently pull at the patterned top layer and it should begin to separate from the plain backing, leaving a layer of what amounts to lining paper on which to hang the new design. Sometimes, however, this paper is too damaged to use effectively as lining paper and if this is so, you will have to soak and scrape the paper to reach the smoother layer beneath.

Non-peelable vinyls and other papers need to be dampened to loosen the adhesive before you can remove them. There are several methods of getting the moisture to penetrate the paper's surface. The simplest way is to use the corner of a wallpaper scraper gently to score the paper, taking care not to press so hard as to make indentations on the plaster beneath; alternatively, there are scoring tools which you can simply move across the paper's surface. They leave tiny holes in the paper to allow the water to penetrate effectively without harming the wall.

Next, allow warm, soapy water to soak into the surface. Use a hand-held sprayer or a sponge to apply the solution, working from the top so that the water runs down the wall, presoaking the lower part of the wall. When the water has soaked in properly, you can begin to scrape the wall using a scraper or wallpaper remover, using the sponge to resoak any particularly stubborn areas.

Alternatively, hire or buy a steam stripper, which will almost undoubtedly cut down your preparation time considerably: the heat and moisture of the steam work quickly to loosen the glue.

When you think you have removed all the paper, go over the whole wall again, lightly scraping and wiping away any residue of paper or glue which may still be stuck to the wall. Carefully fill any dents or cracks and deal with any impurities such as mould growth or mineral-salt build-up (see pages 56–57).

Sizing

Size reduces the absorbency of a plaster wall. Thus sizing makes hanging paper easier because the adhesive adheres more readily to the sealed wall. Size should be applied to prepared walls – which have been allowed to dry out completely after soaking or steaming – using a large pasting brush. When you have finished, wipe any drips of size off woodwork using a damp cloth.

Lining paper and cross-lining

If your walls are marred with minor cracks, cover them up with lining paper to provide a smooth surface for paint or decorative paper. Medium-grade paper is normally used on walls; thicker paper is used on ceilings as it is less likely to tear as you put it up. As with decorative paper, follow the manufacturer's directions on the type of size and paste to use and allow the paper plenty of time to dry out, usually overnight, before hanging decorative paper over the top.

If you are going to paint the wall, the lining paper is usually pasted vertically. However, if you were to adopt this method under wallpaper, there is a risk that the seams from the different papers would fall in the same places, and this would cause unsightly ridges. To prevent this, you should cross-line the walls, hanging the lining paper horizontally rather than vertically. The essential method is the same, whichever the orientation: measure the walls, making sure the tape measure is strictly horizontal, and cut the paper into lengths, as you would when hanging a decorative paper vertically. Starting at the top of the wall and working down to the skirting board, hang the paper from side to side.

Stripping old wallpaper

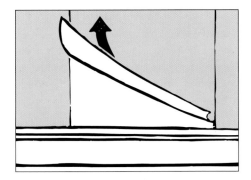

1 Modern vinyl papers are usually designed so that you can simply peel them off the wall.

2 Other papers require dampening. Scoring the surface diagonally with a scraper allows moisture to penetrate.

3 Next, apply warm, soapy water with a sponge or spray. Allow the paper to soak, then peel off with a scraper.

4 Using a steam stripper is a fast, effective way to loosen the glue. The paper can then be removed with a scraper.

Applying lining paper

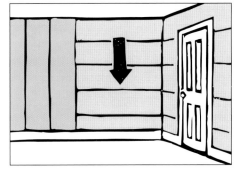

1 If you are using lining paper under wallpaper, the wall should be cross-lined to avoid unsightly ridges.

2 Hang lining paper in horizontal strips; concertina each strip in one hand and unfold it as you go.

Tools and equipment

Preparation

- **Plastic bucket:** for warm, soapy water and to mix size.
- **Sponge:** to soak paper in order to remove it.
- **Hand sprayer:** to soak paper, instead of a sponge.
- **Wallpaper steamer:** a machine that helps to remove paper; ideal when stripping large areas. Expensive, so you may wish to hire it.
- **Scraper:** to score and remove paper.
- **Wallpaper scorer:** a more sophisticated tool for scoring paper.
- **Size:** use the brand recommended by the manufacturer to match the paper of your choice.
- **Wooden dowel:** to mix size.
- **Large decorating/pasting brush:** to apply size.
- **Sponge:** to clean up.
- **Plastic refuse sacks:** in order to facilitate tidying up as you progress with the work.

Planning

Pattern matching

The thought of matching patterns is perhaps one of the most daunting aspects of hanging your own wallpaper. However, so long as you purchase sufficient paper and take some time and trouble with matching it up at the cutting stage, this process is, in fact, relatively straightforward.

A plain paper, or one with a continuous or small, random pattern, such as vertical stripes or a tiny floral print, does not need matching. You can simply cut equal lengths straight from the roll; all you need to remember is to add 10cm (4in) to each length (to allow for 5cm [2in] overlaps at each end).

To match other, more complicated designs, lay the cut strip of paper design-side up on the pasting table, and then lay another strip beside it, matching the pattern as accurately as you can on the adjoining widths, and then ensure that you add the standard 5cm (2in) at each end to the measured matching drop to allow for the overhang – a total of 10cm (4in).

Check, before you cut, that the two drops have the same number of pattern repeats, and that each has an overhang allowance. A straight-match pattern has the same part of the design running symmetrically down each side of the paper. This kind of paper is not very difficult to hang. All you need to remember is, once again, to add enough allowance at each end to line up the pattern exactly; you do not need to match adjoining strips horizontally.

On a drop-match pattern the motifs are staggered, which means that you have to add extra in the cutting: the amount of stagger in the pattern – or length of pattern repeat – is usually indicated on the roll. You could try cutting alternate drops from different rolls, but this may prove more confusing than helpful.

Establishing a vertical

It goes without saying that hanging your first strip of paper vertically is crucial. This is not only because, on a practical level, it will be very difficult to reproduce exactly time and time again an off-vertical hanging line, and gaps and cracks between strips of paper will appear with no hope of correction, but because – rather obviously – most patterns are designed to hang straight

▶ *If you favour a highly co-ordinated look, many wallpapers now come with matching borders and fabrics. It is a good idea, however, to keep the rest of the decoration simple; here the painted floor, plain rugs and understated window treatment provide perfect foils for a 'busy' blue and white wallpaper.*

A few helpful hints

1 Paper in a logical sequence. If there is an obvious focal point, centre your first piece there and work outwards.

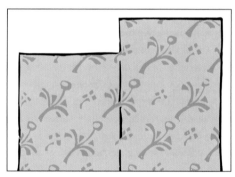

2 If there is no focal point, start to the right of the main window and work clockwise around to the door.

3 To match a pattern, lay a strip on the pasting table and place another beside it, lining up the pattern.

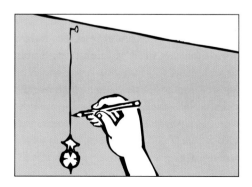

4 It is vital that you establish a true vertical before you start. You can do this with a plumb line or spirit level.

◄ *For those who haven't the time or the confidence to experiment with paint effects, there are now a number of wallpapers on the market that simulate different paint finishes. The subtle stripes of this wallpaper resemble the soft finish achieved by shading, and give a warm, even look to the walls in this smart bedroom.*

Tools and equipment

Tools for papering
- **Tape measure.**
- **Craft knife:** to trim wallpaper.
- **Metal rule/straight edge.**
- **Spirit level:** to check true horizontals and verticals.
- **Pasting brush.**
- **Paper-hanging brush:** to smooth paper into place once it is on the wall.
- **Radiator roller:** to smooth paper into place behind radiators or in awkward corners.
- **Clean household broom:** to hold up paper when applying to the ceiling.
- **Adhesives:** follow the wallpaper manufacturer's instructions. If you have a problem with mould, use a fungicidal paste; you will also need vinyl adhesive if you are overlapping and sticking vinyl wallpaper.
- **Wallpaper trough:** to soak lengths of ready-pasted paper.
- **Plastic bucket:** to mix paste.
- **Pasting table:** any table is suitable, provided it is well covered and at the correct height for you to work at easily.
- **Seam roller:** to smooth the paper seams, once the paper is hung.
- **Wallpaper scissors.**
- **Wooden dowel:** to mix paste.
- **Sponge:** to clean up.
- **Plumb line:** to find a true vertical.

Tools for other wallcoverings
- **Small, sharp scissors and scalpels:** to cut out decoupage motifs.
- **To attach fabric to walls:** staple gun, wooden battens, card to strengthen joins, curtain rods or poles for shirred fabric; mounting track.

and will never look right unless they do. Use a spirit level or plumb line to make sure that the paper is absolutely vertical; do not follow the line of windows or doors as these, particularly in older houses, are not always straight.

To get a true vertical, hang the plumb line by a pin from the top of the wall and mark the line of its fall lightly with chalk or a pencil.

Obviously, it is essential to repeat this process on each wall to be papered rather than assuming anything.

Sequence of papering

There are no set rules about where to start papering; the most important thing is for you to work in a logical sequence around the room. If the room has an obvious focal point, however – a chimney breast in the middle of one wall, for instance – centre the pattern of your first piece of wallpaper on it, and then work outwards from there around the room, in opposite directions, until the two ends meet at the other side, or at a convenient junction – such as a door.

If there is no obvious focal point on which to centre your work, start papering to the right of the main window and work your way in a clockwise motion around the room to the door, before going back to the first drop and working anti-clockwise round to the door. Remember, though, not to use the window frame as a reference for your vertical.

Measuring, cutting and pasting

When you are calculating the number of rolls of wallpaper you will need, it is best to err on the side of generosity and to buy all the paper at the same time, from the same batch.

To work out the number of rolls you need, measure the height of the walls and add 10cm (4in) as an overhang allowance, and the length of the paper's pattern repeat if there is one. This is the length of each drop. Divide the total length of a roll (usually 10m [33ft]) by the length of your drop to discover how many drops you will get from one roll (A).

Measure the distance around the room and divide that figure by the width of a roll (usually 52cm [20½in]) to find out how many drops you will need to paper the room (B).

Then divide the number of drops required to paper the room by how many drops you will get from one roll of wallpaper to calculate the number of rolls (C) you will need to complete the job (B÷A=C). Round up to the next whole roll and add a roll in case your arithmetic is slightly inaccurate.

Time

Hanging wallpaper is time-consuming and should not be hurried. When you are planning the job, overestimate the time needed simply as drying time – after stripping, after lining, after papering – in order not to risk a feeling of frustration creeping in later, which would increase the potential for disaster.

Cutting

Remember always to allow an extra 5cm (2in) at each end of the length of paper for trimming to fit. And always cut before you paste.

Having first established a vertical line on your wall, measure the wall from ceiling to skirting board. Unroll your wallpaper roll on the table and measure out the overall length of a strip, including the overhang allowance. Mark the pasting table itself to avoid measuring each strip. Using a try square, mark a line at right angles to the edge of the strip at the appropriate length and cut straight along the line, using wallpapering scissors.

If you have to match the pattern, cut the first length and then turn the paper right-side up to match the pattern on the adjoining length, before adding on the extra 5cm (2in)

▲ *Highly decorative papers need not be reserved solely for the bedroom – they can also be used to great effect in other parts of the house. This wallpaper in a strong green, printed with a delicate trellis of dew drops and roses, has an old-fashioned charm, and complements the soft lavender panelled walls of the room beyond.*

Calculating the number of rolls

British wallpaper

Wall Height	Distance around room (inc doors and windows)												
	9.1m	10.3m	11.6m	12.8m	14m	15.2m	16.4m	17.7m	18.9m	20.1m	21.3m	22.6m	23.9m
	30ft	34ft	38ft	42ft	46ft	50ft	54ft	58ft	62ft	66ft	70ft	74ft	78ft
2.45m (8ft)	5	5	6	7	7	8	9	9	10	10	11	12	12
2.75m (9ft)	6	6	7	7	8	9	9	10	10	11	12	12	13
3m (10ft)	6	7	8	8	9	10	10	11	12	13	13	14	15

Calculations based on roll measuring 52cm (20½in) x 10.3m (34ft)

US wallpaper

Wall Height	Distance around room (inc doors and windows)												
	9.7m	11m	12.2m	13.4m	14.6m	15.8m	17.1m	18.3m	19.5m	20.7m	21.9m	23.2m	24.4m
	32ft	36ft	40ft	44ft	48ft	52ft	56ft	60ft	64ft	68ft	72ft	76ft	80ft
2.45m (8ft)	8	9	10	11	12	13	14	15	16	17	18	19	20
2.75m (9ft)	9	10	11	12	14	15	16	17	18	19	20	21	22
3m (10ft)	10	11	12	14	15	16	17	19	20	21	22	23	25

Calculations based on roll measuring 45cm (18in) when trimmed x 7.3m (24ft)

Measuring, cutting and pasting

1 Lay the paper out on the table and measure the first length, marking the cut-off point with a pencil.

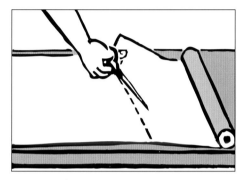

2 Use a pair of long wallpapering scissors to cut off the first strip.

3 Square up one long edge and one short edge with the sides of the table and apply the paste from the centre.

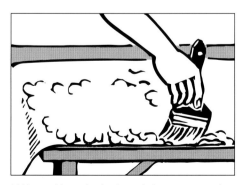

4 Using a wide pasting brush, work the paste outwards to the edges. Make sure the paste is applied evenly.

at each end of the length before you cut across the width. Number each length on the reverse side, in order to avoid any confusion about the order you need to follow to match a pattern accurately when you come to hang the lengths. Mark an arrow on the back of each piece indicating the top on a matching paper, if there is no obvious right way up.

Pasting

First, set up your trestle or pasting table. If possible, position the table so that you will face the light when you are pasting; this will make it easier to identify areas that lack paste – they look dull rather than shiny.

Mix up the paste and lay the paper pattern-side down on the table. Keep the table clean to prevent getting paste on the right side of the paper. Distribute the paste evenly or it will bubble up. Start pasting from the centre and work outwards to the sides, applying the paste with a wide pasting brush.

Check whether the paper requires time for the paste to soak in before it is hung. Leave the paper until it is quite supple before you hang it, but note how long this takes to keep the soaking time constant from length to length to prevent variations in stretching.

Bubbling may have been caused by too much paste. More often, it is the result of not having allowed the paper to soak for long enough; always read the manufacturer's instructions and allow sufficient soaking time. If you need to repair one or two bubbles in a drop, use a sharp craft knife to pierce the bubble. Smear a small amount of paste behind the opening with an artist's paintbrush and use a paper-hanging brush to smooth the paper back into position. Wipe the excess paste away with a damp sponge. This is only practical for a few bubbles; if your paper has a rash of bubbles, the only remedy is to remove the drop and rehang it.

Ready-pasted and foamed vinyls

Ready-pasted vinyl is probably the best paper for an inexperienced decorator, as its tough surface means that it is less likely to tear and stretch as you work. Half-fill a wallpaper trough with water and place it next to the part of the wall where you intend to start

papering. Measure and cut the paper. Roll up the length, with the pattern facing inwards, and immerse the paper fully in the trough.

Follow the manufacturer's instructions on soaking time, then lift up the paper by its top edge with both hands, carefully allowing the water to drain back into the trough. Position the first length on the wall, making sure that it is straight against your vertical guideline (see pages 82–83), and then smooth it with a clean sponge rather than a brush; it helps to absorb some of the excess water.

Some papers and borders are not only ready-pasted, but they do not require soaking either. Their self-adhesive coating becomes exposed as you pull it from the roll and you can stick them directly onto the wall. Further to its advantage, the adhesive takes a while to form a strong bond, so if you make a mistake in hanging, the paper can be repositioned quickly, without a problem.

Hanging ready-pasted vinyls

1 Roll ready-pasted vinyl pattern-side inwards and soak in a wallpaper trough. Unroll and apply directly to the wall.

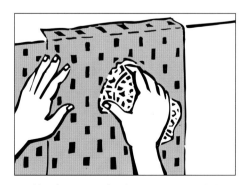

2 Position the paper so that the patterns are matched and smooth it down with a clean sponge.

Hanging standard lengths

Hanging paper along a smooth run of wall is fairly straightforward, but ensure that you have the paper the right way up. This sounds obvious, but it is easy to make this mistake when dealing with lots of large drops.

Making a concertina

When you have pasted the entire length of your measured length of wallpaper, checking that there are no areas where the paste is thin or dry, take the pasted paper (see pages 84–85) and loop it into a concertina shape, making the folds about 75cm (2ft 6in) long. When you get to the end of the paper, fold it back against itself so that the pasted sides are touching to ensure that this does not stick to the wall as you work your way down.

If you are only working with a short length, fold the ends into the centre, but be careful not to crease it as you go.

Hanging the paper

Hang a length of wallpaper from the top of the wall, brushing it into place and then trimming it to match exactly the join where the wall and ceiling meet. Only after finishing the top do you work your way down to the bottom, brushing that into place and trimming it to fit in the same way.

Leaving a 5cm (2in) overlap to run up onto the ceiling, unfold the top half of the first fold of your concertina and offer up the paper against the top of the wall. Ensure that the side of the paper is vertical, running exactly down the line of the plumb line. Do not forget to check that you have an overlap.

Smooth with a brush, working from the middle of the paper outwards, brushing firmly into the junction between wall and ceiling. Run the rounded edge of the wallpaper scissors along the crease to make a distinct mark.

Peel the paper away at the top far enough to reveal the crease you have just made and cut neatly along the line of the crease with your scissors. Smooth the paper back onto the wall with the paper-hanging brush; it should fit the wall neatly now. Wipe off any excess paste, and discard any offcuts too small to use elsewhere, throwing them in the bin to keep wayward paste to a minimum.

Undo the folds one by one as you work gradually downwards, and continue to brush the paper from the centre outwards, being careful not to let the hanging paper crease; if a crease does appear, however, and if the paste is still wet, gently pull the paper away from the wall at the point where the crease has occurred and carefully reposition it. On the other hand, if it is dry, cut open the crease with a sharp craft knife, and proceed as you would to repair a bubble (see pages 84–85).

Do not stick the bottom in place yet. Unfold the last piece at the bottom and repeat the creasing process for the top of the wall to trim the bottom edge. Wipe away any excess paste with a sponge before it dries. Continue to hang lengths of paper along the wall until you reach the corner. Press down

▶ *If you have never attempted wallpapering before, start with a wallpaper that has an uncomplicated pattern, such as these wide stripes. A simple design makes joining the edges a relatively easy task. Stripes, like a plain paper or one with a small, random pattern, do not need matching up so it is simple to cut lengths straight from the roll.*

Hanging the first lengths

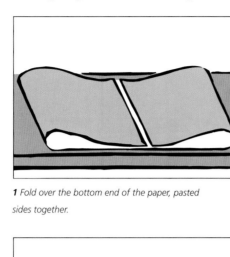

▲ *Few things look fresher than stripes: their uniform crispness lends them to most rooms in the house. Blue and white are perfect for this nautical-look bedroom, where they combine with a co-ordinating border and fresh paintwork to create a look that is pulled together but calm and unfussy.*

the joining edges using a seam roller. If the seams of paper are pulling away from each other or the wall, the paste has not been spread to the edge of the roll. Lift the edge slightly with a knife and apply a little paste to the edge with an artist's brush. Press smooth again with a seam roller.

If you are using ready-pasted paper, it is advisable to run a small artist's brush loaded with some vinyl glue along the seams of paper as a matter of course. Smooth it into place to create a strong, clean join. And after hanging four full strips, go back over the seams with a seam roller. Check the surface for any paste and remove with a damp sponge. It is always easier to remove adhesive immediately than after it has dried.

1 Fold over the bottom end of the paper, pasted sides together.

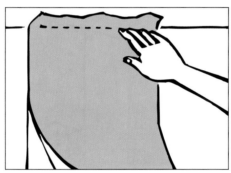

2 For long lengths, loop the paper backwards and forwards into a concertina shape.

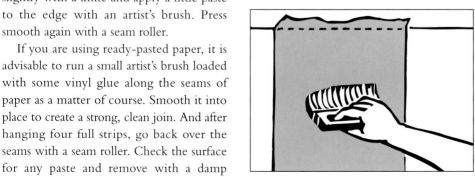

3 Place the top of the paper at the top of the wall, leaving your 5cm (2in) allowance to run up to the ceiling.

4 Smooth the paper with a wide brush, working from the centre outwards.

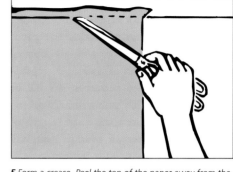

5 Form a crease. Peel the top of the paper away from the wall and trim it before smoothing it back on.

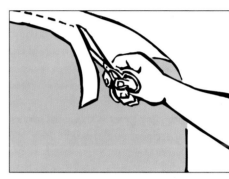

6 Carefully trim the edge of the paper with scissors to ensure a clean finish.

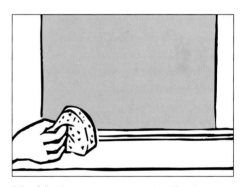

7 Carefully wipe away any excess paste with a clean sponge before it dries.

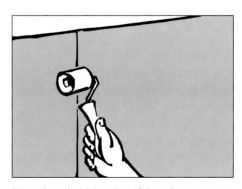

8 Press down the joining edges of the wallpaper using a seam roller.

Turning corners

When you have worked your way along a wall, you will arrive at a corner. Papering around corners requires taking the paper around the corner edge and overlapping it with a new length of wallpaper, regardless of whether the corner is internal or external. Given that you will be working with two strips from the same length of paper, and creating an overlap, you will inevitably lose some of a pattern repeat. However, a slight loss of pattern match is not always noticeable.

Internal corners

Measure from the edge of the last full width of wallpaper to the corner at the top of the wall, then halfway down, and once more at the bottom. Add 2.5cm (1in) to the longest measurement for the overlap.

If you are using paper with a small pattern or vertical stripes, you should adjust the width of your overlap to the width of the pattern repeat to make it easier to match on the facing wall.

Take a cut length of paper and cut it to this width. Leaving the offcut on the pasting table, paste this narrow strip in place using the standard method, but smoothing the cut edge around the corner. Run a seam roller along the cut edge to ensure it is firmly fixed in place against the wall.

Next take the offcut and paste it. Then, using a plumb line or spirit level, you should establish the vertical on the new wall; it is vital that you do this for each new wall as corners are seldom 'true', or square, and your paper will be hanging well out of true by the time you return to your starting point if you do not – a small problem after four corners can appear rather large!

Finally, taking great care to butt it up right into the corner and ensuring that it is positioned vertically, hang the offcut on the internal wall, matching up the pattern if necessary.

External corners

Smooth the paper up to the edge using the paper-hanging brush and ease it around the corner, this time without brushing it firmly into place. In this instance, you

Internal corners

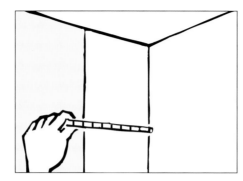

1 Measure from the edge of the last full width of wallpaper to the corner at the top, midway and bottom.

2 Add 2.5cm (1in) to the widest measurement for the overlap and cut out. Paste and smooth around the corner.

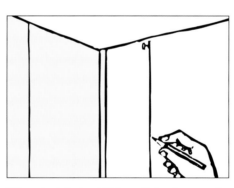

3 Use a plumb line to establish a vertical on the new wall at the width of the offcut.

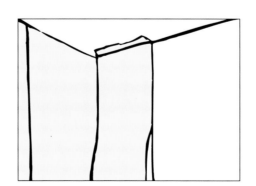

4 Hang the offcut, taking care to position the edge very close to the corner and to match the patterns.

External corners

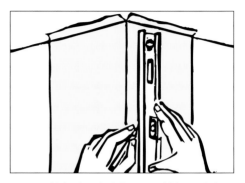

1 Use a spirit level or plumb line to establish a vertical 2.5cm (1in) from the corner. Mark the line with a pencil.

2 Cut along the pencil line with a craft knife, using a straight edge as a guide.

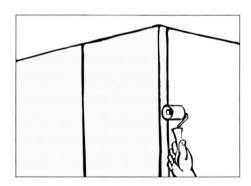

3 Run the seam roller along the edge leading to the corner to fix the paper in place.

4 Finally, hang the offcut, positioning its edge close to the corner and lining up the pattern if necessary.

◀ *Broad stripes are a good choice for a room with sharp corners. Here a striped wallpaper accentuates the neat angles of the chimney breast, while its muted colours create an air of restrained grandeur, ideal for a formal drawing room.*

▼ *In a heavy-use area such as a hallway, staircase or kitchen, it's sensible to use a wallpaper with a tougher finish, and consequently a longer life. In this case, a hard wearing vinyl has been used below the dado rail and a standard patterned paper above.*

should rub your hand down the angle of the wall to make a firm crease along the paper. Slit the overlap allowance to allow the paper to move around the corner without buckling. Use a plumb line or spirit level to establish a vertical about 2.5cm (1in) from the external corner and use a straight edge or metal rule to mark the line in pencil. Using the straight edge and a sharp craft knife, cut the paper along this line. Gently remove the offcut and place it on the pasting table, pattern-side down.

Run the seam roller down the edge of the paper leading to the corner, ensuring that it is firmly stuck down. Next, if the paste has dried too much, re-paste the offcut and then hang it, positioning its edge very close to the external corner, and taking care to match patterns if necessary. Run the seam roller along the join to try to fix the edge of the paper.

Papering around doors and windows

Once you have mastered basic wallpaper positioning and trimming techniques, it is relatively simple to adapt the techniques to enable you to work successfully around doors and windows.

Doors and windows fitted flush with a wall are relatively easy to paper; the wallpaper merely has to be trimmed back to fit neatly around the architrave or casing. If the door or window is recessed, the increased number of surfaces of the reveal requires more careful fitting – and before that more careful planning. For example, it is important to avoid 'seams' falling on the external corners of the reveal, so establishing and checking the correct starting point before you hang a single strip of wallpaper is very important. All you need to do is adjust your chosen starting point by 5cm (2in) to the right or left as necessary. It is easier to paper the wall with the reveal first, before the rest of the room.

▲ In an irregularly shaped room, wallpaper with a small, regular pattern or a narrow stripe is the best option. In this attic bedroom, the paper extends all the way up to the window in the eaves, playing down the room's awkward proportions and creating a sense of harmony.

Flush doors and window frames

When papering along a wall that includes a door or window, you should hang drops until you have one that will overlap the obstacle. Hang this length, letting it fall over the door or window frame. Cut away the excess paper to within 4cm (1½in) of the architrave or window casing and discard the offcut. Then cut diagonally into the paper towards the corner of and as far as the outside of the frame or architrave and smooth the paper with a brush. Press the paper firmly against the architrave or casing, and form a crease with the rounded edge of a small pair of scissors, before peeling back the tongues of paper and trimming along the creases. Always take particular care when working on the corner as it is really quite easy to tear the paper at this stage. Finally, brush the trimmed edges back into position around the frame.

Recessed windows

When papering around recessed windows hang the first strip of paper to one side, overlapping the window.

Trim and fit at the ceiling level as you would a normal drop, and only then make a horizontal cut at the soffit (the horizontal recess above the window), and another at the window sill, using a sharp craft

Fitting mouldings, sills and recesses

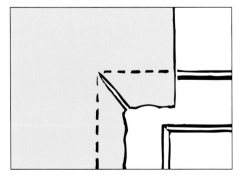

1 To fit a door or window frame: cut away excess paper, leaving a 4cm (1½in) overhang. Cut towards the corner.

2 Form a neat crease around the frame, then peel back the tongues of paper and trim before repositioning.

3 Steps 1–2 also apply for window sills. Take extra care when tackling corners; it's all too easy to tear the paper.

knife. Carefully wrap the paper around the corner into the reveal. Continue to work along the top of the window as if you were papering a flat wall, but using short strips and taking the ends around, under the soffit, to the window frame. Stop when you get to the point when your next strip will be full-length, and turn your attention to beneath the window.

Now hang short lengths from under the sill to the skirting board, using a standard hanging technique. Having hung the same number of short strips as you did above the window, hang another full-length strip that overlaps the reveal. Adopting the same procedure as before, cut the paper horizontally at the soffit and sill, and wrap it neatly around.

Fill in the unpapered spaces in the corners of the soffit with offcuts, matching patterns as best you can. Cut a patch big enough to fit the space with overlap allowances on all four sides.

Crease and trim the paper according to standard practice at the window frame, and tuck in the other edges in turn: firstly under the short strip at the top of the window, and then – rather as you would on a corner – under the wrap-around on the side of the reveal, and finally under the paper on the wall, on the edge that is proud of the recess. Be particularly careful when you lift the corner of the original paper, and add paste before brushing it flat again if the original paste has dried.

▲ *Papering around door frames is not as daunting as you might imagine. This regular fleur-de-lys wallpaper would have been relatively easy to line up. The pattern also helps to draw the eye away from the unusual slope of the walls and complements the handsome walnut furniture.*

Dormer windows

When working in a room with dormer windows your first task will entail deciding which parts of the dormer should be papered – which parts are to be considered walls and which parts ceiling, and thus which sections should be papered and which painted to reflect that differentiation.

Start at a central point beneath the window itself, working out to either side. Hang short strips from the junction of the slope to the floor, creasing and trimming according to standard practice.

You may wish to leave the wedge-shaped walls projecting outward at right angles to the window painted, but if you wish to paper them, these vertical walls should be tackled next. Leave an allowance and take it around the corner; the paper on the sloping roof will butt up to the corner for a neat finish.

Finally you should tackle the sloping roof sections, taking great care to match the drops with those already in place. This may mean that the first length of paper will not be a full-width drop. Below the window, measure outwards from the side of the window to the first seam. Cut to the exact width of your measurement and your drop from top of sloping roof to floor should now align.

It will be neater to tuck the lower edge allowance on the sloping roof section under the top trimmed edge of the half-wall than to trim it, but you could also consider a border at this junction (see pages 96–97).

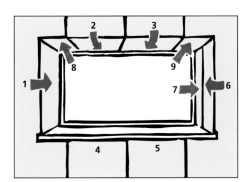

4 *To fit a recessed window: start with an overlapping strip, then hang the longer drops above and below the window.*

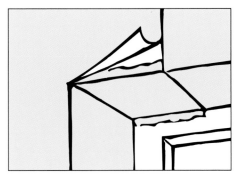

5 *Finally, return to the unpapered recesses and fill with offcuts, tucking the strips beneath the adjoining lengths.*

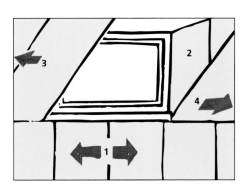

6 *To fit a dormer window: start at a central point beneath the window and work outwards.*

Papering around obstacles

▶ *Papering around light switches can be problematic but there are several options. You can paper around the switch, fix a perspex switch plate that allows you to see through to the wallpaper beneath or, as here, carefully match the paper over the plate to create a smooth, seamless look.*

▼ *There is no set technique for wallpapering around a mantel, as each will have its own unique shape and changes of angle. To ensure a neat finish rather than a scrappy, haphazard one, however, always work slowly and methodically, carefully cutting, smoothing and trimming the wallpaper as you go.*

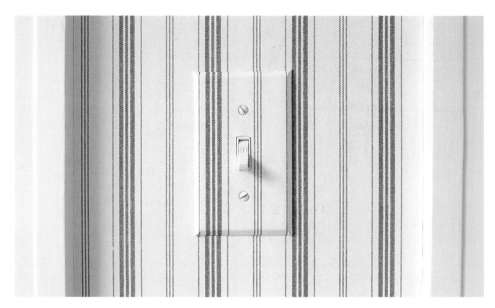

Wall switches and sockets

Before attempting to paper around sockets, switches and any other electrical outlet, always remember to turn off the power at the mains, and allow plenty of time for the paste to dry before you turn it back on again.

Paper over wall switches and outlets and smooth down the wall as usual. Press paper firmly over the edges of the fitting so that it creases. Cut a cross in the paper across the plate, each slit running from corner to corner diagonally. Through this hole, loosen the screws fixing the plate to the wall. Then trim down the flaps of paper to leave an allowance of 1cm (⅜in) all round. Press the paper flat behind the face plate. Tighten the screws again and switch on the power at the mains.

With ceiling rose light sockets, position the paper over the fitting as if you were actually going to paper it into the ceiling. Get an assistant to hold the remaining length of paper against the ceiling with a household broom while you cut a cross in the paper exactly where the fitting needs to fall and pull the pendant through. Trim any excess paper and smooth what remains towards the fitting with a paper-hanging brush. Make a series of small cuts in the paper and use the rounded blade of a pair of small scissors to form a well-defined crease around the fitting. Loosen the plate and press the paper flaps neatly beneath it; secure the plate against

Mantels, radiators and light fittings

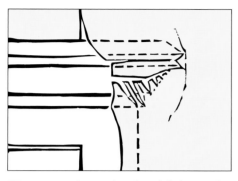

1 To paper around a mantel, work carefully downwards, making new cuts to accommodate each change of angle.

2 Smooth and trim each cut as you go. Smaller and more fiddly cuts may be easier to make with ordinary scissors.

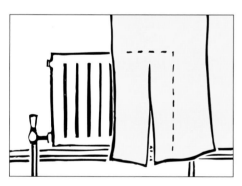

3 To accommodate a radiator bracket, make a cut in the paper to the top of the radiator to form two 'tongues'.

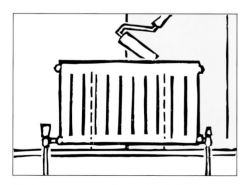

4 Push the two tongues of paper down behind the radiator using a radiator roller.

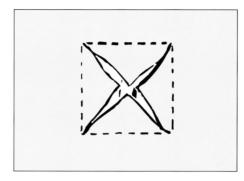

5 To paper over a switch, press the paper over the fitting and crease around the edges. Cut a cross in the paper.

6 Loosen the face plate and trim the paper, leaving a 1cm (⅜in) allowance. Tuck this behind the plate.

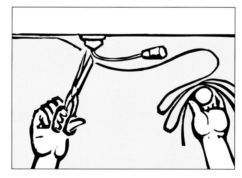

7 Use a similar technique for covering a light fitting by cutting a cross in the paper to pull the pendant through.

8 Make a neat crease around the fitting. Cut v-shaped nicks in the paper and tuck the flaps underneath the plate.

the ceiling. However, do not use this technique with any paper that includes metal in its composition.

Radiator brackets

It is awkward and disruptive to remove central-heating radiators from the wall when you want to paper a room. A better solution, although it can be rather tricky, is to paper around them. Paper the flat uninterrupted wall until you find that the next drop will have to fit behind the radiator.

Measure from the top of the skirting board to the top of the bracket of the radiator, and from the bracket to the edge of the adjoining drop of paper. Remembering to add on the overlap allowance to the vertical measurement and, checking that you are cutting from the bottom and not the top of the paper, make a cut in the paper that will create two 'tongues' in the lower section of your drop; these will accommodate the bracket.

Smooth the wallpaper onto the wall as usual, pushing the two tongues down behind the radiator using a radiator roller. Trim the lower edge at skirting-board level as usual and smooth down with a paper-hanging brush.

Fireplace mantels

Some mantelpieces can be quite elaborate, with lots of extra angles to cut around, but the principle is always the same: work slowly and carefully, cutting into the paper up to each change in angle, and then smoothing and trimming each flap in turn against the solid part of the fireplace, working gradually downwards.

It may be, if the mantelpiece of the fireplace is very close to a corner, that you may find it easier to cut the paper carefully across — horizontally — level with the top of the mantelpiece and then to work in two halves. This avoids the risk of tearing a drop of paper, and can, if carefully done, be all but invisible.

You may also find it easier to make the smaller cuts necessary for an accurate professional finish with ordinary scissors rather than their large wallpapering relatives.

Papering ceilings and stairwells

Your primary concern when you come to paper a ceiling or stairwell should be safety. A platform or stepladder can be extremely dangerous when stretching.

It is vital to avoid stretching too far, and important to work at the correct level. This way, you will work more effectively and expend the minimum of effort, thus making a difficult and awkward job less exhausting.

When setting the height of a stepladder or platform, the ceiling should be about 8cm (3¼in) above your head to make the process as easy as possible.

Ceilings

Ceilings are normally painted rather than papered, but if the surface is slightly cracked you may need to cover it with lining paper. Use a heavier grade of paper, as this is easier to work with and less likely to tear than something thinner. To create a safe work platform, ideally you should hire a couple

of sturdy scaffold boards and rest them between two stepladders or trestles. If the boards bend with your weight, reduce the space between the ladders.

First, mark a guideline: measure the width of the paper and subtract 1cm (⅜in). This gives you some leeway to allow for the walls not being exactly square. Mark this width on the ceiling at opposite ends. Stretch a chalk line across the ceiling, from the marks, and snap it quickly against the ceiling to create a guideline. Use the length of this guideline as your cutting length, plus 5cm (2in) at either end (to allow for trimming). If the ceiling is the same width throughout the room, use the first length as your template. Paste the paper and fold into a loose concertina (see pages 86–87).

Position the platform directly beneath the chalk guideline and brush the prepared ceiling with a coat of size ready for the first strip of paper. Hold the concertina against

▶ *A striped wallpaper makes the most of the sinuous curve of this staircase. A smart rope border adds classical polish and obviates the need for any other detail.*

Hard-to-reach areas

1 Scaffold boards, suspended between stepladders, make a sturdy base for ceiling work.

2 Following a chalk guideline, press, then brush, the concertina of paper onto the ceiling, fold by fold.

3 When papering a stairwell, position the longest drop first, then work outwards to either side.

4 Enlist a helper to hold up the folds while you brush the paper against the wall.

the ceiling with your left hand or a clean household broom and press the first section of paper against the ceiling with your right hand, aligning it with the guideline. Smooth the paper against the ceiling with a paper-hanging brush, remembering to let the allowance overhang against both the end and the side walls. Release another fold of paper from the broom and work along the guideline, brushing the paper from the centre out, until you reach the other end of the room. Run the rounded tip of a pair of scissors around the junction of the wall and ceiling to make a firm crease. Pull the overhang away from the wall and trim the allowance with wallpaper scissors. If you are using heavy-grade paper, it may not crease easily so you might have to mark the join with light pencil before peeling back and cutting.

Smooth the paper back against the ceiling to fit neatly before applying a coat of size to the adjoining piece of ceiling to prepare it for the next length of paper. Butt the next roll of paper against the first; run a seam roller over the join to secure it. And continue, using the same method, across the rest of the ceiling. For papering over electrical sockets, see pages 92–93.

Stairwells

Stairwells are even more complicated to paper than ceilings and again require a scaffold tower or other sturdy support. You can rent a scaffold tower from a hire shop but, alternatively, you can use a series of ladders, steps and scaffold boards. Lean a ladder against the head wall and set up a stepladder on the landing; place the boards between them to create your platform. You can ensure that everything is completely stable by nailing battens to stair treads to stop ladders from slipping and tying the boards to the ladder steps with rope.

You should start papering with the longest drop. Measure it carefully, and remember to allow for the slope of the stairs; you must measure your drop to below the lowest part of the skirting board and then add the usual trimming allowance. Paste it generously so that it does not dry out as you work, fold the length into a concertina as for ceiling paper

▲ *Here, a soft blue harlequin-patterned wallpaper has been used on the walls, archway and hallway beyond so that the space 'flows' from one area to another. This can be very important in narrow or awkward spaces, where careless combinations of pattern and colour can result in a visually 'disjointed' effect.*

and start at the top of the wall. Because of its length and weight, you will need to enlist a helper to hold the lower half of the paper while you position the top half; if you allow it to hang unsupported, it will stretch.

Archways

Hold a drop of (unpasted) paper to the wall, allowing 5cm (2in) at the top, and make a crease along the line of the arch's curve. Cut the excess paper in a neat curve, following the line of the crease, but at a distance of approx. 5cm (2in) from it. Mark the position of the edge of the paper so that you can then measure and cut further drops of paper like this for the remainder of the arch. Only then should you paste the paper and hang it.

Trim the paper around the curve to approx 2.5cm(1in), and then cut small V-shaped nicks into the allowance at regular intervals so that this turnover lies flat when smoothed flat onto the underside of the arch.

Paper the wall on the opposite side of the arch in the same way, endeavouring to match the pattern with that on the adjacent wall through the arch.

Then measure the thickness of the wall and carefully cut a strip of paper to this width, with the standard 5cm (2in) added to each end. Paste it from the bottom upwards, and repeat the process up the other side of the arch so that the two strips meet at the top centre. Finally smooth the strip around the curve, overlapping the 'tabs' and creating a smooth finish.

Measuring the stair angle

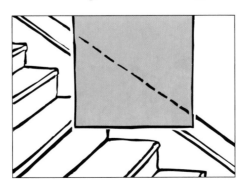

1 When calculating the drops in a stairwell, measure down to the lowest part of the skirting board.

Papering archways

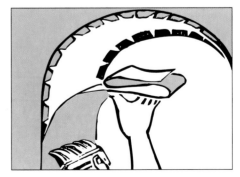

1 Trim, nick and then fold the paper over to fit the curve of the arch. Use two finishing strips to disguise the flaps.

Putting up friezes and borders

▲ *In a room with little or no intrinsic architectural interest, borders and friezes can be used as an admirable substitute. In this child's room, a candy-striped paper in mint green and white combined with a lively border printed with farmyard animals creates a clean yet lively look at minimal cost.*

Plain-painted or papered walls can be transformed with the addition of a border or frieze, and most manufacturers now produce ranges that complement their wallpaper. Borders are usually used to frame a feature in the room, such as a door or window, or to create a feature by forming panels on the wall or ceiling, whereas friezes generally come as a pre-cut decorative feature which can be hung at ceiling or picture-rail height.

Borders that require ordinary wallpaper paste will not stick onto vinyl wallpapers, so use self-adhesive borders for vinyls and special overlap adhesive to apply ordinary ones.

Applying friezes

To use a frieze to create the effect of a cornice, picture or dado rail, first measure the perimeter of the room at the relevant height where you wish to apply the frieze.

Use a spirit level, straight edge and pencil to draw a straight horizontal line to mark where you wish to apply the bottom edge of the frieze. Lay the frieze pattern-side down in the middle of the pasting table and brush on the paste, ensuring that glue reaches right up to the edges. Fold into a loose concertina and apply to the wall, making sure the bottom edge lines up with your guideline. Smooth into place with a brush.

Mitring and joining borders

Use a spirit level and pencil to mark out the shape of the panel. Cut each piece of border paper approx. 10cm (4in) longer than the exterior dimensions of the panel. Apply paste to the strips of border and then apply them to the wall, ensuring that they run accurately along the guidelines you have drawn with a 5cm (2in) allowance at each end, to overlap with the adjoining strip at the corner.

Looking at the overlapping strips as a frame, take your metal edge and position it diagonally on one corner – running from and to the points of intersection – on the outside

Applying paper friezes and borders

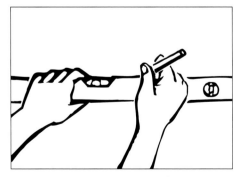

1 Mark a line to denote the base of the frieze using a spirit level, straight edge and pencil.

2 Fold the frieze into a concertina and apply, using the pencil mark as a guide. Smooth into place with a brush.

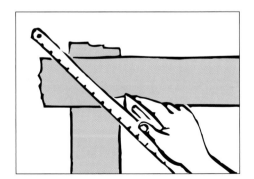

3 To create neat, mitred borders, overlap the two strips and mark a diagonal across.

Fixing a plaster coving

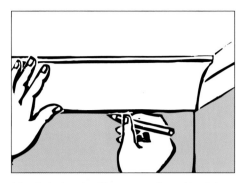

1 Dry-fix the lengths with masonry nails, marking their position with a pencil. Cut extra pieces to fill the gaps.

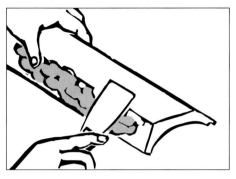

2 When all the pieces have been cut to fit, coat the back edges of the coving with adhesive and press in place.

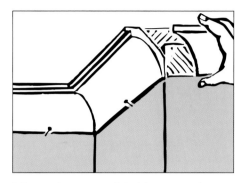

3 Hammer the masonry nails back in to support the coving while the adhesive dries.

and inside edges. Slice diagonally through both layers of paper with a knife to create a mitred corner. Peel off the overlapping border strips and remove the offcut pieces. Smooth the join back together with a brush to create a mitred join.

Authentic period detailing

Using lincrusta panels

Traditionally, these papers were used in panels beneath the dado rail, particularly in hallways or stairwells – sometimes to hide rising damp. Because of the patterned relief surface of these papers, they are ideal for covering cracked walls or for creating a tough surface. Prepare the walls for wallpapering, and cross-line with lining paper (see pages 80–81).

Lincrusta dado panels are bought pre-cut with straight-matching edges so there is no wastage or matching of patterns. Be careful when you are carrying the panels; avoid bending them as this will craze the surface. Before you apply any adhesive, check that panels from different batches are the same length. Soak the panels in warm water before coating the backs with the recommended adhesive. Pay particular attention to the edges. Align the top edge of the panel with the dado rail and smooth down with a soft cloth. Never use a seam roller to smooth the butt joins as this will flatten the pattern.

Never try to turn panels of embossed papers around internal or external corners unless they are rounded, because the paper will probably crack. Cut the wallcovering to finish at the corner and butt up the lengths.

Cornices and covings

Cornices and covings are fixed at the junction between the walls and the ceiling. A cornice is a projecting ornamental moulding while a coving is a plain moulding with a concave profile. Both are manufactured as long lengths that can be cut to size. If you fix a small cornice or coving and it looks rather insignificant, you can make it look grander by adding a narrow strip of moulding along the ceiling edge and painting it to match.

Walls and ceiling must be dry and free of dust before starting work. Then dry-fix the full lengths, supporting them on masonry nails top and bottom and marking their position with a pencil. You will have to cut lengths to fit the remaining gaps; use a fine-toothed saw. Allow extra for mitred joins at external corners (the exact measurements will be indicated in the instructions). Use the templates supplied to cut the mitres.

Lightly sand any rough edges, and then, having removed the nail supports, scratch or sand the areas of the wall and ceiling to be covered. Mix up enough adhesive to use in 45 minutes – the length of time it will remain effective – and butter the top and bottom edges of the moulding with a filling knife or trowel.

Press the lengths of moulding firmly in place between the guidelines. Remove excess adhesive with a filling knife and use it to fill in the joints and mitres. It's a good idea to put the masonry nails back in at this stage to support the moulding while the adhesive dries; they can be removed later.

If you are using a heavy moulding, drive nails through the top edge into the ceiling at each end. Punch them below the surface and cover them with adhesive. Smooth all joints with a damp paintbrush.

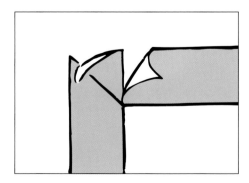

4 Cut across the diagonal through both layers. Peel back the border strips and remove the offcuts.

Applying lincrusta panels

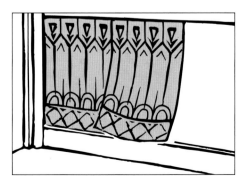

1 Pre-cut with straight-matching edges, lincrusta panels can be lined side by side following a horizontal guideline.

Creating your own papers

▶ *With a little imagination you can create some stunning effects at minimal cost. Here, the fish motifs from a roll of wallpaper have been cut out and stuck on a plain, curved wall to create a bold and lively frieze of fish swimming round. Photocopies, old prints and book illustrations could also be used in this way.*

There is such a huge variety of papers and borders on the market that it would be very easy to forget that you can also make your own, tailoring them perfectly to suit your desired scheme and creating an effect that is unique to you. Many of these home-made decorating solutions are extremely inexpensive to create but will not short-change you on style.

As a clever but effective budget solution, nothing is smarter – or cheaper – than basic brown packing paper. Buy it in a large roll from an office stationer; it comes in rolls 50–90cm (20–36in) wide. Apply it to the walls as you would any wallpaper (see pages 86–87). You need to buy quite a heavy-weight paper because otherwise the wallpaper paste may well soak through the surface making the paper difficult to handle.

One way of making one roll of wallpaper go a very long way is by working in decoupage. The rebirth in popularity of decoupage as a craft has led to an adaptation of the technique for use on walls, so you can now dress up plain walls with borders and motifs cut from a floral or pictorial roll.

Alternatively, you could create your own motifs. Look out for strong images that would be suitable for your scheme and photocopy them in black and white or colour; enlarge or decrease them so that they are exactly the right size; and arrange them on the wall – scatter them at random or place them in a regular pattern. Initially, it is best to do this with an adhesive that allows for repositioning, such as spray mount. But when you are happy with the design, stick the images down with wallpaper

paste. You may also wish to finish off the effect and protect it with a coat of matt polyurethane varnish.

Using the same technique, you could create a Georgian-style print room. Black and white copies of prints, complete with all the attendant bow and ribbon motifs, are now widely available, but you could recreate your own with some inexpensive old prints and photocopied motifs. This finish looks particularly good against strong colours such as golden yellow, terracotta or sharp green.

Walls papered with antique maps or nautical charts are equally striking. Use standard wallpaper paste and paper the entire wall in brightly coloured maps, or use them in panels framed with a piece of moulding or even lengths of rope, to create a nautical theme.

◀ Maps can be used to stunning effect as wall coverings, as shown in this unusual study. Antique maps and nautical charts make striking and original wallpaper and can either be hung in panels or simply papered straight onto the wall with wallpaper paste.

Directory of special finishes

Cork

Available by the roll in a range of natural shades, from light honey to dark brown. Some varieties come with self-adhesive backing. If you are using it in a bathroom or kitchen, seal it with a matt vinyl sealant as it is susceptible to damp.

Flock wallpaper

The wallpaper pattern, often in large repeats, is cut into a velvet pile. Hang as a normal decorative paper but take extra care not to crush the pile with the seam roller.

Foil finish

A metallic-surfaced paper that normally requires cross-lining. It can be used to brighten up and create a sense of space in narrow areas such as hallways. Be aware, however, that it needs a good even wall because its finish serves to highlight any irregularities. **1**

There is no need to limit yourself to paint and paper when deciding what wall-covering you want to surround yourself with. There is a whole range of materials which can be used to wonderful effect. Some of them are expensive; some can be tricky to apply; others require near-perfect wall surfaces to start on, but the striking, unusual effects it is possible to achieve can make all the effort and expense worthwhile.

There are quick, easy and inexpensive alternatives to most of the expensive effects. Would you love to have fabric walls? Are you afraid that it might be too tricky to attempt yourself or that the amount of fabric you would need would make it financially prohibitive? Instead of sophisticated, padded walls, you could choose a less formal look and you could use inexpensive muslin or calico and dye it to suit your scheme. As with all things decorative, it is simply a matter of substituting time, thought and imagination for a limitless budget.

Grass or raffia

It is possible to buy luxurious wall-coverings created by attaching woven grass or raffia to a medium to heavy paper backing. With this type of paper, however, it can be difficult to disguise the seams.   **2**

Hessian

This is purchased in the form of wall-paper with a thick paper backing which makes it easy to hang. As with grass or raffia wall-coverings, hessian's coarse texture makes it difficult to hide the seams.   **3**

Cotton

Some cotton can be stuck directly onto the wall, but it is usually preferable to attach it by first tacking it to battens or by shirring it (see pages 102–103).

Felt

Felt is available in a wide variety of colours. Because of its fairly dense texture and because it is reasonably hardwearing and does not tend to fray, it is probably one of the easiest fabrics to stick directly onto the wall (see pages 102–103).   **4**

Linen

Some of the more densely woven linens can be stuck directly onto the wall. However, for the less experienced decorator, it is probably easier to buy linen in wallpaper form. This is when the fabric is given a medium-weight paper backing to make it much easier to hang.

Silk

A silk wall-covering must surely be the most luxurious of finishes. Woven silk is given a backing of fine paper to create a particularly elegant wallpaper. However, this is not the easiest of papers to hang and it tends to get dirty and soiled rather easily. It is also difficult to disguise the seams.

Using fabric on walls

▶ *Durham quilts in a handsome red and gold stripe make a striking wall covering, adding texture and colour to a traditional interior. Their draught-excluding and sound-proofing qualities make them practical, too.*

Although less usual than paint or paper, there are several advantages to using fabric on walls and ceilings. Like paper, it can cover up minor imperfections in the wall, but also acts as a good heat and sound insulator. With care they can stay fresh far longer than paint or paper. Most fabric finishes can be treated to make them dirt-resistant; later they can be spot-cleaned or vacuumed.

Applying fabric directly to the wall

Many fabrics can be applied directly to the wall but check before you start that they are stain and mildew-resistant. Look out for those with a firm, taut weave that are of medium weight. Felt is a classic choice and comes in a wide variety of strong colours.

The biggest difference between hanging wallpaper and hanging fabric is that with the latter you should apply the adhesive to the wall rather than to the fabric.

Cut the fabric to the required length (plus a trimming allowance), and roll it inwards onto a broom handle for easier handling. Unroll the length onto the wet pasted wall, against a plumbed vertical line, and run a dry paint roller over the surface. To make a seam, overlap adjoining lengths and then cut through both layers with a sharp knife against a straight edge. Having removed the offcuts, smooth back the edges into place.

It is a good idea to conceal the edges of the fabric, which otherwise could fray, with braid or a similar trim. This can be expensive and difficult to remove, so dry-hang several varieties around the walls to make sure you like the effect before you invest.

Some fabrics such as silk, hessian, suede, corduroy and grass cloth are available already backed onto paper to make them easier to hang; in this case the fabric should be treated as paper, so the adhesive is applied to the backing rather than the wall.

Hanging fabric on battens, mounting track and stretch wires

If you are hesitant about sticking fabric directly onto the walls there are several alternatives. The first of these is to fix the fabric onto the walls with a staple gun. The staples can be covered with braid. This is very much a 'quick fix', suitable for rented houses or for short-term solutions. You will get a more professional and elegant finish if you stretch the fabric between wooden battens. Fix the battens along the top and bottom of the wall and attach upright battens along the wall at 2m (6ft) intervals. You may also like to add extra battens in places where you know you will want to hang pictures, or mirrors, in order that you have something behind the fabric into which to fix picture hooks.

For a good, slightly 'upholstered' finish – enhancing the fabric's sound and heat-insulating properties too – you can interline the fabric with bump.

Joining two lengths of fabric and attaching them to a wall sounds complicated but is actually straightforward. It is a technique that is crucial for a professional finish, a variation of which (using only one piece of fabric) is used as the real starting point. Two strips of fabric are placed right sides together over a batten, and a back-tacking strip laid over the top. All the thicknesses are then stapled with a staple gun, and the top layer of fabric brought away from the wall and wrapped over the seam, revealing its right side.

Start by sewing together enough lengths of your fabric to cover one wall – right sides together – allowing for trimming allowances top and bottom, and matching any pattern carefully. Then taking up one vertical edge of your fabric, place it right side down under a back-tacking strip in the corner down the right-hand side of the wall to be covered, as if it would cover the adjacent wall wrong side out. Secure the fabric to the battens by stapling through all the layers.

Take the fabric and wrap it back over the back-tacking strip so that the right side of the fabric is in front of you across the wall. Staple it in place temporarily top and bottom.

Working from the centre upwards and downwards, and gradually outwards, and smoothing firmly as you proceed, staple the fabric firmly in place. Leave a margin all round, then remove the temporary staples and finish off by trimming all edges and covering them with braid. Use quick-drying, non-staining wallpaper adhesive.

If this sounds complex, consider using mounting track to attach the fabric to the walls. This will allow you to attach the taut

Applying fabric to walls

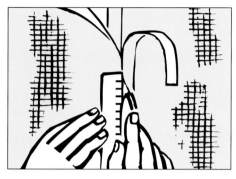

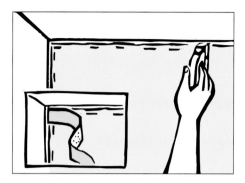

1 Roll the fabric right side inwards around a pole. Unroll onto the pasted wall, following a vertical guideline.

2 For a neat seam, overlap two pieces of fabric and cut through both layers along a straight edge. Remove offcuts.

3 Alternatively, secure the fabric in place with a staple gun. Conceal the staples by edging the walls with braid.

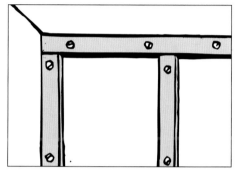

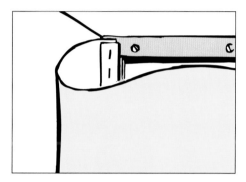

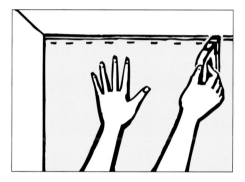

4 For a professional finish, fix wooden battens along the walls at top and bottom and vertically at 2m (6ft) intervals.

5 Have ready enough fabric to cover one wall. Staple one vertical edge right side down under a back-tacking strip.

6 Working from the centre up and down, staple the fabric across the wall. Trim the edges with braid.

fabric neatly without resorting to battens and staples. It comprises long plastic strips with 'jaws' to hide the rough edges, and adhesive plastic strips to hold the fabric taut.

Alternatively, hang the material from the walls from poles or wires. This is a good alternative if you live in rented accommodation as it does not mark the walls and you can take the fabric with you when you leave.

Lightweight fabrics such as sheers and patterned muslin can be hemmed and shirred onto poles or wires attached just below the ceiling and above the skirting board. You should allow approximately three times the wall's width in fabric to create a rich effect. It can be drawn back over the window or door, or another wire or pole can be fixed immediately above them and the fabric shirred over that.

Heavier fabrics such as linen or wool can be suspended from rods or poles and left to hang freely at the bottom. It can be drawn back over windows or doors, if desired, by using fabric or cord ties.

◄ *Using fabric on walls allows you a great deal of versatility; it is simple to customize it so that it is perfect for your scheme. Here, inexpensive calico is stretched between battens and then stencilled with a bold, gold design.*

Tiles, panels and rails

The selection of tiles available today is, quite simply, dazzling. But before you decide on finish, colour or design, you need to consider your surface. Dainty mosaics may look wonderful, but are unsuitable for the heavy-wear splashback area in the kitchen where a more robust tile might be better. Pretty majolica would look just right in a bathroom but wholly inappropriate inside the back door, where a strong surface that can be wiped down easily would be more practical.

Decoratively, tiles allow you to create many different effects, whether your style is coolly neoclassical or decidedly modern. And having the choice of the best looks is not restricted to those with the biggest purses. You could spend a fortune on hand-painted, hand-made, imported tiles, but equally, you could simply buy a handful of expensive tiles and use them cleverly to transform a run of more ordinary ones. Alternatively, you could arrange inexpensive tiles in an interesting way or use contrasting colours to create striking bands across a wall.

Pictorial panels, relief, mosaic, mirror or glass tiles can all be used in a room of little architectural interest to create dramatic focal points that will draw the eye away from the room's more mundane features. Tiles can also be used to emphasize or exaggerate the dimensions of a room. A strong horizontal band of colour, for example, creates an optical illusion of space – so you might want to think about adding a contrasting border tile when you are tiling a small bathroom. By the same token, an oppressively low ceiling can be made to appear higher by creating vertical stripes of colour on the walls.

Tiling is not a mysterious skill; it simply requires a careful and methodical approach. Indeed, it is a relatively easily mastered technique. Walls are seldom straight, blank surfaces but contain windows, alcoves or doors, and these need to be taken into account before you even start tiling or major difficulties will arise.

For your first project, it is probably a good idea to tackle something modest such as a splashback for a sink. This will allow you to perfect your technique and gain some confidence on a smallish area before embarking on a whole wall.

▲ *A delightful combination of textures and materials has been used in this fantasy bathroom. Although the room is small, glass and light combine to add an additional dimension, while the imaginative use of layered wood for panelling adds a back-to-nature feel.*

◄ *Tiles are so durable and versatile, it is a shame to restrict them to bathrooms and hallways. Here, a wall of tiles in various shades of blue creates an unusual backdrop for a soft suede sofa. Glass and tiles seem to have an affinity – as proved by the way the glass coffee table beautifully reflects the tiles in its surface.*

◄ *The gentle sheen of brushed metal provides a surprisingly sensuous wall-covering and co-ordinates wonderfully with the textures in the rest of the room.*

Directory of wall tiles

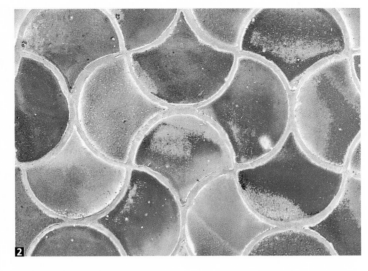

Shapes and sizes

Square and rectangular

Available in a variety of sizes, from tiny mosaic chips to large 30 x 30cm (12 x 12in) tiles. They are generally just over 4mm (⅙in) thick. Square ceramic tiles are the most common type, but for variety in a run of basic tiles, arrange them in a diamond or brick-wall design, or mix with the same type in a contrasting colour. Tiles usually have square or bevelled edges; sometimes they are glazed on one or two edges so that you do not have to use edge trim. **1**

Other shapes

Unusually shaped, hexagonal and octagonal tiles can be used to great dramatic effect either by themselves or in combination with square or rectangular tiles. As with any unusual tile design, plot the effect you want to achieve on graph paper before you start on the wall to avoid errors that will be difficult to correct. **2**

Border tiles

There is now a vast range of dado and border tiles on the market; some are patterned, others plain or with a glazed relief design. These can be used to give a striking and professional finish to runs of plain tiles, or a dramatic band between two large expanses of plain flat tiles.

Textured and smooth

You have to consider more than merely the colour and pattern of tiles when you are planning your scheme. The texture and finish of the tiles plays a considerable part in the overall look of the room. The warmth of rustic terracotta goes very well with unbleached muslin, wooden floors and coarse woollen throws. If you prefer a more streamlined effect, glitzy glass tiles can add some sparkle to stark modern schemes.

Glazed/unglazed ceramic

Glazed tiles have a glossy, waterproof surface; unglazed tiles must be sealed for protection. Acrylic varnish gives a durable surface but wax, though more time-consuming and requiring more elbow grease, gives an infinitely more subtle and beautiful finish.

Vitreous

Glass tiles or bricks are a great way of breaking up a space without running the risk of blocking out light or creating a closed-in, cramped atmosphere in the room. **3**

Terracotta

The warm, natural and earthy tones of glazed or unglazed terracotta combine wonderfully with the naturally-biased elements of today's interiors. Unglazed terracotta tiles will need sealing with wax or polyurethane varnish to make them stain- and water-resistant. **5**

Mirror

These tiles and sheets can transform a cramped space or an awkwardly shaped room, creating a new sense of spaciousness. They come with a self-adhesive backing, which makes this type of tile particularly easy to install. However, you should bear in mind that you will need a com-pletely flat wall if you want to create a perfect, undistorted reflection, otherwise the effect will be ruined.

Metallic

A less expensive alternative to metal cladding on walls, these shiny tiles can look extremely smart, creating the same sort of reflective effect.

Mosaic

These can be stunning, whether covering a whole expanse of wall or interspersed with plain tiles, perhaps as a border. The small tiles, also called chips, are supplied stuck to a square of paper or netting so that they can be attached in reasonably large quantities to the adhesive before the protective layer is peeled off. Although they are occasionally available in a pattern, they are usually supplied in 30 x 30cm (12 x 12in) plain-coloured squares.

Relief pattern

Ceramic tiles with a raised pattern beneath the glaze provide variety in tone and texture in a long run of tiles. Relief patterns are popular for border tiles and are moulded to resemble cornicing for a professional finish.

Pictorial and patterned

Panels of pictorial or patterned tiles can create a stunning focal point on an expanse of wall and need not be expensive if you combine them with a run of co-ordinating plain tiles. **4**

First steps to tiling

The quality of a tiled finish is wholly dependent on good preparation. It is vital to be meticulous with the preparation of the wall and the setting out, because, by the time you get to the end of the wall, what may have started out as a small error can have magnified into a real catastrophe. Once the tiles start to go out of true, there is really no alternative but to take them off and start again.

Calculating quantities of tiles

Working out the number of tiles you will need is quite a straightforward exercise. Assuming you are using square tiles, divide the width of the wall by the width of the tile. This will give you the number of tiles you will need for each row. Then, divide the height of the tile into the total height of the area. This tells you how many tiles will fit down the row. Now multiply the number of tiles across by the number of tiles down to reach the total number of tiles required. To this figure add a further 5 to 10 per cent to allow for breakages. Buy all the tiles you are going to need at the same time, as you would for wallpaper, as there can be slight variations in tone and finish between different batches.

If you are using unusual shapes or hand-made tiles, or will be fixing them in an unusual way, you will need to make yourself a tiling gauge to allow you to estimate quantities accurately. Indeed, this is an invaluable tool whatever the kind of tile you are using.

Making a tiling gauge

A tiling gauge is simple to make and will make your life easier when it comes to deciding on the horizontal and vertical positioning of tiles. It also allows you to know at a glance how many tiles will fit between two points and ensures that you centre tiles accurately over baths or along windows. Make a tiling gauge from a 1.2m (4ft) length of 50 x 25mm (2 x 1in) wooden batten. On a flat surface, lay out the tiles as you will arrange them on the wall, allowing space between the tiles for tile spacers that eventually will be filled with grout. Use a ballpoint pen to mark clearly on the batten the widths of the tiles and the tile spacer/grouting space.

Preparing surfaces

Careful preparation is the key to successful tiling. You need a smooth, clean, grease- and dust-free surface on which to start. Any imperfections in the wall and skimping at this stage will be magnified once you have fixed a glossy ceramic tile on the top or attempted any kind of geometric design.

When tiling on bare plaster, prepare it carefully as you would for painting (see pages 56–57), ensuring there is no mould or damp. If the wall is in very bad condition you may need to consider skimming it with a new layer of plaster. If you are tiling over new plaster, make sure it is absolutely dry and has been sealed with a proprietary primer-sealer. If you are tiling over a chipboard or plywood surface, seal it with a dilute solution of PVA adhesive first.

Keying paintwork

It is very simple to prepare a painted wall, whether it is coated with a water or oil-based paint. All you need to do is to key, or roughen, the surface of the paint with some coarse sandpaper. Wrap it around a sanding block and it will be easier to hold and use. Keying allows the adhesive to penetrate the surface of the wall, ensuring the tiles stick to the wall rather than the painted surface.

When you have finished sanding, use a scraper to get rid of any flaking paint and a damp cloth or sponge to remove any dust from the surface. Allow the wall to dry thoroughly before moving to the next stage.

Removing wallpapers

You cannot tile over wallpaper as it is not stable enough. It is necessary to remove all the layers of old wallcovering so that the tile adhesive

▶ Small mosaic tiles allow you to create surprisingly subtle and intricate patterns. They are also very good for creating startling geometric designs in bands of contrasting colour, as in this chic, modern bathroom.

Tools and equipment

- **Sandpaper:** a coarse grade, to key (roughen) walls.
- **Silicon carbide paper:** to rub down an existing tiled surface.
- **Spirit level:** to establish true horizontals and verticals.
- **Try square:** to indicate exact right angles.
- **Chalk line:** to mark a straight line over a long wall.
- **Tiling gauge:** to measure long runs of tiles.
- **Length of batten:** to support rows of tiles when they are first fixed to a wall.
- **Felt-tip pen or chinagraph pencil:** to mark the tiles.
- **Tile scorer:** most basic tool used for cutting tiles.
- **Score-and-snap tool:** to cut tiles. Easier and more accurate to use than a tile scorer.
- **Score-and-snap pliers:** to cut tiles.
- **Pincers:** to cut irregular shapes in tiles.
- **Tile file:** to smooth rough edges.
- **Tile saw:** to cut curves in tiles.
- **Suitable tile adhesive:** to fix tiles to wall. Various types are designed for different surfaces or purposes.
- **Pointing trowel:** to apply adhesive to walls.
- **Notched spreader:** to spread adhesive.
- **Plastic spacers or matchsticks:** to space tiles evenly.
- **Suitable grout:** to fill spaces between tiles and make surface waterproof.
- **Wooden dowel:** to smooth and shape surface of grout.
- **Decorating sponge:** to clean down tiles and remove excess grout.
- **Cloth:** to polish surface of tiles when tiling is complete.
- **Silicone sealant and gun:** to fill gaps between tiles and bathroom fittings, to create a waterproof seal.

Equipment to hire
- **Electric disc cutter.**
- **Diamond-tipped cutters.**

◀ *Tiles are supremely practical and durable as they are heat and splash resistant, but they can also make a great contribution to the decorative scheme. Here, Mediterranean blue tiles behind the oven and on the floor make a decorative splash and ensure that this kitchen looks stylish rather than merely functional.*

can form a strong bond with the wall surface. For instructions on stripping wallpaper, see pages 80–81. After stripping, make good the wall (see pages 56–57).

Rubbing down old tiles

It is possible – although not recommended – to tile over existing tiles if the surface is sound and smooth. Before fixing your new tiles, roughen the glazed surface with silicon carbide paper in order to provide a key for the adhesive. Then use a slightly damp cloth or sponge to remove any dust from the surface. In some situations, a double layer of tiles may look thick and clumsy. If this is the case, first protect your eyes with plastic goggles and then remove the old tiles using a bolster chisel and club hammer.

Once removed, you will then need to render or replaster the wall before fixing the new tiles, so this will increase the scope of your job enormously.

Tiling plan and preparation

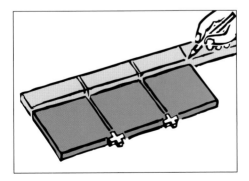

1 Use a ballpoint pen to mark the widths of the tiles and the spacers on the batten to make a tiling gauge.

2 Wearing protective goggles to avoid eye injury, remove the old tiles using a bolster chisel and club hammer.

Planning

▲ *Hundreds and hundreds of tiny tiles look very effective and professional but it can be very tedious matching them up into even rows. Some brands of tiny tiles are available already plastered onto larger squares to make the task less arduous. However, the end result achieves a very pleasing effect.*

Before fixing tiles onto the wall, it is most important to plan where all the tiles will fall – both whole and cut tiles. You can do this using your tiling gauge. If you are planning an elaborate design, work it out on graph paper before attempting to transfer it to the wall.

Setting out

This is the most important stage in tiling, as accuracy here is essential to the overall look of the finished job. First, plan exactly where the whole tiles will be fixed and work out where cut tiles will be the least noticeable. This is a relatively easy task on a blank wall: find the centre of the wall and work out the whole tiles from that point outwards. Most walls, however, contain some kind of obstacle such as a window or door. If this is the case, decide on the room's natural centre point – that is, the point to which your eye is naturally drawn – and start tiling from there. But use your tiling gauge (see page 108–109) to ensure that you are not going to have ugly slivers of tile in obvious places before you lay your first tile. In most cases you will be tiling to the skirting board or floor and it is unlikely that either of these will be level. It is essential that you establish a true horizontal and tile from that to ensure that each row is level. This is called marking out.

Marking out

Using a batten and spirit level, draw a horizontal line along the wall to be tiled, about three-quarters of a tile's width above the floor

Marking out tiles

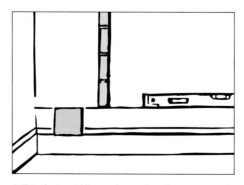

1 Plot a horizontal line no deeper than three-quarters of the depth of the tile. Measure out the tiles with the gauge.

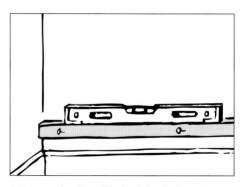

2 To ensure the tiling will be level, fix a horizontal batten to the wall. Check accuracy with the spirit level.

or skirting board. Make sure that at no point is the line more than a tile's width above the finishing level – floor or skirting board. If it is, redraw the line lower down or you will be left with unworkable slivers of tile.

The tiles will need some support while the adhesive dries. Fix a line of battens on the wall with masonry nails, aligning the top of the batten with the pencilled horizontal guideline. Do not fix battens too securely or removing them will be difficult.

Using your tiling gauge, establish where the outer edge of the last whole tile on a wall will be. Mark the wall by snapping a chalk line against it, and fix a vertical batten to the wall, again aligning the inside edge of the batten with the pencilled guideline to mark the edge. Check that the battens form an exact horizontal and vertical before you start tiling.

Setting out tiles

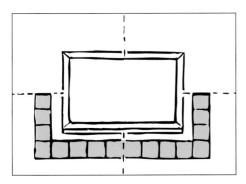

1 To avoid unworkable slivers of tile, the first row should be three-quarters of a tile's width away from the edge.

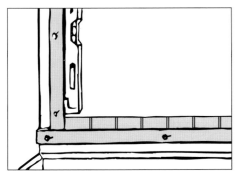

3 Attach a vertical batten to the wall. Check that it is square with the horizontal batten using the spirit level.

▲ *Choosing the right size of tile enables both the curves and straight lines of a room to be emphasized. Tiles are often the first choice for bathroom and shower areas because, once grouted into position, they provide a perfectly waterproof surface that is very easily cleaned – but architects love them because of the design possibilities.*

Fixing whole tiles

Once you have carefully established the horizontal and vertical with your battens and everything is true, you can start tiling.

Fixing tiles

Use the tile adhesive recommended by the manufacturer for the type of tile you have chosen, and spread it out 1 sq m (1 sq yd) at a time with a pointing trowel, ensuring that it is no more than 3mm (⅛in) thick. Start in the corner where the horizontal and vertical battens meet.

Next, take a notched spreader, usually supplied with the adhesive, and distribute the adhesive evenly over the area, but leaving regular ridges. The grooves will create suction when you put the tiles on the wall, thus helping to secure them. If you are using a sealing strip, press this into the adhesive first. If you experience trouble getting it to stay in place, secure it temporarily with a couple of nails.

Press the first tile firmly onto the adhesive, resting it squarely on the tile-support battens. Put a spacer or matchstick against the corner of the tile and place and fix the next tile. Continue to build up horizontal rows in this way, stopping occasionally to check your work by using a spirit level to ensure that the tiles are flush. Wipe any blobs of adhesive from the tiles with a damp cloth.

Having completed the rows of whole tiles, you will need to fill the gaps on the outside edges. To establish where to cut the tiles, take a spare tile and hold it against the previous full tile, glazed side to the wall, so that its outer edge butts up against the adjacent wall. Mark the back of the loose tile with a felt-tip pen or chinagraph pencil at the points at which it meets the fixed tile, and deducting the allowance for the grout that has been made by the tile spacer, use a steel rule to draw straight across the back of the tile.

▶ Mediterranean tiles in a geometric pattern add colour but are also a supremely practical decorative option. In a heavy-wear area, such as below the dado rail in this hallway, the tiles are impervious to bumps, scuff marks and splashes, while providing a colourful point of interest.

Fixing tiles

1 Use the notched spreader to spread the tile adhesive evenly across the wall, leaving ridges.

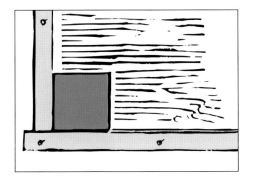

2 Position the first tile firmly into the adhesive, resting it squarely on the support battens. Continue adding tiles.

3 Check tiled rows for both horizontal and vertical alignment with the spirit level.

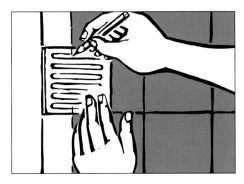

4 Hold a spare tile against the last full tile to find where to cut the final rogue-sized tile so that it fits the wall.

▲ *Plain tiles in a combination of colours can be used to great decorative effect all over your home. In this instance, plain tiles are perfect for this bathroom's understated style and the combination of two colours with white takes the purely functional edge off the room.*

Turning corners

▶ *Tiles can fulfil a variety of functions, as in this bathroom. The stone tile creates a waterproof surface for the shower, while the mosaic tile has a more decorative function, creating a smart dado. The vitreous glass bricks provide essential privacy, while also allowing in the light.*

it is best to apply the adhesive directly onto the back of the tile with a small, notched spreader. This avoids excess adhesive getting onto the rest of the tile.

Internal

At internal corners, you need to overlap one set of cut tiles over another. Work out which edge will be least noticeable when overlapped before you start.

External

When tiling at external corners, you will need to fix an extra batten. This batten should be fixed down the corner, but projecting from one of the walls so that when you fix the last tiles on the other wall, they butt up to the batten. (In effect you are creating an internal corner with the batten.) Then remove the batten and fix the tiles to the adjacent wall so that they butt up closely to the first lot of tiles, with one glazed edge

Firmly score the loose tile with a tile scorer or the wheel cutter of your score-and-snap pliers. Use the pliers to break the tile along the scored line, or snap it against the straight edge of a table or work bench. If you are using a tile-cutting jig, it will have a marking gauge which you can set to the width of the gap before cutting. Do not be tempted, however, to cut all your tiles at once, without measuring gap by gap first, because walls are seldom square and you will waste tiles.

When you need to cut around a more difficult or intricate shape, you should use pincers and bite away a little piece at a time.

Before you fix the cut tile in place, hold it against the gap to check that it fits. If it does, lay it on a flat surface and smooth the cut edge with a tile file. It will probably be necessary to butter the back of the tile with adhesive before fixing it to ensure that it sticks firmly.

Turning corners

Many spaces will require you to tile around corners and across edges. A professional finish here will require a neat and steady hand. Again, when dealing with small pieces of tile,

Cutting tiles

1 Make a score mark across the tile using a tile scorer or the wheel cutter of the score-and-cut tool.

2 Once the tile has been scored it can be snapped apart using the snapping device of the score-and-cut tool.

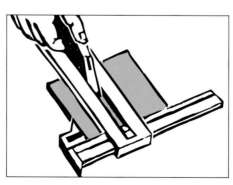

3 On a tile cutting jig there is a marking gauge that you set to the width of the gap before cutting.

4 For cutting round intricate shapes it is best to use pincers, biting away a little bit of tile at a time.

▲ *No one ever said that tiles had to be square. You can use them as creatively as any other decorative tool, as in this bathroom decorated in citrus-coloured tiles. Abstract mosaic patterns are combined wonderfully here with straight runs of tile.*

Turning corners

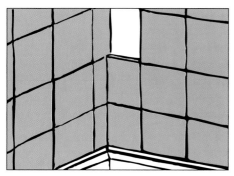

1 For an internal corner, the smaller tiling space should be at the back so that it is least visible.

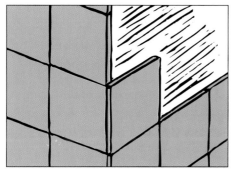

2 For external corners the full-sized tiles on the outside edge should be at right angles to each other.

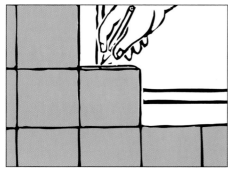

3 For recessed windows place a full tile to the edge and mark the angle which will need to be cut out.

4 When tiling the sill, bring the edge of the closest line of tiles out to butt up flush with the face of the tiled wall.

of the latter tile visible. You may wish to use an edging strip to finish off external corners neatly. If so, you must remember to attach the strip to the corner first before attaching the tiles. They should be fixed to each side of the corner simultaneously so that you can ensure that they are exactly aligned.

Recessed windows

If you are tiling a recessed window but cannot work out how to achieve a neat finish, you should apply and combine the principles you have used for measuring last tiles and for internal and external corners. Tile in rows to within a tile's range of the corner of the window sill and mark the angle which will need to be cut out. Next tile the sill section, bringing the front edge of the closest line of tiles out to butt up flush with the face of the tiled wall – treating it as if it were an external corner. And finally tile the walls of the recess, the junction of the sill and the wall acting as an internal corner.

Tiling around obstacles

Rooms often contain obstacles that are difficult or impossible to move, usually in bathrooms and kitchens, and you must therefore tile around them. Pipes provide a particular challenge for the novice tiler. Make a paper template of the curve you are cutting around and then transfer the pattern to the tile with a felt-tip pen or chinagraph pencil.

To cut around a large curve, such as a waste pipe or basin, cut the paper to the size of the tile. Make a series of parallel cuts in the paper 12mm (½in) apart and then press the paper against the curve of the obstacle. Fold back the paper cuts to mark the line. Draw a line along the series of folds to form a clean curve and cut along the line. Place the template on the tile, glazed side up. Mark the curve on the tile and carefully score along the line with a firm, even stroke.

Place the tile in a vice and cut along the curve using a tile saw. Smooth the edge with a tile file and smear extra adhesive across the back of the tile before fixing to the wall.

For smaller pipes, hold the tile next to the pipe and mark the pipe's exact position on the top and side of the tile. Draw intersecting lines on the tile. Where the lines meet, draw a small circle slightly larger than the diameter of the pipe. Cut the tile in two along the vertical line; score the curve and cut away the tile in the centre of the circle using a tile nibbler. Stick the two pieces of tile on either side of the pipe. To fit tiles around a light switch, hold the tile up against the fixture and mark the position for the

▲ Tiling large areas in one colour is an extremely effective method of creating a feeling of spaciousness. In this instance, beige tiles, relieved with grey details, are co-ordinated with chrome fittings and accessories to create a chic yet functional bathroom which makes the most of its natural light.

Obstacles

1 Make cuts in a tile-sized piece of paper. Press it around the obstacle and fold back flaps. Cut along the fold line.

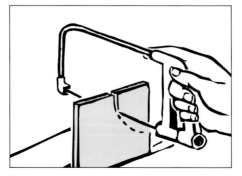

2 Using the template, mark the curve onto the tile. Place the tile in a vice and then cut out the shape with a tile saw.

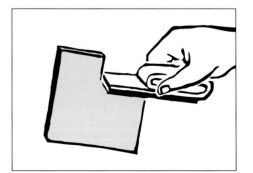

3 Release the tile from the vice and gently smooth down the cut edges using a tile file.

horizontal and vertical cuts with a felt-tip pen or chinagraph pencil. Place in a clamp, and cut down each line with a tile saw. Dab extra adhesive onto the back before securing it.

Finishing off

Many tiles come with a coordinating range of edging tiles. You may wish to incorporate one of these, or to use wooden moulding or plastic trim strips. Wooden mouldings are attached to the wall at the end of the job; plastic strips need to be attached at the beginning, before the tiles. Ceramic coving at the edge of a bath makes a neat, waterproof seal.

Fill in the gaps between the tiles with grout. Allow the adhesive to dry out completely before even thinking about doing this. Follow the manufacturer's instructions as to the drying time; it is usually at least 12 hours and can be as much as 24 hours. Grout can be bought as powder or premixed. Apply with a plastic scraper. Use a waterproof grout and sealant (see below) in areas such as bathrooms and kitchens, where the tiling is likely to come into contact with moisture.

Remember to use waterproof grout for bath and shower surrounds and epoxy grout for work surfaces to keep them germ-free. There are also new stain-resistant grouts available; less likely to pick up dirt, they will thus maintain a fresher appearance for longer.

Force the grout in between the tile joins with the spreader held at right angles to the tile, moving it backwards and forwards as you go. If you scrape off any excess grout quickly,

it can be reused. Before the grout dries, take a damp cloth and wipe off excess. Use a piece of wooden dowel to smooth the grout lines into a slightly concave groove, or wipe over the grout to create a flush finish. When the grout has dried out completely, use a clean, lint-free cloth to polish the tiles.

For authenticity, if you are restoring a Victorian interior, you should follow the style of wafer-thin grouting between tiles.

To finish off the gap between a tiled area and another surface, such as a bath or shower tray, use a silicone rubber sealant or caulk. Apply sealant directly from the tube onto the join, cutting the nozzle to match the size of the join. Squeeze on to the join as you would ice a cake, in a smooth, continuous line, with the tube held at a 45-degree angle to the join. Use your finger or the back of a wet teaspoon to smooth the sealant into the join and use a damp sponge to wipe away excess.

Faults and cures

Uneven tiles

Usually caused by not setting the guide battens against the walls correctly before you begin, this is either a disaster, in which case all you can do is remove the tiles and begin again, or you can decide to live with it.

Cracked tiles

If one tile in a row becomes cracked, remove it carefully with a chisel, working from the centre outwards and taking care not to damage the adjacent tiles. Scrape out as much of the adhesive as you can and use a hose vacuum cleaner to remove the dust and debris. Spread adhesive on the back of the replacement tile and press it firmly into the gap. Wipe off excess adhesive with a damp sponge, then allow to dry and re-grout.

Discoloured grout

Depending on time, inclination and the extent of the discolouring, you can either try bleaching the discoloured grout with household bleach, or you will have to rake out the existing grout with a screwdriver and apply fresh. Alternatively, you could paint the grout with a proprietary grout paint.

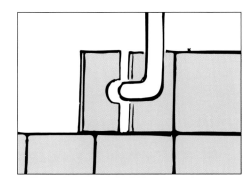
4 To cut out around pipes cut the tile in two along the vertical line. Score the curve and cut away the surplus.

Finishing off

1 Force the grout between the joints of the tiles with the spreader held at right angles to the tiles.

2 Before the grout dries, use a damp cloth to wipe any smears of excess grout from the surface of the tiles.

3 Use a piece of wooden dowel, or similar, to smooth the grout lines into a neat, slightly concave groove.

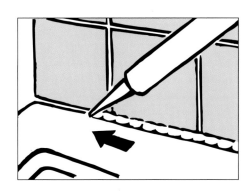
4 Apply sealant onto the join in a smooth, continuous line, cutting the nozzle to match the size of the join.

Wood panelling

▶ *Timber-cladding your walls can be an inexpensive but smart option, particularly if you choose softwood which can then be given a coat of paint to create a smart, durable surface. It is also the ultimate method of disguising walls that are less than perfect.*

Wood panelling can provide a durable and attractive wall surface that is very relevant for today's texture-rich interiors. You can choose from a vast number of grains and colours, and inexpensive softwoods can be transformed with a coat of paint, varnish or wood stain – either a natural shade or one of the brighter colours now widely available.

An added bonus is that timber is perhaps the best disguise for less-than-perfect walls and is an excellent heat and sound insulator.

When ordering wood, avoid unsightly joins by purchasing lengths which are long enough to stretch from floor to ceiling, or from side to side if you are panelling horizontally.

You will also need to allow time for the wood to acclimatize before you start to work with it. Lay the boards flat on the floor for a couple of weeks *in situ*, so they can get used to the temperature and humidity in your house; move them around every few days to encourage the drying-out process. If you

avoid doing this now, the wood may shrink when it is on the wall and you will be left with ugly gaps between the planks.

Types of wood

The most usual woods used for panelling are softwoods, such as pine; they are inexpensive and take paint or stain treatments well, but if money is no object, talk to your timber merchant about available hardwoods. These can provide a much richer effect, and they actually improve in appearance as they get older. Some of the more popular hardwoods used for panelling are ramin, oak, mahogany, meranti and cedar. Cedar has a delicious scent which deters moths, so it is often used to line cupboards and drawers too.

Remember to try to look out for wood from ecologically farmed plantations or hunt for old timber in architectural salvage yards to avoid depleting rainforests.

Attaching the boards

To attach the boards to the wall, you will need to create a framework of 2.5 x 5cm (1 x 2in) battens fixed to the wall about 40cm (16in) apart. If you are attaching the boards vertically, the battens need to run horizontally; for horizontal panelling, attach the battens vertically. You need to add a further support strip at ceiling level; but if you are adding a new skirting board, leave the existing one in place beneath the panelling to act as support. Fix the battens to the wall with masonry nails, or screws and wallplugs, and use your spirit level to check that they really are square.

When you are buying the cladding, look for timber marked TGV (which stands for tongued, grooved and chamfered into a V-joint). This means that the edges are designed simply to slot neatly together when you come to put them on the wall. Alternatively, you could choose something that is a little more decorative; match-boarding, for instance, has a moulding down the edge for a more sophisticated look.

Boards are usually sold in 10cm (4in) widths, but you should estimate on twelve boards to cover a space 1m (39in) wide to allow for overlapping and planing. You can also buy panelling kits, but they are more expensive because they are simpler to fit and come complete with dado rail and skirting board. When you attach the timber, it is important to leave a small gap to allow the air to circulate freely behind the panelling: as little as 1cm (⅜in) will do. This will prevent the timber from warping and the gap is so small it will not be noticeable when you have finished.

With the framework screwed to the wall, place your first board with its grooved edge in the corner. Nail through its face into the support battens, checking that the strip is straight with a plumb line. Tap subsequent boards in place with a hammer and offcut and fix at regular intervals (spaced according to the weight of the wood) either with nails as above, if to be hidden, or with panel pins as below. Before securing the penultimate board, overlap the last board and cut it to width. Spring the two in place together.

It is a good idea to seal wood finishes with wax or with matt polyurethane varnish when you have finished, to avoid staining, particularly in bathrooms and kitchens.

Attaching wood panelling

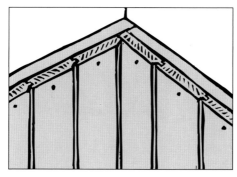

1 TGV cladding slots together as you place the panels up on the wall. Knock them gently so that they abut.

2 Tack panel pins diagonally through the panelling onto the support batten at regular intervals.

3 At a junction with a plain wall, cut the last board to fit, snap last two in place and face nail the last board.

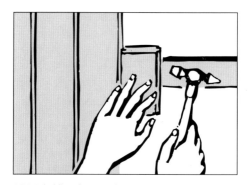

4 Butt join internal corners and either plane a chamfer on the inside edge or neaten with a length of moulding.

5 At external corners plane off tongue to butt square. Finish with dado rail and mouldings, if required.

6 Pack out and remount flush electrical fittings, frame with battening strips, and cut notches in boards to fit.

Detailing for walls

▶ *Rough wooden tongue-and-groove cladding creates an old-fashioned feel in this bathroom. The slightly thicker than usual picture rail attractively finishes off the top of the wooden planks and provides a practical purpose by hanging the bathroom mirror – the alternative would be to drive in nails and damage the wood.*

Dado rails, picture rails and skirting boards

When fitting a dado or picture rail, begin by deciding on the height at which it is to be fixed. Dado rails are usually placed about one-third of the way up the wall, or 1m (39in) from the floor. Or you can use the height of the chairs in the room as a guide. Picture rails should be fitted at a comfortable distance from both the dado rail and the ceiling, but nearer the latter, and their position should enable you to hang pictures where they can be seen from a seated position. This is unlikely to be less than 1.8m (6ft) from the floor.

Once you are satisfied with the proposed height of the moulding, draw a horizontal guideline with a pencil around the room using a spirit level, or ping a chalk line against each wall of the room in turn.

Fitting new skirting boards may well reveal that the floor is not completely level, but most irregularities can be hidden by lifting the board slightly and covering the resulting gap with carpet and underlay, or by nailing a thin or quarter–circle beading along the base of the skirting so that it touches the floor.

Once the mouldings have been cut to length, drill and countersink screw holes at roughly 60cm (2ft) intervals. Hold the moulding in position along the guideline, and mark the locations of the holes on the walls.

Set aside the moulding, drill into the wall with a masonry bit, and insert plastic plugs that will take 45mm (1¾ in) countersunk

Fixing dado and picture rails

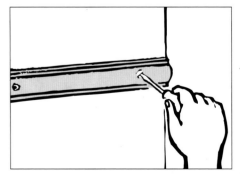

1 Mark position of screws on first, cut length; drill holes and countersinks; secure rail to wall along guideline.

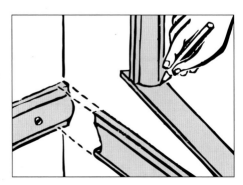

2 For a butt join at an internal corner, scribe rail's profile on back of second length, cut with coping saw and fit.

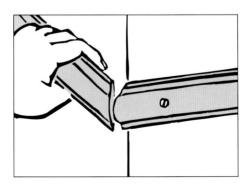

3 Use mitred joints at external corners cutting at 45 degrees; mitre the ends of lengths joining along walls too.

screws. In modern houses, or where the layout of an old house has been changed, the walls may be made from stud partitioning and plasterboard. Where this is the case, you will either have to screw into the timber framing, as above, locating this by tapping along the wall and noting where it sounds less hollow, or you will have to use cavity fixings. It is also possible to buy mouldings in kit form with special fixing clips that allow you to slot the rail into place.

Where two lengths of moulding meet at an internal angle, make a butt joint by drawing the profile of the moulding onto the back of the length that will go on the second wall, at the end that is to be fitted into the corner. Cut carefully along the line with a coping saw, then fit the cut end tightly against the face of the rail on the first wall.

At external corners, use a 45-degree mitre block to cut an angled joint between the two lengths. If the moulding will not fit into the block, mark the cutting line on the face, and continue this along the edge at a 45-degree angle. You can do this accurately by using a combination square, or by drawing a square on the edge where one corner joins up with the line on the face, and making a diagonal cutting line from this point to the opposite corner. Follow both cutting lines as you saw through. Mitred cuts should also be made when joining two straight lengths of moulding. Any small gaps in joints can usually be hidden with wood filler.

Sheet metal cladding

One of the most stylish trends of recent years is the use of metal on walls. The trend originated in cafés and restaurants but has since moved into the domestic interior. Metal provides a chic and durable finish, but it is usually costly and requires heavy maintenance to keep it looking up to scratch: most finishes dull easily and show every fingerprint and scuff mark, so they need frequent buffing with a soft cloth to preserve the smart finish.

Depending on the effect you want to create, consider copper, zinc, aluminium or the even more expensive stainless steel. If you think that a whole metal wall will exceed your budget limitations, consider using it in a more limited capacity – in panels or below the dado rail.

Metal comes in sheets or tiles and should be screwed directly onto the plaster, or onto wooden panels. It is a specialized finish and an expensive material, so you may be well advised to seek professional help rather than embarking on the task yourself.

▶ Polished metal sheets can provide a sophisticated look when combined with other, more traditional materials. This type of room design needs commitment, both stylistically and financially, as it is expensive to achieve and requires a considerable amount of time dedicated to keeping it looking good – every fingermark will show.

FLOORS

▲ *Cool concrete painted a royal blue picks up on the fresh tone of the chairs in the kitchen and contrasts with the warm tones of the pale wood in the foreground. The neat demarcation between the two different materials allows the worker in the office in the foreground to separate work from the comforts of the living area beyond.*

Most decent-quality floor-coverings are expensive, although the cheaper-quality carpets and vinyls are among the most economical floor-coverings currently available. If you are restricted to a tight budget, consider renovating the existing floor (see pages 126–147). The result could look much better than a cheap carpet would and is one of the most potentially rewarding, if challenging, of flooring options.

Houses and some flats built before the 1960s will probably have floors constructed from pine boards, or even oak or parquet. Bald carpets and scruffy vinyl or linoleum may be past salvation but try lifting a corner to see what is underneath (see pages 126–127). People frequently cover up a very good wood floor with a carpet, and what you find could be the basis of a whole new and exciting range of possibilities.

Newer houses and flats and older dwellings that have been extensively modernized may have floors constructed from chipboard or concrete. Although these materials lack the charm of old floorboards they can be brightened up considerably with paint (see pages 138–145). Even concrete can be

Floors and floor-coverings are not indestructible and there comes a day when something has to be done about the threadbare carpet, the tatty vinyl or the filthy, cracked floorboards. Even if the flooring is still in fairly good condition, it may be that you have grown tired of it or, having moved into a new dwelling, you do not share the former occupant's taste. Yet other factors may be involved in the decision to change a floor-covering. Perhaps a dusty carpet that causes uncontrollable sneezing is harbouring a population of house-dust mites and a non-fabric floor-covering would be less allergenic. Maybe a wood floor is looking scratched or the colour is not quite right for a new decorative scheme. Although it may seem that the only solution is to rip up the lot and start again, this is not the only course of action open to you – nor is it necessarily desirable.

The first step when considering a new floor is to examine the options available and to decide whether they are affordable.

▲ *This room has the original oak floorboards often found in much older houses. This type of floor naturally tends to age gracefully and looks good in any environment when just simply waxed and polished; here the floorboards perfectly complement an informal arrangement of pale furnishings that gives an uncluttered impression.*

painted to imitate a more expensive material such as limestone flooring and, of course, it will have the solidity associated with the real thing.

Indeed, there are very few existing floors that cannot be improved by one of the wide range of decorative treatments now available. For instance, floors that really seem past all hope but which are structurally sound can have plywood shapes fixed to them which are then painted or stained, perhaps in imitation of flagstones or marble tiles (see pages 144–145). Such a treatment can transform a rough old floor for very little outlay and will look far more sophisticated than cheap carpet.

Bare wood or concrete is not to everyone's taste; nor is either appropriate to every situation. Fortunately, it is a relatively easy matter to change their appearance completely by adding a new layer of floor-covering. Flooring materials are diverse and within each group there are variations and styles to suit every taste and requirement. All can be quick and easy to install. Hard tiles and stone provide hard-wearing flooring suitable for

anywhere receiving a lot of foot traffic or where water is present (see pages 158–161). Flexible flooring such as vinyl or linoleum, in sheet or tile form, offers softer, waterproof options suitable for kitchens and utility areas, and, if cushioned, is especially kind to the feet (see pages 166–169). Even new wood floors can be laid without much effort or skill (see pages 176–179). And for total underfoot luxury there is today a huge range of carpets and natural floor-coverings – unsurpassed for variety and price range (see pages 182–185).

Varied as they are, all these exciting floor-coverings usually require a sound, level floor upon which to rest in order to ensure that they look good and wear well. Before laying any new flooring the existing floor should be checked for any faults and repaired or prepared as appropriate for the new flooring material (see pages 152–155).

With so many flooring options on offer, there is nothing to stop anyone from having beautiful floors, no matter what the size of their pocket. Free up your imagination and you will achieve surprisingly dramatic effects.

▲ *Natural floor-coverings have become very popular recently due to the wide choice available and their relatively low cost; they also look good in almost any setting. The strong texture of the rush matting here lends relief to the flat features of this room and the neutral colour works well with the vivid colour scheme.*

◀ *Tiles are one of the most versatile flooring materials, being both almost indestructible and waterproof. The handmade ceramic tiles in this shower room give it a more countrified look, the hand-painted tiles on the floor and tiles cut into pyramids on the skirting adding visual interest to an otherwise tiny and plain space.*

Decorating existing floors

Although an existing floor may appear beyond redemption, you do not necessarily have to cover it up with a new and expensive flooring material. As long as the floor is structurally sound, it can either be restored to its former glory or brightened up with a whole range of inspiring decorative improvements. If the floor is covered with an old flooring material, it is always worth peeling this back some way, and in at least two different places, to check the condition of the floor underneath.

Floorboards may look worn and dirty but it is surprising how good they can look when they have been sanded (see pages 134–135) and varnished. For renovation, though, they do need to be in reasonable condition; any damaged boards should be replaced and gaps filled (see pages 132–133). If the colour of the boards is not quite commensurate with the room's decoration, they can be painted or treated in any number of ways. A painted design can look breathtaking and will always be a talking point for visitors.

Cracks and pits in concrete floors can be repaired fairly easily (page 152–153) and then painted with a plain colour or any type of pattern imaginable. Alternatively, a concrete floor can be covered with a pattern of plywood squares which can be cunningly painted to imitate flagstones or a marble-tiled floor (pages 144–145).

One of the few floor surfaces that cannot be easily changed with paint is tiles; the paint will chip off in the hard wear such a floor is likely to receive, especially in the places where tiles are usually laid, such as in kitchens and bathrooms. Unwanted floor tiles must either be physically removed or covered with another floor-covering, such as might be used for concrete. Another surface that does not accept paint is vinyl, because the paint reacts with the plastic and peels off.

Having made the decision to renovate an existing floor rather than to cover it up, the first step is to decide how the finished floor is to look, for this will determine what preparation the floor will need.

Varnished floors

One of the most popular ways of improving an existing floor, and one that can be done quickly and easily, is to machine-sand old floorboards and varnish them for protection (see pages 134–135, 146–147). The result can look particularly attractive if the boards are hardwood, such as oak or ash. It is more likely, however, that an existing floor will be constructed of pine or deal boards. These cheap softwoods were used extensively for flooring up to the 1960s, after which even cheaper materials manufactured from reclaimed wood became standard.

▲ *Sanded old floorboards are an economical and practical choice of flooring, considering how many older homes were built with perfectly serviceable wooden floors. This floor has simply been sanded and given several coats of gloss varnish for a rich, deep shine; bright light pouring through the windows bounces off it.*

One difficulty with old pine floors is that the wood darkens over the years, tending to become a fiery ginger colour. And as the protective varnish coat yellows with age, it exacerbates the hotness of this colour, which tends to clash with many colours commonly used in decorating. Cool blues and greens are perhaps the only colours that sit comfortably with sanded pine floorboards. Thankfully, however, it is an easy matter to alter the colour of pine boards to something more sympathetic to contemporary taste.

Stained floors

Stains (see pages 136–137) modify the colour of floorboards without affecting the appearance of the wood's natural grain. As they always darken the wood, only use stains in situations where this is not a problem. Dark-stained boards are an excellent backdrop ▷

▲ *Painted concrete is amazingly practical and hard-wearing; this bathroom has been painted with an abstract design that not only looks good but is also waterproof, cheap to implement and easily cleaned. The major investment to consider for a floor like this is your own time and patience – and creative skills.*

◀ *Paint is one of the cheapest and most versatile ways of transforming an old floor. This floor has been given a new lease of life with this colourful and boldly patterned floorcloth; originally painted on canvas in a studio it was then transported to this location and installed wall-to-wall. The overall impression is of a painted floor.*

for richly coloured rugs and carpets, although it is important to select a neutral colour rather than a strong one such as mahogany, which would clash with a rug that is predominantly red, for instance. Formal rooms – traditional drawing rooms, dining rooms and libraries – look more sophisticated and imposing with darker floors. As richer and darker colours tend to be used to decorate these rooms, which are often used at night with soft lighting, evoking a more intimate feel, darker floors are a more discreet choice. Of course, a darker floor can also work successfully with a very light room, either for dramatic effect or as a backdrop for darker rugs. And dark colours tend to appear less oppressive the lower down they are used in the room; a dark oak floor can work well with pale walls and furnishing.

Bleached floors

Wood darkens with age; sometimes this can turn the wood very dark, or an unattractive colour, where a lighter colour is more desirable for a more vital and contemporary look. Lightening the wood while retaining its 'woody' appearance can be difficult,

as applying transparent colour will always darken it. Chemical bleaching is one solution to the problem.

Light floors are ideal for informal settings, such as kitchens and eating areas, or in any situation that calls for a fresh and airy atmosphere. Most furnishings will work well with light-coloured floors, as the floor fades against the predominant colours to provide a delicate backdrop. Darker pieces of furniture are accentuated against a light floor, useful for drawing attention to a particularly fine item.

Limed floors

Hardwood floors such as oak or ash can be lightened by using the traditional technique of liming (see pages 136–137). This lightens a whole area generally, but specifically lightens the actual grain of the wood resulting in a very graphic look. Liming is a labour-intensive business but the results are stunning. Staining the wood black, or indeed any other colour, before the liming process is started creates an even more exciting look by combining light and dark tones in a natural, free-form way that virtually becomes the focal point of a room.

▲ *Wood takes paint very well, and both transparent colour that allows the grain of the wood to show through and opaque paint can be used. This wooden floor has been painted with a very loose chequerboard pattern embellished with naive motifs to complement the kilims on the bed – helping create an overall tribal style.*

▶ *A wooden floor has been painted here with the same neutral, pale tones as the walls and ceiling. This approach tends to accentuate the colours of the features and furniture in the room, as the floor becomes part of an all-enveloping, unobtrusive backdrop, punctuated only by the strong lines of the beams and boards.*

Painted floors

Floors that are in poor condition or which are made from very plain materials such as concrete or chipboard can be transformed with conventional paint which will cover any number of blemishes and provide an evenly coloured surface. The floor can be painted any colour imaginable, from white for an ultra-light look to black for the ultimate light-absorbing surface. Neutral greys and beiges are perfect for non-controversial and flattering backgrounds to almost anything.

If plain colour seems a little dull, patterns – anything from simple squares to a painted imitation of an intricate Persian carpet – can be incorporated into a floor. Floors can be stencilled with any type of design (see pages 140–141) or covered with chequerboard squares (see pages 142–143). Even natural-stone looks can be effected to transform concrete or chipboard into a marble or flagstone floor (see pages 144–145).

Painting a floor is quick and cheap, and easily changed if it is not quite right or if you decide you are bored with it. Matching the floor colour to a fabric sample can be effective too, and nowadays, for a modest fee, some paint manufacturers offer a spectrophotometer service that exactly matches a paint colour with a supplied fabric sample.

Sealing

Once a surface has been sanded or stained it needs to be protected against general wear and tear with one of several wood finishes such as varnish or lacquer (see pages 146–147); how heavy-duty the protection needs to be will depend more on the situation of the floor, than on any inherent quality of the raw material.

◀ *If found still to be sound, pine floorboards typically found in Victorian houses are full of decorative potential. They have been transformed here by a subtle painted border that echoes the colour of the stairs while the rest of the floor has been left plain and simply sealed – a straightforward but effectively decorative treatment.*

Directory of decorative finishes

Wood floors can be finished in a number of ways. They can be left *au naturel*, with nothing added or taken away, or they can be coloured with stain or paint. In addition, dark wood can be lightened to counteract the effects of ageing or to highlight the grain. And unless a wood floor has been finished with a floor paint or liming wax, it will have to be protected with varnish or lacquer.

Opaque colour

Opaque colour is what most people think of as 'ordinary paint', which is used for painting walls and ceilings. It is ideal for painting unattractive flooring chipboard and is also useful for poor floorboards that have been repaired with lots of wood filler. Two to three coats will create a pure, unbroken colour that will completely disguise any flaws. Opaque paint is available in an almost infinite range of ready-mixed colours as well as in many finishes and types. It is perfect for very pale colours or if a plain look is desired but darker tones are strong and dominating, which may look heavy if the colour is not chosen with care. Most types of opaque paint can be used on floors but they will usually need the additional protection of a varnish. Oil-based eggshells and gloss paints used in light-traffic areas such as bedrooms may not require additional protection – nor proper floor paint. But water-based paints are the most user-friendly; they have no harmful fumes and brushes are easier to wash out. **1**

Stained floors

Wood stains or dyes are concentrated colours designed to penetrate the wood and effect a dramatic colour change without affecting the appearance of the wood's surface. They are normally associated with types of wood, the idea being that the application of the stain will transform an ordinary pine floor

into something rather more exotic. The reality is that the colour of the wood influences the final colour: the lighter the stain, the greater will be the effect of the original colour of the wood. Stains are also available in quite bright colours, and colours of the same brand can be intermixed. Water-, spirit- or oil-based stains are all so fast drying that it can be difficult to obtain an even finish. Stains always need protecting with a varnish or lacquer.

Varnish stain is an alternative product that stains and protects the wood in one application, although it is unlikely to be sufficiently tough for areas of heavy wear. **2**

Transparent colour

Transparent colour is used to modify the colour of an existing surface, retaining its texture and character rather than obliterating it. It has a much gentler quality than opaque paint, enabling the use of vivid or dark hues without the result looking heavy and solid. Complex and interesting colours can be built up in several coats for a rich and glowing look that is unobtainable with opaque paints. To make up transparent colour, mix artist's

colour into a transparent medium such as a water- or oil-based varnish to create almost any colour imaginable. The colour can be used over the whole floor area or to create a design, an easier task with transparent colour than opaque colour as only one coat is required. If woody colours are used the effect will resemble inlay or marquetry. The only possible disadvantage of using transparent colour is that the floor will always end up darker. **3**

Semi-transparent colour

Also known as semi-opaque colour, this is useful for situations where the aim is to preserve the grain of a wood floor, yet also lighten the colour of the floor. It is a mixture of transparent and opaque colour, usually made up by mixing white paint with a clear varnish. The white pigment in the paint partially covers the existing wood but not to such a degree that the grain of the wood is lost. The pigment has a lightening effect and colour can be added to change the colour of the wood slightly. The final result can look a little milky, depending on how much white is added, but the wood is still very visible. **4**

Liming wax

Liming wax is another product available for lightening wood. It is a white-pigmented wax that is simply rubbed into the grain and buffed with a cloth. Less messy to use than liming paste, it cannot be varnished as no varnish or paint product will adhere to wax. It is essential, then, to rewax the floor once the treatment wears off.

Varnished or lacquered floors

Varnish and lacquer seal plain wood floors with a protective finish. Different sealers change the colour and character of the wood to different degrees and some also change colour with age. Varnish, available in matt, satin or gloss finishes, is the most commonly used sealer. Both traditional oil-based and acrylic varnishes are suitable. They are widely available and easy to apply, whereas hard-wearing floor lacquers usually require more care and entail more work. As a rule solvent-based products bring out the natural colour of the wood better, giving it a richness and depth unmatched by water-based varieties; of the two, however, solvent-based sealers are the less user-friendly.

Bleached floors

Chemical bleaches are useful for lightening wood that has darkened with age, without affecting the appearance of the grain. The chemicals are applied to the bare wood and left to react and lighten the surface. When the wood reaches the desired colour, the chemicals are neutralized and the floor can be varnished.

Another way to lighten the colour of wood is to rub a little white paint into the grain, although this must be done sparingly to prevent the grain being completely obliterated.

Limed floors

Liming is a wood treatment that fills the grain of oak and ash, lightens the surface and gives the texture a very graphic appearance. Oak is particularly improved by liming. Traditionally, real lime was used but it is caustic and damages the skin and nails; more benign alternatives are now available, which have the same effect. They are applied and rubbed off when dry, leaving the grain white. To introduce brighter colours, stain the wood before liming it. But always protect the limed wood with a coat of varnish.

Repairing and preparing floorboards

▶ *These old floorboards are typical of what you are likely to find under an old carpet. Although the boards can sometimes look worryingly uneven and worn, modern sanding machines cut quickly through the wood to provide a smooth and level surface – ready for painting and sealing.*

Estimating quantities

There is nothing more irritating than running out of something halfway through a job and having to stop work to buy extra supplies. Before you start a renovation or decorating job, take time to assess accurately how much of which materials you will need. It is always worth buying a little extra to compensate for mistakes and wastage. Remember to check too on whether you have the correct tools and enough nails.

Replacement floorboards

Although floorboards are usually 18mm (¾in) thick, check the thickness as well as the width of your boards before ordering replacements and specify these dimensions as 'planed all round' (PAR) to the supplier. When calculating the length of timber required, bear in mind that each replacement board must run from joist to joist; the nails holding the boards down indicate the position of the joists. If a large quantity of wood is needed remember that new boards are about 4m (13ft) long, and offcuts may well be too short for practical use. Over-order by about 10 per cent to be safe.

Sandpaper for sanding machine

Estimating how much sandpaper you will need to sand a room is not critical, as the shops that hire out sanding machinery will also supply the paper on a sale-or-return basis. You will need more of the coarsest grade than

of the finer grades; five sheets of grit 24, and two each of grit 40, grit 80 and grit 100 should be sufficient to sand 30 sq m (36 sq yd) of pine floorboards in reasonable condition.

Paint and stain

It is difficult to be precise about paint requirements, but you will require 2–2.5 litres (about ½ gallon) for each base coat for a 30 sq m (36 sq yd) floor.

It is difficult to estimate how much wood stain would be needed to cover the same area as much depends on the type of stain and the porosity of the wood. As a rough guide, however, 1 litre (⅕ gallon) should cover approx. 10–20 sq m (12–24 sq yd).

Varnish and floor lacquer

To seal a 30 sq m (36 sq yd) floor area you will need approx. 2 litres (½ gallon) of oil- or water-based varnish per coat. Floor lacquer does not spread quite as far: 3 litres (⅗ gallon) will be required per coat.

Preparing a wood floor for painting or sealing

Any floor that is going to look good needs to have any defects corrected at an early stage. Damage must be repaired before a floor can be sanded or painted. Old floorboards can sometimes crack along their length and any damaged boards will have to be replaced. Floorboards can also shrink with age, leaving unsightly gaps. The best and easiest way to

deal with gaps between floorboards is to try to live with them; they are part of the charm of an old floor, and on a painted floor the eye tends to focus on the lines of a design rather than on the gaps. But this is not always practical and you will probably have to fill them.

Before sealing, the floor will probably need sanding, a process which removes the top few millimetres of the wood to leave a fresh, clean, ready-to-finish surface. It is not always necessary to sand a floor before painting it, however. A good dirt-removing scrub may suffice, but where old wax or paint needs to be removed, white spirit, paint stripper and lots of work will be required.

Lifting and replacing floorboards

Lifting square-edged boards is comparatively easy. Use a bolster chisel to lever up the board at its end, taking care not to damage the adjacent board. Once it is clear of the surface, support it in this position with a piece of wood and lever the board up with the bolster chisel where it is nailed to the joist. Do not try to lift the board up from the end as it will almost certainly break in half. Repeat this procedure until the damaged area has been lifted; moving to the middle of the nearest joist, support the board and scribe a line across the board – using a try square to ensure the cut is square. Cut the board with a cross-cut saw (see pages 154–155), taking care not to damage adjacent boards. Measure a new board and cut it to fit the removed section. Nail it in place with lost-head nails.

Repairing wooden floors

1 *Lift a damaged board by using a bolster chisel as a lever, and then support it with an offcut of wood.*

Replacing a tongued-and-grooved board is more difficult as all the boards interlock. You will have to cut the tongue off the board to be lifted before levering it up. The easiest way to do this is to cut along the edge of the board using a circular saw (see pages 154–155); to avoid cutting through pipes and cables, set the blade to cut at a depth of 18mm (¾in). You can use a sharp chisel and mallet to start the cut and then continue with a handsaw, returning to the chisel when you reach a joist, but it is much more awkward. Either way, fill the hole with a square-edged board.

Filling gaps

Small gaps can be filled with papier-mâché. Larger gaps that reach from joist to joist should be disguised with a wooden fillet. Measure the gap, cut a corresponding width off the edge of a spare board and glue it in position with wood glue.

If the whole floor is full of gaps it will probably be easier and more satisfactory to lift all the boards, push them tightly together and re-secure them. Number the boards as you lift them so that you replace them in the same order. You will end up with a large gap: fill it with a new board or part of one.

Dealing with nail heads

Remove any old staples and carpet tacks and hammer down any proud nail heads. If you are machine-sanding the floor, you do not have to punch them below the surface, but to save on sanding pads it is sensible.

▲ *It is worth noting that sanding and sealing stairs is a particularly time-consuming and awkward task. Sometimes it is not only easier to leave old floors in their natural state, it is also more authentic. This staircase is made from old pine that helps to evoke a sense of rustic simplicity which is wholly in keeping with the decoration of the rest of the house.*

2 Working along the middle line of the next joist, cut out the damaged part of the board with a cross-cut saw.

3 Fill a gap with a fillet cut from a spare board and glued in position. Tap it flush with an offcut.

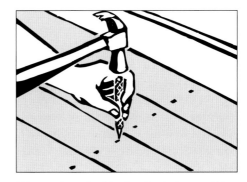

4 Hammer down all nail heads and tacks that are sticking up from the surface, punching them down if necessary.

Sanding and cleaning floorboards

Using a sanding machine

▲ Old pine floorboards here have simply been sanded and sealed. The colour of this type of wood can vary from quite pale to a dark orange: the lighter the shade of the floor, the easier it is to find rugs and other furnishings that work well with the plain unstained wood. The combination here results in an understated and clean look – with a touch of comfort.

1 Tilt the drum off the floor before starting the machine and before each stroke or you will gouge the floorboards.

2 Start by running the machine in diagonal sweeps across the boards with as little overlap as possible.

3 Then run the machine along the length of the boards; the process may need to be repeated two or three times.

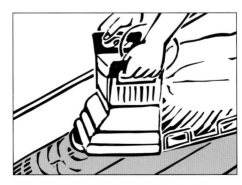

4 Use an edging sander along the skirting boards, echoing the range of sandpapers used for the main area.

Sanding a floor is usually done using two machines, the larger one to sand the main area of the floor and the smaller one for finishing around the edges. The machines are very noisy and produce a lot of dust, so wear ear defenders and a face mask.

Fix a sheet of coarse paper around the drum of the larger machine; fit it as tightly as possible to reduce the likelihood of it tearing during use. Start the machine with the drum raised above the floor. Begin moving the machine forwards and gently lower the drum so that it comes into contact with the floor before the full weight of the machine is lowered down onto the boards. Raise the drum off the floor gently at the end of a cut. This action will prevent the machine from grinding grooves into the floor. Very uneven or badly cupped boards can be levelled more quickly if sanded diagonally first. Once the boards are level, sand along the boards to remove sanding marks from the diagonal cut; this is a bit like mowing the lawn, just going patiently back and forth. Change the sanding paper from time to time as it will wear and its efficacy will diminish, and empty the dust bag when it is a third full in order to prevent the machine throwing out dust.

When the floor is level fix the same grade of paper onto the edging machine. It is worth noting that this machine tugs away from you, which can be tiring for the back.

Once you have done the edges use the next finest grade of paper on the large machine. It is usually only necessary to make three or four passes before moving on to the next finest grade. Alternate with the edger using the finer grades of paper in the same way. Finish the corners and other inaccessible areas with an orbital sander or by hand. On previously varnished floors it may be easier to soften the old varnish in the corners with paint stripper before finishing by hand.

Vacuum up the dust and also take some time to suck up dirt from the gaps between the boards, otherwise your paintbrush will pick up the debris during staining, painting or sealing and spoil the finish.

Preparation for painting

Sanding a floor is necessary only for floors in poor condition, or if you intend to use a stain or transparent finish on the wood. For painting, it is possible to scrub the floor clean with water and detergent and lots of elbow grease! The advantage of preparing a floor in this way is that more of the character of the old floor is retained; a few marks, gently bowed boards and uneven grain add charm to the finished look that is more in keeping with older properties.

If a floor has previously been waxed the wax must always be removed, even if the floor is to be sanded, because the machine may melt the wax and force it further into the floor. Using wire wool soaked in white spirit, go over the floor two or three times to make sure no traces of wax remain and finish with a clean rag.

Old paint can be removed chemically or by means of heat. Take care not to scorch the wood if you are using heat to strip off the paint. Sand off any residue by hand.

If the floor is to be finished with opaque colour, you can fill any holes and knocks with a wood filler because this will not show once the floor is painted. Fill the holes and then sand smooth with sandpaper.

▶ *An oak floor is naturally darker and is generally specially laid for decorative effect rather than simply being part of the basic structure of the building. If a pine floor is still too pale, after you have sanded it and filled any gaps, it can be stained a warmer, more sympathetic shade, which will make the room less stark.*

Bleaching, liming and staining

Colouring wood grain

Bleaching, liming and staining are decorative treatments that can be applied to wood to alter its colouring without losing the unique quality of the grain. Indeed, on the contrary, bleaching and liming emphasize the wood-grain creating striking effects.

Bleaching

The bleached, greyish floors found in old Scandinavian houses create a subtle, sophisticated background that is perfect for virtually any type of furnishing and colour. Although these floors have been scrubbed over the years to the point where the soft part of the wood is worn away leaving the raised and harder central grain, a similar light and airy feel can be achieved on old boards without quite so much time and effort. It can be done either by bleaching the wood or simply by rubbing white paint into it.

There are a number of chemical wood bleaches available, based on either strong acids or alkalis. Always follow the manufacturer's instructions when using them and ventilate the working environment. Wear protective clothing, rubber gloves and a mask. For further product information request a data sheet from the supplier.

To rub white paint into the wood – be it emulsion or undercoat – is a much simpler operation. Use an old cloth to rub the paint in and wipe off any excess with a clean, dry cloth, finishing in the direction of the grain. Alternatively, you can make up a colourwash with a 1:3 ratio of white emulsion to water. Tint this wash with raw umber and ivory black acrylic colour to make a warm grey, and then add raw sienna to warm the colour further. Test the colour on a board in a discreet corner, allowing it to dry before making any final judgements. If it is too opaque, add more water and adjust the colours to suit.

Both these treatments look best when finished with a matt varnish.

Liming

Limed oak has its origins in the mists of time when oak was a common building material. Coating the oak with lime, a powerful caustic material, prevented attack by wood-boring

▲ *Liming a hardwood, such as the ash of this staircase, will transform the natural warm tone of the wood to a cooler, grey colour and will particularly highlight the grain. Thorough preparation of the wood is essential to enable the liming medium to sit in the grain and achieve this distinctive and elegant look.*

bugs such as woodworm. It was soon noticed that this treatment created an attractive finish in its own right. Today, benign alternatives to lime are used.

The wood must be sanded back first to its bare state. Then dampen the wood with a cloth and use a fine wire brush to 'rake' out the grain. Do this by moving the brush gently over the surface in the direction of the grain. The idea is to remove the soft porous woody material that naturally fills the grain without scratching the surface of the wood. Clean the debris off with a damp cloth. Then apply a proprietary liming paste, or a runny paste made from titanium dioxide (available from art suppliers) and water, and brush over

the whole surface, finishing off by brushing across the grain. Allow the paste to dry. Gently rub off the dried paste using medium-grade wire wool. It should come off the surface but stay in the grain. Gently clean off any powder on the surface with a barely damp sponge. Allow to dry and then varnish.

Staining

Stains, available in an extensive range of wood shades and brighter colours, effectively alter the colour of wood to tone in with any decorating scheme – without altering its woody appearance. Either use a commercial stain or create your own by adding artist's colour to a varnish that has been diluted by

Liming

1 Having dampened the wood, move a wire brush gently over the surface to 'rake out' the grain.

2 Brush over the whole surface with the liming paste, working with and against the grain, and finally across it.

3 Rub the dried paste gently with wire wool to remove it from the surface, but leaving it in the grain.

4 Take a dampish sponge and clean off any remaining powder from the surface before the varnishing stage.

▲ *Certain woods, such as pine, cannot be limed, because of the characteristics of their grain. Instead, a pine floor such as this can be given the pale quality of limed wood by a process of bleaching, which actually lightens the wood itself. This look particularly suits the airy atmosphere of a room like this, filled with light and furnished in soft tones.*

one third with its appropriate thinner. If you want a very dramatic colour change, though, it is probably easier to use a commercial stain. Colours can be mixed to modify the final shade to suit a particular room. Complex and interesting effects can be created by applying different colours in layers. For example, mahogany stain can sometimes look an artificial purple red but applying a walnut colour over the mahogany will turn it into a rich, warm glow; such a colour could never be achieved by just mixing the two colours together. Try out the colours first on an unwanted scrap piece of wood to ensure that they are right for a particular room; and bear in mind that the same stain can look quite different on different types of wood.

The best way to apply stain is by wiping it on with a rag, working along one board at a time. This will leave a thin colour, so you must build up to the final colour by applying coat after coat until you are happy with the effect. Stains must be protected with varnish, which will bring out the colour of the wood for a deep, glowing effect. If you are using a varnish stain, treat it like varnish and apply it with a brush rather than a rag.

Staining

1 When applying stain to a floor with a rag, work along one board at a time, building up thin layers of colour.

2 Apply varnish stain with a brush, but work back across your floor moving along one board at a time as before.

Painting floors

▶ *This concrete floor has been painted a primrose yellow before being stencilled all over with a geometric repeat pattern. Although the design looks quite complex it is in fact very simple. The advantage of this type of design is that it has no borders to accommodate, making the whole job much easier – from planning to finished floor.*

types of flooring, the only really limiting factor on utilizing the full potential of floors with paint is that of time.

As the choice of designs is so immense, another problem is knowing where to start, what to do. The key to a successful painted floor is to 'keep it simple'. A room with the minimum of plain, simple wooden furniture and neutral fabric colours could have a blaze of deep colour and intricate pattern on the floor as a stunning focal point, but it would be rare. Most rooms have some mixed colours in the form of fabric and furnishings, others are positively cluttered due to small-space city living. For a floor that is to act as a quiet backdrop to the rest of the room, choose neutral tones; introduce one colour, or perhaps at the most two, that match some other colour in the room. Shades of the same colour look very effective together.

A neutral floor can be transformed by the addition of a simple coloured line acting as a border. For example, the floor could be a soft semi-transparent series of cool cream squares divided by mid-oak parquet blocks. The same colours could be used in the border, delineated by two Gustavian green lines; these would 'lift' the whole design and give the border greater definition.

Painted floors offer the home decorator tremendous scope for choosing colours either to match exactly or to complement other furnishings in the room. The range of commercial colours available is huge and there is an increasing number of so-called historical paint ranges on the market which offer particularly sympathetic and easy-to-live-with hues. In addition, colours can be hand-mixed to offer limitless possibilities. Transparent colours enable you to use quite clear and bright hues that are colourful yet gentle on the eye; a vivid blue that is applied as a diluted wash, for instance, has all the quality of light reflected off water.

Any number of design options provide virtually limitless scope for further improving and manipulating a floor space with paint, allowing for the exercise of personal creative ability. As paint is such a cheap option cheap compared to all the other

▲ *Instead of using an overall design, you can leave the floor basically plain, and just add a border around the edge. Old boards have been left here in their natural state and a simple border added that picks up on the colour of the doorframe and floorcloth, not only offering decorative interest but also helping to unify several elements in the room.*

Floor areas that have furniture and rugs on them can be broken up by being painted with simple squares, or perhaps be given a *faux*-parquet look for greater visual interest. There are opportunities for simple trompe l'oeil: by setting out painted paving slabs as though they were stepped, for example, thus causing new guests to tread with the same care over the floor as children playing hopscotch. Furniture that is arranged to form a central focal area can be enlivened by the addition of a design that fits within that area – large stars or circles enclosing a geometric design, say, or an exotic and colourful carpet.

Large and empty hallways offer uncluttered scope for a central design or a more elaborate repeat pattern. Awkward rooms with too many chimney breasts and obtuse corners can be tidied up by running a border in a straight line in front of these obstacles. Borders look better if they are of a generous width, and squares should not be too small and fussy unless you are trying to recreate the look of hand-painted tiles.

Inspiration for designs can be found in books but frequently the room itself provides its own clue: a simple border on a cast-iron fireplace can be adapted; an interesting cornice design can be mirrored in the floor below; or a motif might be taken from a rug. Perhaps a design seen in a musuem or on an expensive item in a shop can be simplified for the floor. Or you could choose a theme such as the seasons as a starting point. Ideas can be related to a particular style: for example, imagery characteristic of Islam would offer considerable scope. Some people have even taken their company logo and used that, or taken ideas related to a particular hobby such as seashell collecting.

If you want to try floor painting, there are many paint techniques from which to choose; those discussed here are a good starting point. Stencilling allows for easily applied repeat patterns or varied arrangements using cut-outs (see pages 140–141). Painting a floor as a chequerboard is dramatic to say the least (see pages 142–143). And creating fake stone and marble effects on floors provides rustic or sophisticated flooring at a fraction of the cost of the real thing (see pages 144–145).

▲ *This floor has been painted to imitate loosely the style of a rug that fills the whole floor space; smaller versions that sit in the centre of a room work equally well. Various motifs have been stencilled onto vivid bands of colour, so that the floor becomes an integral part of an exuberant and richly decorated room – with highly painted walls and furniture.*

Stencilling

▲ *It is much quicker to execute a complex design with a stencil, and for one like this, it is easier to use a separate stencil for each colour. Aerosol spray paint has been used for this design – quick, but the fumes are unpleasant. Remember, it is not possible to stencil an unbroken line: you will need bridging struts like those at the edge of the central panel here.*

Essentially, a stencil is a template for effectively and quickly transferring a design, even a complex and elaborate one, onto a surface. Each additional colour of the design either requires a separate stencil, or requires one to mask off a different section each time if reusing one stencil for the whole design. Almost any style can be created with stencils.

Borders can vary from delicate natural affairs, with leaves and flowers spilling out onto the main part of the floor, to severely delineated geometric patterns that powerfully define the whole shape of a room.

Stencils are also useful for decorating the main area of a floor. Loose flowing designs can almost blend into each other to provide an overall pattern that is not too overbearing. You can use stencils on top of chequerboard squares. They can even be used to create an intricate chequerboard design or one that incorporates curves and circles. Very small squares or a mosaic type of design can be painted onto a floor in this way with comparative ease.

Specialist shops sell a variety of dedicated stencil paints, but you can easily use your own colours. Acrylic paints are probably the most convenient as they are easy to apply and dry quickly, thereby minimizing the risk of smudging; oil colours, on the other hand, can take days to dry. If the colours are too concentrated, dilute them with the appropriate artist's medium, and remember always to mix sufficient colour at the beginning to complete the job. Standard house decorating paint is too thick and sticky for stencilling.

Stencil designs

There is a comprehensive range of ready-to-use stencil designs on the market – an ever-expanding range – or you can cut your own. Some designs will require little bridging struts to hold the stencil together; you have to paint in the area covered by the struts after the design has been applied. You can mix and match elements from different designs; transfer them into a sketchbook first to see how they will look. It is often useful to do a scale drawing of a design at a more comfortable size before blowing it up on a photocopier to the desired size.

Registration

The purpose of registration is to ensure that the stencil is always placed where it is meant to be and that the second colour is applied in the correct position relative to the first. Draw guidelines in pencil on the floor first. For a border, mark a line the required distance from the skirting board around the room and place the stencil against it as you proceed. An overall pattern will require a grid to keep the stencils correctly spaced.

Registration can be aided by pencilling little marks on the floor corresponding with the exact location of the stencil for each colour; make sure all the stencils are the same size. Ensure that a repeat border has at least one and a half repeats to help with registration, or trace the first design over the second stencil card and match it up at the edges of the painted stencil. Sometimes viewing windows cut in the card are a help.

Cutting the stencil

Stencils need to be waterproof and robust. Oiled card has the advantage of economy and ready availability, but the easiest way of transferring a design onto stencil card is to use transtrace paper. Acetate, a thin clear plastic, is more expensive than card and is not really suitable for intricate designs as it tends to curl up. It is very flexible, though, which means that it bends willingly into awkward corners, unlike card. As acetate is transparent, making sure that the second stencil has been placed exactly over the first part of a design is easy. And transferring the design onto the acetate

Cutting and using a stencil

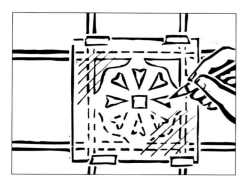

1 Tape your tracing paper in position over the motif you intend to use as a stencil, and carefully copy the outline.

2 Turn the tracing over and tape it in position on a piece of oiled card. Scribble over the outline to transfer it.

3 With a sharp scalpel, on a board, and remembering to leave bridges, cut out the design and registration marks.

4 Tape the stencil in position, using registration marks; apply the paint slowly, building up the required intensity.

5 When the paint is dry, and checking that the design is complete, carefully peel back and lift off the stencil.

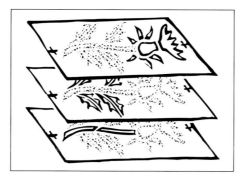

6 For a multi-coloured motif, cut separate stencils for each colour, with dotted guidance lines on each.

7 When re-positioning a border-design stencil, place the stencil in part over the previously painted section.

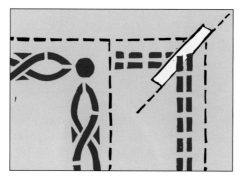

8 At corners, patterns can either be adapted, or mitred – by masking off the approaching patterns at 45 degrees.

is simplicity itself: just tape the acetate to the design and trace the outlines using a fine felt-tipped pen. A thicker, semi-transparent plastic called mylar is now also more widely available: rigid and long-lasting, and facilitating easy registration, this must be an attractive option to consider.

A sharp scalpel is the best tool for cutting out a stencil. Cut it out on either a sheet of glass or a cutting board, taking care not to tear acetate. Card is easier and more satisfying to cut; try to cut it with a bevelled edge towards you. To cut fluently is best, so try to avoid cutting curves in a series of jerks. It is better to stay in a comfortable position and move the stencil as you cut. Cut right into corners, and remember registration marks.

Applying the design

Stick the stencil down with masking tape at the corners so that it cannot move, or spray the back with spray mount which enables the stencil to be peeled up and repositioned several times. Make sure all traces of spray mount are removed from the floor with an appropriate solvent before varnishing.

Use a minimal amount of paint. Dip the tip of the brush into the colour and work it into the brush on some old newspaper or a plate. The brush should appear dry. Stipple the colour over the stencil or brush with a swirling motion so the colour gradually builds up in intensity. Resist the temptation to apply the paint heavily as it invariably seeps under the edge of the stencil. Once the first colour is dry, remove the stencil, then apply a second and further stencils in the same way, using your registration marks as a guide.

Turning corners

Unless they are very linear, border designs do not go around corners so you will need an entirely separate stencil, such as a circle, for the corner. The main pattern finishes just short of the corner and the new stencil is used to fill the space. If the border pattern is to be continuous, lay low-tack masking tape at 45 degrees across the path of the stencil. Work up to and just onto the tape. When it is dry, reposition the tape to the other side of the angle and stencil the other side.

Painting chequerboard squares

Simple squares help break up large spaces and provide the opportunity to introduce two colours to a floor, or two shades of the same colour. And once a simple grid is established the basic alternating squares can be embellished: interspersed stripes could be painted in a variety of arrangements or a stencil design could be added to each square.

With painted squares it is, of course, possible to choose the exact size of the square to suit the scale of the space to be filled. It is easiest to choose a size of square that divides exactly into the floor's area. With a little calculation the squares can be sized to coincide exactly with three walls of any room. In the unlikely event of a perfectly square room, the squares would then fit the fourth wall as well. If you have a number of alcoves, it may be easier – and look better – to paint a central area as a chequerboard and leave a border, in one of the two colours, to stretch to the edges of the room.

Simple squares look more interesting if they are arranged on the diagonal and this is easy to lay out. Begin by setting out the basic grid by following the procedure for setting out tiles (page 156–157). Mark out the basic centre point of the floor, adjusting it if necessary, and establish a diagonal line as described. You can work back from this basic central diagonal to mark out the whole room with all the squares on the diagonal. A chalk line is useful for establishing the basic grid but do go over it with pencil as the chalk will rub off as you walk back and forth over the floor. A soft pencil (2B) gives darker, more definite lines that help give the squares sharp edges, useful if your hand tends to wobble as you paint the edges of the squares.

Applying the colour

Painting the squares is simplicity itself. A 2.5cm (1in) brush is the most versatile tool unless the squares are very large, in which case use a 5cm (2in) brush. Thinned transparent – rather than opaque – colour is the easiest to use. Start by the wall furthest from the door and work back towards it, painting every alternate square. Start by outlining your square – some people like to use the brush sideways on to achieve a straight edge. Then

▲ This hallway has been painted with a simple chequerboard design. The squares have been painted in the same colours as the rest of the woodwork in the room to provide a simple and effective unified scheme, and the skirting board acts as a border for the floor. To reproduce this, paint the whole floor white and then paint the darker colour on as the squares.

Chequerboard squares

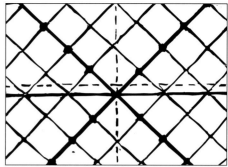

1 Find and adjust the centre point of your floor as necessary and mark out all the squares on the diagonal.

2 Paint the whole floor in one colour, then the second colour in alternate squares. Begin by outlining your square.

3 Having created sharp corners with a fine artist's brush, block in the centre of the outlined square.

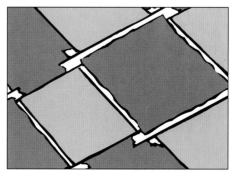

4 Masking tape makes sharp edges easier; but it can be confusing, so be sure to paint only alternate squares.

▲ *This kitchen has been painted in the style of classical tiling. The alternating squares are painted in a slightly darker shade to differentiate between them (in the absence of grout). The border has been painted in a bold green, along with most of the key squares – though the odd one or two are red, for fun and additional interest.*

use an artist's brush to colour in the apex of each corner. Finish by blocking in the centre of each square. When all the first colour is finished and dry, repeat the process for the alternating squares in the second colour. If you are using opaque colour it will be necessary to prime and undercoat the floor first, then to paint the whole floor with the lighter of the two chequerboard colours and finally to paint on the darker colour as alternating squares. If the first coat of the second colour does not cover satisfactorily in one coat you will have to go over the paint again when it

has dried. For sharper edges (or if your hand is very unsteady), mask out the outline of every alternate square with low-tack masking tape, and brush colour over the edges.

Wood stain colours can be used on bare wood for a quick effect. Score along the pencil lines with a sharp scalpel. Paint wood stain as close to the line as you can. The stain will bleed into the wood, rather like ink spilt onto blotting paper, but will stop neatly on the scored line preventing further colour spread. When the colour is fully dry, protect the floor with varnish or lacquer.

Painting *faux*-stone effects

Real marble and stone floors are beyond the means of most people but can be imitated easily and cheaply using paint. Stone-effect techniques look very convincing as they are rarely examined close to; being on such a large scale, the eye takes in an impression rather than focusing on detail. Use painted stone effects where the genuine material would be used. For example, a hallway can be given a palatial air by painting alternating black-and-white *faux*-marble squares or coloured-marble panels over the whole floor. For floors in poor condition, or if you find the texture of cement or chipboard unforgiving, a covering layer of plywood will provide a more sympathetic surface.

The paint techniques used here rely on scumble glaze, a transparent medium that is designed to have colour added to it to create texture for decorative effects such as rag

▲ *Real stone flagstones and plywood squares painted to resemble stone are effectively juxtaposed in this hallway. The floorboards originally beyond the stone were in poor condition; now the gaps between the 'stones' have been grouted for maximum effect and the whole scheme pulls together very happily – with no ugly junctions.*

Creating a *faux*-marble effect

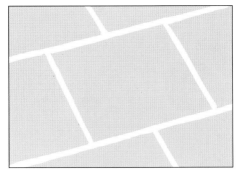

1 *Lay plywood squares as flagstones. Leave gaps for grout between the squares to strengthen the illusion.*

2 *Apply the base coat and leave it to dry. Paint on the glaze and use a rag to break up and mottle the surface.*

3 *With a fine artist's brush, fidget the veins onto the wet glaze, keeping the movement in one overall direction.*

4 *Soften the veins with a soft brush in the direction of the veins, then backwards and then with the grain again.*

rolling and stippling. Slow-drying, and normally diluted with white spirit before use, it is applied over an eggshell base paint. As it has a marked tendency to yellow, take care when using it for pale colours. The addition of a little white undercoat helps to minimize the yellowing. Scumble glaze has to be given a coat of varnish for protection.

Installing plywood 'stones'

Plywood is generally sold as 2.44 x 1.22m (8 x 4ft) sheets, but you can ask your timber merchant to saw these up for you into smaller, more appropriately sized squares – say, 60 x 60cm (2 x 2ft) – to create a chequerboard or flagstone effect. Provided the floor is reasonably level, plywood 6mm (¼in) thick is sufficient.

Allow the boards to acclimatize for 48 hours in the room before laying them, and then lay the plywood following the guidelines for laying tiles (see pages 174–175). If you leave a gap between the squares, you can fill it with a flexible grout or coloured filler reinforced with PVA adhesive to carry further the illusion of a stone floor. Fix the plywood onto concrete using panel adhesive or onto wood surfaces using small panel pins. Prime and paint the plywood and finish with two coats of white eggshell, an ideal base for subsequent paint finishes.

Faux marble

For a simple and discreet finish, marble the floor using one base colour, perhaps with a darker shade for veining. For a darker and more dramatic looking marble, use a dark base colour and light veining. For alternating chequerboard squares or inlaid panels choose two contrasting base colours, either very dark and light squares or a neutral background colour combined with a brighter, more vivid hue.

Find some examples of real marble and copy the colours and the style. Due to the large areas involved, marbling on floors is best kept simple; you are trying to create an impression of the real material rather than a slavish copy. The secret is to get the veining right; once you develop the feel for veining you are almost there.

Oil-based paints make marbling easier. Start by mixing up the base coat as a glaze with 50 per cent scumble glaze and 50 per cent white spirit to the consistency of single cream. For pale grey marble add some white artist's oil colour or undercoat and mix in thoroughly. Mix in a little ivory black; this is a very powerful colour so add only a little at a time. If the colour seems like a thin black rather than a creamy grey add more white until the balance is right. Check the colour on the floor; samples can easily be cleaned off with a little white spirit.

Paint the base colour over an area about 60cm (2ft) square or, ideally, a whole 'paving stone' at a time. Break up the glazed surface with a rag so it becomes mottled. Use artist's oil paints as veining colour, squeezed onto a plate and diluted with a little white spirit to provide a more workable consistency. A very fine artist's brush is ideal for veining. Fidget the veins onto the wet glaze; marble has an overall direction and the veins are angular rather than rounded. Veins never stop abruptly, they either gradually fade into the rock or join other veins. Do not overdo the veining. The last thing you want is something that looks like a road map. Dab off any excess paint from the veins with a rag. So that they become blurry at the edges, soften and blend the veins using a hogs'-hair softener, a very fine-bristled brush available from decorating shops, or, if you are on a tight budget, a decorator's dusting brush. Soften in the direction of the veins first, then lightly against the veins to spread them a little. Finish off by softening with the veins. Allow the paint to dry thoroughly before applying varnish.

Faux limestone

A warm, creamy limestone is the essence of restrained good taste yet can be imitated with paint for a fraction of the cost of the real thing. A floor painted as stone is an imposing yet quiet backdrop that harmonizes well with almost any decorating scheme.

Mix up the base coat as a glaze with 50 per cent scumble glaze and 50 per cent white spirit to the consistency of single cream, using raw sienna and plenty of white undercoat as the colouring, and then add a little

raw umber to 'dirty' the colour. The objective is to mix a pale yet warm cream. Paint the base colour over an area about 60cm (2ft) square or, ideally, a whole 'paving stone' at a time. Stipple the surface to break the colour up into millions of tiny flecks. Use a stippling brush or improvise with a 5cm (2in) brush. Allow the paint to dry.

The second application consists of a light and a dark version of the same colour, to give the 'stone' the appearance of age and wear. Use a well-thinned scumble glaze or a diluted oil-based varnish. Mix some raw umber and a little black to create a dirty colour that takes the edge off the cream. Make up two shades of the same colour, one dark and one pale, for a variable effect. Paint random patches of the two colours together and stipple as you did for the first colour. Use a greater proportion of the darker colour where the floor is subjected to greater wear, near a door, for example, for authenticity.

Creating a *faux*-stone effect

1 Paint on the glaze and then stipple the surface to break up the colour into flecks. Leave this coat to dry.

2 Brush on lighter and darker versions of the same colour in random patches, and then stipple them as before .

Varnishing, lacquering and waxing

Varnishing

1 Apply the varnish generously with a brush, working along the length of a couple of boards at a time.

2 When re-varnishing a floor, you must first clean the surface: use wire wool, water and a sugar soap solution.

▲ *This floor has been finished with a satin varnish. Not only can this more unusual varnish look more flattering than its high-gloss colleague, it also creates a less slippery surface, which is important in a room such as this where a large floor area is exposed, or for a house with young children learning to walk – and run.*

Most decorative floor treatments need additional protection against the battering of countless feet and becoming faded and grey. Sealing the floor with a clear varnish or lacquer will ensure that the floor will continue to look good, last, and remain easy to clean for many years.

Wax, the time-honoured way of protecting floors, builds up an organic layer which protects the floor, smells pleasant and has a rich, deep shine that is renewed every time the floor is re-waxed, providing protection indefinitely. Plain wood floors look particularly good when waxed, because the wax provides a warm mellow colour that appears entirely natural – unlike the more plastic quality of modern lacquers.

Varnishing

Oil- and water-based varnishes can be used straight out of the container but must be stirred thoroughly before use. Oil-based varnish dries slowly, so sealing a floor will take days rather than hours. Acrylic varnish is recoatable after 2 hours, which speeds things up considerably.

If you do use an acrylic varnish, ensure that you use one specifically formulated for floors because the ordinary varnishes are not as hard-wearing as some of the solvent-based products. It is worth checking too that it will not react with any existing floor coatings. Oil paints can take days – if not weeks – to cure properly, and uncured oil paint can cause acrylic varnish to craze.

Start in the corner furthest from the door and brush the varnish on fairly generously, but working along only a couple of boards at a time. When the first coat has dried, apply the second coat in the same way. You should continue to apply varnish until you have a minimum of three coats in low-traffic areas and as many as five coats in rooms that will receive major wear and tear.

Revarnishing

If you are re-finishing a previously varnished floor, you will first have to roughen the surface and dislodge deeply ingrained dirt using medium-grade wire wool and water. Then, using a sugar-soap solution, clean the surface again to remove any remaining grease and wipe clean with a damp cloth. If you are working with newly painted or stained floors, you will only need to vacuum to remove the dust from the floor. If the room has been sanded, ensure that all the walls and any other surfaces are dust-free before varnishing. Open all the windows, as solvent-based products give off strong fumes which can be harmful.

Unless it is very cold outside, a draught will help the sealer to dry more quickly. For a super-smooth finish, sand the sealer with a fine-grade silicon carbide paper before applying the final coat.

Lacquering

Floor lacquers usually consist of two components: the bulk of the product, often sold in 5 litre (1 gallon) containers, and a special hardener or crosslinker that must be mixed with the lacquer before use. Always follow the manufacturer's instructions. And because, once mixed, it must be used within a limited time, calculate how much lacquer will be needed before you mix it (see pages 132–133).

Shake the main component thoroughly in its container and, working to the nearest litre (⅕ gallon), pour enough for the job into a paint kettle. Pour in the appropriate amount of hardener and stir with a small brush. Wait for 5 minutes before using it.

The lacquer can be brushed on in the same way as varnish except that it should be laid on as thickly as possible. Ideally you should use a special lambswool mop, though a roller fitted with an extension handle may be more effective for large areas. Simply pour enough lacquer from the container directly onto the floor and use the roller to distribute it evenly. Several square metres (yards) can be covered at a time. If there are gaps in the floorboards, load the roller from a tray to prevent losing too much lacquer through the gaps. Depending on conditions, floor lacquer can be recoated after 1–2 hours. Three coats are sufficient for most domestic situations.

▲ Floors in bathrooms should be sealed with particular care in order to prevent the wood becoming waterlogged. This floor is finished with a matt varnish, the most discreet of floor finishes. Although matt finishes should be avoided in areas of heavy wear, the effect here is subtle and elegant, and, given the appropriate care, the varnish will survive many years.

Waxing

Sanded floors that are to be waxed should be sealed first with a coat of polyurethane varnish, or a sand-and-seal shellac, to prevent the wax from sinking into the wood. Use a wax specially formulated for floors.

Apply the wax with a cloth, then leave it for 1 hour before polishing it off with a clean dry cloth. Finish by buffing up the wax to a shine with a soft cloth. Re-apply wax as frequently as once a week for high-wear areas such as kitchens; most rooms, though, only need waxing once every few months.

Manufacturers of wood-strip flooring also supply special water-based waxes that can be used to provide additional protection for lacquered floors. These can be brushed or sprayed on and either buffed up when dry or simply left as they are.

Lacquering

1 Work with enough 'mixed' lacquer to cover a quarter of the floor; spread it on quickly , and as thickly as possible.

Waxing

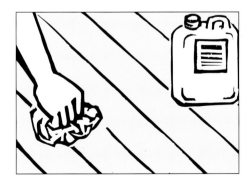

1 Apply floor wax with a dry cloth. When it is dry, and regularly thereafter, buff it up with a cloth.

Laying new flooring

Because flooring materials are so varied, laying a new
floor may involve anything from a few hours of easy work
– involving a few basic tools and common sense – to a
major upheaval requiring specialized knowledge and
equipment, and a serious commitment in terms of time
and energy. Before embarking on a project yourself, take
time to examine what is really the appropriate solution,
and ponder the practical and aesthetic ramifications of
your choice before making a final decision.

The first step is to establish what the existing floor is constructed of. Peel back coverings such as carpet or vinyl to see what is underneath. It is worth checking in more than one place, as it is not unusual to have a cement floor and a suspended timber floor in the same room. Look carefully, because things are not always as they seem. Plain floorboards, for instance, although usually indicative of a suspended wood floor, could also be wood-strip flooring laid over concrete or chipboard.

Next, you have to establish what type of flooring can be laid over the existing floor. Most materials can be laid over all types of floor but in some cases adequately preparing the subfloor can involve additional costs. Most types of flooring can be laid quickly and easily, although some jobs are more complicated than others. It is generally more disruptive, for instance, to lay hard floors (see pages 158–165), than flexible (see pages 166–175) or wood (see pages 176–181) floors. Be prepared for some mess and inconvenience.

Once you know what sort of flooring you are dealing with, you can then decide on what type of floor-covering you prefer and whether it is going to be practical for the situation. Jute flooring looks sophisticated in the right setting, for instance, but is not suitable for a bathroom where water is splashed around. Disappointment will set in quickly when the jute starts to turn black and rot, and deep frustration will soon follow when it is discovered that there is no satisfactory way of cleaning it.

The next stage is to assess the affordability of your preferred material. Measure the room and estimate how much is needed of the product in question (see pages 154–155).

Shop around to find out all the costs involved. Some materials span a wide price band. For example, carpet can be one of the cheapest or one of the most expensive floor-coverings – depending upon quality and type. Some flooring materials are so expensive that it may be worth paying a professional that little bit extra to ensure that the end result justifies the overall cost. Other materials are cheap to buy but expensive to have laid, and, provided you feel sufficiently confident and have the spare time, these are well worth laying yourself. There is also the satisfaction to be derived from working through for oneself from the first glimmer of an idea to the actual creation of the finished scheme.

Fitting might be included in the price, although 'free fitting' is rarely what it claims to be. See what the ancillary costs are, such as underlay and gripper strips or special tile adhesive needed for a problem floor. The savings made by installing the floor yourself may enable you to buy a more expensive material. Check also to see if costly tools are needed to do the job and whether these can be hired (see pages 154–155). Read the relevant sections in this chapter to decide whether you feel sufficiently confident to install the flooring yourself.

Having established which is the most suitable floor-covering, check on availability and delivery times. Most products can be delivered in a week but sometimes a special order is required and delivery can take something like six weeks. Now is the time to obtain the fixing materials and any special tools needed for the job. Either buy them or book the hire of an expensive tool.

A few days before the due delivery date remove the old floor-covering and repair or prepare the existing subfloor. Concrete, chipboard or floorboards may need some attention, dips and bumps to be levelled or cracks to be filled, before new flooring can safely be laid on them (see pages 152–153).

It may be necessary to acclimatize the new material to its new environment for a day or two before laying it in order to ensure a successful job (see pages 144–145, 152–153). Before tiling a floor you will need to mark out guidelines against ▷

◀ *Laying wood-strip flooring is one of the easiest DIY flooring tasks. It is also one of the most versatile in so far as it can be laid over most types of subfloor. The finished floor provides a very practical and easy-to-clean surface, which is particularly important in a dining room like this, where it is likely that food and wine will be spilled.*

▲ *Laying flagstones is the most difficult and disruptive flooring project it is possible to undertake, but will last for ever once it is finished. These polished limestone flags might seem like an unusual choice for a bedroom but in fact work well with the clean lines and warm tones of the fitted furniture.*

which to work. Although the principles are the same for any type of tile, the starting points are adjusted according to whether the room is square, rectangular or irregular (see pages 156–157).

Concrete floors

Concrete might seem an ugly and unforgiving material but, in fact, it provides a perfect base for all types of floor-covering, as long as it is smooth and level. Carpets (see pages 186–187) and wood flooring (see pages 180–181) are easily laid over concrete. It is also an ideal base for tiles (see pages 162–165) and is really the only material with the structural integrity required for laying really heavy materials such as flagstones and brick (see pages 160–161), making it almost invaluable.

Chipboard and plywood floors

These floors are constructed in the same way as traditional suspended timber floors except that boards of chipboard or plywood are used to cover the joists instead of floorboards. They have been commonly installed in housing since the 1960s because of the increasing cost of traditional materials and because man-made boards are easy to lay and very stable. They are also found in older properties where rotten boards have been replaced. Both chipboard and plywood are perfect as subfloor surfaces for most types of floor-covering because they are very smooth and level. Take care when laying very heavy materials over any type of suspended wood floor, however, as the joists might need to be reinforced to take the extra weight.

▲ *Concrete floors are commonly found in newer houses and blocks of flats and can be covered with most flooring materials. Floors as smooth and level as that illustrated here can be easily painted, providing a stylish and economical finish for what is often considered an ugly and difficult raw material.*

▶ *Newer and renovated properties often have chipboard and plywood laid over joists, and this can either make a good base for other materials or be painted easily. At the bottom of the stairs here plywood has been laid as large squares and painted black, so that its appearance is almost indistinguishable from polished slate.*

▲ *Provided that the boards are waterproofed first, wooden decking can be used to define the space occupied by a freestanding bath in a bathroom, and is both a practical and smart design solution. Thin tiles have been carefully laid over well-prepared old floorboards on the rest of the floor, creating an interesting variety of texture in a monochrome room.*

Suspended timber floors

Although pine floorboards are one of the most attractive types of flooring in their own right, they need greater preparation than some other materials before certain types of floor-covering can be laid over them. Wood-strip flooring (see pages 180–181) can be laid directly over floorboards if they are reasonably level. Before laying carpet (see pages 186–187) or flexible floor-coverings (see pages 166–169), however, a hardboard base needs to be installed (see pages 152–153).

Tiles can be laid directly onto boards as long as they are level and reasonably rigid and you use a flexible adhesive; otherwise you can lay 12mm (½in) plywood sheets over the floorboards to provide the necessary rigidity. Special underlays and flexible tile adhesives that eliminate the need for laying plywood are now available; consult your tile supplier. Many stones and slates are available in a thinner tile format which can be laid over timber floors, but thick traditional flagstones should always be laid on a solid base.

Preparing surfaces

Before you lay any new floor-covering, you will need to check that the floor is in good enough condition to receive it. Generally, most flooring requires a smooth, even surface that is free from cracks, dips and bumps. Some may require a new intermediate surface to be installed over the existing sub-floor; it is worth estimating for this before you start, as not only could this hidden cost be a nasty shock if revealed as a necessity halfway through the job, it could actually have an effect on the type of floor-covering you can afford to choose.

Concrete floors

Laying any type of flooring on concrete requires a smooth and level surface – with the possible exception of materials that are bedded on mortar or thick-bed adhesives. Concrete floors are normally finished with a sand-and-cement screed laid over the coarse cement base, and they should incorporate a damp-proof membrane.

Check the level of any dampness present using a moisture meter. If the levels are higher than those specified by the manufacturer for the type of floor-covering to be laid, a damp-proof layer must be added before you begin work. This membrane can either take the form of a polythene sheet or a bitumen waterproofer which would be brushed onto the concrete base.

Special precautions may have to be taken if the floor incorporates underfloor central heating. Tile adhesives may require the use of special additives, and with wood floors allow plenty of room for expansion.

Filling cracks

Cracks in concrete floors are a common problem and are easily repaired with mortar. First rake out and widen the cracks with a bolster chisel and hammer, then dampen the area to be repaired with water.

Mix sand and cement in a 3:1 ratio with water to form a workable mixture and press the mortar into the cracks using a trowel. Smooth the surface level, and allow the repair a few days to dry before you start to lay the new floor-covering.

▲ This concrete floor has been sanded and polished to provide a tough and practical surface that seems more than appropriate in this modern interior. Obviously, a floor in as good a condition as this would need no further preparation were it to be hidden under some sort of covering – whether for practical or aesthetic reasons.

Preparing concrete floors

1 Using a trowel, fill the dampened crack with mortar. Smooth level and leave for a few days to dry thoroughly.

2 Self-levelling compound is applied as a runny paste to a dampened floor. Leave it to find its own level and dry.

Sealing the surface

Concrete floors that are very dusty with the top layer flaking off as a powder should be treated with a concrete sealer or with a PVA general-purpose builder's sealer, diluted with water according to the manufacturer's instructions.

Levelling with compound

Unevenness in concrete floors caused by lots of cracks and shallow depressions less than 3mm (⅛in) deep can be rectified with a self-levelling compound obtainable from builders' merchants. Dampen the floor with water before starting work. Mix the compound with water to form a runny paste. Starting at the corner furthest from the door, trowel the mixture onto the floor to a depth of 3mm (⅛in) using a float. Leave the compound to find its own level and harden off; the floor-covering can be laid the following day.

Wood floors

Replacing chipboard and plywood boards

There is very little that can go wrong with chipboard and plywood floors: damp or leaks, however, can cause chipboard to disintegrate and plywood to swell. If you find that damage has occurred, simply lever up the damaged board and replace it with a new piece cut to the same size as the original.

If you are aware that noise is likely to be a problem in the room below you, lay a sound-deadening material between the existing surface and the new one when you are laying wood-strip or flexible flooring.

Pine floorboards

Boards that have become very cupped with age or that have large gaps between them will ruin virtually all types of new floor covering. Carpets and vinyl will wear on the ridges, ceramic tiles will crack and wood-strip floors will creak and lurch continually unless action is taken. Individual damaged boards can be replaced (see pages 132–133) but an uneven floor should be entirely covered with a layer of hardboard or, if it is in really poor condition, thin plywood, which is more rigid.

Laying hardboard and plywood boards

The same technique can be employed for both hardboard and plywood although there are slight differences in the way they are fixed. Both types of board are normally sold as 2.44 x 1.22m (8 x 4ft) sheets but are easier to handle and to lay if they are cut smaller. Ask your supplier to cut them in half so that you end up with squares with sides of 1.22m (4ft). Allow the boards to acclimatize for 48 hours in the relevant room before laying them. Hardboard can even be dampened with water to allow it to settle more evenly.

In a regularly shaped room, start laying the sheets against the longest, straightest wall and work towards the opposite wall. In an irregularly shaped room, begin in the centre and work outwards; find the centre as you would before tiling a floor (see pages 156–157).

Lay the boards so that the middle of each new sheet adjoins the bottom of the join between the two previously laid sheets, rather like a brick wall. Use small nails, no longer than 18mm (¾in) long, at 15cm (6in) intervals, to fix plywood boards. If laying 12mm (½in) plywood for hard tiles, screw the boards down at 30cm (12in) intervals.

Hardboard should be laid with the rough side facing upwards. Nail it to the floorboards from the centre outwards in a radial pattern so it does not buckle. Space the nails at 15cm (6in) intervals but 10cm (4in) apart at the edges of the sheets. This is less critical for plywood, which is much more rigid.

Determine where to cut the edging boards by placing them (upside down and with one edge against the skirting board) over the last of the laid boards. Using a pencil, mark where the edges of the bottom boards touch the top ones. Cut the boards at these points using a saw and fix them into position the right way up. This technique only works if the edge of the board against the skirting is cut square. If you are using an offcut as an edging piece, ensure that the uncut, square end of the offcut is against the skirting board. Use a profile gauge (see pages 154–155) to transfer the profile of architraves onto the board so that it can be cut to fit, and stop the boards against the doorstop.

Laying hardboard

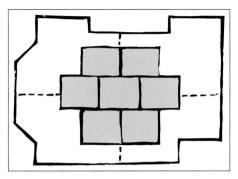

1 In an irregularly shaped room, establish your centre point and work outwards, laying the boards like bricks.

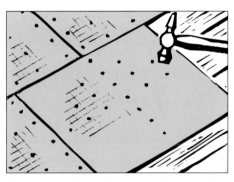

2 Secure the boards with short nails, working in a radial pattern, and with more nails going in at the edges.

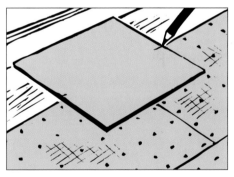

3 Simply turn a board upside down and mark an overlap in order to cut board to fit exactly at the room's edge.

4 Use a profile gauge to produce an accurate pattern to cut when it comes to door frames and the like.

Estimating and equipment

▲ *It is wise not to over-order expensive materials lilke the ash flooring here, so draw a scale plan of the room, taking particular care to be accurate if this room is an irregular shape with obstructions such as kitchen units – and curved-edge stairs – to work into the calculation. It is equally frustrating to underestimate, and can lead to poor colour matches.*

Ordering the right amount of material is vital to ensure that there is sufficient to finish the job neatly. This is particularly important with flexible sheet materials in order to avoid having to make unnecessary ugly seams and because of the risk of colour variations between different batches of material. Whilst over-ordering is simply a waste of money, it is nonetheless essential to order slightly more than you calculate you will need to compensate for the inevitable wastage that arises when you are working around obstacles, and from mistakes and breakages. It is unlikely, for example, that you will be able to find a place for all the half-tiles left as offcuts when you tile the border of a room. Obviously, it is crucial to estimate as accurately as possible to minimize wastage, and to estimate accurately you must measure accurately. Take your time; double-check measurements and sums; and you will probably save both time and money.

Measuring up

It is always worth taking an accurate plan of your room to your supplier, who will know the best way to save material – particularly in awkwardly shaped rooms. However, rooms with square or rectangular walls without any interruptions along them are easy to measure. And to calculate the area, simply establish the width and depth of the room and multiply one figure by the other; this is the number of square metres (yards) to be covered. Most rooms have various obstacles, however: built-in cupboards, chimney breasts and alcoves. In order to include these in your estimate, first measure the width and depth of the unobstructed rectangle forming the room's central part, and calculate that area. Then measure the width and depth of every recess and add these together to calculate the total area occupied by these recesses. Finally add this figure to the first figure to calculate the

Tools and equipment

General tools

In addition to everyday tools, some more specialized implements will be required for preparing surfaces and laying floor-coverings. The more general of these are described below, but task-specific tools will be explained in the relevant sections of this chapter.

- **Straight edge:** length of metal used to ensure edges or lines are straight. Also useful for checking tiles are laid level, and joining up points with a straight line.
- **Chalk line:** length of string that pulls out from a unit rather like a tape measure except that it coats the line with a coloured chalk. Used for marking out straight lines on a large scale. The string is stretched taut between two points and plucked against the surface leaving a line of chalk.
- **Club hammer:** heavy hammer used when brute force is needed. An ideal partner for the bolster chisel.
- **Bolster chisel:** large, blunt, flat-bladed metal chisel useful for tasks as diverse as levering up floorboards, breaking heavy tiles and stone in two and laying carpet.
- **Try square:** used to mark a line at 90 degrees to an edge and for marking the line of a right-angled corner.
- **Trimming knife:** bulky handle holding sharp blade that can be changed when it becomes blunt. Used for cutting flexible materials, such as cork or vinyl, and carpet.
- **Craft knife:** smaller and sharper than a trimming knife. Particularly useful for cutting stencils from oiled card.
- **Trowel:** used for repairs to concrete floors: for mixing small quantities of cement, filling cracks and final smoothing of the repair.
- **Float:** smoothing tool used for screeding. Use a metal plasterer's float for spreading self-levelling compound.
- **Profile gauge:** a series of metal pins that pass through a holder. The gauge is pressed against any intricate areas and the pins are displaced in the shape of the profile. Useful for measuring the profile of architraves when cutting flexible flooring materials.

actual area of floor space to be covered – in square metres (yards). In a trapezoid room, there is really no alternative but to draw a plan to scale on graph paper.

Flexible flooring

For flexible sheet materials you need to order enough material to fit between the two widest dimensions of the room, as the excess is simply trimmed away from any obstructions to avoid making unnecessary seams. Large areas of trimmed material can often be used elsewhere but try to tuck seams away in an unobtrusive corner. Seams should run at 90 degrees to a window as they are less visible in that position. Sheet materials are available in various widths so ensure that the sum of the widths is the same as or greater than the width of the room. The total length of

material required is the number of widths required, allowing for pattern-matching and wastage, multiplied by the length of the room.

Tiles

Calculate how many of your tiles are required per square metre and multiply that number by the number of square metres in the room. Remember that you will have to cut tiles to fit at the edges. Estimate the number of extra tiles you will need by allowing enough to tile one additional strip along half the walls and then add a few more in case of breakages. With larger, more expensive tiles it may be worth calculating if offcuts can be used to

prevent waste. Your final figure will have to be rounded up – tiles are supplied in boxes – so you will probably have tiles left over.

Wood-strip flooring

Calculate how many strips of the desired planking are needed to fit the width of the room. Multiply the number of strips by the length of the room to calculate the total length required. Allow a little extra for cutting as there are bound to be a few short lengths that will be unusable. Pre-finished flooring is sold by the box so your final figure will have to be rounded up to the nearest number of complete boxes.

Tools and equipment

For wood floors

- **Cross-cut saw:** long saw for general-purpose wood-cutting across the grain, normally used for cutting floorboards to length.
- **Ripsaw:** long saw with large, widely spaced teeth for cutting wood along the grain, most often necessary when the last board in a floor is too wide.
- **Tenon saw:** small handsaw with a reinforced back to prevent the blade from flexing and very fine teeth for intricate work.
- **Floor saw:** saw with a curved cutting edge to enable a floorboard to be cut without damaging the boards on either side.
- **Coping saw:** thin blade supported by large metal frame for cutting curves in wood, normally used if a floorboard needs shaping to fit around an obstacle.
- **Chisel:** tool with a very sharp blade, available in various widths. Useful for cutting where a saw cannot be used. Used in conjunction with a wooden mallet.
- **Circular saw:** circular-bladed power saw, useful for cutting wood in all directions.
- **Electric jigsaw:** a small, powered blade supported at one end. Primarily designed for cutting curves in wood, metal and plastic.

▲ *When calculating how many tiles to order, remember to allow for the fact that you will probably be cutting a lot of tiles at the walls and along any diagonal edges. Generally, some of the offcuts can be used elsewhere, which minimizes wastage – at the right-hand end of the diagonal strip here, for instance – but this should not be relied upon.*

Setting out tiles

It is essential to spend a little care and time on setting things out before you start to tile a floor, whether with hard (see pages 158–161) or flexible (see pages 166–169) materials, if you are to prevent problems. Tiles must not be allowed to go out of square, otherwise they will simply not fit together, and you must avoid ending up with an annoying little thin strip of tiles against the last wall.

A regular room

Measure along the two opposite shortest walls to find the midpoint of each. Join these two marks together with a chalk line. Measure and mark 1m (39in) along this centre line on each side of the middle point. Measure 1m (39in) from the middle point at an estimated 90-degree angle. Measure the two diagonal lines between the marks on either side of the middle point and the 90-degree marks top and bottom, and adjust the latter's position until these two diagonals both measure 1.415m (55¾in).

You now have an angle of 90 degrees at the top and bottom. A straight line from these points to the middle of the centre line will meet the centre line at 90 degrees. The diagonals can serve as guidelines for laying tiles diagonally at 45 degrees to the walls.

Use the chalk line to join the midpoint of the centre line with the 90-degree mark and extend this line across the full width of the room to mark the shorter centre line.

From these two lines, dry-lay a line of tiles up to each edge of the room to check that you will not be left with a thin strip of tiles at any point. If this happens, adjust the centre lines by half a tile's width to leave a decent border of tiles.

To ensure that all the tiles are laid without going out of square, it is best to divide up the entire floor into a series of boxes of approx 1 sq m (1 sq yd), starting from the two centre lines. The exact size of the 'boxes' will obviously be determined by the size of your chosen tiles.

When laying ceramic or quarry tiles remember to allow for the grout: about 6mm (¼in) for the smaller tiles and up to 10mm (⅜in) for larger, maybe slightly irregular

▲ Using tiles to reflect the other colours in an interior helps to create a sense of harmony and balance. Here the creamy floor tiles complement the soft pink tiles on the stairs to produce a warm effect, despite the cold, hard character of the raw materials and the predominance of straight edges. Muted colours can also help to create a sense of spaciousness.

handmade terracotta tiles. For example, you could lay thirty-six 15cm (6in) square tiles in a box measuring 936mm (36⅞in), or only nine 30cm (12in) square tiles in a box measuring 918mm (36⅛in). Remember to allow for an extra grout line around the edge of the room. Use the chalk line to mark out your boxes. Once you have marked out the floor with these guidelines, you are ready to start tiling.

An irregular room

The principle for setting out an irregular room is the same as for a regular room

Setting out tiles

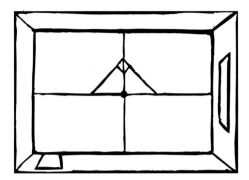

1 Draw a line between the midpoints of the shortest walls; establish a right angle at the centre, as described.

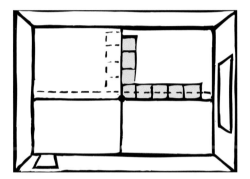

2 Dry-lay tiles out from the centre to each wall. Adjust your centre if there is only a sliver of tile at any edge.

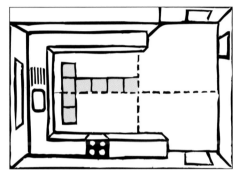

3 Working from your centre point, mark out a grid over the whole floor area, to help you lay your tiles square.

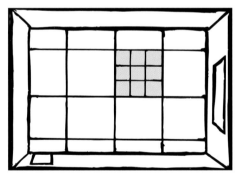

4 In an irregularly shaped room adjust your centre point so that your tiles align with the longest wall.

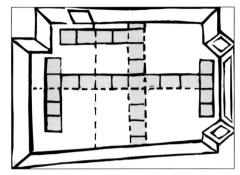

5 In a room with lots of obstacles, lay your tiles square to a door; check for slivers and adjust your centre as usual.

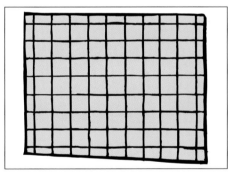

6 You can adjust your centre lines to bisect a dominant feature – a range of units, for instance, or a bay window.

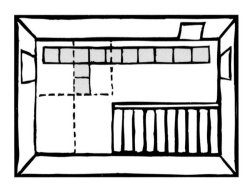

7 To create a border, plan and lay a central area and then fill in the border, with cut tiles against the wall as usual.

8 A diagonally laid central area and straight border has the border laid first, followed by the diagonal panel.

(above) except that you work from the longest and straightest wall. Adjust the position of the centre line so that a series of whole tiles can run from it to the longest wall. If the room is very out of square the final line of tiles – opposite the long, straight wall – will be cut at an angle and will vary considerably in their final size, but visually this is acceptable.

If the room is only slightly out of square, however, you may find that you end up with a thin sliver of tiles that gradually diminish as the room narrows. If this is the case, you should adjust the centre line by half a tile, so that you are basically working with half-tiles at the edge.

In rooms that are very irregular and have no obvious long wall, where to start to tile is really a matter of personal judgement. It is important to identify a feature in the room – the door, for instance – and align the tiles so that they run parallel to it.

If the room has a dominant feature, such as a range of kitchen units that are set out in a U-shape or a very large bay window, run the centre line through the 'U' to bisect it.

Provided the centre lines are at 90 degrees to each other, the tiles will always be square. Always dry-lay the tiles to check that there will be no fiddly bits, or make up a datum rod or tiling gauge (a length of wood with the tile, and grout if appropriate, intervals marked along its length) to save having to lay out the tiles repeatedly.

Setting out with a border

It is necessary to measure from the walls to establish the grid, but adjust the final position of the grid so that there is space for a border all the way around the room.

Either adjust the grid so that there are whole tiles lying against the border on two of the walls, or centre the grid right in the middle of the room and cut all the tiles against the border all the way around the room, provided the cut tiles do not end up being too narrow.

Tile the central area first and finish by tiling the border. Tiles that are laid diagonally should be finished with a border that runs parallel to the walls.

Hard flooring

As their survival in the oldest of our buildings testifies, the most enduring and practical of flooring materials are natural stone and tiles. Stone, marble and slate were once the only hard-wearing flooring materials available and were commonplace on the ground floors of cottages and cowsheds alike, wood being reserved for the gentler life on the upper levels once these were introduced. Tiles have been used since ancient times for the same reasons, but additionally they offer greater decorative possibilities.

▲ *As their shape and texture vividly illustrate, these ancient flagstones have almost certainly been in place for generations. Expensive to lay new today, it is the sort of material we associate with unspoilt country cottages, although flagstones would once have been commonplace in a wider range of houses.*

Indeed, our knowledge of the Roman Empire is derived in part from the patterns and scenes depicted on the mosaic floors of the period, often the only remains of a building and its contents.

Today we have an ever-increasing choice of hard-flooring materials with which to furnish our homes (see pages 160–161). Exotic multicoloured slates and marbles are brought from all over the world, as are dozens of styles of beautiful and vividly coloured ceramic tiles. Even simple terracotta, always a popular choice, is now available in many different shades, shapes and sizes (see pages 160–161); the handmade tiles in subtly varying colours are the best.

The way in which a seemingly straightforward material is manufactured or prepared makes an enormous difference to the atmosphere that it helps to create. The textured surface of riven slate flagstones, for instance, is naturally at home in a simple country room that has been decorated in a traditional style; however the same material can equally be the perfect partner to, say, chrome and modern fittings if used in a contemporary bathroom but first cut into regular squares and honed smooth.

Fairly expensive and very durable, tiles and stone floors are a long-term investment and care should be given to the choices to be made. Hard floors are the preferred choice of those who live in warmer climates for practical reasons as indoors they create a cool refuge from the hot sun, both physically and psychologically. In many countries nearly all interior floors are tiled, with rugs being used to provide decorative relief and to help engender a sense of warmth and luxury.

For those of us who inhabit the cooler regions of the northern hemisphere, warmth is at a premium. In the kitchen and bathroom, however, where tough practicality is just as important, tiles and stone are still ideal. They are both waterproof and virtually indestructible, although dropping china or glass onto tiles or stone will result in a breakage.

Hallways, too, are a perfect environment for hard materials; stone's austere luxury will cause visitors to pause just briefly enough to reflect upon the initial impression it creates. In rooms that combine function with relaxation, such as a kitchen with a dining or seating area, two different materials can be used to demarcate the spaces. Tiles can be used for the kitchen floor, for instance, and wood for the living area. The wood is gentle and welcoming, the tiles provide practicality, and the two materials work well together.

Tone and colour are also important criteria. Brightly coloured tiles can be used as a dominant feature or neutral ones as a backdrop for brighter walls and fabrics or rugs: a cool slate floor simply decorated with a Persian rug in warm reds and blues is an especially rich combination.

Tiles are the perfect material for incorporating borders. Most manufacturers produce a range of complementary border tiles but it is possible to use any tiles as such, providing they fit together. For those with patience, mosaic offers interesting design potential, although it is probably wiser to use it in smaller rooms, and to stick to designs that do not use too many colours. Always use tiles made especially for floors, such as terracotta floor tiles; they are thicker than wall tiles which, being thin, might break.

◄ *Hard flooring is an ever-popular choice for transitional areas like hallways, because they are so practical. Slate tiles here have been laid on the diagonal, which always lends a certain elegance; and the alternation of light and dark tiles – despite being of the same material – is charmingly decorative in its subtlety.*

▲ *Brightly coloured and patterned encaustic tiles provide a visual splash at the right-hand end of the bathroom and contrast strongly with the plain tiles used under the bath and to the left. Interestingly, the pattern painted on the bottom half of the door has been copied from one of the tiles in the patchwork arrangement on the floor.*

Directory of hard floorings

Of all the exciting hard-flooring materials on offer, the most commonly used in the modern home are tiles. Due to a range of manufacturing processes floor tiles offer a wide choice of practical hard-wearing products suitable for most domestic situations. Ranging from natural earthy shades to bright and vibrant colours, they can also be chosen to complement any decor. Terracotta, the simplest and one of the oldest types, remains a time-honoured favourite for kitchens. Quarry tiles, which are at once economical and hard-wearing, are also enduringly popular. Ceramic floor tiles, available in many colours and styles, are perhaps the most versatile. And mosaic, used for centuries to decorate floors, is the perfect material for recreating a design, although simple, coloured borders set against a plain background are the easiest designs with which to work.

In addition, floor bricks can be used to create regular patterns, and stone, whether it be natural or reconstructed, can provide just the right touch for some interiors. Slate, for instance, is a very practical material and comparatively easy to lay because it is so thin; some sheets are hardly thicker than a ceramic tile. Finally, while metal flooring may not be a viable option for most people, it is the ideal material if the ultimate in industrial chic is required.

Terracotta tiles

Unglazed and softer than other types of tile, terracotta is made from extruded or hand-formed clay. It is available in a number of shapes and sizes, from small hexagons to large squares. The colours range from dusky ochres to oranges through to reds. Part of the charm of terracotta is precisely this colour variation, within each tile and from tile to tile, as well as the textural variations of the surface. These porous tiles must be finished with linseed oil and waxed for protection.

Quarry tiles

Quarry tiles are made from extruded or hand-formed clay which is fired at higher temperatures than terracotta to vitrify it, a process that gives the tiles their durability and makes them very hard-wearing and waterproof. The colour range is a little limited; buffs, reds and browns are the dominant tones although white and black tiles have been produced. The tiles usually have a dull satin finish. Variously sized square or rectangular quarry tiles are available – and some 'key squares' too (see pages 164–165).   **1**

Ceramic tiles

Ceramic floor tiles are made from a dust-pressed clay that is fired at high temperatures. Fully vitrified ceramic tiles are the most waterproof of all

tiles, making them suitable for the wettest areas – such as bathrooms. Ceramic floor tiles are not glazed; glazed tiles are normally too slippery unless the glaze has a roughened surface. They may have decorative patterns or little studs on the surface for textural variation and slip resistance. Oxides, added during the manufacturing process, give these tiles the widest range of colours of any unglazed tile – including plain white. Ceramic tiles are thinner than quarry or terracotta tiles and their uniform thickness enables trouble-free installation. They can, however, be polished for a more glamorous look.

Mosaic tiles

Mosaic tiles are tiny, cut from glass, coloured ceramic, terracotta, stone or marble and fixed to a backing sheet for speedy installation. Their appearance varies both according to the material and to whether it has been machine- or hand-cut.   **2**

Encaustic tiles

Encaustic tiles are either plain-coloured or have a decorative pattern applied to their surface which has a soft, matt quality with colours that blend into each other. A design is painted onto a mould using natural oxides and then a plain tile is pressed into the design to transfer the design onto the tile's surface.   **4**

Brick

The bricks that are used for decorative floors are much the same as terracotta tiles. They are, however, thicker, and they do require a solid base. Because of their small, regular size, bricks are perfect for creating patterns: herringbone is traditional but something more individual works equally well.

Limestone

A sedimentary rock formed from coral and shell deposits at the bottom of warm seas, limestone has a considerably varied character which ranges

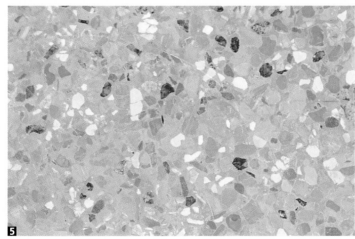

Marble

Metamorphosed limestone, marble is characterized by coloured mineral veins which run through it. It is extremely diverse: for example, Carrara marble is a soft grey interspersed with a blurry, indistinct black veining that is quietly elegant, whereas Brochella marbles are vivid reds and blacks, with colourful swirling veins, perfect for proclaiming wealth and power.

Terrazzo

This is a material manufactured from marble chips bound together with a cement-based adhesive. It is made into slabs or tiles and polished to a high sheen. The colour is dependent on the type of marble used. Different colours can be incorporated into one slab to create patterned borders and centres that simply fit together to complete a repeating or symmetrical design. Traditionally found around the Mediterranean, terrazzo is an extremely hard-wearing material often used in commercial environments. **5**

Quartzite

One of the hardest natural stone flooring materials, quartzite comes in a wide range of plain and variegated colours from soft greys to warmer buffs, as well as much darker colours such as sombre greens and near-black. Quartzite has a riven, slip-resistant surface which, together with its durability, makes it a popular choice for commercial applications.

Metal flooring

The ubiquitous aluminium treadplate is found everywhere nowadays: from the backs of lorries to warehouses. It is available in 2.44 x 1.22m (8 x 4ft) sheets and is easy to lay over an existing floor either as large sheets or cut into tiles. Aluminium treadplate is slip-resistant and non-corrosive. The gleaming surface perfectly complements a contemporary interior.

from almost white and fine-grained through a coarser texture with embedded fossils to very dark greens and blues. It can be finished in a variety of ways, from a rough to highly polished surface. As it is very porous and stains easily it should always be sealed. Antique limestone is sourced from a number of historical sites, but these cannot last for ever. New limestone is more regular and lacks the distressed quality of well-worn limestone – although some suppliers have tried to recreate examples with an aged look.

Slate

A metamorphic rock formed from mudstones and shales, slate splits neatly into thin sheets. Riven slate has a naturalistic, rough and uneven appearance. Typically it is cut into squares or chopped, which gives the edges a complementary rougher look. Slate is usually blue-grey with a silvery quality, although there are some extraordinary colours available too, ranging from pale parchment with warm buff highlights to dark reds and rusts. As slate is so varied it can be used successfully anywhere that calls for a hard-wearing and practical surface.

Sandstone

Sandstone is a sedimentary stone, formed from the grains of igneous rocks. It can be found in colours that range from a soft cream to ochre and warm brick red. As it is hard-wearing, it has come to be associated with flag-stones, most popularly York stone. It is particularly useful in situations where slip resistance is important – in shower rooms, for instance, although it may be too rough for some feet. Its gritty surface can make it difficult to clean too, which also makes it less than ideal for kitchens. **3**

Laying ceramic tiles

▲ *Machine-made ceramic tiles always look smarter if tile spacers are used when the tiles are set into the adhesive, to ensure that joints are evenly spaced and neat. This type of tile is easy to cut cleanly, which is a useful characteristic if a lot of cuts need to be made – around obstructions, for example, or if the tiles are laid on the diagonal.*

Modern ceramic floor tiles are regularly shaped and quite thin, making them easier to cut than other types of tile. If you are laying the tiles on a timber floor, prime the floor first with either a general builder's PVA adhesive or a special tile primer for wood floors. If the floor is at all uneven or insufficiently rigid, first cover it with plywood or WBP (Weather and Boil Proof) chipboard (see pages 152–153).

Laying the tiles

Begin by setting out and drawing up a grid of 'boxes' across the floor (see pages 156–157). Mix up the tile adhesive according to the manufacturer's instructions, adding any special additives for greater flexibility if you are covering a wood floor. Tile adhesive has a limited pot life, about 20 minutes, so do not mix up more than you will realistically be able to use in the time available.

Lay your first tile in the corner furthest from the door. In order accurately to position this tile, dry-lay a line of tiles from the centre point to the far wall along the centre line, and then draw a line at right angles to the centre line along the far edge of the last whole tile. Dry-lay tiles along the new line and, in the same way as before, draw a line on the far side of your last whole tile at right angles to your guideline. Providing this line is parallel to the centre line the last tile you

dry-laid is your 'first tile'. Only spread the adhesive over an area of approx. 1sq m (1sq yd) at a time. Using the recommended side of a notched spreader or trowel, apply the adhesive to the correct depth, normally approx. 3mm (⅛in). Depending on the adhesive being used, it may be necessary to butter the back of the tile with adhesive as well. Press the tile into position with a slight twisting motion; it is important to bed the tile into the adhesive without any air gaps. For neat and even joints, usually 6–12mm (¼–½in), use plastic spacers between the tiles. Continue laying the tiles in the first marked square, checking the tiles are level with a spirit level and straight edge. You need to work fast, as you have a very limited amount of time to reposition any tiles that are incorrectly laid. If any adhesive gets on the surface of a tile clean it off immediately with a damp cloth; ensure too that the joints are adhesive-free.

When the first grid box has been laid, apply adhesive to the second and continue laying tiles along the far wall. Then complete the second row of squares and continue laying the tiles in rows of boxes, working back towards the door. Allow the tile

▲ *Wide joints look particularly effective when used between small tiles. They are also helpful if the tiles are not all the same size: different-sized gaps are less noticeable than different-sized tiles. Two widths of joint have been used here deliberately, adding to the charm of this arrangement of handmade and painted tiles.*

Laying ceramic tiles

adhesive to dry thoroughly before walking on the tiles. Conventional adhesives usually need at least 24 hours although fast-setting adhesives can take only a few hours.

It will probably be necessary to cut tiles around the edges of the room to fit; if you lay the tiles on the diagonal, you will need to cut at least one in every two tiles. Ceramic tiles can be cut using a tile-cutting jig.

To determine where to cut a border tile place a whole tile over the last laid whole tile. To allow for the grout, place a tile on its side between this tile and the wall and place another tile up against it. Mark the middle tile with a soft pencil where the tile above it ends. Place the tile in the jig and cut along the marked line. Butter the back of the cut tile and press into position. Continue until all the border tiles have been laid, leaving the four corners until last in order to cut them accurately.

Where a tile has to go around an architrave, use a tile nibbler to chip away the edge of a tile. For pipes, the tile will have to be cut in half and a semi-circle nibbled out of each half to take the pipe; or you could cut a notch into one edge. When laying the two halves, leave only a thin joint between them so the cut is less noticeable when grouted.

Grouting the tiles

When all the tiles have been laid and the adhesive is dry, fill the tile joints with a tile grout suitable for floors. Conventional grout is a powder mixed with water according to the manufacturer's instructions. It is available in colours ranging from off-white to dark grey. For tiles laid over wood floors, remember to mix in a flexible additive.

For food-preparation areas an epoxy grout is a good idea because it is extremely hard and easily cleaned. Epoxy grout consists of two components that are mixed together, and then a powder filler is added to bulk it out. Always follow the manufacturer's instructions. Pour the grout onto the surface and spread it into the joints with the aid of a rubber squeegee, working on small areas at a time. After 15 minutes, clean any excess grout off the surface with a damp cloth. Once the grout has hardened sufficiently, polish the tiles with a clean, dry cloth.

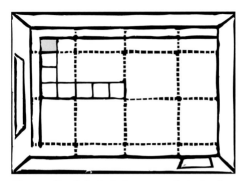

1 Lay your first tile in the furthest corner: dry-lay two lines of tiles from the centre to find the correct position.

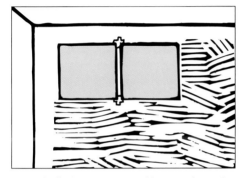

2 Spread adhesive over a manageable area and press the tiles into position; use plastic spacers for even joints.

3 Working fast, continue to lay tiles to complete the first marked square, checking frequently that they are level.

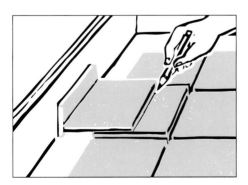

4 Cut border tiles accurately using the simple method described, remembering to allow for grout at the edge.

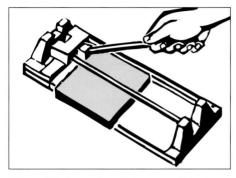

5 To cut all the border tiles effortlessly and efficiently, place the marked tile in a jig and press the lever to cut.

6 The cut border tiles will need to be 'buttered' with adhesive before being pressed into position.

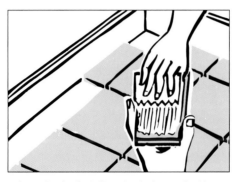

7 When the adhesive is dry, pour grout onto the surface. Spread it into the joints a small area at a time.

8 Any excess grout should be cleaned from the surface with a damp cloth, before it is polished.

Laying terracotta tiles

Larger and heavier than ceramic tiles, terracotta tiles need a thicker adhesive bed, especially if the tiles are handmade and vary in thickness, or if they have bowed during manufacture. The method described here can be used for other types of tile such as quarry or slate, the thick adhesive bed being used to absorb any difference in tile thickness. Although a sand-and-cement mix can be used for many heavy tiles, it is not really suitable for terracotta tiles. Because they are very porous, they may react with the cement to cause efflorescence – when the soluble salts come to the surface as a white stain. Use a thick-bed adhesive, which can be applied at any thickness from 5mm to 2.5cm (¼ to 1in). Thick-bed adhesive can happily be used on an uneven floor base and dries very quickly, in some cases enabling tiling and grouting to be carried out in the same day. Very uneven surfaces, however, should be prepared as described on pages 152–153.

The principles for marking out and laying the tiles are much the same as for laying ceramic tiles (see pages 162–163). You start in the furthest corner, having located the centre point and adjusted it, and having marked up a grid which will help to keep you straight. Mix up the tile adhesive according to the manufacturer's instructions. Some types of thick-bed adhesive are simply poured onto the floor and spread out to an even level with an appropriate type of spreader, and then the tiles are laid straight onto it. Other types of adhesive require the back of the tile to be buttered with adhesive as well: always follow the manufacturer's directions. Handmade tiles may vary slightly in size and thickness, so apply more adhesive to the backs of the thinner tiles and allow a wide gap, approx. 12mm (½in), between the tiles; any variations in size will be taken up within the joints. It is important to keep an eye on the marked-out grid to ensure the tiles are laid square and to keep checking the tiles are level with the spirit level and straight edge. Once the central area of the floor is finished, fill in the border – i.e., lay all the whole tiles you can before cutting your border and corner tiles.

Cutting tiles

The easiest way to cut terracotta tiles is with an angle grinder fitted with a stone-cutting wheel. Cut a groove into the tile to two thirds of the tile's depth and then snap it in two. The cutter will, if required, cut or grind through the whole thickness of the tile –useful for cutting awkward shapes out of a tile to go round pipes and other obstructions.

▶ *Rectangular quarry tiles have been laid in a staggered pattern like bricks in this high-ceilinged, cool white sitting room. Great care must be taken to avoid letting the tiles go out of line. These particular tiles are richly variegated which creates decorative interest on the floor without the need for any major planning effort.*

▲ *Old, handmade tiles look very effective in this kitchen; they can be very tricky to lay, however, compared to machine-made tiles. Remember that the joints between handmade tiles must vary in width in order to allow for slight variations in tile size, and bear in mind that handmade tiles can vary in thickness too.*

Laying terracotta tiles

1 Spread adhesive over approx. 1sq m (1sq yd) to a depth specified by the manufacturer, using a notched trowel.

2 Some adhesives require the back of the tile to be 'buttered' as well, to make both contact surfaces tacky.

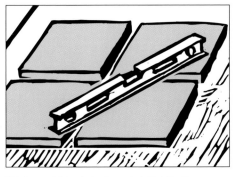

3 Using a spirit level, check regularly that the tiles you have laid are level, and certainly after each grid box.

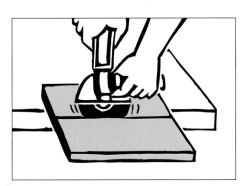

4 It may be possible to cut some tiles with a jig but most will need the power of an angle grinder.

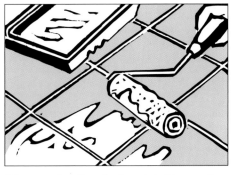

5 Terracotta tiles will need to be sealed with a coat of boiled linseed oil before they are grouted.

6 Grout the joints of porous tiles with a pointing trowel: fill the joints and avoid spilling grout on the surface.

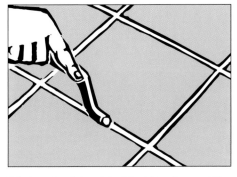

7 Push grout well down into all the joints – to support the edges fully. Use a metal pipe to create a concave finish.

8 Apply wax with a cloth after a secondary coat of sealer, and when dry, polish it off with a rotary floor machine.

Sealing

Terracotta and quarry tiles are very porous and must be sealed before you add grouting in order to provide a hard-wearing and easy-to-clean surface. Ensure the surfaces of the tiles are free from dust and any traces of tile adhesive. Brush one coat of boiled linseed oil over the tiles with a brush or short-haired paint roller. It is important to apply an even coat to avoid the risk of streaking. The oil will soak into the tile, the surface losing its gloss 2–10 minutes after application. If it appears matt in less time than that, apply the oil more liberally. Allow the sealer to dry and then grout. A second coat of sealer should be applied after grouting.

Grouting

Grout terracotta tiles with a grout that is suitable for wide joints; porous tiles are grouted using a pointing method rather than by simply spreading the grout over the surface as you would for ceramic tiles. Fill the joints using a pointing trowel, and avoid spilling any of the grout onto the surface of the tiles. Finish the grout by making it slightly concave; bend a round metal pipe into a convenient shape and use that.

Some types of handmade tiles benefit from 'slurry grouting', a technique which fills in all the pits and dents to create an antiqued appearance. Mix up the grout to a creamy consistency and grout as you would ceramic tiles (see pages 162–163), ensuring that the grout fills all the crevices. Clean the excess grout off the surface with a damp sponge.

Finishing off

Apply a second coat of seal once the grout has thoroughly dried, using the oil more sparingly than before as the tiles will be less porous. Any excess oil that does not soak in after 20 minutes should be cleaned from the surface of the tile. After the oil has had time to soak into the tiles fully, which usually takes a few hours or overnight, the tiles can be waxed. Use a proprietary floor wax and wax the floor twice. The new floor should then be waxed once a week for the following month in order to build up a smooth and hard-wearing, yet mellow surface.

Flexible flooring

Probably used in more environments than any other type
of floor-covering and usually overlooked, flexible
materials are the unsung heroes of the flooring world.
Consisting of just a thin layer, only a few millimetres
(fractions of an inch) thick, they add colour and texture to
any floor, transforming it at a stroke. Their tough
practicality, economy and easy maintenance ensure their
presence in locations from the kitchen to the factory floor
and they are ubiquitous in hospitals, airports and factories.

Although they are usually laid in the more demanding areas of the home – the kitchen and bathroom – flexible materials can be used in any room and would be a particularly sensible choice for a hallway. In practice, these materials should never wear out in a domestic situation.

Linoleum, the forerunner of more modern materials such as vinyl, was once all that many people could afford to lay over their floorboards to increase their practicality while at the same time enhancing their appearance. In its most usual manifestation, a dreary brown colour, it was used in many public buildings. Linoleum virtually disappeared as domestic flooring with the introduction of the more versatile PVC flooring known as vinyl, but having only recently shed its traditionally dowdy image, it is currently undergoing a real renaissance. It has brightened up considerably and now offers a dazzling array of bright and cheery colours that look bang up to date.

Due to its ready availability and particularly extensive potential for decoration, vinyl has been the flooring material of choice for many years. It is possible to add far more colour and design to the surface of vinyl than of linoleum and consequently it is made in a wide range of patterned, flecked and marbled hues, as well as in imitation of expensive natural flooring materials. In some cases it is hard to tell apart from the real thing. Indeed, it can be even more expensive to buy than the real thing, the vinyl version often being chosen because of its low maintenance and because it is warmer and softer than its natural counterparts, such as stone.

Rubber, another material that has recently increased in popularity as a domestic floor-covering, is extremely durable. It recovers from minor surface nicks and resists burns, so it continues to look good for longer than other flexible flooring products. The raised and studded non-slip surface of rubber makes it an appealing material.

Cork has, in the past, been a very popular natural product, although in recent years it has gone slightly out of favour. In the right setting, however, it can still prove extremely practical. Available in a small range of natural colours, it is a very attractive choice, and worth considering for any budget-conscious scheme with a bias towards the environment.

Flexible flooring materials are available in either sheet or tile form and are so thin that they never cause problems with raised thresholds. As sheet floorings can be tricky to install, it may be worth having more expensive material laid professionally. A large sheet is heavy and awkward and can be difficult to manoeuvre in a room. And just one small slip of the knife can spoil what would otherwise be a perfect finish. Linoleum also contracts and expands unpredictably, which can make it difficult to fit. Vinyl is easier to lay than other sheet materials (see pages 170–173).

Tiles are among the easiest flexible products for the amateur to lay at home. They are also easier to use creatively than the sheet equivalent: installing borders or key squares, for example, is a comparatively straightforward matter (see pages 174–175). Vinyl and linoleum can both be cut and inlaid with different-coloured pieces of the same type of material. With linoleum this can either be done when the floor is laid or later, when you want to brighten it up, when you can inlay shapes. Some vinyl manufacturers provide a very comprehensive range of designs for inlaying, either off the shelf or to special commission.

It is possible to create complex borders and designs for vinyl and linoleum using sophisticated cutting technology but the more intricate designs do require professional installation by highly skilled practitioners.

◀◀ Modern linoleum is not only supremely practical but is now available in an excellent range of contemporary colours. It can be inlaid to create very intricate designs: indeed, an extravagant abstract inlaid design in watery blues and greys provides the main point of visual interest in this plain white panelled bathroom.

◀ Cork is a very practical material; its natural golden colour will warm any room – both decoratively and physically. The raw material usually appears on the market as tiles, although these can be made of granulated cork, or arranged as simple patterns within a tile format, as is illustrated in this kitchen.

Directory of flexible floor-coverings

All the various types of flexible floor-ing are hard-wearing. Quality varies from product to product within each category and prices vary considerably, particularly amongst vinyls, ranging from fairly reasonable to very expensive. Flexible flooring materials are either sold as tiles which can be laid in patterns, or in sheet form that is available in various widths up to about 4m (13ft). Once a decision has been made regarding type, choosing a particular colour or pattern will obviously be the next hurdle, and the potential for having fun is huge, so versatile is the modern raw material.

Linoleum

A completely natural product with excellent environmental credentials, linoleum is made from linseed oil, organic fillers, such as wood flour, and minerals such as chalk and coloured pigment. The ingredients are mixed into a paste, rolled into sheets with a hessian or fibreglass backing and then baked for three weeks. The result is a hard material with a slight sheen. Linoleum is available in a comprehensive range of hues, either plain or marbled with additional colour. Plain, coloured linoleum has a rather dead quality that shows marks easily, and should only be used if a very unobtrusive floor colour is required. Being naturally anti-static and anti-bacterial, linoleum is ideal for industrial and hospital applications.

Linoleum is very versatile. It can be inlaid with other colours, offering infinite design permutations. **1**

Vinyl

Made from PVC (polyvinyl chloride), vinyl is a tough and flexible plastic material. It is available in various thicknesses depending on the type of environment in which it is to be used. The simplest vinyls are made from a single thickness of coloured vinyl that is then marbled or flecked with streaks

of a secondary colour; alternatively, several different colours can be blended together. More elaborate vinyls are made in layers, a plain backing with a patterned layer fixed over it. The top layer can be clear while coloured flecks are embedded over a different base to give a subtle three-dimensional look; these silicon carbide flecks give the material excellent anti-slip properties and also a glittery appearance. The most sophisticated designs are made by sandwiching a printed sheet between the backing and a clear facing. This printed sheet often carries images of natural materials which, depending on the quality, can be startlingly realistic or an obviously faked pastiche. The surface of vinyl is usually smooth, although it can be textured for greater slip resistance or better to imitate the texture of natural materials. The wear layer is often treated in order to make it very low-maintenance as a floor-covering, or even harder-wearing.

Vinyl can also be inlaid. Many domestic vinyls have a cushioned back for a softer and more comfortable feel. **4**

Rubber

Rubber flooring is made from both synthetic and natural materials with mineral fillers and pigments added for colour and body. It is so flexible that it can take sharp knocks and cigarette burns without sustaining serious damage; thus it is used in situations where an extremely hard-wearing surface is required. The surface can be either smooth, or studded or ribbed, which, although mainly intended for slip resistance, gives the material a unique decorative quality that is part of its appeal. It has a slightly softer, more substantial quality than vinyl and provides a practical surface that is easily cleaned. It is also very stable, which means it will not shrink or deteriorate significantly over time, and is available in a range of plain colours as well as marbled and granular styles. **2**

Cork

Cork is a natural product derived from the bark of the cork oak tree; once the bark is gathered, the tree will grow a new bark which will be ready to harvest again nine years later.

Cork has many practical advantages over some of the other flooring materials. It is durable and can be very economical to lay. It is an excellent insulator so it always feels warm to the touch. And it is a good sound barrier; indeed, cork can be laid as an underlay for other types of flooring to provide greater sound insulation. It is available in sheets or, more commonly, as tiles of various thicknesses.

Cork tiles can either be made from strips of cork veneer fixed over a compressed cork backing or be simply granulated and pressed together with an adhesive which gives the product a speckled appearance; different-sized granules produce different surface textures. Naturally brown in colour, cork is available in a limited colour range.

Tiles of different hues can be combined, thereby offering some design flexibility. Tiles that are not adhesive-backed are stuck down onto the floor using applied adhesive.

Cork tiles are supplied either pre-finished with a varnish or plain, in which case they will need to be sealed after installation. Some tiles are sold laminated and are particularly hard-wearing and maintenance-free. Laying unfinished tiles, on the other hand, can present problems because the material is prone to bubbling. If you decide to use cork tiles in a potentially wet environment, it is a good idea to give the tiles an extra coat of varnish once they have been laid, to fill any small gaps between tiles and making the whole floor more waterproof. **3**

Laying sheet vinyl

▲ *It is preferable to lay sheet vinyl in one piece, not only because it is less prone to damage than strips, but also because it looks neater. Seams between strips would spoil the clean lines of this room. It is surprising and interesting to note how well this modern grey vinyl sits with old wooden panelling and antique chairs.*

Ideally, sheet vinyl should be laid in one piece so as to minimize the number of seams. These not only look unattractive but also allow the ingress of dirt and moisture that can cause problems in the future. Most sheet vinyls are available in widths of up to 4m (13ft), so only the widest of rooms should require a seam. It is much easier to lay vinyl in an empty room, before kitchen units, for example, or bathroom fittings are installed; the fewer the obstructions requiring fiddly cutting the more likely it is that the end result will have a professional look and be fully waterproof. If you need to remove the vinyl at a later date, just cut around the units or fittings placed over it with a trimming knife.

All sheet vinyl should be unwrapped loosely and left in the room in which it is to be laid for at least 24 hours before laying. This will give the material time to settle and acclimatize to the atmosphere before you start making cuts.

Fitting the vinyl

Cut the sheet of vinyl to size allowing 5cm (2in) extra on all edges. This can be done in a room larger than the one it will be fitted in; if there is not a sufficiently large room available cut the vinyl outside, making sure that it is kept clean. For vinyl that has to be fitted as two strips, unroll it and trim the ends only. It may be necessary to cut more off one end than the other in order to ensure that any pattern matches from one strip to the next.

Choose the longest and straightest wall to work from. Bring the sheet into the room and unroll it diagonally. Then shuffle the material around so it is square to the long wall with a 3cm (1¼in) gap between the edge of the vinyl and the long wall. The material should curve up the skirting boards or walls on the other edges of the room. Check the vinyl is square to the wall by measuring from the wall to the pattern at both ends of the room and adjust if required, and then push a soft broom over the vinyl to ensure that it is flat on the floor and that there are no air bubbles trapped underneath.

Scribing a line

To cut the vinyl to fit the long wall precisely, use a small block of wood pressed against the wall and overlapping the vinyl to first scribe a line. Slide the block along the wall from one end to the other, at the same time holding a marker pen against it with the tip pressing on the vinyl. The line should exactly follow the contours of the wall. Cut the vinyl along the marked line using a sharp trimming knife. If you are feeling confident, you can simply run the knife along with the block of wood (instead of the pen) to cut the vinyl directly. Push the cut edge against the wall; it should fit perfectly.

Cutting corners

To enable the vinyl to lie flat, make relief cuts at the corners. At external corners simply press the vinyl against the base of the skirting

Laying sheet vinyl

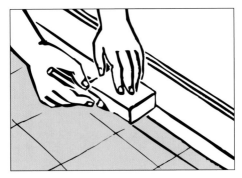

1 Using a block, scribe a line along the edge of the vinyl with a marker pen, following the contours of the wall.

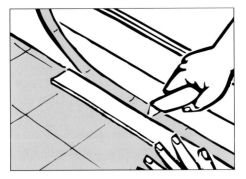

2 Cut the first edge of the vinyl to fit exactly by cutting along this marked line with a sharp craft knife.

3 At external corners, press the vinyl into the base of the skirting board, and make a series of relief cuts.

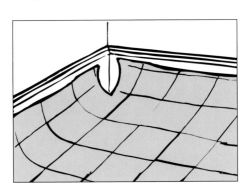

4 At internal corners, cut the corner off the vinyl as described at the measured point to let the vinyl lie flat.

5 Using a paint scraper, push the vinyl right into the base of the wall; create a series of flaps to aid neat trimming.

6 Alternatively, if you are confident, push the vinyl with a metal ruler and cut along its edge in one stroke.

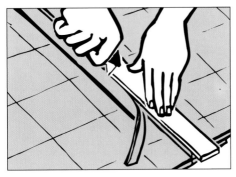

7 Cut through two overlapping pieces of vinyl to create an invisible seam, preferably along the line of a pattern.

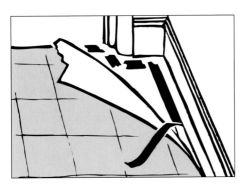

8 Secure the trimmed vinyl sheet at strategic points using special vinyl-to-floor double-sided tape.

board and cut up from that point to the edge of the vinyl so that the material lies flat. At internal corners cut off a triangle from the corner of the vinyl so that when the vinyl is folded up, the two flaps of excess material do not overlap. Do this by folding the vinyl back towards the centre of the room by about 5cm (2in) and measure from the corner to the fold. Measure from the fold towards the corner point of the vinyl by the same amount as the first measurement. Cut the corner off the vinyl at the measured point; the vinyl should now lie flat against the wall with neat flaps of excess material along the walls. Trim these by first pressing the vinyl into the base of the skirting board at intervals of 15cm (6in). Use a stiff paint scraper to push the material right into the angle between the skirting board and the wall. Cut along the fold and remove the piece. Repeat this process until you are left with a series of flaps. Pull the material away from the wall and place a straight edge along the base of the flaps, then trim them off so the vinyl fits neatly against the wall. If you are confident with the knife, cut along the edge of the vinyl in one stroke; use a metal edge when you would otherwise use a paint scraper, and cut.

Cutting seams

Where a seam is necessary, lay the second piece of vinyl over the first so that the pattern matches up. Lay a metal straight edge over the two pieces of vinyl where the seam is to be. Try to place the seam on the line of any pattern as the seam will be less noticeable there. Cut along the straight edge through both pieces of vinyl; the edges should fit perfectly together.

Fixing and gluing

Sheet vinyl sold for domestic use is usually the cushioned type that is used without an adhesive, although some gluing is necessary in certain areas: near doorways, around heavy objects that might be moved, dragging the vinyl with them, and on any seams. Use a special vinyl-to-floor double-sided tape or an acrylic vinyl floor adhesive to secure the floor-covering, following the manufacturer's instructions. ▷

Cutting around obstacles

The easiest way of cutting around obstacles such as a washbasin is to make a paper template. Lining paper is an excellent material for this. If necessary, stick several sheets together to make a sufficiently large sheet. Make a release cut in the paper so that you can position the paper around the obstacle with the cut side against the skirting board. Make a second release cut at 90 degrees to the first, and then continue to make a series of release cuts until the paper lies flat around the obstruction. Fold each flap of paper so that it creases into the corner between the floor and the obstacle. Mark the creases with a pencil line, lift the paper away, and cut along the lines to form the template.

Next you must loosely fit the vinyl in order to trim the edge at the skirting board. Make release cuts in the vinyl at 90 degrees from each other, just as in the initial stage of making the paper template. Position the vinyl around

the obstacle and trim it all along the skirting. Then pull the vinyl away from the obstacle. Tape together the first release cut in the paper template so that the shape of the obstacle is clearly defined.

Position the template over the vinyl so that the edges of the paper and vinyl correspond and the release cuts in the vinyl match up with the edges of the hole in the paper. Mark and cut the hole out of the vinyl and then refit the vinyl into position.

Alternatively, adapt the method you employed to fit your vinyl flush to the first wall (see pages 170–171). Use a block of wood as an amateur profile gauge. With a pencil, scribe around the obstacle on the outside of the block onto a paper template. This template will already need to have been roughly cut to fit around the obstacle. Next, place the template over the vinyl (allowing for the depth of the vinyl to the skirting). Line the outer edge of the block up with the

▲ Wide expanses of floor area can take bold patterns or design effects. Here, large vinyl tiles have been used in the same pattern combination in both the kitchen and the neighbouring room, emphasizing the space available. The kitchen walls have been matched to the red tile colour to provide a bold but harmonious link.

Cutting around obstacles

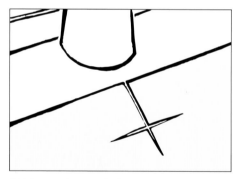

1 Make two release cuts in the paper, at 90 degrees to each other, so that the paper can butt up to the wall.

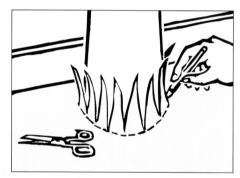

2 Make more release cuts until the paper lies flat around the obstacle. Fold the flaps down, draw a profile and cut.

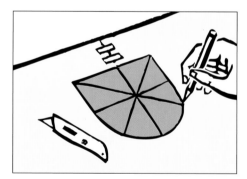

3 Make two release cuts in the vinyl. Transfer the outline of the obstacle using the paper template and cut a hole.

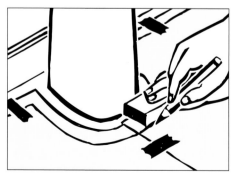

4 Alternatively, use a wooden block to accurately scribe the profile of the obstacle onto your paper template.

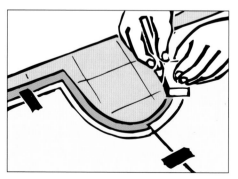

5 Fix the template in position and, with a pen inside the block running around the profile, re-draw the outline.

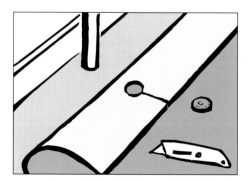

6 To cut around a pipe, make a release cut, mark the pipe's position, and, using a coin as a guide, cut a hole.

pencil line you have drawn on the template and transfer the shape onto the vinyl, by scribing along the inside of the block as you move it around the pencil line.

To fit vinyl around pipes, make a release cut so that the vinyl lies flat at the wall. Measure the position of the pipe and fold the vinyl back from the wall. Measure the place on the vinyl where the hole is to go and mark it using an appropriately sized coin. Cut out the hole and refit the vinyl into place.

Cutting around doorways

Make a series of mini release cuts in the vinyl in the same way as for any corner so a flap fits between the sides of the doorway (see pages 170–171). Alternatively, use a profile gauge to copy the shape of the architrave, transfer this to the vinyl and cut it to fit. Or make a mini paper template. Otherwise, you can fold the vinyl back and carefully cut a sliver off the bottom of the architrave with the end of a long saw, taking care not to damage the surrounding floor. The vinyl can then be slipped underneath the architrave.

Finishing off

For a neater and longer-lasting floor, 'cold weld' any seams to prevent dirt and moisture from getting into the gaps. A solvent-based product, this glues the seams together. Always follow the manufacturer's instructions. Edges can be sealed using a silicone sealant; this is recommended in potentially wet areas such as around the base of a bath and sanitary ware in bathrooms. Fit a metal threshold strip over the edge of the vinyl at the doorway. If fitting mistakes have resulted in gaps at the edges, cover these with wooden beading.

◄ *In smaller rooms with limited floor areas such as kitchens, floors can be made to look bigger by using single-colour wall-to-wall coverings. Because vinyl can be cut to fit small room shapes from one large sheet, it is particularly suitable for kitchens, as food cannot be trapped between cracks and floor-cleaning is much easier.*

Laying linoleum and cork tiles

▶ *In a narrow hallway, work towards the edges of the floor from a centre line running down the entire length of the hall. Plan well and adjust the centre line as necessary before you start. Butt the tiles closely together and trim at the edges. Note the use of a threshold strip at the doorway to prevent the tiles being kicked up and damaged.*

Laying flexible floor tiles is an easy and straightforward job. The tiles are simply butted together without any need to grout or fill joints. They are easily cut to shape and are much easier to handle than their sheet equivalents. Tiles are also more versatile than sheets as they can be used decoratively: by incorporating a border, for example, or creating a focal point in the centre of a room.

With linoleum tiles it is possible to inlay a simple design. A straightforward chequerboard pattern using two colours, for instance, can be enlivened by insetting key squares at the centre of four big squares. Ready-cut designs can be purchased for laying or you can cut and lay your own key squares.

Before starting the work, prepare the floor as described on pages 152–153. It is particularly important for the floor to be absolutely level as even the smallest bumps or hollows will be visible on the finished floor and will spoil the effect. For the best result, use a latex smoothing compound.

If you are not using self-adhesive tiles, your supplier will advise you as to an appropriate adhesive. Unsealed cork tiles should be finished with a varnish as for floorboards (see pages 146–147).

Laying the tiles

Set out the floor as described on pages 156–157, although you should not really need to mark out a grid to cover the whole floor: being machine-cut, flexible tiles should – providing you follow the main guidelines – butt up against each other and remain square right up to the edges of the room. Begin in the centre and work towards the walls.

Use the correct adhesive for the materials. As a general rule, a water-based acrylic adhesive, which is free from unpleasant solvent fumes, is quite suitable. Spread the adhesive with a notched spreader of the size recommended by the manufacturer and covering only the area that you can comfortably tile before the adhesive spoils. Roll the adhesive smooth with a paint roller wetted with adhesive to minimize the risk of the adhesive pushing up under the tiles and showing through as ridges.

Self-adhesive tiles are much easier and less messy to lay. All you have to do is peel off the protective backing paper and place the tile in exactly the right position, before pressing it down firmly.

Place the first tile on the intersection of the two main guidelines and press it down from the centre outwards to expel any air that might be trapped beneath which could cause bubbling. Butt the next tile firmly against it and press it down. Clean off any adhesive from the surface with a clean rag. Tile one side of the room, laying the tiles in a pyramid pattern and working towards the wall. If the tiles that follow the main guidelines are correctly positioned, all the subsequent tiles

▲ *Particularly convenient to lay are the cork tiles that come with a self-adhesive backing, but no cork tile is difficult. Remember that unsealed tiles should always be varnished, and that prefinished tiles benefit from a coat of varnish if they are being laid in an area where they need to be regularly mopped – kitchens or dining areas.*

Laying soft flooring tiles

should fall into place precisely; with factory-cut tiles there are always two edges to work from, ensuring that the tiles are laid square.

Fitting border tiles

When all the main tiles have been laid, start laying the border or edging tiles. Place a tile exactly over the last whole tile in a row. Lay another tile on top that so its edge butts up against the skirting board. Mark a line along the opposite edge on the loose tile underneath. Cut this latter tile along the marked line using a sharp knife and a straight edge; the trimmed-off piece should fit neatly into the border. Repeat the procedure for each of the rest of the border tiles. Any obstacles can be dealt with in the same way that they would be if you were laying sheet vinyl (see pages 172–173).

Laying key squares

Key squares not only add interest to a bland floor, they make a simple chequerboard pattern more sophisticated, and introduce a new colour into a flooring scheme with relative ease. If pre-designed, ready-cut materials are not available locally, you can cut your own key squares.

You can use the same technique to cut out other shapes such as stars, but remember that cutting out complicated shapes is a highly skilled operation and that it is all too easy to end up with gaps between the inlaid pieces. Before cutting up a floor, practise on some scrap pieces first or stick to simpler shapes.

Mark out the square onto stencil card and cut out the shape. Divide the square into four equal triangles with a pencilled cross. Place the stencil over the intersection of four tiles making sure it is correctly positioned with the lines of your pencilled cross aligning exactly with the lines between the tiles. Using a fine pencil, trace the outline of the key square onto the tiles. Then cut out the outlined square using a sharp knife; cut along the lines as carefully as possible and gouge out all the linoleum within the square. Use the same stencil to mark out a square on the linoleum you intend to inlay. Carefully cut out this square and glue it firmly into place in the appropriate position on the floor.

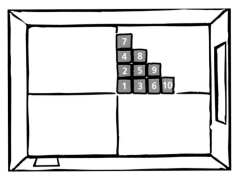

1 Having established and adjusted your centre lines, start to lay your tiles from the middle and work outwards.

2 Spread the adhesive with a notched spreader; the glue must not be so ridged as to affect the surface of the tiles.

3 Alternatively use adhesive-backed tiles; they are less messy to lay. Peel off the backing and press into position.

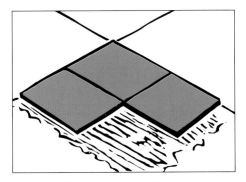

4 Position the first tile at the two guidelines' intersection and work outwards, smoothing out any trapped air.

5 To cut a border tile, lay one tile on the last whole tile, another against the wall, and mark the loose tile.

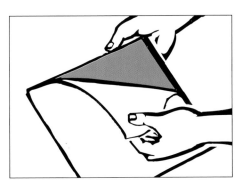

6 Cut along the marked line; the piece you trim off should fit neatly into the space at the border.

7 To position a key square, place the stencil on the intersection of four tiles and trace the outline in pencil.

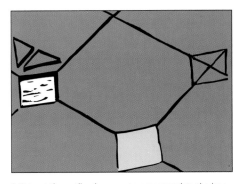

8 Cut out the outlined corners to accommodate the key square, spread glue on its back and press into position.

Decorative wood flooring

Wood has long been used for flooring, as it is so readily
available as well as being an easily worked and practical
material. Diverse, beautiful and with a natural complexity
and depth unmatched by most other flooring, it is a
material with infinite appeal. Its practical, easily cleaned
and durable surface always feels warm and welcoming.
The distinct elegance and luxury of new decorative wood
flooring probably makes it the only flooring material that
will look right in virtually any room in the home.

It is perhaps unwise, for practical considerations, to install wood floors in very wet environments; a bathroom that is continually soaked would not be an ideal place for a wood floor.

New sanded and sealed wood, without any distracting gaps between the boards, is particularly at home in a modern and minimalist interior, which relies on simple, clean shapes and the use of natural materials for maximum impact. But wood also suits any style of contemporary room. A more traditional, country room, on the other hand, might look better with old, wide boards that have moved and twisted over the years, leaving gaps and some imperfections. Yet, such is the never-fading appeal of wood that this type of floor could equally suit a more up-to-date scheme. And wood always ages gracefully, in most cases darkening and gaining character as the decades pass.

Each type of wood has its own distinctive colour and grain, ranging from pale ash to the near black of ebony, although this is too rare today to be used for flooring. In between are a multitude of warm browns, reds and rich beiges. Furthermore, wood can be stained for additional colour variations. The grain can be almost plain, with a few small flecks, or have wild, swirling patterns with great diversity in the colouring. The degree of patterning is dependent upon the type of wood but varies considerably within species. The plainer knot-free examples tend to be more expensive than types with a busy grain and some imperfections.

The colour range of wood is such that it will live happily with most other types of furnishing. The hues are generally muted and neutral. Plain wood is usually sufficiently interesting to be left as it is, although it provides the perfect backdrop for loose-laid rugs when a little extra splash of colour and warmth is desired.

Fortunately, wood is one of the easier flooring materials to install. Traditionally, wood planks are laid over timber joists but these days floating floors are widely used. All that is required to create a brand new floor in a matter of hours is for pre-finished boards to be fitted together over an existing subfloor.

Manufactured wood floors are nearly always made from a hardwood, even if the real wood element is only a thin veneer. The lighter-coloured hardwoods are traditional wood types such as ash, maple and beech. Beech and maple have a particularly unobtrusive grain, ideal for rooms where a light and plain-looking floor is wanted, which would not add any textural detailing to a room. Oak is a darker hardwood with a particularly interesting grain and it is widely used for flooring. Other darker woods such as walnut are sometimes used for floors, too, as are more exotic species such as mahogany and teak, which are a rich golden-red colour. Take care when choosing wood types; tropical hardwoods are likely to have come from non-sustainable primary forest.

All woods can be stained to change their colour. The lighter woods such as beech are frequently stained or have a semi-opaque lacquer applied, to lighten their colour even further. If you want a rich and warm tropical wood, a stained European variety can actually make a very satisfactory alternative. Quality can vary; the more expensive grades are sold knot-free and uniform in colour while the cheaper qualities can vary considerably in colour from board to board. All the hardwoods are sufficiently tough for domestic use, although some, such as maple, are much harder than others. The laminated products can be even harder than solid boards because the middle layer is designed to cushion shock. New pine, however, is very soft and can be dented easily.

◄ *Modern wood-strip floors have a clean simplicity that suits contemporary taste particularly well; the pale and neutral tones of the floor here show off the furniture without any unnecessary distraction. Available in a wide variety of colours and textures, wooden floors are stylish and practical and will complement almost any room.*

▲ *This room is perhaps typical of modern informal living. The floor is light-coloured with a discreet grain that provides an easily cleaned, non-allergenic surface which is warm and inviting at the same time. Largely unadorned, there is a rug to provide extra colour and comfort while the rest of the furniture sits easily in the scene.*

Directory of decorative wood flooring

Manufactured decorative wood floors of all types can be supplied either unfinished or pre-finished. Unfinished floors are plain, bare wood, so that the floor is installed before it is sanded and lacquered. Although the wood is initially cheaper to purchase, the finishing costs must be added on when you are deciding what you can afford. Because installation is much quicker and less disruptive, pre-finished floors are very popular. A major advantage of pre-finished floors is that the finish is applied in factory-controlled conditions and is even. An acrylic lacquer is frequently used and this can be several millimetres (fractions of an inch) thick or have a subtly textured surface for greater slip resistance. Some pre-finished floors have wear guarantees lasting as long as 25 years, although guarantees of 5 to 10 years are more usual.

Solid wood

A solid wood floor consists of planks of wood laid across joists or over an existing subfloor. Traditionally, the boards would have been quite wide and straight-edged but most modern solid wood flooring is tongued and grooved. Tongued-and-grooved boards eliminate draughts from under the floor and make any shrinkage and movement of the planks less noticeable. The main advantage of a solid floor is that it can be resanded several times, making it an excellent long-term proposition.

Load-bearing wood flooring should be at least 18mm (¾in) thick, although wood being fitted over an existing subfloor can be as thin as 1cm (⅜in). Most manufactured hardwood floors are made up of quite narrow strips, 57–83mm (2¼–3¼in) wide, which means that any shrinkage is less noticeable because the gaps are smaller, and any warping of the boards is less pronounced. The boards can be either finished or unfinished. **1**

Wood-block flooring

This type of flooring comes as tongued-and-grooved solid wood blocks 2cm (⅜in) thick, which can be arranged in a variety of patterns. The most common arrangements are herringbone and double herringbone patterns with a straight border two blocks wide around the edge. There is also a brick arrangement, in which the blocks are laid side by side in a staggered fashion, or a basket weave, when alternate blocks are laid at 90 degrees to one another. The blocks have to be laid on an existing subfloor using a bitumen-based adhesive to make a very durable floor that can be resanded many times. **4**

Laminated wood floors

This is man-made board constructed of several layers. The top layer is a veneer of decorative hardwood but the layers beneath are usually either plywood or blockboard, or sometimes cork. The great advantage of a laminated-board floor is that it is relatively cheap to produce because the hardwood layer can be as thin as 1mm (¹⁄₁₆in), although it is normally more substantial than this. Another advantage is its potentially greater directional stability because the laminated construction minimizes the movement of the boards once they have been fitted. Laminated-board floors are available in thicknesses ranging from 6mm (¼in) up to 20mm (¾in). The heavier grades can be sanded down several times.

This type of floor is generally pre-finished with a hard-wearing layer of lacquer. The finished effect is very similar to a solid floor although each 'board' is often actually two or three times wider than the laid floor would suggest in order to facilitate speedier installation. Some laminated floorings have become so sophisticated that it is debatable whether they are wood floors at all; there is one product available as 3mm (⅛in) strips that are glued down rather like vinyl tiles, the real 'wood' element of the floor being an extremely thin sliver of the product. **3**

Parquet

Parquet floors are made up of individual wood blocks, which were traditionally 6mm (¼in) thick but

which are now usually 10mm (⅜in) thick. They are available in different sizes and types of wood.

Parquet can be used to create the same types of pattern as wood-block and even more complex designs such as 'parquet de Versailles'. The blocks can either be fitted to the subfloor individually or they are supplied as panels ready to be laid. There are some elaborate and sumptuous designs

which are, in fact, marquetry floors made up from small pieces of dark and light woods. The wood is laser-cut to size in a factory and comes ready to fit with a cotton backing that is glued onto the subfloor. Finely detailed borders are also possible: a Greek key pattern, for instance; and complex arrangements of stars and repeat patterns can be used over an entire floor. Needless to say, this type of floor is hugely expensive and definitely requires professional installation, but it is one of the most beautiful floorings available. **5**

Wood mosaic panels

Wood mosaic is a very economical type of flooring. The small wooden blocks are either fixed to a backing material that holds the whole pattern together, or the blocks can have a paper fixing on their face that is removed after fitting.

The blocks are arranged in various simple patterns: basket-weave pattern, for example, or Haddon Hall. To fit wood mosaic, the panels are glued to a subfloor, normally in the same way as flexible tiles (see pages 174–175), although some are available with a self-adhesive backing. In addition, some types of mosaic panels are tongued and grooved so that the tiles slot together without the risk of high spots (one panel sitting proud of others) developing. Mosaic panels are supplied either pre-finished or sanded ready for subsequent varnishing. **2**

Laying wood-strip flooring

The easiest type of wood flooring to lay is a floating floor where boards are fixed together but not attached to the subfloor underneath. The boards can be either solid or constructed of laminated-layers and are available in various thicknesses. The thicker boards last longer but do obviously raise the level of the floor more noticeably.

The subfloor needs to be reasonably level, although it does not have to be perfect. The new flooring can be laid over existing floor-coverings, even on a fitted carpet if it has a firm, close pile. Indeed, laying a floating floor over an old carpet in an upstairs room will increase the sound insulation between that floor and the room below. Equally, you can lay an underlay of some sound-insulating material such as cork – or a special foam. Concrete floors must be dry. If there is dampness coming up through the floor, it may be necessary to install a damp-proofing membrane (see pages 152–153).

Most wooden floors require a 10mm (¼in) expansion gap around the edge, but check with your flooring supplier. Ideally, the gap is covered by the skirting board but if it proves too disruptive to remove the skirting board before laying the floor, the gap can be covered subsequently with wooden beading, or it can be filled with a cork strip. The boards should be laid parallel to the longest walls, so if the room is square, it is up to you which way you lay the boards.

Normally, the boards of the first row are laid full width and the boards of the last row

▲ *The direction of the planking here draws the eye down the corridor into the room beyond. This not only looks better but is easier to install too. Floors such as this wood-strip floor can be laid on almost any surface, providing it is smooth and level. For a neater finish lay the floor first and then fit items such as kitchen units and skirting boards.*

are sawn down their length to fit. It is worth measuring the room before you start in order to calculate how wide this last strip will be, because if there is only room for a thin strip, the floor will look more balanced if you saw the first boards down the middle before you start, making both the first and last strips cut strips of a similar width.

Laying the floor

Start laying the boards against the longest and straightest wall. Place 10mm (¼in) wooden spacers against the wall for the expansion gap and lay the first board against them, with the grooved edge facing the wall. Apply a little wood glue to the tongue on the end of this first board. Slot the next board against the

Laying wood-strip flooring

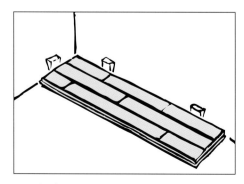

1 Lay the first board against wooden spacers, with a little glue on the end and the grooved edge facing the wall.

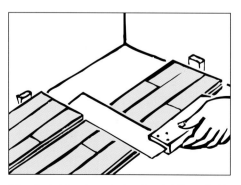

2 Turn the last board round, place it against the wall with a spacer, mark it in line with the laid board, and then cut.

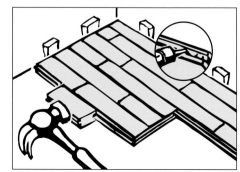

3 Use a hammer and an offcut gently to tap the glued second row of boards home securely.

Laying wood-mosaic panels

1 Adjust your centre point so that as many border tiles as possible can be trimmed in whole blocks.

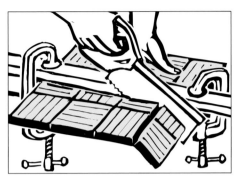

2 If you have to cut through the middle of a block, clamp the panel in place on a workbench and use a tenon saw.

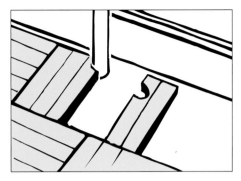

3 To fit neatly around a pipe, separate two blocks from the backing, cut two semi-circles and re-position snugly.

end of the first board and continue until you reach the last board along this row. To cut this board to fit, turn it round and place it against the wall, allowing for the expansion gap, with the tongue end facing the tongue end of the board already laid. Using a try square, mark the board to be cut in line with the edge of the laid board. Cut the board with a tenon saw, glue the tongue on the end and slot the cut board into position with the cut end facing the wall. Position wedges at both ends to prevent the boards from moving.

To prevent the joint lines creating lines across the room, which would spoil the floor's appearance, lay the boards with staggered joints – like bricks in a wall. Use the remainder of your first sawn board as the first board of your second row, with the cut end facing the wall. Apply a 10cm (4in) run of wood glue at 60cm (24in) intervals into the groove and push the board firmly into posi-

tion. Using a hammer and softwood block or an offcut slotted into place, gently tap the board home. Wipe off any glue from the surface of the wood with a damp cloth. Continue working across the floor until you reach the penultimate row.

Position the first board of this row without any adhesive and then lay the last board on top so that it butts up against the wall allowing for the expansion gap. Run a pencil along the edge of the top board to mark the board beneath it. Remove the board and saw carefully down its length along the pencil line. Next glue the uncut board in place and finally the cut board – to complete the floor. Knock wedges into position to hold the floor tightly together until the glue has set.

To fit the boards around a radiator pipe, mark the board where the pipe will go and drill a hole (allowing room for expansion). Cut a V-shaped slot from the edge of the

board to the hole. Lay the board and glue the cut-away piece back into place. The easiest way of fitting boards around an architrave is to place an offcut against the architrave and to cut away the base of the architrave. The board can be slid underneath the architrave for a neat finish. Alternatively, use a profile gauge (see pages 154–155) and cut the board so that it fits the profile of the architrave.

Laying wood-mosaic panels

Wood-mosaic panels are easy to install. The technique employed is similar to that used for laying flexible tiles (see pages 174–175). You need to use an adhesive specially formulated for wood-mosaic panels, unless you decide to lay self-adhesive panels, in which you case you simply need to peel off the backing.

As the tiles are harder to cut than flexible tiles, try to adjust your centre lines so that at least some of the tiles around the edge can be trimmed in whole blocks – by merely cutting the backing between individual blocks. Where cutting through the wooden blocks is unavoidable, you will have to clamp the panel between a workbench and a wooden batten to immobilize the blocks and then use a tenon saw.

At a doorway, cut the bottom off the architraves as described for wood-strip flooring; or use a profile gauge and cut out the profile using a coping saw. The panels can be made to fit neatly around pipes by separating them from their backing at the point where the pipe is to go and then cutting two semi-circles out of the blocks. Once fitted, these are held in place by the adhesive backing.

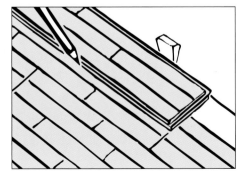

4 With the last board on top of an unglued penultimate board, mark the latter's edge on the board beneath; cut.

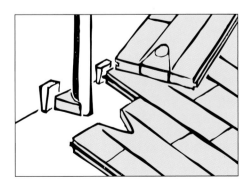

5 Mark the position of a pipe; drill a hole in the relevant position; cut a V from there; fix both cut piece and board.

Soft floor-coverings

In cooler climates carpet is favoured for its warmth
and is used widely for anywhere that requires bright
colour and pattern, combined with a luxuriant quality.
Once a luxury only for the better off, the invention of
synthetic materials, coupled with steadily rising
standards of living in the industrialized countries, has
brought carpet within the reach of most people.
Ironically, nowadays, carpet can be one of the cheapest
and most practical flooring materials available.

Good-quality carpet is still costly and specially dyed, and woven wool carpet remains one of the most expensive of floor-coverings. Most wool carpets contain a proportion of nylon to increase their durability but cheaper carpets are generally made with a higher percentage of synthetic materials and are more loosely woven than traditionally made wool carpets. High-quality carpets, though, can be made from synthetic materials as well.

Carpet is, in fact, very hard-wearing and is suitable for most environments, including those that have to endure very heavy foot traffic; it is widely used in commercial applications. It is not suitable, however, where there are likely to be spillages – kitchens and bathrooms, say. If carpet is used in a demanding environment, it will need more expensive, specialized care than would a hard floor.

As carpet is such a forgiving material, the tendency in some countries has been to lay it in almost every room, but in recent years the sophistication of modern heating systems has meant that the sense of warmth afforded by carpet is no longer so important, allowing other materials, particularly wood, to gain in popularity. The recent increase in allergies to dust mites, which carpet harbours by the million, has also caused more people to turn to alternative flooring materials. For some rooms, however, carpet will always be a sensible and popular choice of flooring. Indeed, nothing can beat a fully carpeted bedroom in winter, feet sinking into the soft pile, warm and softly reassuring, even noise deadened to a soft hush. Inner sanctums – living rooms, studies – unlikely to be tainted by mud benefit too from that special sense of luxury.

Carpet is available in a huge range of colours and types. Darker colours are more suitable for areas, such as hallways, where dirt is likely to be brought in from outside, and you can choose from a vast range of neutral colours for a simple backdrop to an overall decorating scheme. Or you can make the carpet more of a focus. Borders, repeat patterns and central motifs are all easily incorporated into a carpet design. Stair carpet is available nowadays with attractive borders which can add restrained interest to an otherwise plain flight of stairs.

◄◄ The cool austerity of bare brick is considerably softened by the warm, deep pile of a traditional wool carpet. This carpet has been made on a traditional narrow loom and has alternating strips of patterned and plain carpet with the same background colour, the strips indicating that this is a traditional Axminster or Wilton carpet.

◄ Natural floor-coverings have become very popular recently. This formal drawing room is enlivened by the gutsy texture of rush matting which looks perfectly at home with all the different elements in the room. Note how this floor-covering is not fitted but stops just short of the walls, the edge being finished with braid.

Carpet is not the only type of soft flooring. Natural floor-coverings are increasingly popular, because they can provide a room with an elegant and sophisticated backdrop and are excellent for showing off colourful rugs. They are derived from plant fibres woven together to form a mat.

The fibres of natural floor-coverings are often left undyed, so they take their colour from the plant from which they are made. They may be bleached to offer a lighter, more neutral look. Although some plant fibres will not take dye, others can be dyed very successfully; sometimes an interwoven coloured weft gives the material a subtle hint of colour whilst retaining its overall natural, undyed look.

Part of the appeal of natural floor-coverings is their very definite texture. Some are quite soft and can be woven into fine patterns; others seem rough and hairy. These are used to create textured and robust patterns.

Natural floor-coverings are economical to buy but they do not always wear well and they can be very difficult to clean. It is worth buying matting that has been factory-treated with a stain inhibitor, although latex backing also makes day-to-day care easier and the matting can be laid like rubber-backed carpet.

There is also a range of wool-based floor-coverings made in new ways to consider. These combine the practical advantages and underfoot softness of carpet with the character and look of natural floor-coverings.

Directory of soft floor-coverings

Soft floorings fall broadly into two types: carpet, which is made from wool or a number of man-made fibres; and matting, which is made from plant fibres. The names given to carpet refer to the way the carpet is made rather than the materials used in its manufacture. The two broad categories of carpet are woven carpet, in which the pile is woven through a backing material, and non-woven carpet, in which the pile is attached to the backing by various methods using adhesives. Natural floor-coverings are plaited and woven to form strongly textured and patterned surfaces. The look and feel of each type of natural floor-covering derives from the special characteristics of the original plant. Incorporating wool fibres in natural floor-coverings is a recent development.

Woven carpet

Axminster

Axminster, one of the hardest-wearing types of carpet, is woven at the same time as the backing material, normally a natural fibre. The pile consists of a series of U-shaped loops threaded through the backing material. Latex or adhesive is often applied to the backing to help keep the tufts in position. A multitude of differently coloured yarns can be woven together into the carpet, giving unrivalled potential for complex colour and design combinations.

Wilton

Wilton carpet is woven at the same time as the backing material. The pile is made from a continuous yarn that weaves through the backing material and appears on the surface as a series of loops. The loops can be left uncut, which is known as 'Brussels weave', or cut to form a straight pile that resembles Axminster. Although the continuous yarn theoretically makes Wilton the strongest of carpets, it limits

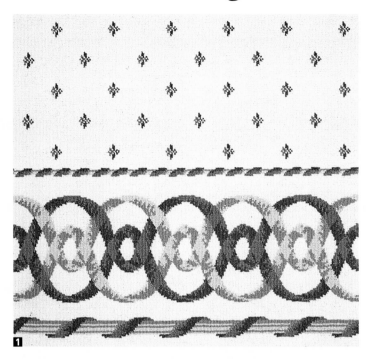

the design potential as only a maximum of five colours can be used together. Wilton can be woven as a textured design with two yarns, usually of slightly different shades of the same colour; one shade is a higher cut pile, the other is shorter and left looped to create a three-dimensional pattern. **1**

Tufted carpet

In tufted carpet the pile material is woven into an existing backing material, usually a synthetic product, and held in place with a latex adhesive, before a second layer of backing material is fixed to the latex for greater structural strength. The backing can be either a natural product, which will require a felt underlay, or rubber, which can be fitted directly over the floor. Although not as strong as traditional types of carpet, the construction of tufted carpet is nonetheless effective and cheap to produce. Due to limited design possibilities, this type of carpet is usually plain or made up of two interwoven colours or a series of very simple dots or crude shapes. Designs can, however, be printed onto the surface for added interest.

Bonded carpet

Bonded carpet is made by fixing the pile to a ready-made backing with an adhesive. It looks similar to a plain woven carpet but uses less pile yarn as this is not woven in and out of the backing material.

Fibre-bonded carpet

In fibre-bonded carpet, fine, synthetic fibres are forced through a backing material with barbed needles, and are then fixed onto a fairly rigid backing, PVC, for example. This construction method produces a thin, coarse carpet without a conventional pile but with a hairy appearance instead. It is often used in commercial interiors.

Flocked carpet

Flocked carpet is made electrostatically: an opposing electrical charge between the pile material and the backing causes the pile fibre to be attracted to the adhesive-coated backing in an upright position, like hair standing on end. Patterns can be printed onto the short pile, which is easily cleaned, making flocked carpet ideal for areas subject to heavy soiling.

Carpet tiles

Carpet tiles consist of carpet attached with adhesive to semi-rigid backing squares. Their main advantage is that a damaged or worn area can be replaced without having to renew a whole carpet. Tiles from underneath furniture, for example, can be swapped with those in high-traffic areas to even out wear. They also allow easy access to under-floor wiring or plumbing. Extra replacement tiles should be purchased with the main batch, as those bought at a later date will almost certainly be a slightly different colour. **2**

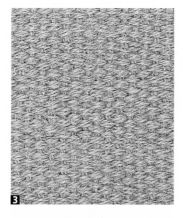

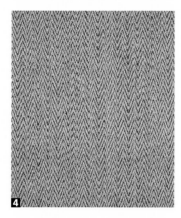

Natural floor-coverings

Coir

Coir is a fibre derived from coconut husks that is spun and woven to make a latex-backed floor-covering. Its coarse and hairy quality makes a strongly textured flooring material which can be woven into many different patterns – basketweave, bouclé, herringbone, diamonds – some wonderfully three-dimensional. Natural coir is a warm brown colour but a more neutral, bleached form is also available. Coir can be dyed with plain colours, or several colours can be interwoven to create subtle two-colour weaves or vividly coloured stripes. Probably most familiar as the traditional doormat, it is indeed particularly suitable for areas of heavy wear such as hallways, as it is easy to clean with a stiff brush and vacuum cleaner. **3**

Jute

Although traditionally used as a carpet backing, jute is one of the finest and softest of natural floor-covering mat-erials. It is made from yarn derived from the fibrous stalks of the jute plant and woven into either a bouclé or herringbone pattern. Naturally a pale neutral brown, it can be bleached to create a very pale cream, or dyed and then woven, rather like a carpet, to create simple coloured patterns. Different weights of yarn create finer or heavier textures. As jute is so soft it is ideal for bedroom floors, but it is not a practical material for areas of heavy wear as it is difficult to clean and develops watermarks if it gets wet. **4**

Rush

Rush has been used as a flooring material since the Middle Ages when it was strewn onto cold flagstones to soften them. The wide, thin rush leaves are plaited and then woven into strips that can be stitched together to cover any width of floor. The edges can be finished with a finely woven rush braid. Rush matting is a pale, warm brown that can look fantastic in the right setting. It is more expensive than other types of matting and should only be used with care in areas of light wear. It should not be allowed to dry out otherwise it will become brittle and crack, so it is perfect for floors that are slightly damp; alternatively sprinkle it with water every week or two.

Seagrass

A grass grown rather like rice in wet paddy fields – hence the name – this is a hard yet smooth fibre that is woven onto a latex-backed floor-covering as a simple or a basketweave pattern. An excellent neutral colour in its own right – brown and beige strands with a definite green tinge – it cannot be dyed; the fibre is impermeable. Wefts of other colours can be worked in, however, to provide a hint of colour. Seagrass is a versatile and practical material that can be used in most situations. Because it is relatively non-absorbent and hard, it does not often stain and dirt is easily brushed loose. Freshly laid seagrass has a wonderful smell rather like new mown hay.

Sisal

From the leaves of a spiky bush rather like a yucca plant, sisal can be spun into yarns of different weights. It is woven into a variety of simple patterns that can look subtle or strongly textured depending on the weight of yarn. Unlike other floor-coverings, strands of sisal can be dyed before being spun, so it can be dyed as a plain colour or interwoven in two or more colours. Different colours are also spun into a single yarn to give the finished product a subtly coloured, metallic quality. It is also possible to paint sisal quite successfully; borders and all-over patterns can be applied either before or after the material is fitted. It is a durable yet gentle material that can be used for most situations. **5**

Wool-based natural floor-coverings

Made from wool-and-nylon mixes or a sisal-and-wool mix, these are a halfway house between carpet and natural floor-coverings. The fibres are spun into a heavy yarn and then woven into various simple patterns, as plant-based floor-coverings would be. There is no loose pile to speak of as the material is tightly woven, the aim being to create the robust texture of plant-based floor-coverings. At the same time wool-based floor-coverings have the advantage of being softer and more easily cleaned than their plant-based cousins. Neutral browns and beiges or subtle, washed-out brighter hues are the most favoured colours. Some have had a herringbone, bouclé or other weave dyed into the pile, which, from a distance, makes them look like textured materials but with an ordinary pile.

Laying carpet

Carpet is made from either natural wool or a variety of synthetic materials – rayon, polypropylene, or nylon – all with different properties that are used according to the carpet's function; the fibres can be mixed to combine their various advantages. Synthetic materials are cheaper than wool, and synthetic carpets can be very hard-wearing although their appearance may be less attractive. They also melt if a cigarette end is dropped on them. Wool is a natural, environmentally friendly product; it wears well and has an excellent appearance and superior insulation properties. Most wool carpets contain some man-made fibres for increased durability – usually 80 per cent wool: 20 per cent nylon. Quality is classified according to the carpet's suitability for a particular purpose: so, 'extra heavy' is very good-quality carpet appropriate for a tough, commercial environment.

All types of carpet are available in a range of widths up to 4m (13ft) to suit different room sizes. Wider, or broadloom, carpet is better for situations where seams are to be avoided, although some people prefer the look of narrow-strip carpet, associated as it is with the more traditional and exclusive methods of carpet manufacture.

The pile of carpet is either looped or straight. Looped carpet is usually woven from one long length of yarn that loops in and out of the backing material, while straight pile is made either by cutting the tops off the loops or by inserting short lengths of material into the backing so that the two ends stick up. Pile varies in length. Short-pile carpets resist flattening more readily. They tend to look good for longer, although this does depend on the pile density and material. Long-pile carpets feel more luxurious, although very long pile has gone out of fashion. One way of making the pile more resilient to flattening is to twist a wool yarn tightly while heating it, rather like crimping hair, before weaving: twist carpet appears more textured than a smooth, velvet pile and is a good choice for areas, like stairs, that have to endure heavy traffic.

Woven-backed carpet

Traditionally, carpet has a jute or hessian backing but sometimes it is woven polypropylene. Woven-backed carpets are laid over a rubber or felt underlay which helps to even out irregularities in the subfloor and also makes the carpet feel softer and more substantial. Rubber feels softer underfoot but felt is more resilient and thus a good choice for an uneven floor or a carpet that needs stitching together. A combination underlay combines the qualities of both.

Laying woven-backed carpet is a tricky task for the amateur; it is, however, a very quick operation for a skilled person and comparatively inexpensive. It is probably not, therefore, worth laying such a carpet your-

Laying carpet

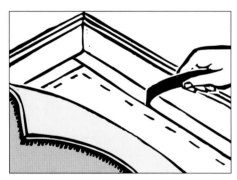

1 Fix underlay and tape to floor. Butt carpet against first wall, trim, and secure – removing backing from tape.

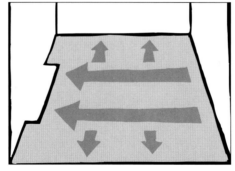

2 Walk the carpet from the fixed edge to the opposite wall, fit, and fix. Work to remaining two edges and fix.

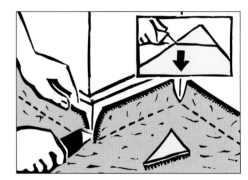

3 Make release cuts at external corners and trim diagonally at internal corners to ensure carpet lies flat.

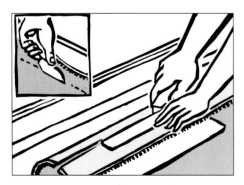

4 To trim, press into base of skirting with bolster chisel to score, turn back, and cut – on a board, along metal edge.

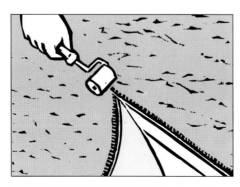

5 To make seam, bed one edge on length of carpet tape, butt up the next piece, and bond with seam roller.

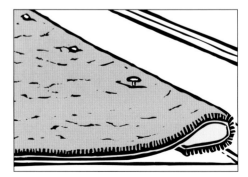

6 Alternatively, cut carpet slightly oversize, turn under and staple or tack through the double thickness to fix.

self, particularly as if it is not properly laid, unstretched woven-backed carpet will ruck up and wear very quickly.

Rubber-backed carpet

This is a cheaper type of carpet than woven-backed carpet; it has a rubber backing bonded to the carpet, which renders a separate underlay unnecessary. Felt paper is laid over the floor instead to stop the rubber sticking to the surface when the carpet is subsequently replaced. The main advantage of rubber-backed carpet is that it does not have to be stretched over gripper strips to fit. Having simply cut it to size, rather like laying sheet material (see pages 170–173), it can just be taped into position, although you can turn the edges under and tack it down.

Lay the paper underlay and apply double-sided tape down the longest, straightest wall. Keep the tape's backing paper in place, butt the carpet up to the wall, and trim it if necessary. Remove the backing paper from the tape and stick down this edge of the carpet. Stretch the carpet across the room to the opposite wall, fitting carefully at corners with release cuts, as necessary. Walk the carpet flat and trim this opposite edge to fit, before securing on a strip of double-sided masking tape as before. Finally, walk and stretch the carpet flat to the other sides of the room, and trim and fix these edges in position with tape.

Use a bolster chisel to press the carpet into the base of the skirting, and score a line along this junction. Turn back the carpet and cut along this line against a metal straight edge on a board. To make a seam, bed one edge onto a length of carpet tape and then butt up the first edge of the second strip. Press down the edges firmly with a seam roller.

If you prefer, tacks or staples can be used to fix the carpet edges. Having cut the carpet oversize, turn under excess and tack through the double thickness of carpet.

Laying carpet tiles

1 Mark the direction of the pile, place tile face down over the gap and mark the overlap by making slight nicks.

2 Cut tile, as marked, with a sharp knife on a board. Border tiles should be secured with double-sided tape.

Carpet tiles

Carpet tiles are very easy to install. The principles for fitting them are the same as those for lino or cork tiles (see pages 174–175) except that carpet tiles should not be glued permanently in place. Use a tackifier adhesive that will fix the tile and yet will still allow it to be easily pulled up and repositioned. Alternatively, in areas where the tiles are likely to move and under heavy furniture, fix tiles using double-sided carpet tape. Make sure the pile all faces in the same direction, following the arrows marked on the back of the tile or running your hand through the pile to see which way it lies.

Border tiles are easily cut to size. Place the tile upside-down over the gap between the wall and the last laid tile, with the tile against the wall. Make two nicks on the tile, one on each edge, adjacent to the edge of the tile underneath. On a cutting board, using a craft knife and metal edge, cut the tile between the two nicks. Reposition the offcut at the wall; it should fit the gap exactly.

▲ The rather stark look of this bedroom, created by the monochrome colour scheme and skeletal, twisted metal furniture, is softened by the addition of a thick, highly textured carpet with a woven diamond pattern. An expanse of snow-white carpet can create quite a dramatic effect, but bear in mind that such carpets rarely look spotless for long.

Laying natural floor-coverings

▶ *Sisal is versatile; it can be woven robustly, as here, or it can be finely woven. This basketweave sisal matting is installed in a similar way to a fitted carpet using gripper rods so that it fits neatly against the walls, and does not ruck up when the chair is moved. But natural floor-coverings are glued rather than stretched into position.*

simply butted together, although the use of an extra adhesive bond is recommended on the joints. Always lay the floor-covering with the pattern of the weave running in the same direction. Unroll the floor-covering in the room in which it is to be laid at least 48 hours before fitting to allow it to acclimatize.

Laying the underlay

Begin by nailing or gluing the gripper strips into position 6mm (¼in) away from the skirting, with the gripper spikes facing the walls. Use a tackifier adhesive to secure the underlay to the subfloor. This type of adhesive does not go solid to form a permanent bond, but stays slightly tacky so the floor-covering can be lifted at a later date without damage to the subfloor. Apply the tackifier adhesive with a notched trowel or paint roller according to the manufacturer's instructions. Allow the adhesive to dry to clear, as specified by the manufacturer – depending on conditions, approx. 40 minutes. Unroll the underlay over the adhesive with the rubber side down and trim it to fit against the gripper strips; each length of underlay must butt up against the one already laid. Go over the floor with a carpet glider or a long-handled soft broom, pressing down firmly to ensure a good bond. The natural floor-covering can be laid over the underlay immediately.

When you buy a natural floor-covering – unlike many carpets – you will have to pay quite a bit extra for fitting and underlay. The labour cost can be much higher than for conventional carpet-laying because carpet fitters tend to dislike laying natural floor-coverings. As the underlays can also be quite expensive, laying your own natural floor-covering can make a significant saving.

Before embarking on such a project, however, bear in mind that some aspects are tricky. For example, some materials can be difficult to cut to size. They have to be glued to the underlay, which is stuck to the subfloor, and then gripper strips are installed to help hold the floor-covering in place and minimize any shrinkage. It is possible to lay natural floor-coverings without an underlay but the finished result will not be as com-

fortable to walk on and any slight irregularities in the subfloor will quickly manifest themselves as wear ridges.

Plan the laying before beginning work. Natural floor-coverings come in strips 4m (13ft) wide so that all but the largest rooms can be laid without a seam. Remember to add 7.5cm (3in) on to each edge for trimming. Any seams should run along the longest side of the room. Rooms more than 4m (13ft) wide will require another strip of floor-covering. If the extra width required is less than 2m (6ft 6in), you can order a strip half the length of the room. This can be cut down the middle and laid end to end for greater economy although it will mean that there will be an extra seam to live with.

Natural floor-coverings require no complicated sewing of seams. The seams are

Laying the floor-covering

Cut the material roughly to size, allowing an extra 75mm (3in) on all edges for trimming. If the room is more than 4m (13ft) wide, start at the wall furthest from the door and lay the material loosely into position on the floor. Mark the edge of the floor-covering with a pencil or chalk line as a rough guide for the application of the adhesive. Roll the floor-covering back on itself and away from the wall, without moving the whole piece, and exposing half the floor area. Use a suitable notched spreader and apply the correct amount of permanent carpet adhesive to the underlay. Some of the rough-backed floor-coverings, such as coir, will require the use of a coarse spreader which applies a greater quantity of adhesive in order to ensure a strong bond. Your supplier will advise you.

Laying matting

Carefully roll the floor-covering back over the wet adhesive and go over the glued area with a carpet glider to press the material into place. Now roll the unglued half of the floor-covering back on itself and repeat the process on the other side. If a second strip of material is required, only apply the adhesive within 20cm (8in) of the marked line. The second strip should be cut to length allowing the same extra 7.5cm (3in) for trimming, as described above. Then overlap the second piece over the first by 7.5cm (3in) and cut the excess from the wall, again allowing a margin for trimming. If a third strip is needed, the trimming will only be necessary on the final length.

The second strip can be glued into place as described for the first length starting from the seam. Remember to leave a 20cm (8in) strip at the seam without glue. Finally, glue the half-strip adjacent to the wall.

Trim the excess from the walls with a sharp knife, taking great care not to cut yourself with the knife or snag your hands on the gripper strip spikes which are very sharp. Fold the material against the skirting board and cut it along the base – against a board to protect the skirting – ensuring that you allow enough material to tuck into the gap between the gripper strip and the wall.

Trim the seam or seams using a straight edge and knife. Cut through both of the overlapping strips at the same time for a perfect finish. Place a piece of hardboard or plywood underneath the floor-covering to prevent the knife slicing into the underlay. Cut edges do not need binding because the floor-covering is backed, which prevents fraying. Fold back the edges of the seams and apply adhesive to the underlay and press the edges firmly down. Go over the whole floor again with the carpet glider or broom, or a roller, to ensure the floor-covering is firmly bedded into the adhesive. Finally, use a bolster chisel to press the material home at the edges for a neat finish. In a doorway a binder bar is a safe and easy option. Fix the bar in position adjacent to the doorstop, mark the position of the centre line on the floor-covering and trim. Press it in place under the bar with a bolster chisel.

1 Secure gripper strips close to skirting, spikes facing the wall; if nailing in place, use cardboard to protect skirting.

2 Apply tackifier adhesive with notched trowel up to the strips to fix the underlay to the subfloor; let dry to clear.

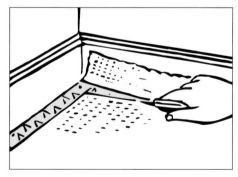

3 Lay the underlay rubber-side down and trim to fit against gripper strips; press firmly for good bond.

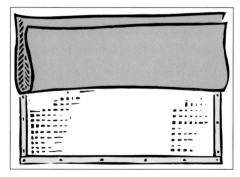

4 Roll back material on itself, apply adhesive on exposed half, roll back matting, and press. Repeat with other half.

5 Taking care to avoid gripper spikes, trim excess with sharp knife at base of skirting against a protective board.

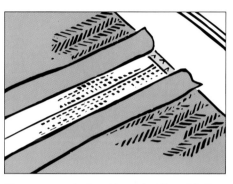

6 For a seam, overlap two strips, and cut through both layers onto a board. Fold back, glue and press into place.

7 Use a bolster chisel to tuck the trimmed floor-covering snugly into the gripper strips at the edges for a neat finish.

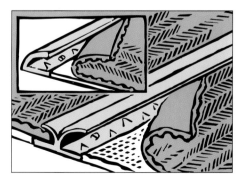

8 Cut binder bar to length with a hacksaw, nail in place, trim floor-covering to fit and press home with a chisel.

Unfixed flooring

The weaving of carpets and rugs is an ancient tradition
embraced by virtually every society in the world at some
time, whether small independent groups of nomadic tribes
or a large collective society. Rugs and carpets are made for a
far greater diversity of reasons than any other type of floor-
covering. Rugs afford warmth and a degree of comfort for
people inhabiting colder climates and mountainous regions
and also make an important aesthetic contribution to any
environment regardless of its physical location.

Most carpets and rugs are constructed from one of two types of weave. Tapestry or flatweave rugs have no pile. The weft is woven over and under the warp threads and pulled tight. Pile or tufted rugs, on the other hand, have a softer and more luxurious surface and are made by knotting individual strands of wool into the warp. In tufted carpets, the number of knots per square inch determines the fineness of the weave. Carpets with a high number of knots per square inch can incorporate intricate curved or floral designs and will also feel softer to the touch, while those with a lower density of knots per square inch are generally characterized by geometric designs.

Traditionally, carpets were dyed with natural dyes derived mainly from local plants, but today both chemical and vegetable dyes, or a combination of both, are employed. Natural dyes are considered superior because they give softer and more attractive colours that age gracefully, although it is possible to find exceptional chemically dyed rugs that have the same qualities.

Most countries have their own distinctive design traditions. Carpets from the East usually follow a design style and colourings peculiar to the tribe or region of origin of the carpet. Designs in the West tend, instead, to reflect the style of a particular period. Architects and designers have often tried to design rugs and carpets alongside their more usual occupations: Morris, Voysey and Mackintosh, amongst many others, all produced a wealth of rug designs. Today rugs can be very modern and free-form in style; many are arguably artworks for walking on.

Because a large carpet is inevitably a major focal point, it is better to purchase a fine rug first and decorate a room around it than the other way around. Carpets look best when placed over a neutral background; both wood and natural floor-coverings such as seagrass make a perfect backdrop, and stone can also look very sophisticated. Rugs can be used to provide a simple focal point or relief in a large floor area or to provide a greater sense of warmth and softness on an otherwise hard and unrelenting flooring material.

Buying carpet and rugs

Buying a carpet is something that should be approached with great care. Beware of spending a huge sum on a carpet because the carpet trade is like the secondhand car market: some carpet dealers can only be described as of somewhat dubious character. It can be extremely hard to tell if you are buying a genuine antique or a modern copy; equally, it can be difficult to distinguish between natural and chemical dyes, and the former would nearly always add to a carpet's desirability – and price! It is better to go to a reputable dealer who will give you a fair deal. It is also probably more sensible to buy a carpet from a reputable source on home territory than when on holiday; it may well be possible to secure a bargain when travelling but equally you might end up with something that could be purchased more cheaply and easily at home.

Backings and fixing

Although it is possible to put a rug straight onto the floor, it will last longer and will not move around if it is placed on an underlay. This is particularly important on wooden floors, as rugs are potentially dangerous if not held in place. The underlay used with fitted carpet can be used but the corrugated types should be avoided for thinner carpets, especially the thinner flatweave rugs like kilims, because you will see and feel the corrugations through the carpet. Generally, dedicated rug underlays are better, as these are specially designed to prevent the carpet physically moving on the floor.

While giving added protection from high heels and general wear and tear, particularly if the carpet is lying on a hard surface, underlay will have the added benefit of giving the carpet a softer feel. Thinner varieties can be obtained for use over a fitted carpet.

◄ Wall-to-wall carpets are not everyone's preference, but while bare floorboards are wonderful in summer, they can look cold and stark during the winter months. This is when rugs, the most adaptable of all floor coverings, come into their own. This thick, hard-wearing rug with a chequerboard weave would help to ward off winter chills.

▲ A quirky interior, with more than a touch of the surreal, called for an unusual floor covering. This white rug decorated with parallel lines of black spots has a trompe l'oeil twist: the two spots in the centre have been cut out and replaced with plastic veneer to give the illusion of wooden flooring beneath.

Directory of rugs and carpets

Flatweave carpet and rugs

Kilims

Kilims are flatweave rugs made from wool. The term usually applies to rugs that come from an area stretching from Eastern Europe through Turkey and Iran to as far east as Afghanistan. For many years considered the poor relation to hand-knotted carpets, kilims became popular in the 1960s when the bold, bright colours and simple geometric designs appealed strongly to the hippie culture of the time.

Kilims can be woven much more quickly than a tufted carpet – important to nomadic peoples who were constantly moving on. Designs are much simpler and more geometric than those of the knotted carpet because of the limitations of the type of construction. Kilims frequently contain a series of slits, which occur when one colour of yarn adjoins another along a warp thread. Designs incorporating a series of long vertical lines are thus avoided as the length of resulting slits would weaken the kilim. Usually created using horizontal and diagonal lines with very short verticals, designs vary according to origin: Anatolian kilims are very colourful with particularly abstract geometric patterns, whereas traditional eastern Bulgarian kilims have a predominant black background characterized by floral motifs rendered in pinks, beiges and gentle yellows. **1**

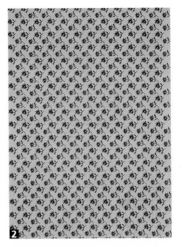

Dhurries

The dhurry is the traditional flatweave rug of India. Dhurries are made from cotton rather than wool, giving them a slightly harder quality than a kilim. As the dyes are taken up differently by the yarn they tend to be less brilliantly coloured than their wool cousins. Traditionally there were three types of dhurry: the bed dhurry was placed under a mattress; the prayer dhurry was divided into a series of prayer niches; and the room dhurry was intended for use in rooms. This latter type was the largest and could be enormous. The finest dhurries were woven in Indian prisons between 1880 and 1920 – an enlightened policy designed to relieve the monotony of prison life. Sometimes carpet designs were copied from imported Persian or Afghan carpets by prison warders or their wives, or new designs were drawn. Because of the influence of colonialism, traditional folk design tends to be watered down. Mosques or Hindu shrines appear frequently, although they tend to be quite geometric due to the construction of the dhurry. Today, dhurries are manufactured in factories for the Western market and are characterized by insipid pastel colours and sparse designs.

Needlepoint

Needlepoint is the sewing of a yarn, usually wool, using a variety of different types of stitch, into a ready-made canvas backing. During the eighteenth century in England needlework carpets enjoyed some popularity. Copies of traditional designs are made today in needlepoint as very few of the originals survive, along with designs associated with other types of carpet, in the style of the French Aubusson, for example. The origins of this particularly elegant and sophisticated style were tapestry-woven carpets made almost exclusively for French royalty and aristocracy, which as a consequence makes the originals rare and extremely valuable.

Needlepoint is also used in the recreation of other eighteenth- and nineteenth-century European designs and for creating original work as well, although many of the rugs are likely actually to be made in places such as China where labour costs are low. **2**

Tufted carpet and rugs

Gabbeh

The gabbeh is a rug woven by the tribes of southern Iran. They are quite unlike more traditional Oriental carpets as they are woven for personal use in a much freer and more spontaneous style, their designs often taken from the weaver's immediate surroundings. Animals, birds and people and simple shapes such as diamonds or the tree of life also feature, the motifs often being used more sparingly than on traditional carpets with larger areas of plain colour. Largely made in factories now to satisfy Western demand, gabbehs are made from either natural or dyed wool, left unclipped and shaggy.

Floral carpets

A 'floral' carpet is a carpet that makes use of curvilinear design, as opposed to rather more geometric representations and patterns. This can only be achieved by the use of a very high density of knots per square inch,

4

5

which produces highly complex and fine designs. Carpets of this type, such as the 'Persian' carpet, are manufactured in more organized workshops from designs produced on paper by a designer. It is then woven into a carpet by a weaver who has little to do with the design process. Carpets made in this environment used to be produced almost exclusively for sale and export, often for the Western market. They are characterized by highly sophisticated and intricate designs of a very delicate nature, often produced using very dark and rich colours.

Geometric carpets

Geometric carpets are principally produced by tribal peoples, either nomadic or living in villages. The designer is also the weaver and the carpet design is made up as it is woven, although unlike the gabbeh mentioned above, the design uses traditional patterns and motifs. Each of these carpets is unique and is made for the use of the particular tribe. Some will be made for sale, and this is becoming increasingly common today as these smaller peoples enter the

global economy. Tribal carpets originate from a huge area stretching from Turkey through Iran to Afghanistan. Each region or tribe has its own distinctive designs and colour range, although some motifs are universal and are also utilized in floral carpets.

The reason for this type of design is cultural and is in some part due to the difficult conditions under which the rugs are made. Tribal rugs are less formal and looser in style than floral carpets. More folk art than classical art, this type of rug is rather more suited to contemporary interiors than the manufactured carpets; consequently they are much in demand.

Contemporary carpet

These are modern carpets produced by artists and designers – art for the floor. They are produced for their own sake as purely decorative pieces, unlike some of the more traditional types of carpet. Designs vary widely according to the style of the individual designer, and can be entirely free-form and expressive, or more representational, either with or without borders. Some of these rugs are woven in the tradi-

tional carpet-producing areas of the East using hand-knotted wool and vegetable dyes, like the more traditional carpets of these regions. There are very few hand-woven carpets produced commercially in the West today as labour costs are so high. This type of carpet may well be made in China or India, or in other parts of the East, and indeed, most patterned rugs (whether designed or plain) originate from these areas.   **4**

Fabric rugs

Rag rugs

The early American settlers living in more remote areas produced many of their own goods, rugs being one such item. These people were very frugal and consequently were very good at recycling materials. As a result they made rugs from strips of cloth obtained from clothes that had reached the end of their useful life and wove these into rugs of several different types. Rag rugs were the most common type of rug and were made from narrow strips of cloth that are woven on a loom, rather like a flatweave rug. The rug can be made from a fabric of one colour or other colours can be incorporated. Rugs of this type have a simple knobbly appearance that is a very

cheap and effective way of covering up a bare floor. Today, rag rugs are easily found, but are likely to be made in places such as India.   **3**

Braided rugs

Three or more strips of cloth are plaited together to form a braid rather like a person's hair. These braids are then joined together to make a rug. This type of rug would be started in the middle and worked outwards, with more braided lengths added to the outside of the rug until the desired size was reached. This type of rug was often circular or oval. The colour of the rug is dependent upon the colour of the cloth used in making the braid. The overall colour of the rug is controlled by varying the colours of the fabric used in each subsequent braid and in this way a pattern can be built up. Today this type of rug is often machine-made, although it is possible to make a rug at home in the same way that the original settlers did.

Hook rugs

Hook rugs are pile rugs made by pulling a yarn or a strip of fabric through a backing material using a hook. The pile is made from a series of fabric loops that can be varied in height to create either a firm, close pile or a longer, more shaggy look. The pile lengths can be varied on the same rug to create a more sculptured appearance. The hoops can be clipped in the same way as a Wilton carpet to create a soft, more velvety feel. Quite complex designs can be achieved using this technique, depending on the density of the hoops and the number of colours used. Representational rugs, more abstract patterning, or copies of oriental designs can be tried. Hooped rugs can look more sophisticated and less folksy than the other types of rug made from recycled materials, but this will obviously be dependent on the design used.   **5**

Floorcloths

Floorcloths are an alternative to conventional carpets and rugs. They are really the forerunners of linoleum which, in turn, was displaced by vinyl. Floorcloths were popular in the eighteenth century as they could be painted to imitate expensive pile carpets. Sailcloth was the material generally used; it was given many coats of linseed oil to create a very heavy and durable surface. Floorcloths could be left plain or painted with a design. They were used in corridors and hallways, indeed any area of heavy wear that would have quickly ruined a carpet or rug and in the servants' quarters where a real carpet would have been considered extravagant. The great advantage of a floorcloth is that it can be painted with any imaginable design at minimal cost. Moreover, it is a surprisingly hard-wearing 'carpet', making it an excellent choice for a hallway runner. And it can be made to fit any particular room's shape.

Making a floorcloth

Preparation

A floorcloth is really a blank canvas onto which any design can be painted, rather like an artist paints a picture, except that the floorcloth requires a protective coat of varnish once the design has been completed. Artist's canvas can be used but it is probably better to visit a theatrical scenery supplier and buy the canvas from them, or to buy cotton duck, as this is a satisfactory, inexpensive alternative.

You can make a very large floorcloth as it is possible to buy cotton canvas up to approx. 9.5m (10½yd) wide and any length, although some of the cheaper alternatives may be a little narrower. You will need to buy a piece of canvas slightly larger than you expect the finished floorcloth to be because the canvas will shrink by approx. 7.5 per cent once it has been primed. You will also need to allow 2.5cm (1in) extra all round to fold under as a hem – to make a neat edge.

It will be necessary to find a space larger than the floorcloth in which to work comfortably. Begin by ironing out any creases in the canvas with a conventional steam iron. The canvas should be stretched before priming otherwise there is a risk of it rucking

▲ *A floorcloth makes a stylish and original alternative to a carpet or rug. The turquoise blue used here was probably specially mixed to offset the warm ochre used on the walls, while laying the cloth over grey colourwashed boards shows off both the colours and the design to maximum effect. In fact, the floorcloth forms the focal point of the room.*

up unpredictably once it has been painted. A frame like an artist's stretcher can be made up to the required size using 5 x 2.5cm (2 x 1in) timber and the canvas fixed to that; otherwise pin the canvas along the edge to an existing smooth and level floor using plenty of drawing pins, though these will leave small holes. The canvas should be sized before painting; traditionally, artists use an animal skin glue that is purchased in granular form. A quicker and easier alternative is to brush the canvas with a modern PVA adhesive and then let it dry. Now prime the canvas with

two coats of ordinary acrylic wood primer/undercoat, allowing two hours between coats; it is a good idea to give the underside of the canvas a coat too as this will give the floorcloth greater rigidity. The canvas will shrink so that it becomes very taut. Only at this stage can the drawing pins be removed, or the canvas be taken off its stretcher. Use a metre rule and pencil to mark out the size and shape of the finished floorcloth and additionally mark a second line about 2.5cm (1in) away from the first line towards the edge of the floorcloth. Cut away any excess material beyond this line. Use a sharp craft knife and a long metal rule and score along the first line – very gently, just to break the weave of the fabric – and cut diagonally across each corner on the marked line. Apply a fabric adhesive or PVA up to the marked edge and fold it on the scored line to give a neat, finished edge. The floorcloth is now ready for painting.

Painting the floorcloth

Almost any design can be painted onto a floorcloth; as usual, the only limiting factor is the skill and patience of the painter. Indeed, there is no reason why a full-scale painting cannot be created on the floorcloth; it is, after all, a blank canvas. It is probably better to stick to conventional rug designs used on a floor or to copy a picture of a real rug that you particularly like but cannot afford to buy. Simple chequerboard or grid-type patterns can be painted rather as they

would be on a wooden floor: decide on the width of the border and mark it out using a pencil and ruler and then mark out the squares onto the centre of the floorcloth. If the floorcloth has one predominant background colour, paint the entire piece with that colour first before marking out the design. Floorcloths should be easier to paint than real floors as they are usually smaller and more manageable; the smallest floorcloths can even be painted on a table. More complex designs will need to be carefully planned and drawn out on the canvas, while complex borders or repeat motifs may be more easily painted using a stencil (see pages 140–141). As with painted floors, the paints themselves do not take any wear so you can use either artist's oils or acrylics, both for tinting colours and for painting in fine detail. You can use either oil- or water-based paints, either as opaque colour or, for a softer, more washed-out look, semi-transparent tones.

Finishing

Once the paint has dried, the floorcloth must be varnished. Use an acrylic varnish or an oil-based polyurethane, but remember that this latter will yellow with time. It is better to avoid floor lacquers as these are very hard-wearing but rather brittle and may crack. The floorcloth should have at least three coats of varnish – or more, if it is going to be subjected to especially heavy wear.

Once the varnish has dried, the floorcloth can be placed in its final location. If this is a hard surface (wood or tiles), it is best to stick the floorcloth down with a few squares of double-sided carpet tape to minimize skidding and to prevent the edges of the floorcloth from being continually rucked up, which will eventually cause the edges to curl and the paint to crack. Or try attaching an underlay as you might to a rug, because this will not only prevent slippage but also give the floorcloth a more luxurious, padded feel.

▲ Floorcloths make particularly effective runners, though they can be made to fit any space. The plain yellow floorcloth warms the walls in this hallway, while the one in the foreground is embellished by a simple and effective design that picks up on the wall colour for a delicate balance, making it the epitome of discreet classical style.

Making a floorcloth

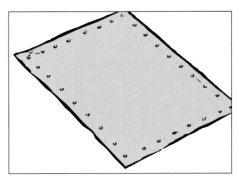

1 Having ironed the canvas to get rid of any creases; fix it flat with pins along the edges – or on a stretcher.

2 Size the canvas as described, brushing on the glue and leaving it to dry, before priming it with undercoat.

3 Cut away any excess canvas outside the scored line on the sized, shrunk canvas, leaving a turn-under allowance.

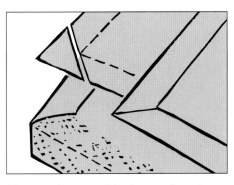

4 Cut across the corners of the allowance diagonally; turn under the glued, trimmed edge to make a neat finish.

WINDOWS
& DOORS

One of the wonderful things about windows and doors is that they are architectural. Good windows have structure and form which relate to the history of your home, its date and style. They genuinely have that often misrepresented quality, 'character'. Your windows may be things of beauty: elegant multi-paned Georgian sashes, Victorian with an interesting pattern of glazing bars, or rolled-steel casements original to an Art Deco house or block of flats.

Even a plain one-over-one Victorian sash, a row of pretty cottage casements or a handsome pair of modern wooden French windows can have proportions and an honesty of appearance which make the windows a pleasure to look at. Large plain windows in a contemporary building with a modernist or industrial look are equally attractive in a different way. Windows should be decorated in a decisive style which is sympathetic to, though not necessarily imitative of, their particular period and setting.

Doors, too, come in innumerable shapes, sizes and styles. Flush doors (a relatively modern invention) are flat on both sides. Panelled doors have recessed sections, often

▲ *A modern flush door is painted a strong dusky blue, the same colour as the bedroom walls. The cylindrical steel knob reinforces the clean simple lines of this ex-workshop in London's Spitalfields. The radiator, painted to contrast with its background, becomes a feature rather than being disguised as one might expect.*

edged with moulding: two or six panels if Georgian or Georgian-inspired, four if Victorian or Victorian-inspired, three if early twentieth century. Cottage doors, made to varying degrees of sturdiness and sophistication from planks, the simplest usually being the oldest, are known as battened doors.

In spite of their significance and tremendous potential, windows and doors are often treated as the poor relations in a decorative scheme. Walls and floors are usually planned first, followed by the furnishings, while the windows and doors are thoughtlessly painted white or cream, or perhaps stained brown and varnished, and expected to merge into the background. This is not to say that in many circumstances white, cream or brown are not exactly the right colours. The point is that whatever colour and treatment you decide upon for your doors and windows, the choice should be a positive one, not a case of 'Oh well, white will do!'

Colour, even strong, vibrant colour, can look wonderful on the wood- or metalwork of doors and windows. It draws attention to them so that they make a greater contribution to the whole look of a room, perhaps reducing the need for elaboration elsewhere.

The original doors in your home are more likely than the windows to have been altered over the decades or centuries in response to changing fashions in interior decoration. Panelled doors were often simply covered on each side with a sheet of hardboard which can be removed and the door restored. If your doors are not consistent with the period of the house, or just do not look right for some other reason, you can simply change them.

Inappropriate flush doors may be replaced by panelled doors of the right size and period. These can be found in reclamation yards, bought new off-the-peg from DIY stores, or made for you by a joiner. Alternatively, you can make flush doors look like panelled doors, at a fraction of the cost of replacing them, by adding mouldings corresponding to the size and position of real panels.

Like doors, windows come in a variety of styles which reflect their history and sometimes their geographic location. A normal

sash window has two panels, one above the other, one or both of which slide up and down. In some areas sashes are to be found which slide from side to side. The panes of sash windows are often subdivided by glazing bars, which generally adds to their interest and charm.

The other most common window type is the casement, which swings open from one side. It is usually part of a series of similar-sized windows, some of which may be fixed in place rather than opening. Like sash windows, casements may be subdivided by glazing bars; a very old casement may be a leaded light, in which the divisions are strips of lead forming small diamond shapes. In a twentieth-century house a casement may be part of a metal window unit which includes a couple of fixed lights below a transom (a section which also swings open but is hinged at the top) alongside the casement.

◄◄ *In the charming inner hallway of an English country house, sage-green paint unifies several doors of different styles: one is a ledged and braced cottage door, one four-panelled, and the other has glass panes in its upper half.*

◄ *Large sash windows, painted plain white and uncluttered by curtains or blinds, make a strong contribution to the cool, airy atmosphere and pared-down look of this drawing room in a French country house.*

Other interesting window types include two which let light in through a roof. The dormer is a vertical window which with its housing breaks through the line of a sloping roof, usually in an attic room. A skylight or rooflight is usually overhead, following the line of the roof. The porthole is, as you would expect, a round window.

Windows are usually dressed with curtains or blinds. Practical and visually pleasing, they offer exciting opportunities for using fabric of almost every type, as well as rugs, blankets, saris and other purpose-made textiles.

Internal shutters are an often overlooked alternative to curtains and blinds. Handsome and clutter-free, they cut out draughts, noise and light with great efficiency, give a house added security and take up little space when folded open. Although curtains can be drawn across them at night, shutters can be splendid enough in themselves to require no cover-up. Sensibly, they are gaining popularity again.

▲ *Two pairs of dramatic arched glazed double doors allow light and (when open) fresh air to flood into a living room in Umbria in Italy. Outside, a simple iron balustrade across each window contributes to the modern look and prevents the possibility of anyone falling out.*

You are fortunate if your house has its original folding or rolling wooden shutters, which may be nailed up waiting to be rediscovered. If the original shutters are missing, a joiner can be commissioned to make new ones, or you could make them yourself if you have the necessary carpentry skills.

There is, of course, no requirement for you to cover your windows at all. Shutters, curtains, blinds or anything else are used for a number of reasons, such as privacy, draught exclusion and visual appearance. But if a window has none of these requirements, and especially if it is well proportioned or looks out on a striking view of countryside or rooftops, leave it bare. This will be particularly effective in a room with a fresh, clear-cut, simple look.

Not all windows are situated in external walls or the roof, nor are they always see-through. A window in an internal wall gives

▲ *Typically, tall sash windows in an eighteenth-century house would have had hinged shutters which folded back neatly during the day. When closed at night they excluded draughts and lent a degree of security. Nowadays, shutters can be made by a carpenter to fit almost any window – at a price.*

▶ *A simple, blue-framed dormer window, adorned only by a plain white roller blind, looks out over a pantiled roof and into the greenery of trees. Dormer windows push out through sloping roofs in order that rooms in the eaves might receive adequate light, a little extra space and some non-sloping headroom.*

'borrowed' light to the room beyond. A glazed door does the same job; it might have been originally designed as such or it could be a traditional panelled door with some or all of its panels replaced with glass.

Plain clear glass is usually the obvious choice for most windows because it lets in the most daylight (which is, after all, the point of a window). But there may be windows in your home – on the stairs or overlooking a less-than-beautiful view, for example – where this need not be the primary consideration. A window which looks out into a dingy basement yard or other depressing sight, for instance, could be replaced with tough glass bricks which block the view while letting in plenty of light. (It is possible to have an interior, or even exterior, wall built using these bricks, which are usually associated with industrial buildings of the early twentieth century, to allow daylight

▲ *Light floods through this renovated warehouse in Anvers, France, thanks to an expanse of metal-framed interior window which even has its own opening casements. Double doors are left bare on one side, painted white on the inside only. External windows are veiled with unbleached linen.*

into a room.) Alternatively, the clear glass of the window could be replaced with a type that you cannot see though.

Rooms such as bathrooms and lavatories call for glass which provides privacy, such as patterned glass. This could be embossed, where a raised pattern has been stamped onto the glass, or etched with a flat pattern. Etched glass is now manufactured in a variety of fairly traditional all-over designs. A plainer alternative is frosted glass. Where a window is in two sections one above the other, as in a subdivided casement or a sash, you can install frosted glass in the bottom half only for privacy and still get maximum light through the top. You can quite easily make 'frosted' glass to your own design using a self-adhesive plastic (see pages 222–223).

Yet another approach would be to commission an artist to design and make patterned glass which would be unique to your home. Alternatively, you could create your own design, perhaps incorporating your initials or something else with special meaning for you, and have it sandblasted onto a pane of glass by a local glazier.

Coloured panes and window shelves are two further assets you could use in planning the decoration of your windows. They can be used to create a degree of privacy or to mask a view, as well as for their intrinsic decorative qualities. You can either replace the existing panes with coloured glass or paint colour onto it (see pages 222–223).

Window shelves - strips of toughened or laminated glass - are fixed like shelves across a window in the depth of the wall. Coloured glass objects look radiant exhibited there, or you could display a collection of items connected with the use of the room – shells and toy boats in the bathroom, perhaps, or antique cookery equipment in the kitchen.

Decorative finishes for window frames and doors

The technical advances made by big industrial paint
companies, combined with the recent upsurge of interest
in historical colours, traditional finishes, and in 'old-
fashioned' and organic varnishes, stains and paint, has
created a huge choice of materials with which to finish
doors and windows in any decorative scheme.

An increasing number of specialist companies, most of which offer a mail-order service to customers, have nurtured the renewed interest in paints and interesting finishes from the past as well as the enthusiasm for organic products and natural finishes. Many small manufacturers are proud of their particular products, which include items such as biodegradable varnish and milk-based paints.

Before making a choice about the type of finish and colour you want for your doors or windows, it is well worth undertaking some research to find out more about the range of available products. The first step is to visit a well-stocked decorating shop, where you can read information on the paint cans and pick up manufacturers' information and colour cards. Also ask specialist suppliers for their product literature.

An option for stripped woodwork in good condition is to leave it bare or treat it with a protective varnish or sealant, or to nourish it with oil or wax (see pages 218–219), so that the natural beauty of the grain contributes a decorative element. If the colour of the wood is unsatisfactory in any way, it can be modified with the application of a wood stain (see pages 218–219). This can be a conventional 'wood' colour or a more brightly tinted shade to complement any overall colour scheme. Many stains are widely available in the usual DIY and decorating stores but some specialist companies make stains that can be diluted as much as you want to produce a washed-out look on wood.

Paint is the most wonderful stuff and it can be used in a number of ways to draw windows and doors into a decorative scheme. In addition to conventional painting techniques, special treatments can be applied to create different effects (see pages 210–211), including a distressed finish, in which previous coats of paint are allowed to show through worn-away areas, chips and scratches in the top coat.

Among so-called 'new' colours are many vibrant shades inspired by eighteenth- and nineteenth-century house·decoration. These colours look magnificent on woodwork, emphasizing the architectural qualities of doors and windows. They are equally impressive whether the tone of walls and other features is pale, in which case they stand out, or strong, in which case colours on the woodwork add richness and variety to the overall look.

Some unusual modern paints which have caught the imagination of interior decorators can be used to create striking effects. Metallic-coloured spray paint, for example, was designed for re-touching exterior car paintwork but it can be applied in all-over swirls on a suitably primed door or with a stencil to create a pattern on doors or on fabrics for dressing windows. Paints designed for use on metal include all-in-one rust inhibitor, metal primer and top coat. They are easy to use and practical for metal windows and doors.

The choice of paint may have changed, but many of the old techniques for applying it have not. Whichever method you use, the aim is to have a smooth surface without blemishes at the end of the process. You could slap your paint on without any thought for technique, and as long as you work quickly and apply the correct thickness then the result will probably be perfectly satisfactory to the untrained eye. But the great attraction of techniques tested by use over a long time is that they work, and last (see pages 210–215). It is worth following them if you are serious about decorating because they are more likely than not to give good results with a minimum of fuss and mess.

Getting set up for decorating doors and windows involves little financial outlay. Compared to other decorating materials, paints, stains, oils and varnishes are inexpensive, though the cheapest is not necessarily the best; cheap paint contains extenders which fill up the can on the shelf in the shop but reduce its covering power at home. You do not need any special clothing (except for safety gear if you are using chemical strippers), just old, comfortable things which you do not mind getting splashed. The most expensive items are likely to be electrical equipment, such as a hot-air gun for stripping old varnish or paint, and a set of good-quality brushes. View these as an investment, to last you for many years.

▲ A pair of Spanish-style wooden doors has a flower motif carved into each panel, and paintwork which is so distressed that it remains in only a few mottled patches. Doors bought from reclamation yards sometimes still have attractive layers of old paint.

◄ In this house belonging to a designer of woven textiles, the colour scheme uses old-fashioned paints in sumptuous colours from the English National Trust range: dead flat (matt) oil on the doors and woodwork, and estate emulsion (which has a chalky rather than a rubbery finish) on the walls.

Preparing surfaces for decorative finishes

▲ *The doors and windows of this room have been painted with hard-wearing high-gloss oil-based paint. The better the surface preparation before painting, the smoother and longer-lasting the finished surface will be. In this case, the quality of finish is very important, as imperfections would be highlighted by the bold colour.*

How much preparation doors and windows require before they can be painted, stained or varnished will depend on whether they have been previously finished. What needs to be done to previously finished wood- or metalwork is dictated by the condition of the finish and what you want to cover it with.

The putty on windows must be sound before they are painted on the outside. Check the putty's condition before you paint and replace any that is dry, cracked or missing.

Discoloured patches in stripped woodwork can be bleached, as can large areas of wood that are an unsatisfactory colour, in preparation for a finish. Use specialized wood bleach, available from decorator's suppliers.

Preparing new wood

New wood requires relatively little preparation before paint, stain or varnish is applied. It must be clean and dust-free, however, as any debris will spoil the finish. Rough areas should be sanded and the dust wiped off.

Before new wood can be painted, the knots must be sealed with knotting solution to prevent them from seeping resin, which can stain the paint even after it has dried. It is a good idea to remove some of the resin before sealing the knots. To do this, apply heat using a hot-air gun to encourage them to weep, then wipe away the resin with a cloth soaked in white spirit. Apply the knotting solution with a small brush and wipe clean with methylated spirits. Two coats are ideal (it is quick to apply as it dries very fast), but one coat will suffice.

Preparing previously finished wood for painting or varnishing

If the existing finish is painted and in good condition, and door panel mouldings, architraves or glazing bars have clear edges and are not clogged with paint or varnish, wash the surface thoroughly with sugar soap or liquid sander (see pages 206–207). Rinse well and dry. If you are not using liquid sander, lightly sand the surface with sandpaper or wet-and-dry abrasive paper wrapped around a cork block to create a key for the new paint to grip, and to soften the edges of any chips in the finish prior to touching them up with primer/ undercoat. Bad chips may need filling and re-sanding. Always fill after the first coat of primer or primer/undercoat has been applied, as this helps the filler to grip.

If the existing finish is oiled or waxed, the wood will need thorough washing down before painting (see pages 206–207).

Paint or varnish in poor condition will have to be completely stripped and the woodwork freshly primed and painted. Dry, flaky paint can be brushed off with a wire brush or dislodged with a scraper. The surface must then be sanded, with extra attention being paid to any stubborn patches of old paint. For large areas use an electric orbital sanding machine.

Hot air gun: Thick, gungy paint that is clogging mouldings can be removed using a hot-air gun or by applying a chemical paint remover. If you use a hot-air gun, keep it moving along the wood to avoid scorching

Preparing painted surfaces

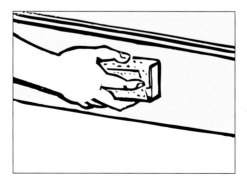

1 Use a sandpaper block to smooth surfaces and provide a key for painting. Work along the grain of the wood.

2 If the paint is hard to shift, or if large areas must be removed, an electrical orbital sander may be helpful.

and scrape off the melted paint immediately. Use a shavehook on any mouldings. Take care not to let hot paint fall on you. It may be advisable to wear cotton gloves for protection. Catch the scraped paint in a metal container such as an old baking tray and throw it away later, wrapped in old newspaper, in an outdoor bin, to prevent the possibility of fire indoors. When stripping glazing bars, add an attachment to the hot-air gun, with a rounded flat plate to one side, to protect the glass from the heat and the danger of cracking it.

Chemical paint strippers: Liquid and paste chemical paint strippers used in conjunction with scrapers and shavehooks are available for removing both oil- and water-based paint. On windows and doors use either a paste or a non-drip liquid or gel stripper. Other liquid strippers will, of course, run off vertical surfaces. Brush on the liquid and wait until the paint softens. Paste stripper is especially good for mouldings. Apply a thick layer and leave it for several hours. Once the stripper has had time to work, scrape and peel off the old paint and then wash down the surface. It is advisable to follow the manufacturer's instructions for application, removal, disposal of waste and, above all, safety to yourself. Paint strippers are necessarily corrosive, so protect yourself with goggles, gloves, and long-sleeved and long-legged workwear when using them, and keep the work area well ventilated. You may also need to wear a mask.

◄ *Rubbing back old paintwork creates an attractive distressed finish you may decide you don't want to paint over. Sanding has created uneven, rough patches of colour on this door and table, giving them a convincing look of age which complements the colourwashed walls.*

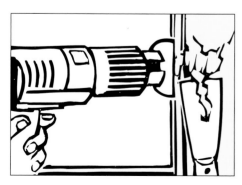

3 *A hot-air gun softens paint so that it can be scraped off. A heat deflector allows the gun to be used near glass.*

4 *Liquid stripper also softens paint. Brush it on, wait for it to work, scrape off the paint and wash the surface.*

5 *A paste remover is especially good for mouldings. Leave for several hours before peeling off, then wash down.*

Wood veneer and French-polished wood should never be cleaned in this way. Instead, use a specialist wood cleaner or, if the grime is superficial, wipe with a cloth dipped in a warm solution of water and malt vinegar, well wrung out so that it is barely wet. Wipe dry immediately.

Preparing new metal

Before painting new metal or finishing it with blacking, ensure it is completely dry and free from rust and grease. Rusty patches must be cleaned and cured with rust inhibitor before metal primer or paint is applied, unless you are using an all-in-one rust-cure paint.

▲ *The stripped pine sash windows and panelled window surrounds in this city bedroom help to create a clean, uncluttered feel. Their pale finish is emphasized by the milky whiteness of the limed floor, and is enhanced by the unlined calico curtains. Together, they provide a neutral background for the antique chair and bed.*

▶ *Rusty metalwork requires a fair amount of preparation before it can be painted: scrubbing down, cleaning, treating with rust killer and metal filler, and sanding. A little effort, however, pays dividends, and a smooth paint finish on a well-prepared surface can make once dilapidated metal frames look flawless.*

Preparing previously finished wood for staining

Because stain cannot penetrate paint, wood that has been painted must be completely stripped before stain can be applied; any overlooked patches of paint will give a blotchy and unsatisfactory result. Use a chemical stripper in liquid or paste form.

To remove any stubborn patches of paint that may remain after the initial stripping, scrub along the grain using wire wool dipped either in white spirit or in more of the chemical stripper.

Preparing previously finished wood for oiling or waxing

Before re-oiling, re-waxing or painting woodwork that has previously been oiled or waxed, clean it thoroughly to remove all the old waxy/oily deposits. Scrub the surface (not a veneered or French-polished surface) with steel wool dipped in white spirit, following the wood grain, then wipe down with a clean rag or paper towels. You may have to repeat this action several times. Finally, wash and dry the woodwork ready for treatment.

Preparing previously finished metal

If paintwork on metal window frames is in good condition it can be repainted with relatively little in the way of preparation. Just wash it with sugar soap or a solution of soda crystals, rinse and dry. Then sand the paint lightly, with fine sandpaper wrapped round a cork block, in order to create a key for the new coat of paint. Before starting to paint, thoroughly clean off any dust.

If the paintwork is in poor condition, however, it will require considerably more work before it can be repainted. Be sure to protect your eyes with goggles before brushing off all the loose material – rust as well as paint – using a sturdy wire brush. Next, scrub the metal with a solution of sugar soap or soda crystals, and rinse. Wipe down the entire surface with white spirit on a clean rag to remove any remaining grease. When it is thoroughly dry, paint rust killer onto bare or rusty patches, paying special attention to ensure it thoroughly permeates fixing boltheads, hinge areas and joints. When this has dried, fill holes and depressions in the framework with metal filler. Allow this to dry, then sand all over to create a smooth, even surface for painting. If priming the surface first, use a primer formulated specifically for metal which contains rust inhibitor.

Alternatively, strip off the old paint completely using a chemical paint stripper suitable for metal, and wire wool. A hot-air gun is of no use when stripping paint off metal, as the heat is absorbed by the metal, and the result is to bake the paint on.

Tools and equipment

The preparation of doors and windows for a new finish requires little in the way of specialist tools and equipment. In addition to the items described below you will need a screwdriver for removing ironmongery and door furniture before starting work.

- **Knotting solution:** an oily sealant made from shellac and methylated spirit which is painted onto the knots in new timber, especially pine, to prevent them weeping resin (see pages 204–205), which can stain a paint finish.
- **Sugar soap or soda crystals:** washing existing paintwork with sugar soap or old-fashioned soda crystals dissolved in hot water is a marvellous way of removing dirt and grease, and even decades of caked-on grime.
- **Liquid sander:** a solution for cleaning surfaces prior to applying a new finish. It is particularly useful for cleaning and smoothing intricate mouldings and corners.
- **Sandpaper or abrasive paper:** essential at every stage of preparation to feather the edges of cracked or flaked paint or varnish; to create a key on existing finishes ready for the next one; to smooth and level dried filler after application; and between new coats of paint for a really glossy result.
- **Wire brush:** extremely useful for removing flaky paint and rust from metalwork.
- **Hot-air gun:** the cleanest, neatest and, some say, the safest way to strip paint is using a hot-air gun. Shaped rather like a hairdryer, this machine melts paint, even layers deep, which can then be scraped off with a scraper or shavehook. Some have integral scrapers and heat deflectors which allow paint to be stripped near glass. When it is fitted with an attachment shaped to channel the heat away from the panes, it is an ideal tool for stripping paint from glazing bars of windows. Never pass your hand in front of a hot-air gun to test how hot it is, as it will burn.
- **Shavehook:** a triangular tool for scraping narrow surfaces. The type with curved edges is designed to be used on the curved profiles of mouldings and glazing bars.
- **Chemical paint stripper:** powerful paint strippers can be used for removing paint. Special strippers are available for stripping paint off metal windows. Use these with wire wool. Whatever type of chemical paint stripper you use, whether a paste or a liquid, always protect eyes and hands. Cover arms and legs, however warm the weather, and carefully follow the manufacturer's instructions for safe storage and disposal of chemicals.
- **Rust killer:** preparations can be painted onto metal windows and doors where rust has pitted the metal. Clean the areas to be treated of all rust and paint on the solution. Fill the crevices with metal filler to create a smooth surface before painting.
- **Filler:** often necessary when renovating wood or metal to repair damaged surfaces. It is normally applied after the priming stage. Use the right sort of filler for the material you are working on. If mixing a filler up yourself, rather than using a ready-mixed type, be sure to add thinner in exactly the correct proportions, as directed by the manufacturer.

Preparing to paint

▲ *Narrow double doors are useful for dividing two rooms which interconnect and are often used together, as they look more welcoming and create less of a barrier when open than a single, full-sized door. Here, a panelled effect is suggested with roughly applied white paint.*

To work out how much finish you need to buy, measure the surface area of your windows or doors to get a rough idea of the area that needs to be covered, and check the estimated coverage details on the cans. Check, too, whether the finish requires any treatment: for instance, some paints are sold in a slightly concentrated form and need to be thinned with white spirit or other thinner before application.

Most are applied with brushes although some, such as stains, can be put on with a cloth. It is worth having a few improvised tools to hand in addition to the necessary decorating tools. An old spoon, for instance, is useful for lifting paint-can lids, especially ones that have been resealed for a few days.

Equipment choices for different paint effects

Always buy the best brushes you can afford, preferably natural fibre and ideally pure hog's bristle. Check that each brush is well made, with no loose parts and with a solid pad of flexible, springy bristles. You need a selection of paintbrushes for different jobs. Another point to remember is always to use a brush of the appropriate size: one that is too big will not get the job done any more quickly. For painting windows and doors you will need a 2.5cm (1in) decorating brush for mouldings, a similarly sized cutting-in brush for glazing bars, a 5cm (2in) brush for flat areas on panelled doors and a 7.5cm (3in) one for flush doors. Look after your brushes properly and they will last for many years.

For creating decorative effects with a glaze, brushes in different sizes will be useful. They are used dry. A bristle grainer, for example, is invaluable when dragging (see pages 210–211), and a wallpaper-paste brush can be used to soften up lines. Combs are used for patterning glaze. These can be bought, made of steel or rubber, but can be customized easily from cardboard. For an even effect, cut the teeth evenly across the comb, or to create a freer effect, cut less symmetrical teeth. Rubber rockers for patterning a wood grain are like curved rubber stamps and are, quite literally, rocked over and through tinted glaze to produce *faux bois* finishes.

Lining brushes are useful investments for ensuring a stable flow of paint over a long distance and are especially suitable for painting *faux* panels. Sable and polyester lining brushes are best used for thin washes; try ox- and hog-hair ones for thicker paints. Sword-liner brushes have bristles that taper away to a point and these brushes are used for such effects as marbling, lining and detailed work.

Paintbrushes must be dry and clean before you begin a job. If a brush is new, work it against your hand to encourage the loosest bristles to drop out. More loose bristles can be removed by dipping the brush in water and then painting this onto newspaper or a rough surface such as an outside wall. Next, wash the brush thoroughly in warm soapy water, rinse well and squeeze out most of the water. To speed drying, spin the brush between your hands before suspending it with its bristles hanging downwards.

When you buy your brushes, drill a hole through the wide part of each handle (not through the metal) large enough to take narrow-gauge dowelling. Cut sections of dowelling long enough to sit on top of a jar and to extend each side so you can store the brushes suspended from the dowelling with their bristles hanging downwards when not in use (see pages 224–225).

Cleanliness

Cleanliness is important when applying any finish. When wet or tacky, surfaces can act like magnets to dust and dirt, which will spoil the final finish into which you have put so much effort. So even if you think your doors and windows are already clean, wipe them down again with either a clean cloth that is barely damp or a tack rag immediately before beginning decorating. Remove dust from the crevices of mouldings on doors and windows after sanding filler or paint. A vacuum cleaner with a brush attachment is useful for this.

To prevent dust and pieces of dried finish, especially paint, dropping into the can when you open it, clean the can before removing the lid, brushing loose bits out of the rim. If debris does fall in or if paint has formed lumps, strain the contents of the can through a piece of fine cotton muslin stretched over

▲ *Wide double doors look majestic when closed and create a generous, welcoming space when open. These examples have been painted in two colours, grey on the frame and mustard on the panels, both drawn from the curlicue pattern painted on the walls.*

another clean container. Always remove the skin on paint, however thin; do not be tempted to work it into the paint in the hope that it will disappear.

Cloths and neat rags without trailing threads are useful for wiping up spillages and drips but they must be clean to avoid transferring dirt onto fresh paintwork. Tack rags, for wiping surfaces clean, can be bought from DIY or decorating stores.

Protecting yourself and your furnishings

Lay protective sheeting everywhere, even where you think splashes will never reach. Fine plastic sheeting is impermeable but can be slippery and cannot be satisfactorily repaired if torn. Decorator's fabric sheeting, used by professionals, is available in sheets of various sizes and weights.

It goes without saying that you should wear old clothes; they are going to get splashed with paint. Do not wear wool, as wet paint will pick up the fibres. To protect your hands during decorating work, it is worth using special protective handcream, available from decorator's suppliers. This gets into creases and cuticles and is as effective a barrier as wearing gloves, but with none of the disadvantages. You simply wash it off when you have finished painting, leaving cuticles and creases clear and clean.

Using paint

▶ *There is no paint so shiny and hard-wearing as good quality oil-based gloss. The deep-blue gloss used in this country-style kitchen-cum-dining room is practical as well as decorative; it can be wiped down and will withstand the onslaughts of dirt and condensation.*

Paint choices

Oil-based gloss: Tough, hard-wearing and shiny, oil-based gloss paint is best applied in several thin coats (a minimum of two) rather than one thick one. Drying time is 12–16 hours although it may take several weeks, depending on the weather, for the paint to harden completely.

Oil-based silk: Oil-based silk paint has a smooth, silky finish that is not as shiny as full gloss paint. It is made by most industrial manufacturers but is given different names according to the brand. Drying time is 12–16 hours.

Oil-based eggshell: Oil-based eggshell has a smooth, hard-wearing surface and a slight sheen. It gives a more elegant finish than gloss. Drying time is 12–16 hours.

Flat oil: Also known as dead flat oil, it has a chalky, totally matt finish. Until recently it was considered to be exclusively a profes-sional paint. Now more readily available from specialist paint companies, almost all of which offer a mail-order service, rather than from regular DIY or decorating stores. It is well suited to the woodwork of doors and windows. Drying time 6–12 hours.

Water-based (acrylic) gloss: Although not as brilliant as oil-based gloss, acrylic or water-based gloss paint has other advantages. It does not smell strongly, it dries quickly and it gives a good shine. It can be painted on more thickly than oil-based gloss, but needs immediate working out as it dries rapidly. It is easy to wash off hands and brushes with water and soap.

Paint on woodwork

Both oil- and water-based paint can be used on woodwork. Traditionally, bare wood is prepared for top coats of paint with both primer and undercoat. Primer seals the wood and smoothes any slight blemishes. Undercoat, which can be coloured, gives a solid ground for the first top coat. All-in-one primer/undercoat is popular. The acrylic form dries quickly and can be painted over with oil-based paints as well as water-based ones.

Paint on metal

Metal requires special primer, filler, paint, thinner and cleaner. It is best to use products from the same brand. The more specialized paints do not need undercoat, and have rust-proofing qualities. They also need only one coat for complete coverage. For a really chalky, matt black finish on metal, consider using blackboard paint.

Applying paint

Paints need to be stirred thoroughly with a clean implement before use. A piece of wooden dowelling is ideal. However, do not stir non-drip paint or it will lose its non-drip qualities. If you do so in error, cover and leave the paint for several hours to stabilize.

Working with a heavy can of paint can be difficult and dangerous. Decant a proportion of the paint into a smaller paint kettle, or a clean metal or plastic container with a handle.

Loading the brush

Dip the end third of the bristles in the paint. A length of string stretched across the top of a paint kettle is useful for removing the excess. You need enough paint to work with, but not so much that it will dribble or form wrinkles as it dries. Read the instructions on the can for any additional advice about the particular paint you are using.

Whatever type of paint you choose to use, the way you load your brush and apply the paint can make all the difference to your technique and the finished paintwork. Avoid painting doors and windows during hot and humid weather, as the paint will not dry properly and there is a likelihood of moisture becoming trapped between coats to cause problems later on (see pages 224–225).

Applying paint

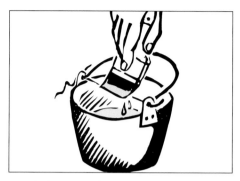

1 Dip the lower third of the bristles in the paint, and wipe off excess on string stretched tightly across the paint can.

2 Paint three downward strokes, parallel but not touching, in the same direction as the grain of the wood.

3 Without re-loading the brush, work over the strokes to spread the paint, at right angles to the original direction.

4 Finish by lightly 'laying off' in the original direction, to remove any brush marks and leave a smooth surface.

First brush-strokes

Start painting at the top. On flat areas, first apply three downward strokes of paint, parallel with each other but not touching and painting along the grain. Without reloading, work over these downward strokes crossways to spread the paint, until it forms a solid block of colour.

Finish by 'laying off' in the original downward direction, with the grain of the wood, gliding your brush lightly over the surface. The point of laying off is to remove any marks made by the bristles of the brush, leaving a smooth surface. Reload and paint further sections in the same way, blending the paint over adjoining sections.

Special paint effects

Special paint effects can be applied to the woodwork of doors and windows to bring further interest to otherwise plain paintwork. Effects such as dragging, combing and woodgraining are achieved using a choice of tools, from decorating brushes to special rubber rockers, in order to pattern a further layer of paint or glaze over a base coat of oil paint.

Apply a base coat and leave it to dry. Tint transparent scumble glaze, mixing 1 part glaze to 3 parts white spirit. Add 1 part white oil-based eggshell per 20 parts of glaze; and add artist's oil paint to add colour. Mix up enough for all the woodwork you want to cover. While the glaze is still wet, lightly drag a wide decorating brush over the surface.

Dragging involves just that: dragging a decorating brush such as a bristle grainer through the top layer of tinted glaze so that the patterning of the brush strokes remains visible when dry. Combing with a special wide-toothed comb is particularly effective, if a substantial proportion of the tinted top coat is combed away, allowing a contrasting coloured undercoat to show through.

Woodgraining may be done using a special rubber rocker patterned with a woodgrain effect or, for a more impressionistic effect, using a lining brush to pull thin distressed lines over the base coat in a pattern similar to the veining of marbling. The technique for using the rocker is first to rock and then to gently drag it through the glaze.

Dragging

1 Apply glaze over the base coat, then drag a wallpapering brush through it to leave a brush-stroke pattern.

2 Follow the direction of the grain roughly or the effect may be too mechanical.

▲ *A top, coloured glaze wash can be dragged, as here, or treated using a range of other techniques – including combing and woodgraining – to create subtle paint effects. The soft colour combination of blue over cream on this cupboard door makes a clear visual link between the woodwork and the marble splashback behind.*

Painting windows

Painting a window is a fiddly job that should not be rushed, yet it needs to be done in one session to avoid ugly joins in the paintwork. Start early in the day and leave the window open so that the paint will be dry enough to close the window at night; do not attempt to paint in windy weather as dust will blow onto the wet paint and spoil it. Immediately before starting work, remove handles, stays and catches and clean the panes thoroughly so that dust or dirt cannot transfer onto the wet paint.

Applying the paint

If you are using an oil-based paint, remember to build up the paint in layers, beginning with a wood primer, progressing to an undercoat and then finishing off with one or two layers of top coat. Use a 2.5cm (1in) brush for flat areas and a cutting-in brush, which has an angled tip for painting mouldings and glazing bars, of the same size. Apply the paint downwards, along the grain if painting wood. Without reloading the brush, lightly work over this, making sure that paint (but not too much) gets into all the grooves of any mouldings. Finally, glide the brush down again, ensuring that the paint on all the surfaces is smooth and even.

Protecting glass

To protect window panes from paint, either use a paint shield or stick decorator's or masking tape on the glass close to the glazing bars or frame. Whichever method you use,

Painting around glass

1 A paint shield is invaluable when painting window frames, to avoid getting paint on the glass.

▲ *A dramatic use of colour draws the eye: vibrant blue on the wall and emerald green on the window. Despite having been built up in layers, the paint around the window has become worn with age, but far from offending the eye, this softens the brash green and adds to the window's charm.*

The painting sequences for casement and sash windows

1 To paint a casement window, follow the numbers, painting the opening windows first.

1 To paint a sash window, first reverse the position of the sashes, then follow the numbers.

outer sash. Now paint the upper cross-rail of the inner sash, the vertical bars of the inner sash and finish off with the top runners and behind the cords, the frame and sill.

Casement windows

Fix the window open with a piece of wire wound around a nail tapped into the bottom of the opening casement. First paint the glazing bars and rebates, next the upper and lower rails, then the hinge stile and this window edge. Follow with the outer stile, and finally the frame and sill.

Shutters

Because of their similarity to doors, treat shutters as if they were a panelled door, taking care to wedge a whole shutter open before you start work. Leave the window itself open (unless it is windy) to help the paint dry.

---

let your paint overlap onto the glass by about 1mm (1⁄16 in) to seal the join between glass and frame and protect it from damp.

A paint shield is a piece of shaped metal or plastic with a fine edge along one side. While you paint, you hold the fine edge against the glass, almost touching the glazing bar or side of the window. When using a paint shield, wipe it frequently to prevent it causing smears.

Stick masking or decorator's tape around the edge of the glass close to the wood. Wide decorator's tape, which is half self-adhesive and half plain paper, is the easier tape to remove when painting is complete. Peel away the tape before the paint has dried, otherwise it may take some paint with it.

Sash windows

Begin by reversing the window positions so that the bottom sash is pushed up and the top sash is pulled down. Paint the meeting rail and the vertical bars of the outer sash as far as is possible. Next, paint the area beneath the inner sash and the runners. Following this, paint the lower cross-rail and the underside of the inner sash. Leave to dry. Reverse the window positions and start by painting the upper cross-rail of the outer sash, and then the remainder of the vertical bars of the

▲ *This roomy colonial interior boasts an abundance of divided louvred shutters. They are ideal here, behind the desk, where their versatility can be exploited to advantage. One half of the shutters can be closed to shade the eyes while air and sunshine can still stream in above or below to refresh and inspire the mind.*

Painting doors

Like windows, doors should be painted in one session to avoid leaving visible joins in the paintwork. Remember that, as with all decorating, you will be able to see your handiwork more clearly in natural rather than artificial light. Cover the floor underneath a door and wedge it open firmly so it won't wobble as you paint. Before getting down to work, remove knobs, handles, catches, escutcheons, fingerplates and any other ironmongery. Have an old screwdriver handy for cleaning out the groove of hinge screws after painting them.

Paint the edges of a door outwards, towards the corners, to prevent paint being drawn off by the corners of the wood and running down in dribbles. On panel doors use a 5cm (2in) brush for stretchers and a 2.5cm (1in) brush for mouldings. For a flush door a 7.5cm (3in) brush is suitable.

Furniture

Metal fittings should be cleaned (see pages 226–227) and coated with an appropriate paint, always making sure that moving parts and screw holes are not clogged.

Wooden door knobs, especially cupboard knobs, can be painted to match a colour scheme. Use a hard-wearing paint such as oil gloss or enamel, apply several thin coats and consider a final coat or coats of yacht varnish to help protect them from wear and tear.

Panelled doors

Always working with the grain, first paint the mouldings around each panel, then the panels themselves. Next paint the centre stiles, the cross-rails including those above and below the panels. Now paint the stiles down each side of the door, then the edges, and finally the door casing (jamb and door stop, and architrave) if these were not painted at the same time as the skirting board. When you paint the outside edges of the architrave use a paint shield (see pages 212–213) to prevent paint getting on the wall.

An old-fashioned technique for painting panelled doors is to use slightly different tones of the same colour on different parts of the door. By painting the panels the darkest shade, the frame the lightest and the mouldings a shade in between, the architectural features of the door are made more noticeable. The door looks like a three-dimensional object rather than a two-dimensional one.

Flush doors

The best way to paint the large flat expanse of a flush door is to mentally divide it into six or eight equal parts, two across and three or four down, rather like the sections in a bar of chocolate. Start by painting the top left section, then the top right, then the next left, then next right, and so on down to the bottom of the door. Paint each in turn, blending the wet edges together as you work down the door. Paint the edges, jamb and architrave as for panelled doors.

Flush doors can offer greater and more varied opportunities than panelled doors for extravagant painting styles. Their flat sides

▲ *Panelled doors provide the opportunity for having fun with colour. Here light and dark blue paints have been used to make a striking entrance to the room. In times past, the panels were painted in slightly different tones of the same colour to provide a subtle sense of depth.*

The painting sequences for panel and flush doors

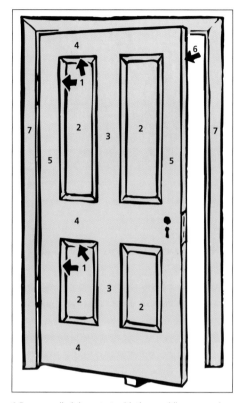

1 For a panelled door, start with the mouldings around the panels, and then follow the sequence of numbers.

▲ *The frame of a metal glass-panelled door is painted black, drawing attention to the geometry of the glass. The squareness of the panels contrasts pleasingly with the generous curve of the red-painted wall in front of it. Glass blocks above this wall serve to create an internal window as well as echoing the panels of the door.*

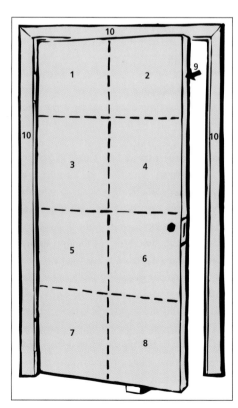

1 Work down a flush door from the top in imaginary sections, blending wet edges together before they dry.

lend themselves to all-over designs such as the eye-bending geometric patterns found in the work of pop artist Bridget Riley or the blown-up cartoons of Roy Lichtenstein. Some of the most famous examples of door painting can be seen at Charleston Farmhouse in Sussex, where the artists Vanessa Bell (Virginia Woolf's sister) and Duncan Grant used every surface, including the doors, as a canvas. You can find inspiration for making up your own designs or pictures almost anywhere.

Glazed doors

Glazed doors can be painted following the sequence recommended for panelled doors, starting with the area around each pane of glass. If the door is multi-paned or entirely glass except for the frame, treat it like a large casement window instead. Protect the panes from splashes with tape or a paint shield (see pages 212–213).

Protecting the floor

Use a paint shield or a piece of cardboard under the door frame to prevent the brush picking up dust from the floor and to protect the floor from paint. This is applicable when painting skirting boards too.

Protecting the floor

1 As well as keeping paint off the floor, card under a door or skirting board stops dust from spoiling the finish.

Further ideas for painting doors

▲ *Brilliantly coloured high-gloss paint has been used here: flame in the hallway area and bright Matisse blue woodwork inside the room. While with the door open the effect is busy, vibrant and full of contrasts, when the door is closed no blue will be visible from the landing.*

Two-colour doors

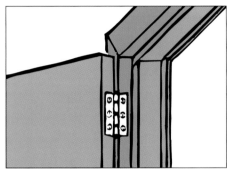

1 Use two different colours, but make sure that none of the wrong colour is visible when the door is closed.

Different colours on either side of a door

It often happens that a door needs to be painted in different colours on each side, corresponding to the decoration of the rooms or areas it links. It does not matter which side you paint first, but it is important that every part of the surface you see on one side of the door matches.

For the purpose of description, imagine the door opens from a passage into a room. On the opening side, paint the architrave, the frame up to and including the edge of the door stop, the leading edge of the door and the door face in one colour. On the other side, where the door faces the passage, in the second colour, paint the architrave and frame up to and over the doorstop, the hinged edge of the door and its other face.

Faux panel effect for flush doors

To lift the flatness of a flush door, painting *faux* panels creates an effective three-dimensional illusion. First measure up your door. Determine the number and size of the panels you want, and the dimensions of the *faux* rails and stiles. Measure and draw in the panels in pencil directly onto the surface. Mix up two shades of the chosen door colour, one lighter than the other, and then apply the darkest shade to each of the panels. When dry, paint the rest of the door in the lighter colour, beginning with the centre stiles, progressing to the rails, and finally paint the outer stiles. When completely dry, you can paint in the shading at the sides of the panels to give the panels depth. You will need a further darker version of the

Painting fake panels on a flush door

1 Measure and draw panels with a pencil before painting them in a slightly darker shade of your chosen colour.

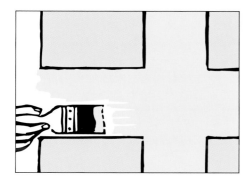

2 When the panels have dried, paint what remains in a lighter shade, in the usual order (see pages 214–215).

3 When the door is dry, paint the 'mouldings' with a fine brush, using a ruler; make sure the corners are mitred.

4 Taking note of the natural light source, use a lighter shade on two sides to reinforce the illusion.

◀ *Several faux panels have been incorporated here to create a simple, triumphant and humorous trompe-l'oeil door – complete with cat flap, letter box and bolts. The reliance on lines without shading in the panelling, and the strong, joyful colours used, complete the effect, proving that stylish interiors can also be witty.*

original colour and a paler version too. Establish in which direction your light source (real or imaginary) will hit the door. The tops of the panels and the sides closest to the light should be lined in the darker tone; the bottoms and further sides in the lighter tone. The thicker the lines you draw, the deeper your panel will appear to be. It is not advisable to make them too thick. You must judge this to suit the proportions of the panels you have created and choose the width of your brush accordingly. A fine brush is recommended. Use a wooden or plastic ruler with a bevelled top. Turn the bevel against the door so that it stands proud of the surface. Line the ruler up with the edge of the panel, rest the ferrule of the brush on the inside edge, and drag the brush gently along it. You will need to mitre each corner, so be sure to let the paint dry before attempting this in the corner where the two tones meet. If you do not feel you have a steady enough hand to use a ruler, you can create the lines by applying strips of low-tack masking tape and painting between these instead.

Finishes for woodwork

Doors and windows that are made of wood do not have to be painted to look good or complement a decorative scheme. They can be left bare, completely stripped of old paint, varnish or any other finish to allow the beauty of the grain to be admired. The two possible disadvantages of leaving wood unfinished are that it is not protected from dirt such as greasy fingermarks and that the stripping process may have left the wood dry and even slightly rough. The wood of old doors which have been industrially stripped in hot chemicals is likely to be in the worst condition; cold chemicals do not do nearly so much damage but are more expensive. Sanding will help and may even cure a roughened surface. In addition, there are a number of finishes that can enhance or seal bare wood to protect it from dirt. Before choosing a particular type of finish, do some research to make sure the finish will achieve the results you want.

Before applying any coloured finish, practise on a piece of wood of the same type until you get the right effect. Where more than one material needs to be applied in succession, use products from the same brand to avoid incompatibility and later problems. Always follow the manufacturer's instructions.

Staining

There are many different types of stain, all of which you wipe onto the woodwork with a wad of cloth, except for mouldings when, for greater accuracy, it is better to use a brush. Quick-drying stains can be tricky to apply evenly, so try out the colour first on a spare piece of wood. If staining a door, lie it flat before you start, so that the colour does not run. Wood must be clean and completely free of other finishes before application.

Water-based stains give the brightest and best colours. DIY shops tend to favour shades of brown, which reflect natural wood colours. Oil- and spirit-based stains are also available. Household dyes in many colours are widely available, and today, various types of coloured stains can be bought from specialist paint suppliers. Some sell pigments or concentrates with which you can mix up your own colour; some stains are concen-

trated and can be thinned to the shade you want, giving anything from an intense colour to a washed-out effect. You can also make your own stain by seriously watering down emulsion so that the grain will show through when it is brushed onto the wood. A stain does not give wood protection from wear, so consider adding a varnish or sealant; seal either the whole door or window, or only the areas around handles where fingers may eventually make dirty patches.

Varnishing

To protect bare or stained wood from becoming marked, you can paint it with a varnish or sealant. Varnish is available in a clear form, coloured in shades of brown or tinted with more interesting colours. Some types have three alternative finishes: gloss, silk and matt.

Oil-based varnish that is billed as 'clear' generally has a yellowish tinge that will become more yellow with age or in direct sunlight. Acrylic (water-based) varnish is clear and does not yellow with age. In steamy rooms, oil-based varnish is better. For extremely hard-wearing qualities, look for varnish containing Teflon. It should be noted that coloured varnishes are very difficult to remove, should you ever want a change.

Varnish is simply brushed on. For a really smooth finish, rub down with sandpaper between coats.

Oiling

Bare wood doors can be nourished and given a soft, mellow glow with specialist oil or even stale olive oil. All oils will darken the wood to some degree. Linseed oil mixed equally with button polish will give a slight sheen. Some finishing oils are waterproof. Rub oil into the bare wood using a soft cloth. Except for some special finishing oils, oil does not protect against dirt and spillages.

Waxing

Wax is not waterproof and may pick up grime unless the wood is first treated with a sealant. Colour can be added to clear wax such as beeswax by melting it gently with artist's oil colour. This should be allowed to

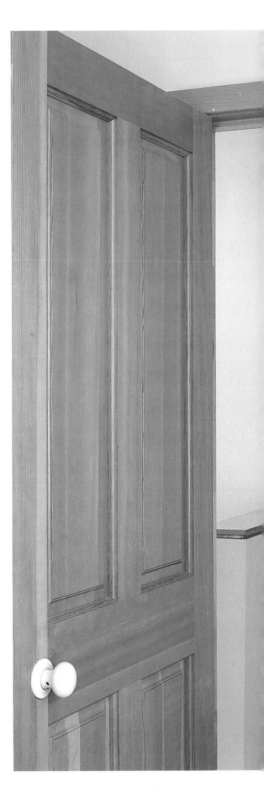

▲ *Varnish, whether clear or tinted, will allow the grain of the wood beneath to show through. Where the colour of the walls is bold, doors in good condition will often look their best left unpainted. Using wax, stain or varnish, as on this landing, the light wood of door, floor and ledge becomes a major, brightening and cohesive feature.*

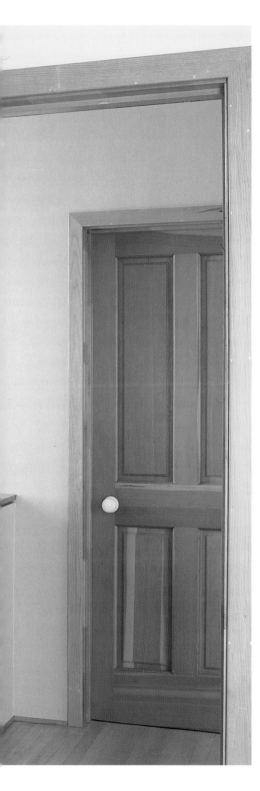

cool before application. Alternatively, you could use a coloured shoe polish.

When polished up, wax gives a glossier finish than oil but, like oil, it allows the grain of the wood to show through. Wax does not protect against dirt and spillages.

Bleaching

Wood can be lightened to give a soft, sun-bleached effect, like that of driftwood. Use specialized wood bleach available from good decorator's suppliers.

Liming

Especially suitable for oak and other woods with a distinctive grain pattern, this milky finish lightens and adds interest to natural wood. Liming wax and liming kits are available from specialist paint and wood product suppliers. They come with clear instructions, but the process basically involves opening the grain of the wood by scrubbing along it with a wire brush, cleaning, working in the liming wax, wiping off the excess and polishing the dried wax. The wood must be clean and completely free of other finishes before application.

Staining the wood between cleaning and liming will make the liming more noticeable. You can also obtain a similar effect to liming by repeatedly painting bare wood with coats of watered-down white or lightly coloured emulsion then wiping it off. This finish will need sealing with varnish.

▶ *If you feel that carrying out the liming process properly sounds too long-winded, or too complicated, try the cheat's method: a similar effect can be achieved quite easily by painting bare wood with several coats of watered-down emulsion, wiping off the excess each time, and then sealing with a coat of varnish.*

Using paper, fabric and metal

In addition to the more conventional ways of painting or finishing doors described earlier (see pages 214–219), there are several exciting treatments which can be applied to them. With a little imagination and a bit of flair, any door can be transformed into a work of art by decorating it with painted patterns or large pictures.

Doors can also be covered with materials as diverse as different types of paper, fabric or even sheet metal.

Papering doors

If you do not feel up to devising an all-over design yourself, you can cover a flush door with virtually any kind of paper and varnish over it. The door and paper both need to be clean and the type of adhesive used should be appropriate for the job.

To create a bright and jolly, even kitsch, look, inexpensive paper items such as the covers of fashion or interiors magazines and brightly coloured packaging of food products – especially those from other parts of the world – can be used. The latter would be particularly appropriate in a kitchen.

For a more sophisticated look, you could use black and white or delicately coloured paper such as old sheet music, pages from out-of-date road atlases or maps, newspapers (which will yellow), old prints bought from a street market, photocopies of prints in a book or even old letters.

Textile cover-up

Another approach is to face the door with a single piece of fabric such as green baize, coloured felt or vinyl 'leather', using decorative brass-headed upholstery pins. Obviously the material needs to suit the overall decor of the room.

The material can be cut to the exact size of the door and glued on all over with an adhesive appropriate for the fabric. It must be smoothed out to ensure it is bubble-free and the edges must be turned back, if necessary, and securely glued down. Alternatively, the material can be slightly padded and secured with tacks. This gives a more generous, sophisticated look and is easier to remove when you want a change.

▲ Metal foil has been applied to the surface of the door to provide an unusual and extremely eye-catching focal point in this silver-themed room. Applying metal foil to wood is a straightforward – if time-consuming – job, but the results are worth the effort. Finish with a layer of clear glaze to prevent damage to the foil's surface .

▲ Large, square, black metal studs appear at intervals around the raised parts of a pair of handsome panelled doors – and in the corners! Although the studs have been used sparingly, their effect is impressive and the overall look of the doors is reminiscent of those found in a medieval castle. Heavy knobs provide the finishing touch.

A padded door

First remove the door handle and then paint the edges of the door and a few centimetres around the edges of the front of the side you are covering. Choose a colour that tones in with the facing material. Cut a piece of wadding slightly smaller than the size of the door. This wadding could be a length of curtain interlining or a piece of leftover carpet underlay. Fix this to the door using tacks or a staple gun (available from hardware stores to suit various sizes of staple).

Before attaching the facing material over the wadding, mark the door at regular intervals around the edge where the tacks are to go. Cut the fabric slightly larger than the door. Turn back the edges so that you have a panel of fabric the same size as the door. Press these edges, if appropriate for the fabric, and then glue or sew them down. At the same time, cut off the bulk of the material at the corners and fold back, first along one edge and then the other, to mitre them.

Decorative tacks for attaching this fabric panel can be bought from suppliers of upholstery equipment in a variety of designs and sizes, including the traditional brass-coloured domed-top type. Alternatively, simply attach the fabric to the door with a staple gun, then hide the staples by gluing a braid or edging over them.

Attach the fabric to the door, making sure the material is hanging straight. Fix a tack (or staple) through the centre top of the material into the middle of the top of the door. Make sure that the tension is just right – not too tight and not slack – and position the second tack through the centre of the bottom of the material into the middle of the bottom of the door.

Finish attaching the fabric along the top, bottom and lastly the sides, always checking tension and (using the weave if there is one) that it is straight. Place a tack in each corner for a neat finish. Other tacks can be placed on the door face in lines to make a pattern or a panel effect.

Cut a small hole through the layers of fabric for the spindle of the door handle or door knob. Fix the door handle or knob back in place.

Sheet metal

For a really dramatic, industrial-style finish, face a door with sheet metal such as zinc or stainless steel. This is not a difficult job, but requires care, and the end result can be stunning. Begin by measuring the door precisely. Then find a steel stockholder who will supply you with a single panel of metal and cut it to size. From the wide choice available, choose a metal and finish you like, bearing in mind that a lightweight flush door may only be able to support a thin sheet of metal. The optimum thickness is 1mm ($\frac{1}{16}$in).

When the piece is to be cut, specify that the corners must be cut exactly square, and the sheet must be without scratches or blemishes. Handle pieces with extreme care as the burred edges can cut, and smooth the edges with heavy-duty wet-and-dry paper.

You can attach the metal to the door using a wide range of finishes and sizes of fixing, including escutcheon pins, drive pins, round-head screws, pop rivets and even tin tacks. The choice of fixing is entirely personal, as the finishes are equally effective. Pop rivets give a particularly pleasing industrial look and are applied with a pop riveter, which is available from hardware and DIY stores.

Whichever fixing you select, begin by drilling a small hole through the metal and into the wood, using a drill bit of the same diameter as your fixing or slightly smaller (experiment on a scrap of wood). If you are hanging a new door, you can attach the metal before hanging it, to make working along the bottom edge easier. Otherwise, attach the metal at the top first so it hangs down while you fix the rest. Use an adhesive suitable for gluing metal to wood, or double-sided tape, to ensure that the edges of the metal sheet stick properly to the door. Attach the metal with fixings applied in any pattern you choose, perhaps by using a combination of sizes or types for a more elaborate effect.

To make a hole for the door-knob fitting, first drill a small hole in the metal, to act as a guide, then a larger hole with a 1.5cm ($\frac{1}{2}$in) drill bit. If you are in any doubt about your ability to do this correctly, there is always the option of getting a professional to fit it for you.

Metal sheeting and rivets can of course be used to transform the doors of cupboards anywhere in the house, but it is not necessary to use real metal to create the look. Metallic paint is effective too. Car paints are available from car goods suppliers in a range of colours as well as the silvery grey associated with real aluminium or steel.

◀ *Rich red leather has been used to cover the outside of these impressive doors, made even more stunning by arranging rows of brass studs in various rectangular forms to provide a panelled-door effect. Upholstery tacks or studs could be used to achieve a similar effect.*

Making a padded door

1 Cut a piece of wadding slightly smaller than the size of the door, and attach its edges with a staple gun or tacks.

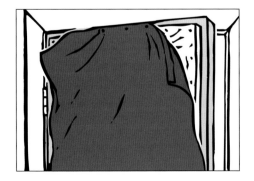

2 Cut the fabric slightly larger than the door and turn the edges over. Start fixing at the centre top of the door.

3 Finish attaching the fabric at the top, then the bottom, followed by the sides, using fixings at regular intervals.

Effects for glass

Frosted glass

▶ *While preserving privacy and yet allowing natural light to filter in, different types of glass combine happily here around two sides of this walk-in shower: glass blocks divide it from the bath, while the door has been etched. A similar effect to this chequerboard with palm trees can be achieved with a frosting technique.*

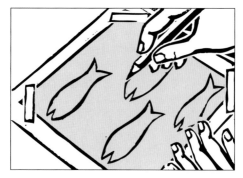

1 Lay the design underneath sticky-backed plastic, transfer the design and cut it out with a craft knife.

2 Once the design has been cut, peel the sticky plastic off the backing and stick the shapes onto the window pane.

3 Stipple the paint solution onto the surface of the glass, overlapping it onto the edges of the plastic shapes.

4 When the paint is dry, peel the plastic shapes away from the window to reveal the clear glass underneath.

Frosted, patterned and coloured glass have long been used for window panes to give privacy or simply to add a decorative aspect to a window. Coloured glass has been popular for centuries and since the early nineteenth century homes have been decorated with coloured, cut, etched and painted panes. Coloured glass can be used to make windows and glazed doors more interesting and it becomes really beautiful when sunlight streams through it, creating pools of tinted light on walls and ceilings. Frosted windows are useful where light needs to be admitted to a room where an element of screening is also required.

Frosted glass

Interior designers use a wonderful cheat, without embarrassment, to create a patterned frosted window – frosted-effect self-adhesive plastic. It is available in a variety of weights

and finishes from sign-writing, specialist decorating shops and even hardware stores. The plastic can be used in sheets to cover a whole pane of glass or cut out to create individual designs. When creating a design this way, you will need to take into account to which side of the glass you will fix the plastic. In a bathroom, where condensation may get between the glass and the plastic, it may be preferable to apply the design to the outer side of the door. If this is the case, make sure that your original design has the image in reverse.

For a different frosted effect, self-adhesive plastic (not necessarily frosted) can be used as a mask, and around it a mixture of white paint and varnish can be stippled. Begin by drawing your design on paper (bear in mind that the shapes you cut out from it will represent the unfrosted part of the final window). Use a fine black marker. You could pin the paper to the window and draw *in situ*. Where there are two or more windows beside each other, the design could be made to flow across them in one unified image.

Tape the finished drawing to a hard horizontal surface. Tape the self-adhesive plastic over the design, trace through it and cut out the shapes from the plastic with a craft knife. To transfer a complicated design to the window, it may be worth taking care to cut through the plastic only, not the backing, in order to keep the pieces together. Alternatively, tape the design to the back of the window and align the cut-out plastic pieces on the other front. Either way, the glass must be scrupulously clean and dry. Peel the plastic design(s) off the backing sheet and rub down onto the glass, being careful not to catch or lift the edges.

Mix up equal quantities of white gloss oil paint and matt polyurethane varnish (you will not need a great deal: three tablespoons of each will be enough for quite a large window). Having fixed the design to the window, apply the paste, using a stencilling brush, with a light stippling action. Leave until completely dry before removing the plastic from the window. A craft knife will be needed to lift the corners of the plastic. Finally protect the pattern using a spray acrylic aerosol varnish, which will coat the design effectively.

Painted glass

You can install a window or panel of real stained glass that has been specially designed and made for you by a craftsman, but a much cheaper alternative is to paint a glass panel in imitation of a stained-glass window. You can obtain special glass paints for this and fake lead strips or special relief paste for separating the colours from art shops, but you can also use artist's oil colours, thinned to a greater or lesser extent with linseed oil and turpentine or white spirit and mixed with a small amount of polyurethane varnish.

Draw your design first on paper. It need not imitate traditional stained glass found in churches and Victorian houses. Look at contemporary art and abstract stained glass for inspiration. It may be wise, on a first attempt, to keep to simple geometric shapes.

The best method for achieving this is to paint a piece of glass, keeping it flat to avoid colours running, and replace the existing glass in a window with this new piece. However, it is possible to paint on glass *in situ*, provided the paint is kept sufficiently viscous. The glass must be completely clean, free from grease (including fingermarks) and dry.

Lay the design behind the glass and secure it in place with masking tape. Use special relief paste to demarcate the outlines of the

design, using your drawing beneath as a guide. Fill in the areas with paint using a fine artist's brush. Take care to avoid the paint running by ensuring there is minimal paint loaded on your brush. Thin layers can be built up if necessary. If you make mistakes, either remove the paint while wet with a clean rag dipped in white spirit or scrape it off when dry. When the design is completed, allow the paints to dry thoroughly before spraying with polyurethane varnish.

◄ *The panels of this kitchen door have been painted red and yellow to create an idiosyncratic effect that adds the finishing touch to this personalized, madcap kitchen. Once the glass panels are prepared or in place, an effect like this is easy to achieve with glass paints. Even small areas treated in this way will enliven a space instantly.*

Painted glass

1 Tape the design behind the glass, trace out the design on the glass with leading paste and leave it to dry.

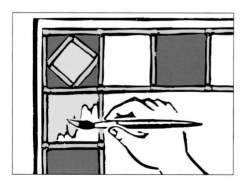

2 Using an artist's brush, fill in the areas between the leading paste with specialist paints formulated for glass.

Cleaning up and problems with paintwork

Tools and equipment should be cleaned and put away before the finish dries on them. Close a can by placing a piece of wood across the top of the lid and tapping it with a hammer. Throw away dirty rags in an outside dustbin, preferably a metal one, after chemicals have evaporated. Clean metal tools such as shavehooks with water or white spirit and put them away.

Cleaning and storing brushes

If you take the time to care correctly for your brushes, you will greatly extend their life. Wash brushes used for water-based paint or wood stains in water. For brushes used for oil painting, wash in white spirit to loosen the paint then wash in warm soapy water; proprietary brush cleaner is expensive but worthwhile if you have invested in the best brushes. Rinse cleaned brushes thoroughly, then work them against a clean rag to get the worst of the water off.

For overnight storage, suspend brushes with oil-based paint on them in water, with the brushes clear of the bottom, by a wire through a drilled hole in the handle. For shorter-term storage, wrap in foil or clingfilm to keep them wet.

For long-term storage, when brushes are clean, shake any excess water off the brush and place a rubber band around the bristles to help it to keep its shape as it dries. Rest it on its side. When completely dry, wrap brushes in paper and store in a dry place.

Cleaning up paint spills and splashes

Paint on glass is quite easy to remove. Let it dry and then scrape it off. Dry paint on the floor is more difficult. On wood, scrape it off carefully as for glass, taking care not to scratch the surface. It may be necessary to sand a paint blob very carefully, trying not to damage the surrounding wood and, if necessary, touching up the floor with scratch cover or other wood treatment.

Paint on a carpet is extremely difficult to remove. If the paint is only lightly on the surface of a carpet with a pile, it may be possible to snip away the top of fibres when the paint is dry. If it has soaked into the carpet,

▲ Gloss paint can look stunning. These panelled walls and wooden door have been given a glossy sheen in a warm shade of cream which reflects the incoming sunlight. However, if undercoat or primer is incorrectly applied, a top coat of gloss can end up looking dull. If this happens, wait for the paint to dry, sand and clean it, then re-apply the gloss.

you can try removing it with a strong dry-cleaning fluid, but this may spread the colour. If the stain cannot be removed, it will be necessary to cut out and replace a small square of carpet.

If you get paint on a recently painted wood surface, lightly sand the surface and touch up with the appropriate colour. In certain situations, if a blob of oil paint has splashed onto a water-based paint for example, it may be necessary to prime the patch before repainting.

Paint problems

Blistering

This will occur if moisture has been trapped between the layers of paint. To correct, strip off the offending layers (this is not difficult if the blistering is extensive, as much of it will simply peel off) and re-apply the paint. Blistering may also occur if the wrong type of paint has been applied – for example, a water-based paint over a layer of oil-based paint – so check that your paints are compatible.

Wrinkling or sagging

If you apply paint too heavily, it will begin to sag. To resolve this, wait until the paint is dry, sand sufficiently heavily for a smooth surface and re-apply the top coat. Alternatively, strip off all the top coats entirely and re-apply the paint less heavily.

Dribbles

This is a consequence of too much paint on the brush. If you notice a dribble or 'run' as you are painting, work across it with your brush before the final laying off (see pages 210–211). If the dribble has begun to dry, leave it until it is completely dry, then sand it down and touch up as necessary.

Undercoat showing through

This could happen for a number of reasons. Either the wrong colour undercoat has been used (too dark for a pale top coat or too pale for a dark top coat) or the top coat has been applied too sparingly. You may even have forgotten to add a second top coat. To rectify, paint on another layer or two of top.

Storing brushes used for oil painting

1 For long-term storage, wash brushes first in white spirit to loosen the paint, then in warm soapy water.

2 For overnight storage, suspend unwashed brushes in jam jars filled with water, or wrap in paper or clingfilm.

▲ *A beautifully smooth paint finish in vivid yellow draws the eye towards this window frame and the garden beyond. Few of us have so steady a hand that we can paint a window frame without leaving splashes on the panes. Fortunately, paint is easily removed from glass; simply wait for the paint to dry, then carefully scrape it off.*

Foreign bodies stuck in the paint

Wet paint will trap anything that touches it, such as clothing fibres, dust specks or small insects. Experts usually recommend leaving the paint until it is dry, then sanding and touching up with paint. But if the paint is wet and the foreign body is just one item (a fly or paintbrush bristle, for example, rather than a cloud of dust) you might feel confident enough to have a go at removing it in one neat swipe with a clean rag.

Crazing

This will appear if one layer of paint has been applied before a previous one was completely dry, or if the paints are not compatible. Unfortunately the only way to correct crazing is to strip off the paint completely and re-apply.

Paint will not dry

This occurs for several reasons. Either the paint was not stirred properly before application, the surface was not clean, or the weather is too hot and humid. Try opening the windows for a few days, if possible. If this does not work, you will have to strip off the paint and re-apply, this time making sure the surface is absolutely clean.

Gloss looks dull

This is caused if the primer and/or undercoat was improperly applied (or omitted) or is not completely dry. Alternatively, the top coat could have been applied during frosty or exceptionally cold weather. You will have to wait for the paint to dry completely, then sand lightly, clean the surface thoroughly and apply another top coat during normal weather conditions.

Brush marks show

This will occur if cheap brushes, which are more likely to leave brush marks in paintwork than better-quality ones, were used and/or the paint was applied too thickly and not laid off properly (see pages 210–211). To address this problem, sand, wash and dry thoroughly, then re-apply the top coat using a good-quality brush, and taking special care with your technique.

Directory of window and door furniture

Doors and windows are equipped with various fittings to facilitate their movement and security. Generally referred to as 'furniture', these fittings may be unobtrusive or more decorative and in a style to suit the period of your home. Except for some door knobs and handles, they are usually made of metal, including iron, brass and chrome.

Additional paraphernalia can be fitted to doors to perform various functions, including providing security with bolts and locks. A front door might also be fitted with a spy hole, a knocker, a letter plate and house numbers, with a bell nearby on the outside wall. These items can be handsome or elaborate antiques, reproductions or interesting modern designs, or anything in between so long as they are appropriate to the door in scale and design.

Doors

Knobs

Door knobs are twisted to operate the opening mechanism, except for those on cupboards which are designed to be pulled. Traditionally, they are made of iron, brass, glass, china, plastic or wood, and are sometimes finished in other materials like copper or chrome. Some eighteenth- and nineteenth-century examples are elaborately decorated and mounted on interestingly shaped back plates. Contemporary designs range in shape and type from sleek steel to coloured resin 'shells'. Old knobs can be bought from industrial stripping workshops, second-hand markets and junk or antique shops. **1**

Handles

Because of the pressure exerted on them, handles are usually made in fairly robust materials such as iron, brass or plastic. Their design ranges widely.

Rim latches and locks

A rim latch contains the opening mechanism of a door in a metal box which is fitted to the door's surface. The box may be plain and painted black (as are most modern ones) or it may be more decorative. Brass rim latches and locks are available in imitation of antique ones that were fitted to the doors of important rooms in the eighteenth and nineteenth centuries. Rim latches have an appealingly unpretentious appearance especially suited to old houses and cottages but do not seem to have caught the imagination of contemporary door furniture designers in the way that knobs and handles have.

Because they can be prised or kicked off a door, rim latches are less secure than mortise latches (below) and therefore not generally acceptable for exterior doors. **3**

Mortise latches and locks

A mortise latch or lock is fitted into the thickness of the door and is thus hidden from view. Insurance companies generally specify the type of mortise lock acceptable to them for exterior door security. **2**

Thumb latches

A thumb latch is the type of fastening mechanism that is appropriate on battened cottage-type doors. You grip a vertical handle while pressing down on a protruding iron (or wood, if the latch is wooden) plate just above it. This raises the sneck which lifts the bolt (known as the 'beam') to open or secure the door. All the mechanics of the fastening are on the surface of the door, which gives the thumb latch a special charm and interest.

Escutcheons

These are the small plates, sometimes with a swinging flap for draught exclusion, which surround keyholes. Door handle back plates often incorporate an escutcheon.

Finger plates

These are narrow rectangular panels placed vertically above and sometimes below a door knob. They are designed to protect much-used doors from greasy fingermarks. Antique ones are made of the same variety of non-porous materials as door knobs; modern ones are just as likely to be made of plastic, resin or a metal such

4

5

as stainless steel. Few people today bother with finger plates, as modern paints have excellent wash-down qualities, but they do serve a purpose, especially for a bare wood door, and add smartness. You can decorate a clear glass or plastic finger plate by painting it on the back before attaching it to the door.

Hinges

Hinges are barely noticeable, except for the elongated type used on battened cottage doors. Often shaped and decorative, these are usually painted black, in contrast to the colour of the door. The recessed hinges used on a panelled or flush door are usually either brass, in which case they should not be painted, or iron, which can be painted. It is advisable to remove paint from the screw heads so that they can be unscrewed easily at a later date if necessary. **4**

Portière

This is an ingenious fitting which aids draught exclusion around a doorway. Consisting of a hinged metal curtain pole attached to the wall at one end and the door at the other, it hangs a curtain across the inside of the door and opens with it.

Windows

Sash fasteners

These secure the two parts of a sash window, pushing them apart vertically and together horizontally. By pushing the sashes firmly into the frame, the action also cuts out draughts. Sash stays come in a variety of designs, most commonly traditional styles made either from iron, which you oil or paint, or lacquered brass, which you do not.

Casement fasteners

Casements require two fittings, a fastener at the side and a stay along the bottom which not only helps to keep the window closed but also allows it to be left open without flapping. Perhaps the prettiest design widely available is the rat-tail, which ends in a spiral shape.

Metal casements often have a cockspur fastener, where the part that turns onto the window has two or more teeth, allowing the window to be fastened open just a fraction for ventilation.

Espagnolette

This is the long bolt that fastens a pair of French windows. A handle, fitted on one of the windows, turns the bolt, which shoots up and down into the window frame. **5**

Restoring metal fittings

Door and window furniture can be cleaned then restored with household metal polish, paint stripper or old-fashioned recipes.

First wash the item thoroughly with soap and water or a solution of soda crystals, to enable you to establish its condition. Then clean it up: old lacquer can be removed with acetone; soak iron fittings in paraffin before scrubbing with wire wool to remove rust; wash chrome with a solution of washing-up liquid and a small dash of ammonia; de-tarnish brass by rubbing it with a half-lemon sprinkled with salt. Finally, polish the item with a product appropriate to the material in which it is finished. If you like a bright finish and do not like polishing, add clear acrylic lacquer.

Curtains

Besides their obvious practical merits of draught exclusion
and the creation of privacy, curtains are popular in homes
because they create an aura of comfort and a pleasing
atmosphere. As soon as curtains are hung up at the
window of a bare room, they make it look like a home.
Furthermore, they can be used to create almost any effect,
depending on the type of fabric and how it is used: sheer
floaty curtains are romantic; enormous padded ones are
grand and pretty; checked ones are fresh and cottagey.

When deciding upon the type of curtains for a room, it is important to bear in mind the overall decorative scheme. Its design and the colours used in it will reflect your personal style and preferences.

Considering the options

There are many factors to take into consideration. Look at the room carefully. Study the size, shape and position of the window or windows and take into account the period and proportions of both the window and the room. In a period house, curtains can reflect the style of that period or not, as you choose, but they tend to look better if they are in sympathy with the architectural proportions of the room. Small curtains that only just cover a window will look silly in a Georgian or Victorian room with a high ceiling, for instance, as will a neat cottage casement puffed up with an over-sized, over-grand window treatment.

It is possible to have more than one style of window treatment in a single room, creating more visual interest and giving the opportunity of using a more extravagant or expensive fabric than you might otherwise consider. For example, where there are three windows in a row, the middle one could have generous, billowing, floor-length curtains while those to each side could be fitted with a handsome Roman blind (see pages 260–265) made of the same fabric. This would create a sophisticated and dramatic effect using about the same amount of fabric as skimpy curtains for all three windows.

A window does not necessarily have to have two curtains. One may be enough if a window is hard up against a wall on one side or if several windows are close together. In the latter case an extra curtain at the other end of the row will balance appearances when they are drawn back during the day.

Light and warmth

Another important consideration to bear in mind is the direction the room faces and how light and warm it is as a result. Where there is plenty of direct sunlight, a single, large curtain could be fixed across the top of each window, for example, and pulled back to one

◀ *This window is framed with layers of fabric in the same colours – terracotta and cream – but in different patterns: the Roman blind in a simple check is edged with the same tasselled braid as a cushion, while heavy interlined curtains are made from bold stripes edged with green.*

◀◀ *The ultimate no-sew curtain, this diaphanous fabric floating in the breeze has been cut to double the length required and hung over a slender pole outside the door, to filter bright sunlight. White, rough-plastered walls and blue-painted woodwork on the doors and windows contribute to the seaside look.*

side during the day. On the other hand, if the room is dark and faces away from the sun, the amount of light available can be maximized with curtains that pull back completely clear of the window. Lining the rebate with mirror will reflect more light into the room and can make narrow windows appear wider. To warm a room, soft sheer curtains can be used to filter cold light, while heavy, flanking overcurtains create a cosy effect.

Curtain lengths

Naturally, curtains can be any size you choose, but most often are one of three lengths: sill, below sill or floor.

Floor length

Floor-length curtains either just skim the floor or billow onto it. They look generous, generally make a stronger visual statement than short curtains and, at their most magnificent, can be stunning. They will show off a beautiful or large-patterned fabric to best effect and they will balance a handsome pelmet, beneath which short curtains would look silly. They make sense for a window that is taller than it is wide, especially if it is exceptionally tall and narrow or if it comes down to the floor. They may also be more appropriate to the period of your house, if for instance it is Victorian with sash windows or even Georgian. Floor-length curtains window, including the sill, is completely hidden. They also look more generous than curtains that only just touch the sill.

Shorter curtains which barely graze the sill are practical in a kitchen or bathroom, although a blind would perhaps be a better and more economical choice.

Budgeting

Whatever your style preference, your budget is also a significant factor. It will influence your choice of fabric, which varies widely in cost, as well as the amount of material you can afford to buy. Even on a limited budget, however, extra-long, extra-full curtains are not out of the question, for they can be made of inexpensive fabric and can be left unlined. Alternatively, consider other styles of curtain and combinations with blinds (see pages 258–269) which can achieve a similar effect using much less fabric, such as pull-up curtains (see pages 266–267) or a blind beneath a pelmet.

▲ *A length of muslin, tie-dyed in vibrant colours and knotted at each end, is looped over a simple wooden pole. This sill-length curtain is dramatic and will veil a dull view, but won't give draught exclusion or much privacy. The window's exuberant cut-out frame adds to its impact.*

▲ *An ingenious curtain made from pieces of Chinese paper, each decorated with a sheet of gold leaf and glued to a string of natural hemp pulled down with a weight. The paper is hung in carefully staggered rows so that the pieces do not touch and the light between them makes a zigzag pattern.*

are also best for draught exclusion, especially if they drape luxuriously on the floor.

Long curtains use the most fabric and are therefore more expensive to make than shorter ones, but you do get more curtain for your effort. Another factor in their favour is that, if you are a beginner and worried about getting your hems straight, even a couple of centimetres out will not show with curtains that drape on the floor.

Sill length

Short curtains look more cottagey than long ones and suit small windows as well as those that are square or wider than they are tall. They either fall a little below the sill or just to it but not quite touching it; a prominent sill, or a window seat, will certainly dictate the latter, as anything longer will not fall straight. Below-sill-length curtains are more effective at keeping out draughts, as the entire

Cost is an important factor when deciding whether to buy the curtains ready-made or to make them up yourself. A halfway measure would be to buy the fabric at a cost that suits you then ask someone else to make the curtains up for you. Other options for keeping costs low are to exercise patience and wait for the sales before buying fabric or ready-made curtains; to visit mill shops and buy direct; to buy, and perhaps re-make, second-hand curtains; or just to modify your initial idea for an elaborate curtain design into something more manageable.

Making up curtains

Making the curtains yourself (see pages 240–253) will obviously save money, but the design needs to be something that accords with your level of sewing experience and the time available. A limited budget can be a blessing, helping you to choose a simple and uncluttered contemporary style that will last. The more frilly and full the curtain, the more complicated it will be to make, the longer it will take and the more fabric it will require.

Suspension

The type of curtain hanging needs to be determined in context, considering all the details of the setting. You must decide whether you want the curtain to hang from rings on a pole or from a track (see pages 232–233), whether this will be left exposed, hidden by a pelmet (see pages 244–245) or set into a *faux* pole. If there is little space between ceiling and window, a pelmet is inadvisable as it will either look thin and mean or crouch down on the window; a pole is preferable in such a situation. If, on the other hand, there is plenty of space, and you want the window to appear taller than it is, a well-proportioned pelmet can help create an illusion of greater height.

Fabric

The choice of fabric suitable for making up into curtains is so huge it can seem baffling (see pages 236–239). Take the overall style of the room as your starting point and first establish which type of window decoration is most appropriate: flimsy fabric for creating floaty effects or for layering; plain fabric, pale or richly coloured, perhaps with a velvety pile or an interesting weave; refreshing checks or stripes; printed graphic motifs; traditional fabric like floral chintz, tartan, printed linen or *toile de Jouy*; picture fabric; ethnic-style fabric like crewelwork, kilim print or Indian hand-blocked cotton; rich silk or damask.

Practical considerations are often involved in the choice of a fabric. Silk, for example, fades and rots in sunlight and washable cotton is useful in a kitchen or bathroom. Scale is another factor: a large window can take a huge print that will look entirely out of proportion on a small window; and conversely a small print will look fiddly on a large window.

Trimming

Trimmings can make all the difference to curtains but they must be used with great care (see pages 238–239). A contrasting braid or ribbon set back from the edge of a plain curtain or blind gives it weight and definition. A substantial fringe along the bottom of a pull-up curtain or Austrian blind can transform it, making it look serious and luxurious.

Lining

The final but important consideration is whether or not to have a lining (see pages 248–253). Lightweight, unlined curtains are the simplest to make, while lined curtains keep out light and draughts better and look more substantial. Curtains can be lined in two main ways. Heavy interlining is like solid padding between the front and lining fabrics; locked-in lining means the curtain lining is invisibly attached at intervals to the front fabric. Professional curtain makers say these hang better than loose-lined curtains, which are the simplest to make (see pages 250–251). Detachable linings are versatile as they can be taken off for laundering, or removed in summer to give the curtains a lighter effect.

◄ *Draping elegantly on the floor, these unlined curtains have an integral valance and are tied to a slender wooden pole. Because the curtains are made from pre-shrunk calico, and the valances, edging and ties from pre-shrunk linen union, these curtains can be machine-washed without problem.*

Directory of poles, tracks and accessories

Poles

Curtain poles are intended to be seen and to make a strong visual contribution to the overall look of a window and its dressing. They are altogether bolder and more demonstrative than curtain track, which is designed to be discreet and often hidden behind a pelmet or valance. Made in either wood or metal, there is a huge range of poles to choose from.

Poles are made in various diameters and are sold by length to suit your requirements. Pole kits, with brackets and rings included, are widely available. The poles come in set lengths and can be cut if required.

Wooden poles

Wooden poles are often finished at either end with a finial. Both poles and their rings (where these exist) can be painted, stained, oiled or waxed.

Natural wood suits many interiors. Plain black, grey or white looks discreet, or you could paint the pole to match the walls, the woodwork or the curtain fabric. For something as grand as richly coloured brocade, a gold-painted pole would be dramatic. Wooden poles without rings can be used with handmade cased or looped headings, for example. **1**

Lightweight rods

A variety of rods can be used to carry lightweight curtains and sheers, including wooden dowelling, plastic net rod and brass café rod. These slender rods are well suited to small windows and look good with cased, slotted and other headings that do not have rings. They take up little space and are therefore useful where the top of a window is just below a low ceiling. Light rods with a bracket and hinge at one end can be used in a dormer or other deep-set window; instead of drawing back the curtains the rods swing open during the day.

1

2

4

Metal poles

Metal poles and any rings are generally made of brass, iron or steel. Steel and iron poles, often painted black, could be painted any colour. **3**

Faux poles

Although a *faux* pole, or corded pole, is made to resemble a brass or wooden pole, it is not really a pole at all. It has track set into it, with rings masking the runners. A hidden pulley system opens and closes the curtains, which helps protect the fabric. An overlap arm can be used with *faux* poles.

Tracks

Curtain track consists of a rail and sliding runners into which the curtain hooks slot. Made of either plastic or metal, it is available in a huge variety

of subtly different types and weights. Some are fitted with a corded pulley system which helps protect fine or delicate fabric from wear and tear. Some have an integral valance rail.

As track takes up little space, it is particularly useful in situations where there is almost no wall space between the top of a window and a low ceiling. It can be bent to fit around curves such as bay windows. When the curtains are pulled back, however, track will show unless it is hidden by a pelmet or other covering.

The length of track required is governed by the bulk of the curtains and the extent to which you want them to draw back from the window during the day. You can buy track in kits or you can buy all the parts separately according to your needs. The sliding runners are sold separately. **4**

Metal track

Stronger and longer-lasting than plastic, metal track is probably a better choice for heavy curtains, the weight of which may pull plastic track from the wall. If fitted with a corded pulley system, metal track provides the easiest way of drawing curtains around bends; in such cases it is best fitted professionally to ensure accurate results. Track can incorporate an overlap arm to allow one curtain to overlap the other when closed. Metal track can be painted with enamel paint.

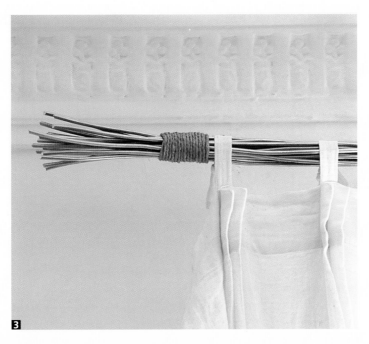

3

Cording sets

A cording set is useful if the curtains are especially fragile or fine as it removes the necessity of pulling on the curtains to draw them closed. Sets can be bought with track or separately. Electric curtain track is also available. This has a small motor at the end of the track which draws the curtains, activated either at the touch of a button or by a remote control unit.

Draw rods are a simple alternative to a cording set. These are plastic rods, one attached to the leading edge of each curtain, which allow curtains to be drawn manually but without the fabric being handled.

Valance track

This can be bought with track, or separately and added on later to most types of curtain track with the help of brackets and extension arms. Plastic valance track is easy to bend to shape.

Weights

These can be sewn into the hem of a curtain to give it added weight and help it hang well. They come in two forms: buttons and tape. Buttons are round weights with holes in the middle for sewing in place. If it is not sewn in position, a button weight will, in time, gradually move along the bottom of the curtain. Leadweight tape consists of a narrow tube of fabric containing small cylindrical weights which is placed in a continuous line along the bottom of the curtain hem.

Cord tidy

This small plastic shape solves the problem of what to do with the strings of a heading tape after the curtain has been gathered up. The strings are simply wound around the cord tidy, which is then tucked into one of the pockets in the tape. The strings should never be cut off; if they are, the curtain heading cannot be pulled flat for cleaning or alterations.

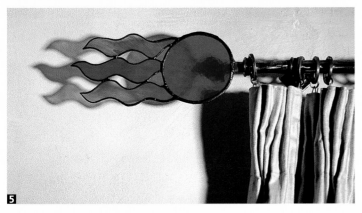

5

Plastic track

Plastic track is easier to fit than metal and adequate for light- to middle-weight curtains. It is easily bent around gentle corners, the ideal type for this being that with a metal core, as this keeps its shape better than track that is made entirely of plastic. Plastic track cannot be painted successfully.

Accessories

Rings

These are used with a curtain pole. If you buy a pole kit, the brackets and rings will be provided; otherwise, buy as many rings as you want separately, checking that they fit the pole, but not too tightly or they will be difficult to draw across. Allow for a ring at each end of the pole, between the bracket and the finial, to secure the outer edge of each curtain. **2**

Curtain clips

These small curtain rings, with a decorative clip at the bottom instead of a hole for a hook, are most suitable for lightweight curtains. Before the clips are attached to the curtain fabric, the top edge of the fabric needs to be turned over twice and hemmed, with the raw edge of the lining, if any, sewn in under the hem. Clips should be attached to the top of the curtain at intervals, with one at each end.

Sewn-on rings

Sew small brass, metal or plastic rings to the curtain top at intervals, with one at each end. These are not suitable for heavy curtains, where the rings might pull and tear the fabric.

Hooks

In addition to standard plastic and metal curtain hooks which slot into heading tape and then into the runners or rungs, there are several clever types with special uses. Among these are the combined hook and slider, and the combined valance hook and glider. With the latter, the valance is divided and draws back with the curtain during the day, rather than remaining across the whole window like a pelmet.

Finials

A decorative finial is usually fitted onto each end of a pole. They finish the pole with a flourish and need to be in proportion to the pole. A fiddly little finial on the end of a stout pole, for instance, will look silly. There is a wide choice of finials, including balls, spear heads, arrow ends, curlicues, rams' heads, pineapples and many more, in a range of materials and finishes. **5**

Fixing poles and tracks

Fixing poles

Poles are designed to be face-fixed to a wall with support brackets, one at each end and possibly an additional central bracket. Some poles can be end-fixed by slotting them into side wall fixings.

A bracket prevents the rings moving any further along the pole, so the position of the end brackets (and indeed the length of the pole) depends on the fullness of the curtain and how far back from the window you want the curtain to pull. A frequent mistake is to place the brackets too close to the window. As a guide, fix brackets at least 15cm (6in) out from the window frame on each side, and allow about 10cm (4in) between the bracket and the finial. The outer curtain ring sits between the bracket and the finial to hold the curtain in place when drawn.

The pole should be installed parallel with the top of the window, unless this is wildly out of true with the line of the ceiling, in which case you can position the pole either strictly level, using a spirit level, or somewhere in between level and parallel with the window, whichever looks better. The pole should be high enough above the window for the curtain to cut out light at the top, but not so high that there is a great expanse of wall between it and the top of the window.

If you would like the curtain to fall further into the room than the brackets allow – perhaps to clear a deep window sill or to fall in front of a blind – mount each bracket on a wooden block. The blocks can be finished in the same way as the wall, with paint or paper. As the brackets (or brackets and blocks) will be bearing considerable weight, ensure that they are securely fixed to the wall with long screws.

Fitting lightweight rods is easy as the ends can be slotted into small metal brackets with integral sockets, either recessed or face-fixed. Telescopic rods are also available; they have an internal spring that enables them to expand to fit the window. Dowelling, being less rigid than a proper curtain pole, needs to be well supported in the middle to prevent it sagging. A small decorative hook of the type onto which you loop a tie-back will do the job. Generally speaking, the thicker the

▲ Simple cotton curtains are hung with iron rings sewn directly to the top of the curtain. The rings are then strung on a narrow iron pole with decorative curled finials. Because the pole is narrow and the curtains long and therefore quite heavy, the pole is given added support by a central bracket.

▶ Pretty gingham curtains are ideal for the kitchen of a country house. They are hung from a standard curtain track which is concealed by a covered fascia board. The board has been decorated with the same fabric as that of the curtains, and extends down behind the ruffle but in front of the track.

Fixing poles and tracks

pole, the further it can go without a central support, but even a full-sized pole may need one if it is required to carry heavy curtains.

Fixing track

The height at which track is fixed depends on the look you want and whether there is to be a pelmet. It can be attached either to the wall or to the ceiling.

Track is attached to the wall by brackets which can be either of fixed size or extendable to the required length. Supplied with track kits or bought separately, extendable brackets are useful if you want the curtain to stand clear of a blind or net curtain that will hang behind it. They can be screwed directly to the wall or to a wooden batten fixed to the wall, which will spread the load. Special brackets also allow more than one track for a layered effect.

Track should be fitted at least 5cm (2in) above the window and 15–40cm (6–16in) beyond either side of the window. To fix it, first screw the brackets to the wall, making sure they are level and spaced at regular intervals. Use a hacksaw to cut either

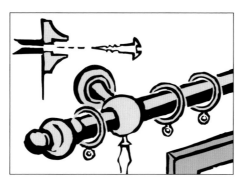

1 Poles are held by matching brackets, screwed onto the wall. Use wall plugs if fixing onto a masonry wall.

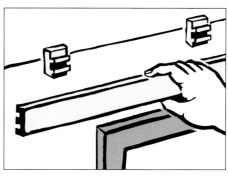

2 To fix track, draw a horizontal line with a spirit level to show the drilling position for the supporting brackets.

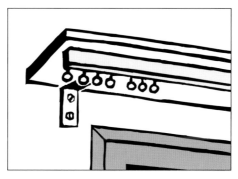

3 Pelmet boards are supported by right-angled brackets screwed to the underside, behind the curtain track.

4 To conceal the curtain track, make a small fascia board and cover it with the same fabric as the curtain.

plastic or metal track to the exact measurement you require. Clip the track to the brackets and then secure it to the wall according to the manufacturer's instructions.

When the window has a pelmet or a similar covering, the track can be attached either to the wall or to the base of the pelmet board. Its position should be far enough back from the front edge to allow room for bunching of the curtains when they are drawn open, but not so far back that the track is visible when looking up at the pelmet. The exact position depends on the bulkiness of the curtains. For unlined cotton curtains the track can be only 5cm (2in) from the front; heavy, interlined curtains will need to be hung further back.

Track can also be hidden when the curtains are drawn open by use of a fascia board attached to the front of a pelmet board. This is a narrow piece of wood or buckram, faced with the curtain material and attached with Velcro, tacks or glue around the edge of a pelmet board or to the front of the track.

The track is fixed behind it to the pelmet board or wall; the curtain hooks loop into the runners, and the gathered frill of the curtains stands up in front of the fascia board to cover it when the curtains are closed.

Returns

To exclude light and draughts properly, curtains on track may need a return. This is a permanently fixed section of the curtain that blocks out the gap between the end of the track and the wall. If the track is attached to the wall by short brackets, very little light and few draughts will get through, and so a return may not be necessary. If the brackets are longer, make a fixing for the end of the curtain with an eyelet screw. If there is no pelmet board, either fix a block of wood to the wall for this purpose or use a special track return kit. This includes an arm which goes at a right angle to the end of the track and into which the curtain is hooked. Alternatively, plastic track with a metal core can be bent back to create a return.

Directory of fabrics

There is a vast range of fabrics suitable for curtains and blinds. Before choosing one, it is a good idea to spend some time in a well-stocked fabric shop or department, during daylight hours. Take any fabrics you particularly like the look of to the window to see their colour and finish in natural light; artificial lighting alters colours considerably. The shop will give you a tiny piece to take away. You can order a larger sample of anything you really like, but you will probably have to pay a deposit for this.

When you are ready to buy your fabric, take your measurements and calculations with you in case you need to consult an assistant about quantities. Be sure to buy enough fabric in one go, rather than having to go back later for more, as colour quality may not be identical between batches.

The following descriptions will help you decide which fabric is right for the curtain effect you want.

Sheer fabrics

Sheer and flimsy fabrics are suitable for curtains intended to diffuse and filter light as well as create privacy during daylight hours. They are too delicate to form blinds, but you can hang a plain, ungathered panel at the window. They can be combined with a heavier curtain in front, a blind behind or a frame formed by a lambrequin.

Pretty and elegant, voile is a very fine, sheer fabric printed or woven with a pattern or pictures. Ordinary nylon net comes with a ready-made hem down one side and a channel for inserting wire down the other and is sold in different widths. Lace makes a charming window covering, especially if you can find a picture panel or antique piece that fits your window. Embroidered cotton is a charming patterned alternative to lace or voile. Muslin, a loosely woven fine cotton, is less see-through than other sheers. It drapes well but crushes easily. **1**

1

2

4

Plain fabrics

Unpatterned twill is usually a pure cotton fabric with subtly interesting textured weaves; the most attractive of which are, arguably, the herringbone and waffle patterns. Slubby fabric is often hand-woven and therefore has irregular threads which give it an attractive roughness.

Calico, available in various widths including some wide enough to curtain most windows without joins, is an inexpensive plain cotton fabric suitable for customizing, but wash it first to shrink it and remove the dressing before applying any paint.

Pure linen, and linen-and-cotton mixes known as linen union, are strong, long-lasting and hard-wearing fabrics which take dye superbly and hang well. Available in various weights, they look marvellous made up into curtains and blinds. **4**

Checks and stripes

Of all patterns, checks and stripes are the most cheerful and unfussy. There is a huge variety of designs and colours available, and they generally mix well together in a room, especially alongside a traditional print such as floral linen or *toile de Jouy* (see opposite).

range. Horizontal stripes are less common than vertical ones, but they do have many of the same qualities, although they will not help a dull, low window look any taller.

Originally designed to keep feathers inside mattresses, ticking has a distinctive stripe. It is available in variously coloured stripes on white or cream, and has become popular as an inexpensive and hard-wearing soft-furnishing fabric.

Traditional patterned fabrics

Due to their long history and historical associations, traditional fabrics add a certain grace and gravitas to a room. They also remain among the most beautiful patterned fabrics available.

Floral prints are quintessentially English. Among the most charming are those that have a faded look, as if they have been around for generations. Florals mix well with other patterns, such as stripes, which can freshen them up and prevent them looking fusty. Chintz, a glazed cotton printed with flowers such as roses and peonies, is the epitome of English style. **3**

Toile de Jouy is a distinctive picture fabric, generally showing pastoral scenes, printed in a single colour on white or cream.

Provençal prints, based originally on imported seventeenth-century Indian-printed fabrics, are decorated with flowers and abstract motifs printed in black and distinctive rich colours like egg yolk and bottle green. They make a strong impact, combining a rustic farmhouse feel with the exoticism of Provençal heat, harsh sunlight and scented air.

Jacquard has a pattern woven into it, often of flowers and leaves, and a slightly silky finish.

Paisley, a popular fabric design that originated in Scotland, has a swirling pattern of rounded shapes that curve into a point; it generally comes in rich and strong colours. **5**

Geometric patterns always look good made into blinds, although they must be printed straight and cut square for a successful result.

Gingham is a jolly check formed from coloured stripes woven on a white background. Available in a dazzling range of alternatives, checks can be anything from quiet, woven in two subtle shades, to loud and boisterous, combining several bright colours.

Madras cotton is a brightly patterned cotton check originally from India.

Wide stripes can look stunning and create a strong graphic image when formed into a blind, draped over a pole across the top of the window or made into floor-length curtains. **2**

Narrow stripes are more restrained and will contribute a quiet elegance to an interior. They mix well with floral prints and checks in the same colour

Tartan, the Scottish hallmark beloved of Queen Victoria, who decorated whole rooms with it, has a sober, masculine feel. The colours are mostly rich and resonant, though some are rather drab and disappointing. **1**

Graphic print fabrics

Sometimes sharply defined, sometimes loose and painterly, but generally fresh and uncluttered, images such as stars, heraldic motifs, circles, triangles and letters of the alphabet are favoured motifs for this sort of fabric. Colours vary from pale and subtle to knock-out brilliant. Many are manufactured in several colourways, with curtains in one colour, say, to be combined with a pelmet in another – the pattern being the unifying force.

Picture-print fabrics

These have picture images scattered across them and the best are wonderfully fresh and attractive. Because of their content, such as circus performers, boats, animals, cups and saucers, fruit and vegetables, classical motifs or playing cards, some are better used in one type of room than another. Some designed for children's rooms are particularly delightful. **2**

Ethnic fabrics

These can add variety and interest to almost any style of interior, not only those with an ethnic feel. Indian crewelwork, woollen chain stitch worked on a creamy cotton background, usually depicts birds and leaves in light shades of blues, greens and pinks. Kilim print is strongly coloured printed cotton with bold and distinctive geometric patterns drawn from kilims, woven cotton and wool rugs made in central Asia. Hand-blocked Indian cotton can be fragile, so it needs to be handled with care.

Rich fabrics

These gorgeous fabrics are useful for creating a grand or sumptuous interior and an aura of luxury. Pure silk is the most lustrous of fabrics but varies greatly in type, quality and price. It is available in a dazzling choice of colours, some shot through with another colour, some overprinted with

Interlinings

For luxuriously thick curtains that will drape well and provide good draught protection, use interlining. Bump, the heaviest, bulkiest type, makes curtains look luxurious. It gives excellent protection against cold and, indeed, heat, when sewn into curtains. Lighter domette can be used with lighter fabrics and gives body to Roman blinds and pelmets. Synthetic, the lightest of all, can be slightly see-through. Its main virtue is its cheapness, but its other good points are that it should not shrink when cleaned, and it will not cover you with fluff during sewing.

Trimmings

Interesting trimmings can transform a handsome curtain into something really special. A ribbon, 1.5cm (⅝in) or more wide, adds interest and definition if you choose a contrasting colour and set it back from the edges of a curtain or blind. Braid is a looped and woven trimming available in a multitude of colours and designs, some of which are wonders of textile engineering and fiercely expensive. A braid with pompoms, sewn along the leading edges of a pair of simple muslin or sheer curtains, will completely transform them. Fringing, too, comes in endless variations of colour and design. One of its best uses is at the bottom of an Austrian blind or pull-up curtain (see pages 266–267). When the blind is pulled up, the fringe looks pretty against the light; when let down, it gives weight and definition to the bottom edge. A pelmet or blind with a shaped bottom edge can be made to look positively exotic if tassels are attached to hang off each downward point. Some ready-made edgings incorporate beading. Alternatively, you can sew or string individual beads along the edge of a sheer curtain for added weight, detail and a delicate touch of colour. **3**

a pattern, some woven into checks or other patterns. Although it is not hardy enough for blind making and it rots in sunlight, it should not necessarily be excluded from curtain-making, but it must be used with care and forethought. **4**

Damask can be made from silk, cotton or man-made fibres. It has a woven, two-tone pattern, usually of intertwined leaves and/or flowers. Really grand damask comes with appliqué and/or embroidery added to the surface. Like damask, brocade has a woven pattern but in more than the one colour.

Velvet, the most luxurious of fabrics, has a pile which must always lie in the same direction, otherwise the colour will look different. Available in a whole range of colours and patterns, it is incomparably sumptuous and invaluable for creating an atmosphere of comfort and elegance. The thickness of its pile makes it unsuitable for making into blinds. Plush has a pile like velvet, but it is longer and less closely woven. It was particularly popular in the nineteenth century for tablecloths and as curtains in a multi-layered window treatment.

Lining fabrics

Coloured linings are available in a range of colours to match or contrast with almost every fabric. Although some are certified fade-proof, the safest choice is always cream or white. There is also a choice of qualities, the best having a certain amount of body that will survive cleaning.

Blackout, a special fabric for excluding light, is available in various weights, the heaviest of which can be difficult to work with. Thermal lining, known as milium, is coated on one side with aluminium and gives excellent thermal protection without adding bulk to curtains in the way that interlinings do.

First steps to making curtains

Measuring up and estimating quantities

Measuring up a window and estimating how much fabric is required for the curtains need to be done accurately. To work out how much fabric you need, the formula is to multiply the number of fabric widths required by the working length of the curtains, plus any allowance for a pattern repeat. For how to determine these lengths, see below.

Having established the style of your curtains, it is easiest to take the measurements for your fabric once you have installed the pole and rings or track and runners (see pages 234–235) from which they will hang. Tracks and poles must be fixed with enough room either side of the window to accommodate the curtains when pulled back (heavy fabrics will need more than light fabrics), and should be fixed at least 5cm (2in) above the window.

If you want to purchase your fixings and fabric at the same time, you must estimate the positioning of your track or pole and the depth of any rings as accurately as you can.

Since you will not know the width of your fabric, or the size of any pattern repeat, until you have chosen it, you will have to do most of your calculations in the shop. Take your measurements and a calculator.

Measuring for fabric widths

To calculate the number of widths of fabric you need, first measure the length of the pole or track (A) (not the window). For a track with an overlap in the middle, add on the amount of the overlap. Add as much as necessary to cover any returns at the sides (from the track back to the wall).

Multiply this curtain-width measurement (A) by the multiple required for your chosen curtain heading (see pages 244–245). Add 7.5cm (3in) per curtain (i.e. 15cm/6in for a pair) to allow for turnbacks, then divide this figure by the given width of your chosen fabric. The resulting figure is the number of widths of fabric you need. Round up to the nearest whole number of widths. (If your figure is only just over a whole number, you might consider rounding down rather than up because of the large amount of wastage involved, especially if your fabric is costly.)

▲ *A wall of light-flooded windows is curtained with a sheer lightweight fabric edged with bands of colour in a slightly heavier fabric. Joining widths to make wide curtains is much easier if the fabric has no pattern, but the seams must be neat on both sides if the fabric is see-through.*

Measuring for working length

The length of fabric depends on the chosen length of the curtains, plus any allowance for the hanging, depending on how much it will be covered by the top of the curtains.

For a pole and rings that will be totally in view, measure from the bottom of a curtain ring. If, however, you want a ruffle to cover part of the rings, start from where the top of the ruffle will be.

For a track, which should be hidden when the curtains are closed, measure from just above the top edge of the track. If the track is to be hidden by a pelmet, measure from the runners. If it is to have a fixed, non-drawing heading, measure from the top of the piece of wood across the top of the window to which the curtain will be attached. In all cases add 4cm (1½in) to allow for the turnover at the top of the curtains.

Measure down to the sill (B), below the sill (C) or to the floor (D). For curtains that

Measuring up for curtains

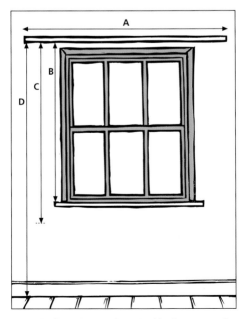

1 Curtain dimensions are determined by the amount of window clearance at either side and the length desired.

Tools and materials

For measuring up and fixing
- **Step ladder.**
- **Steel tape measure:** use a long metal tape rather than a fabric one which might have stretched with use, and measure in centimetres.
- **Notepad and pencil:** for recording the measurements.

All curtains

To make up curtains, plenty of space – ideally a large table – is essential. If the table is not large enough, lay a big board on it to provide a larger work area.

- **A sewing machine, and supply of needles:** any machine with a pedal action or electric pedal control will do so long as it does a straight running stitch.
- **Fabric, lining, interlining and trimming** (although all of the last three are optional).
- **Thread:** for tacking (in a dark colour if the fabric is light, light if it is dark); and also for sewing – plenty of it in a colour to match the front fabric. Always use thread of the same fibre and similar weight as the fabric itself.
- **Weights:** to help curtains hang well, weights can be inserted in the hem. Alternatively, a special weighted tape can be sewn on.
- **Sharp scissors:** in various sizes.
- **Dressmaker's pins:** these must be sharp and rust-free. Glass-headed ones are more easily noticeable and less likely to get lost in the curtain. Do not leave pins in fabric for long as they might leave holes.
- **Tailor's chalk:** for marking cutting lines.
- **Steam iron:** to press material flat before and after making up.

Keep your sewing equipment orderly, tidying up at the end of each day so that you can find things when you start again. A tray or box in which to keep all loose equipment is useful. Heavy weights for holding fabric in place, such as bricks wrapped in scrap interlining and sewn into scrap cotton, are a good idea. Sew a handle on the top of each for easy lifting and moving as you work.

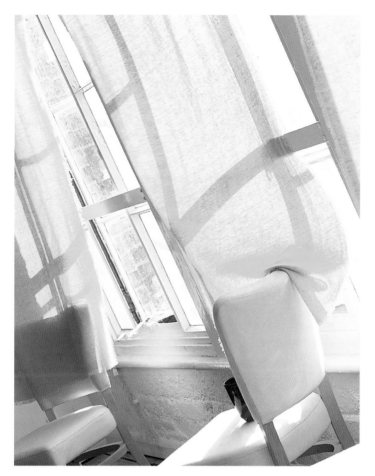

◀ *Where there is a large expanse of window, an economical and contemporary option is to have curtains which hang completely flat when closed. These can be made specially or ready-made textiles such as shawls, throws or tablecloths can be used for instant effect.*

will drape on the floor add 15–25cm (6–10in), depending on how much curtain you want on the floor; for ones that will just skim the floor deduct 6mm (¼in). Finally, add a hem allowance of 16cm (6½in) for lined curtains or 10cm (4in) for unlined. The total figure is the working length of the curtain.

Pattern repeats

Patterned fabrics have a 'repeat', the distance between the point where the pattern begins and the point where it ends before being repeated. When a fabric has a repeat, you will need to allow extra fabric in order to match the pattern across joined widths of a curtain and also across two curtains. To calculate the extra fabric needed, round up the working length of the curtain to the nearest whole multiple of the repeat measurement. For example, if the working length is 1.95m (76¾in) and the repeat is 20cm (8in), round the working length figure up to the next multiple of 20cm (8in), i.e. 2m (78¾in).

▲ *Another economical method of covering large windows is to hang curtains made from different fabrics whose colour and texture contrast interestingly, all finished to the same length. The fabrics might be inexpensive in themselves, like the blue cheesecloth, or bought cheaply in sales or as remnants.*

Cutting, matching and joining fabric

▲ *A simple yellow and white striped cotton has been cleverly transformed by dividing the curtains into bands with the stripes going alternately down and across. The bands of fabric are separated by a narrow black stripe. For added visual interest, a checked Roman blind hangs behind each pair of curtains.*

Cutting fabric

Iron the fabric smooth to make it easier to measure. Cut this to the individual lengths you require, ensuring that both top and bottom raw edges are cut straight – at 90 degrees to the selvedges. With loosely woven fabric and linens, a weft (crossways) thread can be drawn out enabling you to cut along the line left by it in the fabric. For other fabrics you will need to use a set square.

Plain fabric

Measure out your lengths, marking each cutting line with pins at each side on the selvedge. If necessary, use a metre (yard) stick to align the two marks and, using tailor's chalk, draw a line to cut across the fabric. As you cut each length, mark the top of the fabric with a safety pin. Fold each length neatly or roll it onto a cardboard tube to prevent it getting creased or crumpled. If you are making two curtains, then you will need to divide the number of widths in half at this point (e.g. 4 widths = 2 curtains of 2 widths each; 3 widths = 2 curtains of 1½ widths each). The total width of fabric you need rarely coincides with an exact number of fabric widths. If the discrepancy is small, it may be preferable to absorb some extra width by taking it up in the curtain heading. Certainly for unlined, fine fabric, distributing excess fabric in the spacing of the folds as it hangs is less of a problem than for a heavy fabric with a box-pleated heading.

If you do need to remove excess fabric, trim a width at the outside or back edge of each curtain, never at the inside or leading edge. Similarly, if a width of fabric is being split into two to make up the required total width, add the part width to the outside or back edge in the same way.

Patterned fabric

Before you start work, check for faults and misprinting. The fabric should be cut following the grain. If the pattern is not square to the selvedge or is printed off the grain, consider returning it to the shop or adjust your cutting to follow the pattern.

Try to arrange a patterned fabric so that the bottom of the curtain falls at the end of a repeat. Mark a line across the fabric along the base of the first pattern repeat, then mark a second line for the hem allowance – 16cm (6½in) below for lined curtains, 10cm (4in) for unlined. Cut on this second line. For full-length curtains that are to hang from a pole, where the pattern will be less gathered up than when using heading tape, you might prefer to have the complete repeat at the top. In this case, you will need to measure your lengths from the top of the fabric down-wards. Draw your first line across the fabric at the top of the first pattern repeat, then a second line 4cm (1½in) above that for the heading allowance. Cut on the second line.

It is important that the pattern matches across the widths and across both curtains if there are two. Line up the first cut length against the uncut fabric, matching the pattern exactly before cutting a second length.

Joining widths

Plain fabric

To join the drops, pin right sides together along the edge. Tack along each seam then sew, 1.5cm (⅝in) in from the edge, from the bottom. Press flat. For unlined curtains, you can make a flat fell seam. Having pressed the seam flat, trim back one seam allowance to half its original width. Fold the other one over to cover it, then fold under this edge of the seam allowance to enclose the raw edges. Top stitch through all the layers. This will show on the front of the curtain.

Patterned fabric

To join patterned fabric, fold under and press a 1.5cm (⅝in) seam allowance down the side that is to be joined of one length of fabric. With right sides facing upwards, place this over the unfolded seam allowance of the second piece, matching the pattern horizontally and pinning it in place. This should be tacked using ladder stitch. With a knotted thread starting under the fold, stitch up through the fabric and across the join and down through the bottom piece and back up through the fold. Repeat to form horizontal 'ladder' stitches across the join. To machine stitch the seam, place the right sides of the fabric together and stitch in the usual way.

Cutting, matching and joining fabric

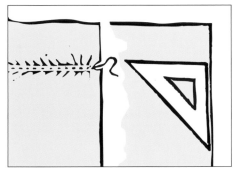

1 To get a straight, right-angled raw edge, pull out a weft thread, if possible, or place a set square on the selvedge.

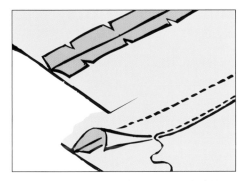

2 Either press seams open, or trim back one side, fold over the other to enclose the raw edges and top stitch.

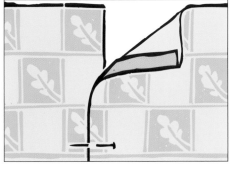

3 To join patterned fabric, fold under one seam allowance, place it over the other, matching the pattern, and pin.

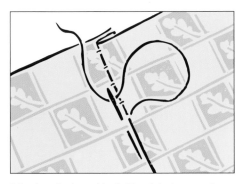

4 Hand sew in place with a ladder stitch, then turn the top piece back and machine stitch along the seam line.

▲ *In this grand window treatment, fixed linen curtains have a cased heading made from the same bold stripe as the blind behind, and the linen has been carefully matched to ensure the pattern works perfectly across the seams. The curtains' static heading allows the curtains to drape beautifully, and the decorative pole and finials complete the effect.*

Gathered headings

The way that the top of the curtain is gathered or folded into a pattern of pleats is referred to as the 'curtain heading'. The type of heading affects how the fabric falls when the curtains are closed as well as the amount of fabric required to make the curtains.

For substantially interlined, heavyweight curtains, the heading is best made by hand, with the pleats and hooks sewn in individually. This is a job for a professional or someone with experience of making curtains. The usual way for amateurs and beginners to arrange the top of curtains is to use ready-made, woven heading tape.

Heading tapes vary in depth and stiffness, according to the type of gather. They have strings threaded through them for gathering up the curtain, and pockets into which the hooks - by which the curtains are suspended from the pole or track - are inserted. An alternative to pull-cord tapes are those tapes with which you use prongs to form the gathering. These are easily removed for cleaning.

Heading tape is sold by the metre (yard). The length required is a little more than the total fabric width required for each curtain.

Types of heading tape

Different multiples of fabric are suggested for the tapes listed below. The range of multiples for some tapes allows a choice between the minimum amount of fabric required to make the heading look respectable and the maximum amount for a generous look.

Standard: This tape gives a shallow, gently gathered heading suitable for lightweight, unlined curtains. Depending on how full the curtains are to be, the fabric width required is 1½ to 2 times the length of the pole or track. The tape should be sewn 2.5cm (1in) from the top of the curtain – so that the curtain will cover any tracking or partly cover the rings of a pole – or it can be sewn closer to the top to allow it to hang below the rings on a pole.

Pencil pleat: Wider and more robust than standard heading tape, this gives a much deeper, smarter, more regimented gather, pulling the fabric into regular, rounded pencil-shaped pleats. Suitable for most types of curtain, it is available in several widths and requires a fabric width of 2¼ to 2½ times the length of the track or pole. There are three

Gathered headings

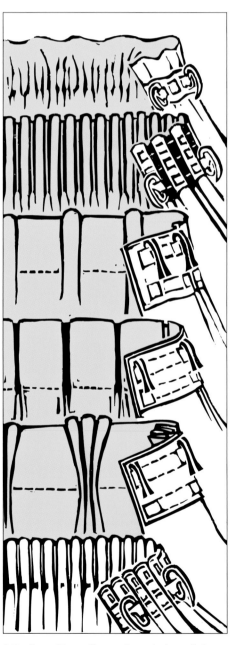

1 Headings with tape (from top): standard, pencil pleat, cartridge pleat, box pleat, triple/pinch pleat and net pleat.

▶ *The triple-pleat heading, also known as a French or pinch pleat, is fixed in place on this small window, giving the curtains a handsome finish. Having fixed curtains is a practical choice in this situation, as there is no space on the right into which the curtain could be drawn back.*

Heading tape

1 Turn under the heading allowance, place the tape in position and knot the strings under the cord.

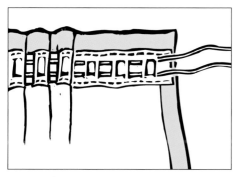

2 Hold the free cords in one hand and push the heading along until it is pleated to the required amount.

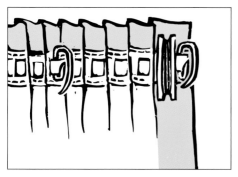

3 Insert hooks at each end and space the rest evenly along the curtain; tie the strings around a cord tidy.

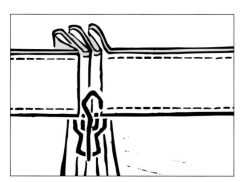

4 For triple pleats, insert one prong of a pleater hook in each of four pockets. Skip one pocket, then repeat.

rows of pockets, to offer a choice of hanging heights. The tape should be sewn 3mm (⅛in) from the top of the curtain.

Cartridge pleat: Cartridge pleats are single, large, regular, rounded pleats spaced between flat stretches of fabric. They give curtains sophistication, especially heavy floor-length ones. When pulling up the tape, match the pleats evenly across both curtains if there is a pair. Avoid having a pleat at either leading or back edge; these should hang flat. Cartridge pleats require a fabric width of 2½ times the length of the track or pole. The tape should be sewn 3mm (⅛in) from the top of the curtain.

Box pleat: Like cartridge pleat tape, this tape gives regular, tailored pleats, but these are flat and tucked behind the flat fabric rather than in front of it. Box pleats are suitable for all types of curtain, especially heavy, lined ones. When pulling up the tape, match the pleats evenly across both curtains if there is a pair. Box pleats require 3 times the length of track or pole, and the tape should be sewn 3mm (⅛in) from the top of the curtain.

Triple or pinch pleat: This tape gives regular, fanned, triple pleats at intervals across the curtain. Known as French pleats, these produce a handsome, tailored look for formal lined curtains and are available in several depths. When pulling up the tape, match the pleats evenly across both curtains if there is a pair. This tape requires fabric twice the length of the track or pole and should be sewn 3mm (⅛in) from the top of the curtain.

Net: This is a discreet, lightweight tape for net or sheer fabrics, combining pockets for hooks and loops for wire. It can be sewn to the top of the curtain either way up, depending on how much of the curtain you want to stand up above the hooks. Alternatively, wire or a rod can be threaded through the loops. Net tape can take a fabric width 2 to 3 three times the length of the wire, pole or track.

Attaching heading tape

Heading tape is sewn onto the top of the curtain back, once the curtain has been

▲ An otherwise plain triple-pleat curtain heading has been given the added decorative detail of a self-covered button on each of the pleats. This accentuates the pleats, but in a restrained way. The narrow curtain rod is carefully placed above the window to ensure it does not mask the charming plaster roses on the cornice.

made. Lay the tape over the raw edge of the turnback (see left for position) and pin and tack in place. At the inside edge of the curtain, unthread the strings for about 2.5cm (1in), then knot them underneath. Fold the tape end under to cover the knots; tack in place. Repeat on the outside edge of the curtain, but leave the cords free and on top of the tape. Machine stitch the tape in the same direction along both edges to avoid puckering. Machine stitch over both the tape ends, making sure the needle doesn't pass through the strings at the outside edge.

Gathering

Gather the curtain by holding the loose strings and pushing the tape along until it is sufficiently pleated to measure the length of the pole (for a single curtain) or half the length (for a pair). If you are using track with an overlap, allow for this. Coil then knot the loose strings or wrap them around a cord tidy (see pages 232–233). You can then insert the hooks, one at each end of the curtain with others spaced evenly between them.

Handmade headings

Headings can be created for hanging curtains from poles without using a heading tape. They include pierced headings, looped, tie-on and cased headings. Except for cased headings, each of the headings described below needs to have a loop, eyelet or tie at or very near each top corner to prevent the ends from drooping. When buying fabric for a curtain with looped headings you will need the same width of fabric as the length of the pole, and for pierced and tied headings, approximately twice the length of the pole, depending on the fabric and the way you wish the folds to hang. If in doubt, ask for advice at the point of purchase.

Pierced heading

Pierced curtains have metal-rimmed eyelets inserted along the top of the curtain through which a thin pole is threaded. Use an inexpensive eyelet kit bought from a DIY or hardware store. The eyelets should be positioned on the wrong side of the hem, approximately 10cm (4in) apart.

If you are using an eyelet kit, practise on a spare piece of fabric before making the holes in the curtains. Place the fabric over the die provided with the kit and, using the narrow end of the tool and a hammer, punch a small hole in it. Assemble both parts of the eyelet around the hole. The washer part should be uppermost, on the wrong side of the material, with its closed side upwards. Using the wide end of the tool, hit the washer sharply with a hammer. When you feel confident enough to make the eyelets in the curtain, use the position marks you have made on the curtain to line up the eyelet tool. To avoid later ripping of the fabric, the top of the curtain can be reinforced first with binding, cotton webbing or ribbon.

Looped heading

A looped heading has lined fabric tabs sewn into the top of the curtain through which the pole is slotted. Bearing in mind the total width of the curtain, determine how many tabs you want and their width. The finished width of each should be approximately 5cm (2in), so to make them, double the width and add 3cm (1¼in) for a seam. To establish how

▲ Cheerful, cottagey sunshine-yellow gingham curtains, unlined to let through the light, have been given an interesting heading. There is an integral valance to give the heading some weight, and the fabric ties that attach the curtain to its pole are extra long so that they hang down, looking a little like ribbons.

long the tabs need to be, measure the circumference of the rod or pole and then add 5cm (2in) for ease, plus 3cm (1¼in) for seams.

Cut out the strips of fabric and fold them in half lengthways, right sides together, and sew 1.5cm (⅝in) seams. Turn the tubes right side out and press them flat with the seam in the middle of one side. Loop the tabs and sew them together with a 1.5cm (⅝in) seam. Sew them to the right side of the fabric, 1.5cm (⅝in) from the top and with the loops hanging down.

Cut a strip of fabric for the facing 7.5cm (3in) deep and the same width as the curtain, plus 3cm (1¼in). Sew a small hem along one long edge of this. With right sides facing, pin the other, unhemmed edge to the curtain, along the attachment line of the loops, 1.5cm (⅝in) from the top edge. Tack and then stitch this strip in place along the top edge, catching in the loop bases as you go. Sew small hems at each end of the strip so that the strip aligns perfectly with the curtain.

Fold the facing strip over to the back of the curtain, with the wrong sides

Headings without tapes

1 A pierced curtain has metal eyelets spaced along the top, and the curtain is threaded onto a narrow pole.

2 Tabs of fabric are looped over and sewn onto the top of the curtain. A facing strip covers the seam line.

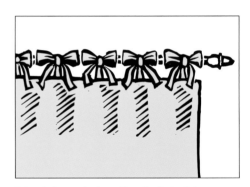

3 A variation on the looped heading is the tied-on curtain, where fabric strips are tied into bows.

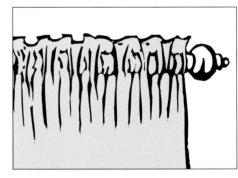

4 A cased or slotted heading can be sited at the top of the curtain or set down to form a ruffle.

Making the headings

1 Using an eyelet kit, place the fabric over the die, and hit the narrow end of the tool with a hammer.

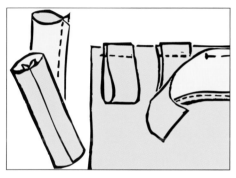

2 Fold strips of fabric in half and seam. Place along top of curtain, stitch in place, then cover with facing strip.

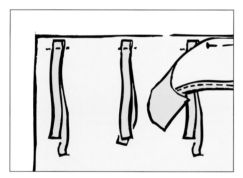

3 Stitch pairs of ties evenly across the curtain top, then cover with a facing strip as for the looped heading.

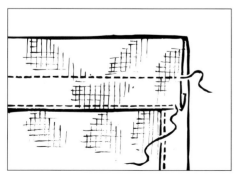

4 Fold a double hem deep enough for the slot and frill (if wanted) and stitch on either side of the slot.

together. Press so that the loops stand up at the top of the curtain. Slip stitch along the bottom edge and sides of the facing.

Tie-on curtains

Ties can be sewn into the top of the curtain in the same manner as the tabs of a looped heading and tied around a pole. Loose ties – made of ribbon, raffia, string, or 'invisible' fishing line – could be inserted through the eyelets of a pierced curtain instead of a pole.

Cased heading

A cased heading (also known as a slotted heading) is made by forming a channel or slot to take the curtain pole. At its simplest

▲ *These stunning gauzy linen curtains have been given texture and interest by making horizontal pleats throughout their length. The pleats, which hang loose, are quite narrow at the top and increasingly wide as they approach the bottom. The curtains have cased headings at the top and drape on the floor.*

this can be made at the very top of the curtain heading, or it can be placed just down from the top of the curtain so that a ruffle stands up above it. For this, fold a double hem deep enough for the slot and any frill, and first tack and then machine stitch along either side of the slot, in the same direction. The size of the slot is dictated by the diameter of the pole, which should fit easily, without the fabric being too tight or slack. You need a total fabric width of up to 2½ times the length of the pole, plus turn-backs. Curtains with cased headings cannot be drawn back easily, so they are well suited to sheers or nets which are intended to hang down permanently or be draped to one side.

Other headings

For lightweight curtains, make a double hem at the top edge and simply sew small brass rings at intervals along it for threading onto a pole. Alternatively, you can buy special curtain clips – essentially rings with decorative clips at the bottom – which clip onto the top of the curtain (see pages 232–233).

No-sew curtains

It is possible to make curtains without sewing a single stitch. All you need are tools and materials such as fabric glue, pinking shears, hammer and nails or a staple gun and staples, an eyelet tool or curtain clips. For curtains that make use of either of the latter two items, fold and glue a wide ribbon or tape over the raw edge at the top of the fabric to finish and reinforce it.

For all these curtains, use a fabric that is wide enough to cover the window without needing joins and, if possible, one that has a self-coloured selvedge. You can leave the edges plain or you can cut, turn back and glue decorative borders such as zigzag, scallop or castellated patterns.

Draped fabric

A very simple curtain style consists of a length of fabric, twice the height of the window, just thrown over a pole, with one or both layers draped to one side. To prevent the curtain sliding along the pole, reinforce and nail or staple the fabric at intervals to it.

Unlined curtains and sheers

Although they are often considered the poor relations of the curtain world, unlined curtains are among the most versatile, and in the right situation they can be beautiful. A single thickness of lightweight fabric will not excel at excluding light or draughts, but it has its own positive qualities. It will drape easily over a hold-back or on the floor. It can diffuse sunshine, creating privacy without blocking the light, and it can make an important contribution to a layered window treatment.

Natural fabrics

Linen, cotton twill, slub cotton and calico all work well when made into unlined curtains, as do lightweight, purpose-made textiles such as striped cotton sheets, Indian hand-printed

cotton bedspreads and saris with glittering woven borders (but remember that pure silk fades and even rots in sunlight). You can create your own decoration on an unlined cotton curtain by painting or drawing on it with special fabric paints or pens.

Sheers

Net, voile, lace and muslin are not intended to be lined, so they can be used to veil a window rather than to cover it up. They can be difficult to handle, especially if they are made from certain man-made fibres. If you find that they are slippery, try placing strips of tissue paper between the two layers you are sewing together and under the sewing machine foot; you simply tear the paper away

▶▶ Two layers of muslin, each a different brilliant colour, are sewn together across the top to create a magical curtain which drapes and billows beautifully. Natural fibres such as cotton can be dyed colourfast at home in a washing machine with household dyes.

▶ The single, flat, white unlined curtain that masks this window can be draped back to either side during the day. Braid strung with ornaments, laid flat across the top, adds visual interest and reduces the curtain's starkness and severity.

afterwards. Use lightweight thread with sheers. Some of these fabrics have a top and bottom hem already sewn into them and are sold off rolls in different lengths to suit the heights of standard window sizes. Just buy the amount you need for the width of your window.

Washing unlined curtains

Unlined curtains can be washed, a process not advised for lined curtains because the different fabrics shrink at different rates. A sensible idea is to pre-wash the fabric so that

Making the curtains

Unlined curtains are the easiest curtains of all to make yourself, especially if you have chosen a fabric that is easy to handle. With sufficiently wide fabric you may not even have to join drops, just hem around the edges and sew on heading tape or rings. If you do have to join drops, remember that the seams will be seen on the back of the curtain. You can use an open flat seam, but a French or flat fell seam that turns the raw edge in will give a much neater finish.

Once the widths are joined and any excess at the sides trimmed, turn in and press a double 2cm (¾in) hem on each side of the curtain and a double 5cm (2in) hem along the bottom, inserting leadweight tape (special weighted tape) if you want to give the fabric a bit of added weight.

To mitre the corners (which gives a neat, short diagonal seam where the side and bottom hems meet), unfold one turn of both the bottom and side hems but mark the limit of the double turns with pins on the edge. Fold the corner up diagonally, through the corner point of the curtain and the points marked with a pin. Refold the bottom and side hems to form a neat mitre. Finish these hems and the diagonal join with slip stitch. Do not cut the fabric across the corner, because it's possible that you will want to alter the curtains in the future.

Measure the finished curtain length up from the hem and mark the line with pins. Turn over the excess at the top, folding in the sides at a slight angle as you do so to form a neat edge. Press it and then trim back the fabric if necessary so that the heading tape will cover the raw edge. Snip the hems at each side on the fold line to ease the material. Attach the heading tape and gather up the curtains (see pages 244–245).

You are now ready to hang the curtain on its track or pole. The outermost hook on each curtain goes into a fixed hole to anchor it in place. This is either an eyelet screwed into the pelmet board or into a wall-mounted wooden block, or the end hole in a track; alternatively, on a curtain pole, it is the ring on the pole between the end bracket and the finial.

any shrinkage happens before you make the curtains. The disadvantage of this, however, is that you remove the finish or dressing that helps protect it from gathering dust.

An alternative to pre-washing is to cut the curtain extra wide and long, so that it drapes on the floor, gather it tightly at the top when first hung, and wash it only when absolutely necessary. When you rehang it, any shrinkage in the length will be absorbed by the billowing bottom, and you can gather the width less tightly across the top.

Making unlined curtains

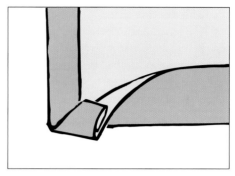

1 Turn a double 2cm (¾in) hem at each side and a double 5cm (2in) hem along the bottom. Press.

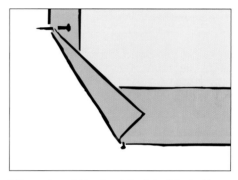

2 Open out one fold and mark the limit of the double hems with pins. Fold diagonally through both pins.

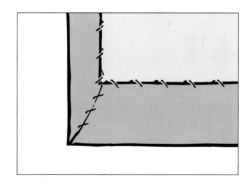

3 Refold the edges to form a mitre, and slip stitch the diagonal join and both hems.

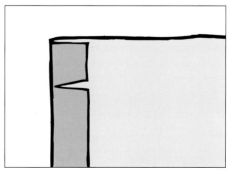

4 Finally, hem the top of the curtain, snipping into the hem along both sides of the fold line to ease the material.

Loose-lined curtains

Making the curtains

In these loose-lined curtains, the lining is attached to the front fabric at the top and sides only and so hangs loose, rather than the front and lining fabrics being sewn to each other as in conventional locked-in lined curtains. The easiest way to make loose-lined curtains is by the 'tube method', so called because a tube is made with the front and lining fabrics. These are the easiest type of lined curtain to make. (To make curtains with a locked-in lining, follow the instructions on pages 252–253.)

Join drops and press seams open on both the front and the lining fabrics (see pages 242–243). The lining fabric should be about 10cm (4in) narrower than the front fabric and 8cm (3¼in) shorter. Finish the bottom of the lining by machine stitching a double 5cm (2in) hem. Then lay the fabrics right sides together, with the bottom edge of the lining 18cm (7in) short of the bottom raw edge of the front fabric. Machine stitch the sides of the curtain, taking a 1.5cm (⅝in) seam allowance, with the edges of the lining and front fabric aligned, stopping well short of the top and bottom to allow for mitring.

You now have a tube of fabric. Turn it right side out and press the sides so that the front fabric comes round to the back an equal amount at each edge. One way of doing this is to mark the middle of the wrong side of both the front fabric and the lining with tailor's chalk, then match the marks when pressing the edges. Make a double 8cm (3¼in) hem on the front fabric, which will sit behind and just be covered by the lining, sewing in leadweight tape or weights, and finish the corners with mitres (see pages 248–249). Alternatively, if you are a perfectionist or there is any doubt about the pole, track or floor being exactly level, tack the hem and hang the curtains. After several days, make any necessary adjustments to the hem and finish with slip stitching.

To finish the top of the curtain, measure up the finished length from the hem and mark the line with pins. Turn down the front fabric along this line. If necessary, trim back any excess front fabric and trim the lining so that it fits neatly underneath it. Turn in the sides of the turnback (see pages 248–249) and attach the heading tape (see pages 244–245). Gather the heading to the required length and neatly tie up the loose strings. Finally, hang the curtains.

If the curtain is designed to hang straight, fix the folds by a process known as 'dressing' or 'draping' the curtain. To do this, pull the curtain closed and arrange the fabric into folds. Do this by tugging the hem in line with the pleats at the top of the curtain, and then running your fingers down the length of the curtain to create full-length pleats. Keeping these in place, carefully draw the curtain back. Using tape or strips of scrap fabric, gently tie the curtain in several places

▲ *These luxurious, heavy curtains are fixed at the top, but are looped back during the day to reveal their contrasting lime-green lining. Coloured lining can be made in any fabric, plain or patterned, so long as it has sufficient body to support the front fabric and is colourfast in sunlight.*

▶ *The plain lining of these striped curtains has been extended round to the front, to make a contrasting edging along the top and down the sides. Each curtain is hung from its own iron rod, and the rods are placed at different heights on the wall, which cleverly allows a considerable draught-excluding overlap.*

Lined curtains

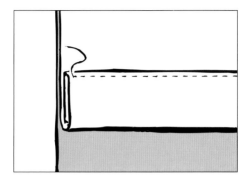

1 Machine stitch a double hem on the lining then place it on the main fabric, 18cm (7in) up from the bottom.

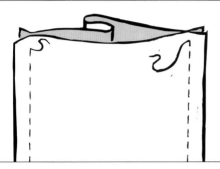

2 Machine stitch the sides of the curtain, stopping short of the top and bottom to leave room for mitring.

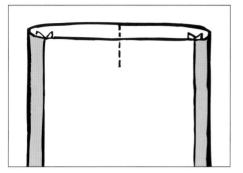

3 Turn the fabric tube right side out, and press the sides, matching the centre points of both fabrics.

up its length, starting near the bottom. Leave it for as long as possible, a few days at the least, to ensure the folds are fixed.

Detachable linings

Detachable linings can be removed in summer or for cleaning. Make up the front fabric and the lining as for two separate unlined curtains (see pages 248–249). The lining does not need to be so fully gathered as the front curtain. Sew the top of the lining into special tape designed for the top of detachable linings. Shaped in profile like an upside-down 'Y', the raw top edge of the lining fabric is inserted within the open bottom section of the tape and sewn along its bottom. Curtain hooks are then looped through the top of this tape, before being hooked through the heading tape at the top of the front curtain fabric, and into rings or runners on the pole or track.

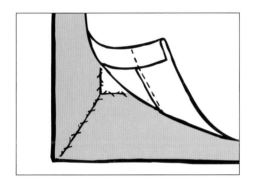

4 Unfold the hem and refold the hem and side seam into a mitre. Slip stitch the diagonal join and the hem.

5 Close the curtain and use your hands to arrange the folds. Tie them in place and leave for a few days.

Detachable linings

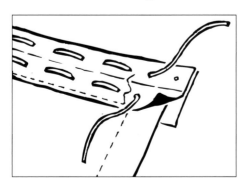

1 Place the edge of the lining between the two halves of the lining tape, overlapping and turning under the ends.

Locked-in lined curtains

▲ *Lining and interlining sewn into curtains give the front fabric greater body so that it hangs in handsome folds like these boldly checked silk curtains. The additional layers also increase the curtains' efficiency at excluding sound, light and draughts, when drawn closed.*

Locked-in lined curtains

Locked-in lined curtains take a little more time and more hand stitching than loose-lined curtains, but the result is worth it. Once you have mastered this technique, an option is to add a layer of interlining between the lining and the main fabric (see opposite).

Buy the front fabric and the lining in the same widths if possible. Cut all the lengths and join the seams of the front and lining as usual (see pages 242–243). Cut the lining 8cm (3¼in) narrower than the front fabric and 8cm (3¼in) shorter.

Making the curtains

On the main fabric, fold over and press a 4cm (1½in) turning at both sides and a double 8cm (3¼in) hem, mitring the corners and inserting weights as you go (see pages 248–249). Herringbone stitch the side turns and slip stitch the hem.

You are now ready to attach the lining. Machine stitch a double 5cm (2in) hem along the bottom of the lining, then lay it in place on the curtain, wrong sides together. Check that the lining is centred on the curtain, and about 2cm (¾in) from the bottom. Fold the lining back on itself so that there is a fold formed along the centre. Use lock stitch to attach the lining to the front fabric along the line of this fold. Sew from the top to the bottom edge, making a stitch every 10–15cm (4–6in). Pick up only a thread or two of the front fabric so that the lock

Locked-in lining

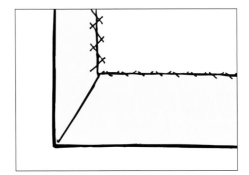

1 Turn back the side and bottom edges of the front fabric, mitring corners, and herringbone stitch in place.

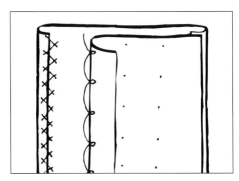

2 Lay the lining on the curtain, wrong sides together, and lock stitch to the front fabric down the centre.

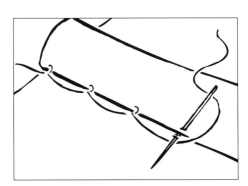

3 To lock stitch, pull up only a few threads from the main fabric so that the stitches do not show on the right side.

stitch will be invisible on the finished curtain. The sewing needs to be loose, without any tension, so use a single long thread for each row, rather than knotting together shorter lengths as you work. Use thread that matches the front fabric. Continue lock stitching along the widths and the half widths. Repeat for the other half of the curtain.

Turn under, press and slip stitch the edges of the lining to the turnback of the front fabric, so that equal amounts of front fabric show at each side. Slip stitch the bottom edge of the lining to the front fabric, unless the front fabric hem is tacked for final adjustment after the curtains are hung. In this case do not sew the bottom edge of the lining until the front fabric hem has been sewn.

When the lining is attached, complete the heading by turning back the front fabric and sewing the heading tape over the raw edge in the usual way (see pages 244–245). You can now gather up the curtain, hang it and dress the folds (see pages 250–251).

Interlined curtains

Interlined curtains undoubtedly look smarter than any other type of curtain. Not only is their appearance magnificent, but their bulk and weight make them extremely efficient excluders of draughts and light. They are also heavy and so should be hung only from the strongest, well-fixed track or pole.

Making interlined curtains is a big job, requiring concentration and immense patience

▲ *Lining needs to be made from a sturdy fabric to support the front fabric, especially when the curtains are made from heavy woollen twill. The weight of these curtains is increased by the pleats in the front fabric, so that the rods from which they hang have to be exceptionally securely fixed.*

You need plenty of table space, plenty of time in which to work undisturbed and plenty of experience in curtain making. The difficulty is in keeping everything flat and straight so that the curtains hang straight and smooth at the end. Padded weights help, and some people also use large bulldog clips.

Making the curtains

Joins in the interlining need flat seams, made by overlapping the material by 2cm (⅜in) and zigzag stitching over the cut edges. Cut the interlining to the exact size of the finished curtain (i.e. smaller than the main curtain fabric, which will have hem allowances). Fold in the side turns and hem allowance on the curtain fabric and press, then unfold them and place the interlining inside the creases.

Attach the interlining to the main fabric with lock stitch, as for the lining, but when you complete each row, lock stitch the bottom edge of the interlining along the hemline, from the last vertical row of lock stitch to the one you have just completed. Now fold and sew the turnbacks down each side of the curtain with herringbone stitch. Trim the hem allowance down to 10cm (4in), then herringbone stitch this to the interlining. Attach the lining as before.

Hems and edges can be padded for a more substantial look. Cut the interlining wider and deeper than the finished curtain. Turn back the edges and hem of the interlining, first lock stitching the lines of these folds to the edge and hem creases on the front fabric.

Interlined curtains

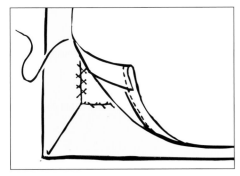

4 *Turn under the edges of the lining and slip stitch to the turnings of the curtain, around three sides.*

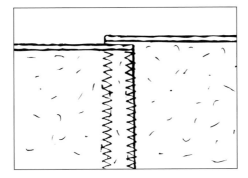

1 *Join widths of interlining by overlapping them and machine zigzagging over the cut edges.*

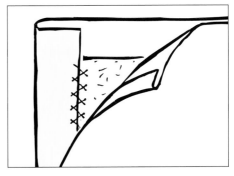

2 *Interlining is inserted between the front fabric and the lining, and attached to the front fabric with lock stitch.*

Pelmets, valances, swags and tails

▲ *This shaped pelmet with a zigzag bottom edge makes a dramatic impact when the curtains are open and the points are outlined against daylight. Covered in the same fabric as the curtains, the pelmet is deep enough not to look skimpy, without blocking out much light from the window.*

The space above curtains offers plenty of scope for decorative interest. If you decide against having a pole, then a world of pelmets, valances and other ornamental toppings, such as swags and tails, opens up. All manner of designs and fabrics are possible.

Pelmets

A pelmet can be made of stiffened fabric or plain wood, fixed onto a board, or shelf, that is then fixed to the wall. The simplest fabric-covered pelmet is rectangular when looked at face-on, and covered with the same fabric as the curtains. More exciting alternatives might have a shaped lower edge, such as scallops, zigzags or castellations. Some pelmets have a shaped upper edge too. A pelmet can be decorated with trimmings such as ribbon, braid, tassels or fringing, while a large window can be made grand with a pelmet formed from magnificent swags and tails.

Using a different fabric from the curtain material for a heading can make an attractive contrast and is an opportunity to use a more expensive fabric than you could afford for the curtains themselves. It could have similar colours but a bolder pattern, perhaps, or a pattern that will be shown off to greater effect when flat on the pelmet rather than lost in curtain folds. Checks give definition to striped curtains, while stripes give a refreshing finish to floral cotton curtains. Alternatively, use a plain fabric with a contrasting edging, or create your own fabric design, using appliqué, embroidery or paints.

Pelmets

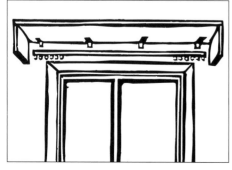

1 A pelmet board is fixed above the window so that the pelmet will eventually conceal the curtain heading.

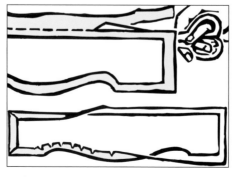

2 Fabric is attached to the stiffened pelmet shape and the edges are turned over to the wrong side.

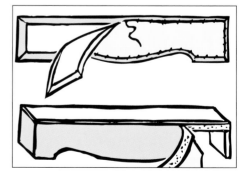

3 Lining is slip stitched to the back, then the pelmet fixed round three sides of the board with Velcro fastener.

Valance creator

1 Feed fabric through the spiral hooks from back to front, pull into a loop and secure the tail behind.

2 The finished ruffles hide the supporting hooks, and the whole result gives a 'swag and tail' effect.

A wooden pelmet can be made from solid wood, plywood, or MDF (medium-density fibreboard), which is easier to saw into interesting shapes than timber. It can be painted, or it can be decorated with glued objects around the edges or in patterns: shells, rope or beads, for example.

Making a pelmet

Cut a 10cm (4in)-deep pelmet board from 12mm (½in)-thick plywood, making it the length of the curtain track plus about 12cm (5in) to give 6cm (2½in) clearance at each end. Glue and screw end pieces to form returns, if desired. Fix the pelmet board to the wall just above the window and track using angle brackets fixed at 20cm (8in) intervals, making sure it will conceal the curtain heading.

Cut out the pelmet shape from stiffening material, making it long enough to fit around the sides and front of the pelmet board. The traditional stiffener is buckram, which is sewn in place with interlining. Iron-on buckram

is also available. PVC self-adhesive stiffener can also be used, and makes the job a lot easier. It has graph backing paper, enabling you to cut your own designs easily, and several printed designs that can be followed. The single-sided type of self-adhesive stiffener, which has peel-off strip on one side and integral velour backing which acts as both lining and Velcro on the other, requires no lining; but the double-sided type, which sticks to both front fabric and lining to give a neater finish, does.

Cut out the same shape from the main fabric, adding 3cm (1¼in) for a turning all round. Attach the stiffener to the wrong side of the fabric. Turn the fabric edges over, clipping into the curves and corners so that the fabric lies flat. Cut lining fabric 1.5cm (⅝in) larger all round than the pelmet shape. Turn

and press this allowance under and attach the lining to the back of the pelmet, slip stitching it to the main fabric. Attach the pelmet to the top edge of the board using Velcro – where necessary stapling or tacking the hooked half to the board and the soft half to the back of the pelmet.

Swags and tails

Hung from a pelmet board, swags and tails create an illusion of continuous drapery. Made up in many forms, swags and tails range in complexity from one swag to many and from pleated ones cut from several pieces of fabric to gathered ones made from a single piece of cloth. Swags and tails are best suited to full-length curtains on large windows.

Lambrequins

A lambrequin is the name given to a flat fabric shape which frames the window. Usually hanging down at the sides, it can front a blind or simple net or lace curtain, or it can stand alone at a window where no curtain is necessary.

Valances

In addition to being made into pelmets and lambrequins, fabric can be gathered or sculpted into folds or pleats, making a type of short fixed curtain known as a valance. An attached valance is a decorative fold of fabric which hangs down from the top of the actual curtain, giving you the best of both worlds as you have a handsome curtain top and you can hang the curtains from a pole.

Fabric can also be draped across the top of the window, with or without curtains or a blind. It should be lined to give it body and support, and can then be arranged over and fixed to a pole or rod (separate from the curtain pole if there is one), wooden or metal curtain hold-backs or some other prop.

A 'valance creator' is a curly-ended bracket around which fabric can be wrapped. It is fixed to the wall above and to each side of the window. Feed the fabric through from the back of the spiral to the front, in a loop, with the tail secured to the back, hanging down. The loops of fabric, creating gathers, hide the brackets of the valance creator.

▲ Unsewn fabric, draped in an elegant curve across the top of this narrow window and finished with a puff at each corner, makes a charming unstructured swag. Such an effect is easy to achieve with a 'valance creator' and is an appealing alternative to the tortured folds of some more sophisticated window headings.

Tie-backs and hold-backs

▶ *A pair of original and amusing fabric tie-backs have been created by taking conventional curtain restraints and sewing mother-of-pearl buttons all over them. These twinkle in the light from the window, echoing the spots of glitter on the curtains themselves.*

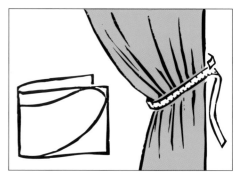

1 Use a tape measure to calculate the dimensions of the tie-back, then make a paper pattern of the exact shape.

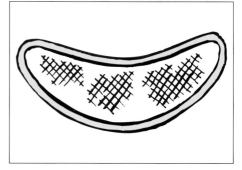

2 Cut two pieces of stiffener and four pieces of fabric, adding a seam allowance. Iron on the stiffener.

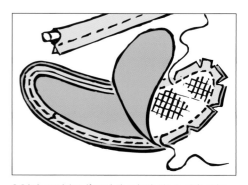

3 Stitch on piping, if used, then both pieces, right sides together, leaving an opening for turning.

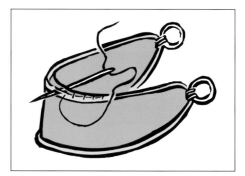

4 Turn right side out, slip stitch closed, then sew on rings at each end, or in far enough so that they are hidden.

During the day, curtains are drawn back to let as much light as possible into a room or to reveal other layers of curtain dressing such as lace, net or a light-diffusing blind. The curtains either hang straight down or can be restrained by tie-backs or hold-backs fixed to the wall at the sides of the window. Tie-backs are made of fabric, rope, cord or any other soft material that can be tied, and hold-backs are made of metal or wood.

A tie-back can be decorated with anything that can be sewn or glued to a suitable backing, threaded onto cord or plaited into a rope, and which is sufficiently resilient to withstand the daily business of being undone and done up again. Beads, for instance, can be sewn or threaded; a fringe of corks can be threaded together; roses and leaves made from brilliantly coloured velvet or glazed cotton can look stunning; a plait of hessian rope looks rugged and is well suited to fabrics such as unbleached calico or natural linen.

Fabric tie-backs

A fabric tie-back consists of two shaped pieces of material sewn together with a layer of buckram or other stiffener sandwiched in

between. This is fastened to a hook or loop on the wall by means of brass rings or ties sewn into each end. The fabric could be the same as the curtain or the pelmet, or of another design entirely. Edges of tie-backs can be defined by binding them with a contrast fabric, known as bound-edge binding, edging them with braid or inserting piping.

Making a fabric tie-back

To make a fabric tie-back, first loop a flexible tape measure around a curtain, drawn open, and hold the ends next to the wall where it will be fixed to find the length. Decide how wide it is to be. Make a rectangular paper pattern to the length and depth you want. Fold this in half along the length and if you want the ends to be rounded or curved, draw these in on one half. Cut through both thicknesses of paper around your shape and unfold the pattern. Pin it around the curtain to check it is the right size, and make any adjustments as necessary.

Use the pattern to cut out four pieces of fabric (two for each tie-back), adding 1.5cm (⅝in) all round for seam allowances. For each tie-back also cut out a piece of stiffener without the seam allowance. Attach one piece of stiffener in the centre of the wrong side of one piece of fabric. The simplest to use is iron-on stiffener.

Place the fabric pieces right sides together and machine stitch along the seam line, leaving an opening to turn the tie-back through. Trim the edges, clip the curves or corners and turn the tie-back right side out. Press flat.

Turn in the open edges and slip stitch the gap closed. Rings can be sewn at each end, or further in so that they are hidden when the tie-back is in use.

Piping on a tie-back

Piping is made by enclosing piping cord in a strip of fabric cut on the bias. The length of fabric strip must allow for piping to go right round the shape, plus an extra 3cm (1¼in) for overlapping the ends. You may find it necessary to join strips in order to achieve the right length. The width of the fabric strip needs to be the circumference of the piping cord plus 3cm (1¼in), i.e. twice the seam allowance. The strip of fabric is folded in half and the cord enclosed within it. The cord should be stitched in as close to the fold as possible, and the raw edges of the seam allowance left.

If using piping on a tie-back, attach it at the point of sewing the two main fabric pieces together. It is stitched to the right side of the fabric at the seam line. To do this, align the raw edges of the tie-back sections and the piping. When the piping turns a corner, a section will need to be clipped out of the seam allowance at that point to ensure the fabric does not kink.

To finish off, turn the tie-back the right way out and sew up the gap with slip stitch, on the inside edge of the piping.

Bound edges on a tie-back

You can use ready-made bias binding, but to get just the binding you want, cut strips of contrasting fabric on the bias. Binding strips need to be twice the finished depth required, plus 3cm (1¼in) for seam allowances.

When making bound edges, cut out the fabric pieces for the tie-back to the required size and attach the stiffener, as previously, to

the wrong side of one piece. This time, place the wrong sides of the tie-back pieces together and machine stitch around the edge.

Fold over 1.5cm (⅝in) along each edge of the binding strip and press, then fold the strip in half lengthways and press again. Open out the last fold and align the raw edge of the binding with the raw edge of the tie-back, right sides together. Sew a 1.5cm (⅝in) seam. Bring the edging over the raw edges of the tie-back and slip stitch the seam on the reverse side along the stitch line, trimming the enclosed edges if necessary. Turn under at the ends to neaten them.

Hold-backs

Hold-backs made of wood are generally shaped something like a mushroom, with a

▲ *Hold-backs are an ideal opportunity for extra decoration and unusual touches. This leaf in thin gilded metal dresses up the plainest of curtains made in inexpensive fabric. It is attached to a thick shank that is then fixed to the wall, providing space in which to fit the curtain so that the leaf can be seen to full advantage. .*

base, a stalk and a round head decorated with carving or gilding, behind which the curtain is looped when drawn open. You can paint or stain a wooden hold-back to match or complement the curtain fabric or the finish of other surfaces in the room.

Metal hold-backs are either fixed or hinged. A fixed one curls out from the wall like an arm, embracing the curtain when it is drawn back behind it. It can look odd when the curtain is closed and it has nothing to hold. This problem can be overcome if the curtain hangs well out from the wall and hides it when drawn closed, without it creating a protuberance in the fabric.

A hinged, hook-shaped metal hold-back has a hinge or ring near the wall which allows it to hang down flat when it is not holding back the curtain. When the curtain is drawn open the hold-back is lifted up and the fullness of the curtain looped into it, so that it stands out from the wall.

Bound-edge tie-back

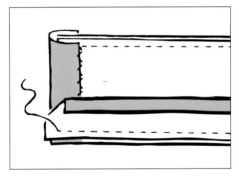

1 *Machine stitch the binding to the right side of the tie-back, raw edges aligning, with a 1.5cm (⅝in) seam.*

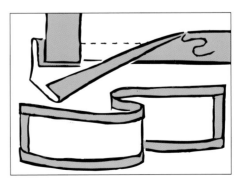

2 *Turn the binding over to the wrong side and slip stitch in place, turning under the ends where necessary.*

Blinds

For many windows in the home, blinds are the simple,
stylish solution. Where a room is small and
space is important, or where there is little room at the
sides of a window, it may be far more appropriate
to fit a flat roller or Roman blind neatly within the
window frame than curtains from a raised track
or pole. Flat blinds will show off fabric well; can be an
inexpensive choice; and if sized correctly and lined,
they can provide excellent insulation.

There are blinds to suit most practical and decorative requirements, ranging from the very basic to the flamboyant. They can be left unlined - the lighter fabrics useful for allowing light to pass through, but hiding an uninspiring view or giving privacy - or they can be lined to improve their light-blocking and insulating capabilities.

Depending on their design, blinds can be hung in almost any room or situation. Crooked windows in old houses are probably the one exception, because blinds do need to be hung absolutely straight and will look odd at a window out of true. For a window that is wider than it is long, two or more blinds fixed side by side work better than a single wide blind which may be too large to operate well.

The most basic of blinds is a piece of flat, lightweight fabric permanently fixed over a window to block out an unpleasant view but allow light into the room. A little more versatile than this, but still simple, is the tie blind, which should only be used where it will not need to be raised and lowered frequently – perhaps in a bathroom. It consists of a piece of unlined fabric to which are attached four ribbons or fabric strips. Fixed at the top of the blind, about a quarter of the width in from either edge, these hang down – two to the front and two to the back – and are tied together at each side under the blind's bottom edge. The drop of the blind is adjusted as required by re-tying the ties at different heights. The blind itself can be attached to a heading board using Velcro strip. A dowel can be sewn into the bottom hem to ensure the blind hangs with a straight bottom edge.

Roller blinds incorporate a sprung roller which facilitates the raising of the blind and takes up very little space above the window. They are useful for any situation where as much light as possible is required when the blind is up, but where they need to be pulled down frequently. They are also practical for windows that are set at an angle, such as in an attic conversion, as the batten at the bottom of the blind can be restrained beneath the window by cup hooks, while the blind itself follows the sloping line of the roof.

◄ An unusual arrangement of translucent white roller blinds in a minimalist interior. One is set into the window rebate and pulls down, while the other larger blind pulls up from a box on the floor and covers the entire window, with a wide margin on each side.

◄ An impressively lofty kitchen-cum-dining room in a modern building has louvred blinds built into the windows, in keeping with the uncluttered interior. The great advantage of louvred blinds is that the amount of shade can be varied when the blind is let down, or the blind can be pulled up completely.

▲ Slatted wooden blinds like these, which roll up inside the pull-up string, can be used as inexpensive room dividers as well as shade and privacy providers. Here they conceal the kitchen in one corner of the sitting room, when let down. They are also a good choice to tone in with the cane furniture and wood-slat doors.

▲ *A single huge blind for this large window space would be too cumbersome to pull up; instead, there are three elegant Roman blinds. The centre one is wider, conforming in size to the window behind, and made from the same green linen as the left-hand chair, while the others are white to match the right-hand chair.*

ridges are hoisted up to fold the blind into its neat pleats. Many people prefer the appearance of Roman blinds to curtains because, while they look equally luxurious (especially if padded with lightweight interlining), they are unfussy.

When drawn up, a Roman blind blocks out more light than a roller blind does, but if it is lined (and possibly lightly interlined) it is as good as a curtain for excluding draughts and light, especially if it fits the window well or hangs so that the edges overlap the architrave or reveal. Because of the reinforced folds stacking up at the back of it when drawn up, the Roman blind requires a certain depth of window in which to operate.

Gathered blinds: Austrian, pull-up and festoon

Quite different from the simple appearance of flat blinds are the various types of gathered blinds which all involve festoons of fabric, some also ruched. The more extravagant of these are suited to a certain type of heavily decorated interior rather than anywhere requiring a fresh, contemporary feel, especially in a small room.

The Austrian blind is pulled up by means of cords and rings like a Roman blind but has a gathered or pleated heading which bunches up into a series of puffs or swags, and does not have the strips of dowelling to form strict pleats. Like the Roman blind, it can provide good insulation and light exclusion. In certain situations – in simply furnished rooms with tall ceilings and windows, for example – it can be used successfully if care is taken to avoid making a place feel claustrophobic. This is especially true if the blind looks like a curtain when let down, falling straight to the floor (or window sill) with no ruches at the bottom. Some people call this type of blind a 'pull-up curtain'.

Similar to an Austrian blind, a festoon blind retains the swags down its entire length when let down. A further variation is known as a tailed Austrian blind, which by omitting cords at the edges of the blind allows the sides to trail and flop down.

Roller blinds offer little in the way of insulation, however, although they will filter bright light and create privacy at night. Because they can be made of spongeable fabric, they are useful in frequently damp rooms such as kitchens and bathrooms. Specially stiffened fabric is readily available for making roller blinds, but ordinary fabrics (except very loosely woven ones) can be used as long as they are sprayed with, or dipped into, a stiffener before being made up.

The Roman blind is the smartest, most regimented of blinds. When pulled up, it folds away neatly in pleats tucked behind each other. The regularity and crispness of these pleats is created by narrow strips of wood, usually lath or dowelling, slotted into a series of horizontal fabric pockets on the back of the blind and creating ridges. When the blind is pulled up by the cords, which run through small brass or plastic rings that are sewn to the edge of each pocket, the

▲ *A series of loosely hanging, narrow Roman blinds, made from natural textured linen, make a strong and witty impact on this series of folding glass-topped doors. Each blind is knotted at the bottom and covers a pane of glass, emphasizing the door's shape and the number of panels.*

Fabrics and finishes

Fabrics for blinds need to be chosen with some care. Because an Austrian blind makes an impact through its puffed-up fullness, it should be made with a plain fabric or one with an unfussy pattern, such as stripes.

The simplicity of the roller blind and the regimented form of the Roman blind also call for fabrics which are plain, either with an interesting texture or patterned in a graphic style. Before deciding on a particular fabric, imagine, for instance, how a Roman blind would look once pulled up into its pleats. Alternatively, picture fabric is fun on a roller blind in a bathroom or kitchen, and fresh patterns like stripes and checks look good on any type of blind. Flat blinds are better for large patterns than ones with lots of folds.

The fabric used for making any type of blind must be cut absolutely straight or it will look shoddy once it is finished and hung. If there is any sort of pattern on the fabric, make sure it is arranged symmetrically across the blind. It must also be printed true. Examine your chosen fabric carefully before starting to make the blind, and if it is faulty in this or any other respect, return it immediately to the shop.

Interest and definition can be added to a blind with a band of contrasting fabric or trimming set back from the edges. If this trimming is to be continued across the bottom of a Roman blind, the last flap of fabric has to be made extra deep so that the bottom border is not hidden when the blind is pulled up.

A roller blind can be made more interesting if it has a shaped bottom edge, coming down at an angle, for example, or cut in a pattern of points or castellations. The shaped part hangs below the bottom batten, and the string should be attached to the batten rather than the shape below it.

Non-fabric blinds

Blinds do not, of course, have to be made of fabric. They can be constructed from cane, bamboo, wooden slats, paper and even metal, and are widely available in many styles, designs and colours (see pages 268–269).

First steps to making blinds

► *A neat and restrained use of a Roman blind. This one is tucked inside the architrave of the window and is made from plain white linen which allows sunlight to glow through it, making it appear almost luminous, as well as matching the pure white paint on the window and the restrained pattern of the walls.*

Measuring up for blinds

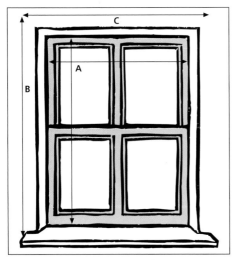

1 Measure the height and width of the window, either inside the recess or to cover the architrave.

Measuring up and estimating quantities

Decide exactly where the blind is to hang, then measure up, as follows, to find the finished dimensions and the amount of fabric you will need for your blind.

For a recessed blind, measure the height and width of the recess (A). For roller blind fabric, deduct 3cm (1¼in) from the width to account for the ends of the mechanism within the window frame.

For a face-fixed blind, measure from the top of the hanging system at the chosen height to the sill for the drop (B) (or past the sill for a longer blind), and for the width add 5cm (2in) either side of the recess (C) so that the light will be blocked out. Get extra fabric if you plan to wrap the hanging batten with the same fabric in order to disguise it.

Roman blind construction

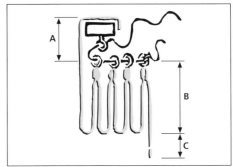

1 A fully pulled-up Roman blind. A = hanging allowance; B = depth of pleats; C = lower flap.

Roller blind

For a roller blind add an extra 30cm (12in) to the length for a hem at the bottom and to cover the roller at the top.

Austrian blind or pull-up curtain

For an Austrian blind allow an extra 5cm (2in) for the turnback at the top and 20cm (8in) for a double hem at the bottom. The width of fabric you need is two and a half times the length of the heading batten plus 4cm (1½in) for turnbacks at the sides. If you are lining the blind, you will need roughly the same amount of lining fabric.

To achieve the curtain effect when the blind is down, make the blind's finished length equal to the distance from the window top to the sill. However, if you want to retain the ruched look at the bottom when the blind is down, make it about 45cm (18in) longer.

Roman blind

Estimating quantities for a Roman blind needs careful working out so make sure you check your calculation. Make a clearly drawn sketch and mark all the measurements on it so that you can refer to them when making up the blind. When measuring up, allow an extra 6cm (2¼in) for the hem and ridge pocket at the bottom and 6cm (2¼in) to wrap over a 5 x 2.5cm (2 x 1in) heading or fixing batten at the top. You will also need to allow 6cm (2¼in) for a 3cm (1¼in) turnback at each side.

For the lining allow an extra 6cm (2¼in) for each ridge pocket for laths about 25 x 5mm (1 x ¼in), and cut it to the same width

Tools and equipment

To make a blind you will need the following materials and equipment. If you are sewing a Roman blind (see pages 264–265) or an Austrian blind (see pages 266–267), you will also need almost all the materials and equipment required for sewing curtains (see pages 240– 241) to create the fabric part of the blind. Roman and Austrian blinds are suspended from a batten, approximately 5 x 2.5cm (2 x 1in) by the width of the blind, which is fixed to the wall with screws and plugs as necessary and can be painted to match the decor or the fabric.

For measuring up and fixing

- Long wooden measure and a set square or T-square: to ensure that marking-up lines are perpendicular to the edges.
- Spirit level, a drill, screws and wall plugs, a hammer and tacks or staple gun and staples: for fixing the blind to the wall.
- Saw: for cutting the roller to size.
- Hammer: for the fitting.

For a roller blind

- A roller blind kit: consisting of a roller with spring, brackets, end cap and pin, wooden lath, cord holder and acorn (or these items bought separately).
- Pencil and masking tape.
- Liquid or spray stiffener: for untreated fabric.

For Roman and Austrian blinds/ pull-up curtains

- Cord, drop weight and wall cleat: for pulling up and lowering the blind.
- Brass or plastic rings: through which to thread the cord on the back of the blind.
- Screw-in eyelets, as many as there are cords at the back of the blind, plus one through which all cords go.
- Sewing machine with zip foot.
- 6, 10 or 12mm (¼, ⅜ or ½in) dowelling or lath, maximum 25 x 5mm (1 x ¼in): enough for all the pocket ridges in the blind (Roman).
- Velcro-backed heading tape or pencil pleat heading tape (Austrian).
- Leadweight tape (optional) (Austrian).
- Fringe or edging material (optional) (Austrian).

◄ A carefully orchestrated scheme of white and washed-out blues, distressed plaster, metal and wood called for an understated window treatment: Austrian blinds in their simplest form, unadorned by fringes or other trimmings, in a crisply striped fabric.

as the front fabric. For wood of different dimensions or dowelling, calculate the amount of fabric needed for each ridge pocket, adding a little extra so that the wood slides in easily.

To work out how many ridges you need, first decide how deep the piece of fabric at the top of the blind will be. This will usually extend above the last pleat by about 4–10cm (1½–4in) and will cover the eyelets and give room for the pleats to lie evenly. The deeper this hanging allowance, the more light is cut out when the blind is pulled up.

Also decide if the lower flap at the bottom of the blind will hang down below the rest of the pleats when the blind is closed to allow the bottom edge of the border, if you have one, to show. Subtract the hanging allowance and the bottom border allowance (if any) from the blind's finished length to give the folding length.

Decide how many pleats would be right for the proportions of the blind. A pleat is usually 20–30cm (8–12in) deep. To check that your imagined pleats fall within this range, and to establish their actual measurement, divide the blind's folding length by the number of pleats you want, plus an additional half-pleat. A full pleat is the complete fold of fabric between two ridges. The extra half-pleat is taken up by the fabric that falls from the last ridge to the bottom edge of the gathered-up pleats.

Having established the number and depth of pleats, you have finally arrived at the number of ridges and ridge pockets you need, which will, in turn, enable you to calculate the length of lining fabric you need.

Roman blinds

▶ *Blinds on the ceiling of a conservatory, as well as at the windows, help to prevent the room overheating in the strong mid-afternoon sun. In winter, the blinds can be completely folded back to allow maximum light to stream into the area.*

Making a Roman blind

Prepare the heading board using a length of wooden batten 5 x 2.5cm (2 x 1in), and as long as the blind's width. Paint it the same colour as the wall or window, or wrap it (ends included) in a piece of the front or lining fabric of the blind. Make any other necessary preparations, such as preparing screw holes with a bradawl, for fixing the batten in place after the blind has been attached to it.

Cut out the fabric and lining to the required sizes (see pages 262–263). Cut the fabric on a straight grain by drawing out a weft thread (going across the width of the fabric) and cutting along this line at the top and bottom of both front and lining fabrics.

Make sure you can easily see and read the sketch of the blind, with all measurements marked on it, which you made when measuring up (see pages 262–263). Refer to your drawing for measurements when taking all the following steps. Mark up the front fabric and the lining, using a right angle or set square to ensure the lines are perpendicular

to the edges of the fabric. On the wrong side of the front fabric, draw the top edge of the blind (the drop line) 6cm (2¼in) from the top, the position of all the ridges down the blind, and the bottom edge of the finished blind. On the right side of the lining, mark the position and depth of each ridge.

Turn back the sides of the front fabric 3cm (1¼in) and press. Turn back the sides of the lining 4cm (1½in) and press. On the lining, sew the ridge pockets in place. Pin and tack every seam with great care before sewing, making sure they are exactly horizontal, as it is extremely important that these are straight; if they are not, the blinds will not hang or move up and down properly.

Lay the front fabric face down and the lining face up, centrally, on top of the front fabric. Match the pockets on the lining to the lines marking their position on the front fabric. Fold the pockets down, pin, tack, then stitch the lining to the front fabric, just above and very near the pocket stitching, using the zip foot attachment on your sewing machine.

Stitch the top edges of the fabric and lining together with a zigzag stitch. Slip stitch the lining to the front fabric down the sides, leaving the pockets free, and stopping 2 cm (¾in) from the bottom edge of the front fabric. Trim the lining to this level. Turn up and press the front fabric 2cm (¾in) from the bottom. Then turn it up again so that the line you drew previously to mark the bottom edge of the finished blind is along the fold. You should have a hem of about 4cm (1½in), which will form the pocket for the bottom ridge. If the hem is much too deep, turn back more at the bottom edge of the fabric. Sew across the hem, near to the fold, either with the machine or, if you prefer the stitches not to show on the front of the blind, slip stitch by hand.

The pieces of wood that will form the ridges (laths) now have to be cut to size. The bottom one needs to be slightly shorter than the width of the finished blind, the others slightly shorter than the width of the lining. Insert these into their pockets and slip stitch the ends closed.

Sew the rings to the ridges (except the bottom edge ridge) in vertical rows spread evenly across the back of the blind at intervals of about 30–60cm (1–2ft), depending on the width of the blind. The first and last rows should be about 8cm (3¼in) in from the edges of the blind. Cut the cord and tie a piece to each bottom ring, threading it up through the other rings in each row.

At the top of the blind, lay the hanging batten on the blind so that the drop line is along what will be the top front edge of the batten when it is fixed to the window or wall. Wrap the blind tightly around to the back of the batten, tacking and stapling along the back to attach it securely. Alternatively, if the weight of the fabric you are using can be borne, the blind can be fixed to the hanging batten by using Velcro or strong double-sided tape.

Screw in the eyelets for the cords to go through before they drop, each eyelet corresponding to each row of rings on the back of the blind, with one extra in line with these near the end of the batten. Thread the cords up through the eyelets and along to one side.

Making a Roman blind

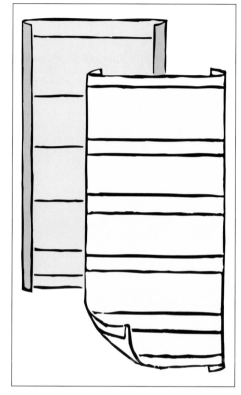

1 *Cut out main fabric and lining to size, plus allowances, and divide up into equal sections for the pleats.*

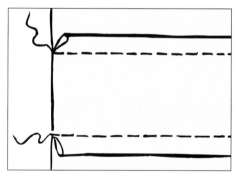

2 *On the lining, match pairs of lines for the ridges, wrong sides together, and stitch along the lines to form casings.*

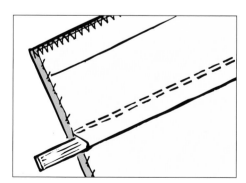

3 *Position the lining centrally on the main fabric and stitch the two together as described. Then insert laths.*

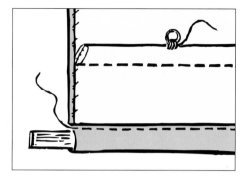

4 *Trim off lining at the bottom edge and turn up main fabric to form casing and sew rings on. Insert the batten.*

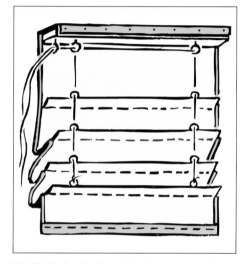

5 *Fix blind to heading board. Attach screw eyes and thread up cord from bottom to top. Fix to the window.*

Fix the heading batten to the window or to the wall using small brackets or fix it directly up into the recess of the window, then fit the cord cleat to the wall. The cleat needs careful positioning: if it is too far forward the cords will catch on the blind and spoil it. Finally, thread the cords through the drop weight, cut them to the same length and knot them.

This is only one style of Roman blind and many other variations are possible. The ridge pockets can be made separately from the lining and then sewn on after the lining has been attached to the front fabric. Alternatively, the Roman blind can be left unlined, in which case the pockets for wooden stiffening are made either from folds in the fabric, or separately, using other fabric which is sewn onto the back afterwards. The pockets can even be placed on the front of the blind, made either in the same material or in a contrasting one. Kits for making a soft-folded version of the Roman blind, made with tapes instead of laths, are available.

For a less bulky look, the wood stiffening at the bottom of the blind can be omitted, to leave a finished edge hanging down. Alternatively, only the ridge at the very bottom of the blind is stiffened to make the folds softer and more bunched up.

◄ *A lovely, crisp white and brown linen Roman blind filters the light from the window. An attractive contrasting border has been added to the edges of the blind and finished with neatly mitred corners. The bottom of the main part of the blind has been decorated with a simple embroidered capital 'A', inspired by the engravings of Albrecht Dürer.*

Roller and Austrian blinds

Making a roller blind

To make a roller blind it is easiest to buy ready-stiffened fabric and a special kit (see pages 260–261). (If you choose to use your own fabric, you will need to treat it with a fabric stiffener. Iron the fabric before you do this.) The roller has a spring fitted into one end and is sawn to the required length before a second fitting is hammered into place. The kit also includes two brackets designed to take each end of the roller, which can be fixed either to the wall above the window or to the sides of a reveal.

Screw the brackets to the wall, the slotted bracket to the left, 3cm (1¼in) down from the top of a recess to allow for the thickness of the rolled-up blind. When fitting outside a recess, or to a window without one, position it 5cm (2in) above and out to each side.

Cut the fabric to the width of the roller, excluding fixtures, and if necessary join widths using flat seams. Use a right angle and a long wooden measure to ensure cutting is perpendicular with the sides and cut the fabric perfectly straight, with the weave.

Assuming the batten for the bottom of the blind is 25 x 5mm (1 x ¼in) thick, make a 4 cm (1½in) hem on the wrong side of the fabric and sew this in position with a zigzag stitch to create a pocket for the batten. Cut the batten to the correct length: it needs to be slightly shorter than the width of the blind, by approximately 1cm (⅜in), so that it does not show. Slide the batten into the pocket and slip stitch the ends. Attach the pull-cord holder to the wrong side of the batten (the same side as the hem).

Cut the roller to fit the brackets and hammer the other fitting into the sawn end. Draw a guideline along the length of roller, perpendicular to the ends, if it does not already have one. Position the fabric right side up and the roller on top with the spring to the left so that the top edge meets the guideline on the roller. Tape it to the roller to keep it steady and tack or staple the fabric to the roller.

Roll up by hand and slot into the brackets, right-hand end first. Pull the blind down to check the spring tension, rewinding by hand if necessary to increase the tension.

Making an Austrian blind or pull-up curtain

An Austrian blind is made like a conventional curtain, except for the finish to the heading and the system of rings and screw eyelets fixed at the back. For a list of requirements see pages 262–263. The description here is for separate rings but Austrian blind tapes can be used instead.

Depending on the weight of the fabric, the blind's heading can be attached to a hanging batten (also known as a heading board) with either Velcro or special Austrian blind track. The track has cord holders which line up above the cords.

For lightweight blinds, use a hanging batten and Velcro. Peel apart the two halves of Velcro and attach the stiff half across the front of the hanging batten with tacks or staples. Special Velcro heading tape, which gathers up in the same way as normal heading tape, but has Velcro instead of pockets, is also available.

For measuring up and determining fabric quantity, see pages 262–263. Make up the blind as for an unlined curtain (see pages 248–249), with leadweight tape in the hem if you want, and attach a fringe or other edging, if you are having one, to the back of the hem. The bottom edge looks more finished with a substantial trimming, like a deep fringe. When the blind is pulled up, this looks pretty against the light; when let down, it gives the bottom edge weight and definition.

To make a lined blind, sew the fabric and lining right sides together round three sides, catching in any fringe or trim between the layers as you stitch. Trim and turn right sides out, press and sew up the fourth side.

If not using special Velcro heading tape, sew on traditional heading tape to the top. Most heading tape types are suitable, but pencil pleats are recommended. Next, fold the blind vertically at evenly spaced intervals, about 60cm (2ft), where you want your scallops to be. The folds mark the positions for the rings. Bear in mind that an Austrian blind looks better with an odd number of swags rather than an even number, and the outermost rings on each side should be placed about 5cm (2in) from the edges.

Making a roller blind

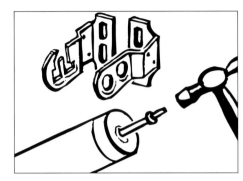

1 A roller blind kit comes with two wall brackets. Trim the roller to length and insert a fitting into the cut end.

2 Make a hem along the bottom and sew with a zigzag stitch. Insert the batten and slip stitch the ends closed.

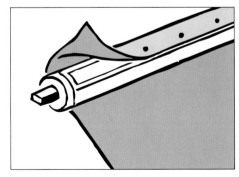

3 The pull-cord holder is attached to the wrong side of the hem with two small screws.

4 The top edge of the blind is fixed to the roller with tacks or staples so that it hangs completely straight.

Sew the small rings at intervals on the back, making sure each row aligns. Note that when attaching the rings to a lined blind, you will need to catch some of the threads from the front fabric as well as the lining. If you are making a blind that retains its ruching when down, you will also have to attach a ring to the cords in the pulley system in order to stop the blind dropping fully at a certain point.

Sew the other half of the Velcro to a strip of matching fabric, or lining fabric, a little larger than the heading. Gather up the heading to the width of the finished blind, and attach the back of this Velcro/fabric strip over the heading tape, turning in the edges. Make sure when sewing the Velcro to the fabric back that it will be at the correct height to attach to the Velcro on the hanging batten, i.e. at or very near the top of the blind.

Screw the eyelets into the bottom of the batten, one corresponding to each row of rings on the back of the blind plus an extra one on the side where the cords will hang down, as for a Roman blind (see pages 264–265). Fix the batten above the window, checking the horizontal with a spirit level. Fix the cleat to the window architrave or the wall.

Tie long cords to each of the bottom rings in each row and thread them up through the rest of the rings above them. Attach the blind to the hanging batten, and thread all the cords up through the eyelets and along to one side. Cut the cords to the same length, thread them through a drop weight and knot them.

▲ *This pull-up blind combines some of the features of a Roman blind and some of an Austrian blind: it is stiffened at the bottom, which means the blind lifts straight, not in festoons, but the folds are not sharpened with battens or dowelling, so it folds and crumples softly as it is pulled up.*

Making an Austrian blind

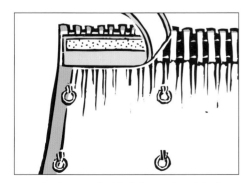

1 *Sew the rings onto the blind, aligning them in both directions. Slip stitch Velcro to the heading tape.*

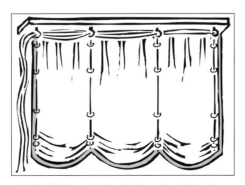

2 *Fix the blinds onto the heading board, and thread up the cords through the rings and screw eyelets.*

3 *Alternatively, special tapes with integral loops may be used. Take care to align the loops across the blind.*

Non-fabric blinds

▶ *Rattan blinds, slung across the glass roof of a garden room, give welcome shade and echo the natural texture and colour of the plaited grass rug on the floor beneath.*

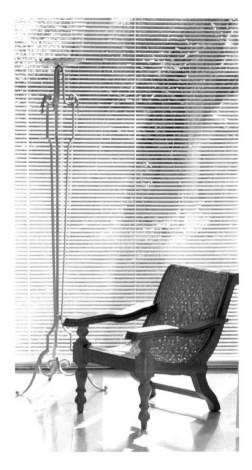

▲ *A massive louvred 'Venetian' blind, made from aluminium alloy strips, filters the bright sunlight at a huge plate-glass window and provides a geometric background for an uncluttered space. The blind's neutrality and plain lines allow the interesting items of furniture, both traditional and modern, to feature without distraction.*

Blinds are made in a number of non-fabric materials. Bamboo, wooden slats, paper, metal and plastic blinds are available to suit all types of interior design styles. Some work on a simple roll-up principle which means they can be a little bulky when rolled up. Others are variations of the Venetian blind mechanism which pulls up neatly to the top of the reveal. The great advantage of this type of blind is that when down they can be adjusted to allow different amounts of light through at the touch of a cord.

Ready-made blinds are sold in a number of standard sizes, and in addition many types can be made up by suppliers to particular measurements and colours. Prices vary according to the materials used and the amount of work involved in making them up. Pleated paper, for example, can be among the cheapest, while metal Venetian blinds or those made with wooden slats can cost as much as fully lined curtains.

Paper

Made from pleated paper, these blinds keep their folds even when they are let down. They fit into the window reveal and so can be used in combination with curtains. They are easy to dust. Some have holes punched through them. Paper blinds are cheap to buy and are available in a wide range of colours.

Cane

Blinds made from whole or split cane either roll up or fold in pleats. They do not screen light completely but are useful in rooms where strong sunlight needs to be moderated, creating a pleasing filtered effect. At night, when a light is switched on, they are virtually see-through from outside. Privacy can be improved, however, by lining them with a simple panel of plain fabric. Make it slightly shorter than the blind and several centimetres narrower on each side, then glue or sew it to the cane across the top at the back. The lining will roll or fold up with the blind when the cord is pulled.

Wood

Blinds can be made from wooden slats, about 5cm (2in) wide, held equal distances apart and controlled by tapes. Adjusting the angle of the slats controls the amount of light the blind allows into a room. The wood may be left natural or stained or painted in any colour. Pinoleum blinds are thin wood strips woven with widths of cotton which diffuse sunlight in a pleasing way; but like split bamboo blinds, however, they can be seen through at night.

Plastic

Plastic strips can be used in the same way as wooden slats. Available in a range of colours, they are easy to wipe clean and therefore useful for kitchens and bathrooms, where soiling can be a problem.

Metal

Usually aluminium alloy strips, these are constructed into blinds in much the same way as wood slats and are traditionally known as Venetian blinds. They are available in a wide range of colours and finishes, including a mirror, striped or graduated finish. Perforated slats are also available to let some light through when the blind is fully closed.

Vertical louvre blinds

Vertical louvre blinds are suspended vertically from a track and linked at the bottom by a chain. They may be made of wood or synthetic flexible strips but are most commonly made of stiffened strips of fabric, often with a textured weave and usually 9–13cm (3½–5in) wide. Usually standing from floor to ceiling, they are drawn like curtains and are useful for shielding large picture windows or patio doors. The amount of light they let through is controlled by adjusting the angle of the louvres.

▲ *This blind is made from primed canvas bought at a theatrical supplier, rolled around a length of wooden dowelling, but it could just as well be made from paper, with the edges reinforced against tearing. The rope is made of natural fibres and similar types are available at any good DIY store.*

FURNITURE &
FURNISHINGS

Whatever the decoration on a room's walls, ceiling and floor, it is the style and coverings of the furniture within that will give the room its definitive character. At its simplest, a room with white walls and white floor, filled with furniture that has been upholstered in sumptuous velvets and bright, glassy coloured silks, will present a very strong, vivid style where colour is king. The eye will be drawn to the forms of the furniture, set off by the neutral, clean background.

The same room can be completely changed by the introduction of a different style of furniture decoration. To achieve warmth and texture in the same room, the emphasis shifts to creamy bleached wood furniture with cream-on-cream textured cushion fabrics and loosely draped white cottons over sofas and chairs, with perhaps a few warm red and terracotta touches – ties for the cushions or a painted chair.

When undertaking the decoration of a room, inevitably the walls and perhaps the floors will be tackled first. And when time, effort and money have gone into major refurbishment, attention to re-covering or redecorating the furniture may not be considered a priority for quite a while. This is a shame, for in addition to contributing in a major way to the final 'look' of a room, the pieces on or in which we sit, sleep, rest, eat, store and work figure as vital practical elements in our lives. It is important to account for these elements, not just in terms of budget and practicality, but also for the impact they make in the room.

Fabric is perhaps the most exciting and versatile way of covering and decorating the surfaces of furniture. Upholstering, wrapping, draping, cushioning – fabric comes alive when used imaginatively. From the finest, flimsiest linen to the most textured and mightiest of brocaded velvet, the potential of fabric for decorating and transforming furniture is unending. In addition to the fabric, there are braids, buttons and trimmings to truly jazz up a piece of fabric, define the curve of a sofa or accentuate the folds of curtains.

Fabric can also be decorated very successfully with paint or dye, in either a fairly controlled way, as with stencilling, or by using

▲ *The bold use of colour creates a dramatic, Middle Eastern effect in this room. The varnished floor provides a neutral background for the rich, jewel-like fabrics draped on the sofa. A contrast is provided by the deep blue of the wall, which is also used around the door frame and featured in the tiles to help link the room together.*

▶ *The strongest features in this room are light and space, which have been accentuated throughout. Furniture is grouped around the room to divide it into functional areas. The use of faded fabrics, the distressed paint effect on the cupboard and evidence of junk-shop finds add a nostalgic, tranquil feel to the room.*

the more random method of hand-painted applications. Paint is also suitable for directly applying to the surfaces of furniture. Natural effects can be imitated or instant 'ageing' techniques applied for those who want a more battered, lived-in feel to their furniture. You can opt for the quick approach by using paint in a very loose way, such as colourwashing where layers are applied and reapplied to create the desired effect. The

finish can be changed easily to suit the mood of the rest of the room, altering the surface paint colour or 'texture' as easily as changing a cushion cover. Other paint techniques require more time and precision and because of this have a more permanent, perhaps less relaxed feel to them – the difference between a scrubbed pine table and an antique mahogany desk. Each has its place – it all depends on the effect you want to achieve.

Balance in all of this is crucial. Avoid over-doing a paint technique or using the same patterned fabric on every item in the room. Less is more. One beautifully colourwashed chair among a collection of pared-down fabrics can often be more effective than a riot of them. Although, in the right place, this too can be wonderful.

The position of furniture within a room is also very important. Don't feel that all large items of furniture should hug the walls – placing them on the diagonal and juxtapos-ing them can give unexpectedly pleasing results. In bigger rooms with numerous pieces of furniture, it helps to think in terms of group arrangements so that there are islands of furniture throughout the room, rather than many individual but slightly lost-looking pieces. Using the same colour, paint and fabric helps to link unrelated items throughout the room. Try different mat-erials, be imaginative – but keep a balance.

▲ *Bleached cream, pale stone and stark white are relieved by a honey-toned floor in this harmoniously elegant room. Fabrics are the dominant feature of the room, together with the abundance of natural light that floods through the window.s The light reflects off the various surfaces to provide a sophisticated and relaxing environment.*

Decorative finishes for furniture

Painting the walls of a room in a neutral colour or shade allows
the furniture free rein to make powerful colour statements.
Using different painting or varnishing techniques, furniture can
be transformed, creating dramatic visual effects within a room.
Wood, with its ability to transform itself with the application of
paint, varnish or wax, is extremely versatile and can be treated
in various different ways within the same room. Metal furniture,
too, can be enhanced with the application of different coverings
and the use of different paint application techniques.

The choice of paint effects is vast: on the one hand, finishes such as fake rust or verdigris (see pages 280–281) on wood or metal can add texture and 'weight', while a simple coat of varnish or beeswax may be applied purely to bring out the natural colour, grain and character of wood. For a subtle colouring effect somewhere in the middle, both varnish and wax come into their own when first mixed with a little powder colour or stain, and paint can produce a superb look when applied as a colourwash.

Built-in furniture – for example, alcove bookcases or cupboards – is often painted along with the rest of the wood in the room – invariably in an unadventurous, light off-white. Try painting such pieces in a different finish, such as a light colourwash or an antiqued finish, for a different effect.

Interesting surface decoration can transform a piece of furniture. A simple, plain chair could be painted in hot terracottas and a wild patterning of bright and bold stencilled borders, or in cool grey – worthy of an eighteenth-century Swedish interior – or in faded cream, russet and gold – befitting a nineteenth-century French salon.

Sometimes it is unwise to give single items of furniture, such as tables or chairs, a dramatic colour treatment if it makes them stand out in awkward isolation; you can, for example, achieve a stylish and harmonious look by simply painting a series of pieces in varying shades of cream.

Colourwashing is a wonderfully versatile way of putting paint onto a wood surface. On bare, untreated wood, diluted emulsion paint sinks in, lightly colouring the wood and allowing its natural qualities and grain to show through. The more diluted the paint, the more the character of the wood will come through. Two colours, one over the other, will give a richer finish. Light colours, especially on pale woods such as pine or light oak, can be used to give slight hints of colour, while a strong wash of inky black on a darker, grainier wood can be equally effective but a bit more dramatic. Rough and quite dark oak boards, for example, can take a fairly dark colourwash. The wash needs to be worked into the surface and, after a few minutes, rubbed a little with a cloth. The deep browns of the wood will show through. A pale, chalky-white colour also creates a beautiful finish on more textured wood. The beauty of colourwashing is that the result is immediate and the technique easy.

With simple variations, attractive and widely different effects can be achieved using colourwashes. Paint narrow chequerboard borders along edges of, or panels in, the furniture. Alternate colours in wide bands across larger pieces. The beauty of this kind of painting is that it provides the opportunity for great adventure and experimentation with colour and texture. Create smart, chic pieces in combinations of subtle chalky whites and bleached blues, or go wild with vibrant orange, mint green and deep indigo.

Metallic paints, if 'textured' a little, can give a wonderfully rich and exciting surface to furniture. Apply silver metallic paint to the prepared surface. Dilute black emulsion with water and a little detergent and, using a damp cloth, dab it over the surface, into mouldings or along edges, to build up a rich patina for dramatic effect. The silver-grey colour looks splendid against rich jewel colours – emerald, orange or deep burgundy. Try painting the legs of upholstered stools in this finish in combination with rich velvets and cord.

◄ *With a little imagination a tired piece of furniture can be given a magical transformation. The two chests of drawers, one wild, bright and abstract, the other more restrained with its seashore motifs and touches of gold, are lively and fun. They blend happily in this bright room – where even the flowerpots are decorated with paint.*

▲ *The beauty and warmth of polished wood show up well in the honey-gold long refectory table. The natural grain and patina of the wood are drawn out with waxing or varnishing and contrast with the bleached-wood effect of the flooring. Against the neutral walls, the table's richness of texture and colour contrasts well.*

Preparing surfaces for decorative finishes

▶ *The worn-out surface of this little cupboard may be the result of age, or it may have been decorated to imitate this state. In either case the effect is very appealing; but should such a piece require repainting or a new decorative effect, the old paint would need to be thoroughly removed and the surface rubbed down and washed.*

Make sure the surface you are to paint has been properly prepared beforehand, otherwise the effort of painting will be wasted. Unless you require a rough, unsanded surface with some of the imperfections that build up with the passage of time, a professional, smooth-looking finish is well worth the effort of good preparation.

Preparing and priming wood

For both wood and metal furniture it is important to remove all old paint and any varnish. Wearing rubber gloves, apply liquid or gel paint stripper with an old paintbrush, following the manufacturer's instructions. When the layers of paint begin to soften and bubble up, you can use a scraper to remove them from the surface – but take care not to scratch or gouge the surface of the wood. Stubborn areas can be rubbed with steel wool. Wash the surface down with either water or white spirit, depending on what type of stripper you have used.

It is possible to go to a professional wood-stripping company to have the item dipped in a caustic solution. It is not a bad idea to use this kind of service where appropriate: for example, to treat a large piece of furniture or an item with many layers of old paint,

as apart from the convenience, the fumes from the caustic solutions used in the stripping process can be overpowering.

Caustic solutions often leave the wood surface discoloured and slightly raised and rough, although a fine-grade sandpaper will restore the surface after several rubbings over. Either use sandpaper directly on the surface, applying pressure with your fingertips, or wrap it around a block. For simple curved mouldings, wrap it around a length of dowel. Before applying a finish, any knots in the surface should first be sealed, as they produce

resin and can cause discolouring of the finished paint surfaces. Apply one or two coats of knotting sealant over any knots, according to the manufacturer's instructions. If the surface needs some filling before applying a finish, lightly sand and apply a proprietary wood filler to match the grain of the wood. When dry, rub it down again until smooth.

Once the surface has been prepared it is not always necessary to prime it. Some finishes first require a layer of shellac and should not be primed. However, if you are going to paint it then it will need priming. This can be done using an oil-based wood primer, which traditionally comes in pink or white. Dilute the primer by using three parts primer to one part white spirit. Then, with a wide brush, apply it liberally over the surface. The next step is to apply undercoat using a clean brush. The surface is then ready for painting.

Preparing and priming metal

Preparing and priming metal are approached in much the same way as for wood, using specific solvents to remove the paint.

Spray paint can be removed with acetone; oil-based paints and varnishes with turpentine or white spirit; and French enamel varnish with methylated spirits. Use steel wool or a firm wire brush to remove the old paint layers and rust. Continue to rub the surface until it is completely smooth and clean. There are special zinc-based metal primers available for preparing the surface of metal for painting. A base coat of red oxide

Preparing wood

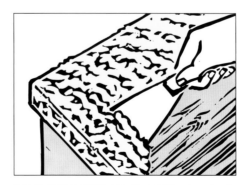

1 Apply liquid or gel stripper with an old brush and wait for the surface to bubble. Scrape off the softened paint.

2 Sand down the stripped surface. Use your fingertips to apply pressure for light sanding or for curved areas.

Preparing and priming metal

inhibits rust and protects metal, so it is ideal for treating garden furniture. Always remember to wear rubber gloves when using red oxide. Apply the primer in a single, even coat and leave it to dry for 24 hours.

Preparing and priming plastic

Wash the plastic surfaces down with a clean cloth and a solution of warm water and household detergent. Rinse the surface thoroughly with clean water, and dry it off completely before painting.

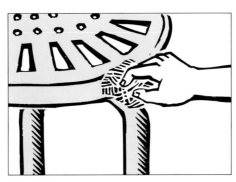

1 Use steel wool or a wire brush to remove old paint layers and rust from the surface.

2 Prime the metal before painting by applying a zinc-based metal primer to the surface. Allow 24 hours to dry.

Tools and equipment

For preparing and priming wood

- **Sandpaper:** in various grades from fine to rough, for removing old finishes and smoothing back wood filler.
- **Overalls, paper mask and rubber gloves:** for protection where the job is dusty and messy and may involve the use of solvents.
- **Flat scraper:** for removing paint.
- **Sponge with rough side, steel wool and small pointed knives:** for removing paint, including paint stuck into deep cracks.
- **Methylated spirits:** for removing French polish or shellac.
- **Paint stripper:** for removing other varnishes and paint.
- **Old paintbrush:** for applying paint stripper.
- **Patent knotting sealant (knot sealer):** to seal knots before priming.
- **Wood filler:** where wood requires filling and smoothing.
- **Undercoat.**
- **Primer.**
- **Sheets of plastic:** to protect the floor.

For preparing and priming metal

- **Methylated spirits:** for removing French enamel varnish.
- **Acetone:** for removing spray paint.
- **Turpentine or white spirit:** for removing oil-based paints and varnishes.
- **Steel wool:** for removing old paint layers and rust.
- **Metal primer.**

▲ *The magnificent red on the bath and curly metal washstand provides splashes of warmth in this cool grey-blue room. Metal furniture, especially if flaked with old paint and rust, requires some attention before painting. The rough surface of the bath was smoothed out after being rubbed, primed, undercoated and then covered with several layers of gloss paint.*

Applying varnish, glaze and stain

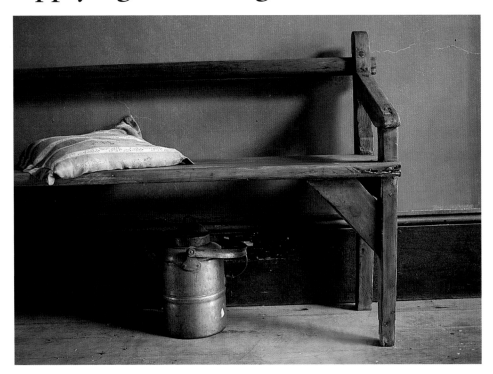

▲ *The natural colour of wood can be enhanced with an application of wax polish. If a bit more colour is required, you could try staining or glazing the wood. This rather battle-scarred bench has come up beautifully after being stained a rich chestnut colour. The intensity of the wall colour helps strengthen the wood's tones.*

Varnishes

Varnishes fall into different categories, depending on the solvent with which they can be diluted. These are: oil-based polyurethane (diluted with turpentine), water-based acrylic (diluted with water) and alcohol-based (diluted with methylated spirits). Oil-based varnishes are available in matt, semi-matt or gloss finish, so choose carefully.

If you are using varnish simply to give a painted surface a good protective finishing coat, there are many household varnishes to choose from. However, polyurethane varnish has a tendency to go yellow. On many finished surfaces this will not matter, but on a pale colourwashed wooden table, for example, it is important not to ruin the effect of the subtle paint colour with the wrong varnish. Oil-based varnishes can be tinted with universal stainers or artist's oil paints.

Instead of oil-based varnish, you can use acrylic (water-based) varnish or those known as 'decorative' or 'copal' varnishes. These are more pleasant to work with, being quick-drying and having one quarter the toxicity of oil-based varnishes. PVA is also a useful varnish – white when liquid and clear once dry. It gives a good protective finish to most surfaces, particularly when using paper.

Shellac is a yellowish-brownish liquid which is not as tough as varnish but can be a useful sealant. French enamel varnish, made from bleached and chemically dyed shellac, looks much the same and can be dabbed on to bright brass to dull it down and give it an aged look. Originally brown, it comes ready-coloured in a wide range of shades and can be successfully diluted with methylated spirits. The liquid can stain and varnish wood in one application, but it dries very quickly so you have to work fast.

Applying varnish

Varnish should be applied with care to any finished surface. To facilitate drying, the air should not be damp so, ideally, you should varnish on a dry, warm day. Make sure the area you are working in is well ventilated and protect all surrounding surfaces with plastic sheeting before starting work.

Many types of brush may be used, including a standard paintbrush, and it is a good idea to experiment with various different types until you feel comfortable with one. Tin 'Glider' brushes are used for applying thin light varnishes; pointed brushes are best for using with shellac; while a chisel-headed lily-bristle brush will do for most other types of varnish application (other than shellac). Treat yourself to a good brush and look after it, cleaning it after every use. Never use varnish brushes for painting.

Coat the first third of the bristles with varnish. Take care not to wipe the brush against the rim of the pot as this causes bubbles. Transfer the loaded brush straight to the surface of the piece, brushing the varnish from the centre outwards. Remove any excess with a clean rag. Apply several coats of varnish, as necessary, brushing each one in a different direction. The final coat, especially if using a gloss varnish, will need a light rubbing down with fine wet-or-dry paper or fine steel wool.

Craquelure

To achieve a crackled surface effect, 'ageing' and 'crackle' varnish can be bought together as two separate bottles – one of which contains slow-drying oil-based varnish and the other quick-drying water-based varnish. These work against each other to create the decorative cracked finish.

First paint the surface of the furniture in a pale oil-based paint. When the base coat is completely dry, apply the oil-based varnish, according to the instructions, to the whole of the area you wish to 'crackle'. Use a soft fitch to ensure the layer is thin and smooth. Leave this to dry for about 45 minutes or until it is tacky to the touch. Apply the second varnish, also over the whole area. This can be left to dry naturally or aided with hot air from a hair dryer. As the top varnish dries, a network of cracks will form. After about an hour, when this process is complete and the varnish thoroughly dry, artist's oil paints or tinted oil glazes can be rubbed into

Craquelure

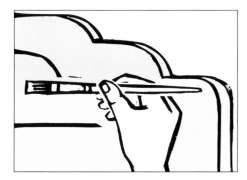

1 When the oil-based base coat is dry, apply the crackle varnish with a fitch. Once dried, apply the second coat.

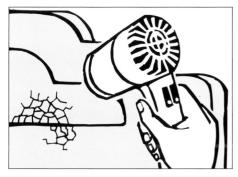

2 As soon as the varnish has dried the crackle will appear. Using a hair dryer will speed up the drying process.

3 When completely dry, rub tinted oil glaze into the surface of the cracks with a soft cloth.

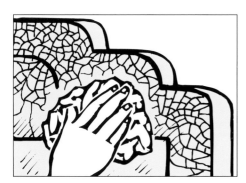

4 Rub off excess glaze with a clean cloth to leave dark cracks on a light background. Seal by applying a varnish.

the surface with a soft cloth so that the tint lodges in the cracks and accentuates them. When you are happy with the degree of colour and overall effect, rub off any excess glaze or oil paint not in the cracks and leave to dry for several days. Once dry, coat the area in shellac and/or an oil-based varnish.

Glazes

Oil glaze (also called scumble glaze) is an extremely versatile substance over paper or wood. It can be tinted with artist's oil paints and, when dry, will be translucent and smooth. Oil glaze behaves like a filmy translucent layer which, even if coloured slightly, will still allow colour beneath it to come through.

Creating an antiqued finish with oil glaze

Mix one part artist's oil paint to eight parts transparent oil glaze to create a murky tint. Antiquing glazes are best applied over a roughened surface so that the colour will sit in the wood grain and any surface scratches and cracks. If you have newly painted wood, you should sand or wire-brush it first to give

it a cracked appearance. Apply the glaze, brushing it out in different directions into a thin layer. Then use a rag to gently rub it off in patches, leaving the glaze in the cracks of the surface to create a mottled effect.

As well as applying tinted oil glaze to plain or painted wood, it can be applied over photocopied images and newspapers that have been glued onto furniture such as screens. This will make paper look as if it is old parchment. Finish off with a coat of clear varnish to give lasting protection.

Stains

Wood stains will colour wood but, unlike varnish, they will not seal it. Wood stains can be used as plain colour or, more decoratively, painted on surfaces in geometric patterns to imitate marquetry. Look at tile patterns in historic houses or church interiors for inspiration. To stain wood, first mark out the pattern by lightly scoring the wood with a knife. This helps to prevent the different coloured stains from seeping into their neighbouring sections. Apply the stain with a brush and allow to dry. Finish with several coats of varnish to seal the wood.

◀ *A painted surface that looks cracked and aged by both time and use can be achieved using the craquelure technique. The gently broken surface it produces, especially when used with paints in pale colours, can be given a further ageing effect with the addition of a coloured antiquing glaze rubbed gently into the surface.*

Applying paint and wax

Paint on wood

Colourwashing

Exactly as its name implies, colourwashing involves the application of a 'wash' of water-based paint onto a wood surface to create thin, transparent layers of colour.

Build up colour and texture bit by bit, painting over previous layers and moving the paint around with the brush. The application of the paint can be quite rough and uneven to give a lively, 'loose' effect. If, however, you want the finish to be quite even, apply a final coat in a paler colour. Take care to 'contain' the unevenness by setting the finished piece of painted furniture against a clean-looking background. Colourwashing with three colours achieves a rich, intense depth.

Colourwash with a wax resist

Painted or colourwashed furniture can be given a slightly beaten-up, weathered look using a wax resist. Wax resists the paint and can be rubbed off at the end of the process to reveal the base layer – whether it is the original wood, or a painted or enamel-varnished surface.

Beeswax polish, or rubber glue that can be removed easily, should be applied over the base coat with a small brush in streaks or blobs. The more worn out the finish you require, the more wax or glue you should apply. Once dried, paint on a layer of emulsion paint and allow this to dry overnight. Then apply subsequent diluted layers. When the last coat has dried, use an old cloth and a scraper to remove the wax or glue, exposing the base and other layers of paint. Finally give the whole piece a light sand.

Wax on wood

Liming

Liming is an effective technique used to enhance the beauty of the wood, leaving a white residue in the grain and cracks and a subtle white sheen over its surface. Choose a wood that has a noticeable and attractive grain. Oak and ash are two good examples of woods that have an 'open' grain and take the white liming paste or wax particularly well. However, if you are prepared to thoroughly wire-brush the surface of a piece of pine furniture (pine has a closed grain), the white waxy residue will be equally effective. All wood surfaces should be lightly wire-brushed first to open the grain. Work the brush in the direction of the grain.

Ready-made liming wax is the easiest to use, and it should be applied using a fairly stiff brush. The idea is to coat the wood and allow the wax to settle in its cracks, splits and grain. Once the wax has dried, smooth over the surface with a cloth, taking care not to lift the wax out.

▶ *The wonderful patina and character of weathered slabs of old wood have been enhanced by using a liming technique. The creamy white wash sits in the grainy surface of the wood, but still allows the original colour of the wood to show through. The white colour scheme of this room is complemented by the use of this technique.*

Colourwash with wax resist

1 Apply the beeswax polish or rubber glue to the surface of the furniture. Brush it on in streaks with a small brush.

2 When dry, paint a layer of emulsion over the surface. Allow to dry again and then apply further diluted layers.

3 After the final layer has dried, use an old cloth and scraper to expose the base and other layers of paint.

▲ *This truly majestic piece of furniture has intricate metalwork encrusted with old peeling paint and rust, which wonderfully complements the rich textures of the kilim and the velvet of the cushions and upholstery. Aged paintwork can be re-created effectively by paint techniques which imitate rusted, bleached or otherwise battered surfaces.*

Paint on metal

Verdigris

Pale-green-topped buildings are a common site in most towns and cities. The sea-green colour is the naturally occurring corrosion of copper, brass or bronze. Verdigris, as the effect is called, takes time to develop and although items can be left outside for the weather to do its work, it is possible to cheat and achieve authentic-looking verdigris by using paint and paste.

The technique is suitable for metal or plastic items such as picture frames, candlesticks and lamp bases, and for furniture, but it has to be worked onto a horizontal surface as the paste will not stick to a vertical one. If you are working on a metal-framed table, for example, you will need to do each part of the frame separately, turning the table so that the painted surface is always horizontal.

The base for the work should be a bronze-brown colour, so first paint the item with a suitable shade of paint, French enamel varnish or shellac and allow this to dry. Apply a wash of deep-green emulsion (diluted one part emulsion to four parts water) and leave this to dry. If necessary, apply a second coat.

You now need to make up two verdigris pastes, one using mint-green emulsion and the other a pale blue. Mix methylated spirits into each of the paints (one part spirit to two parts emulsion). Using a sieve, mix in plaster powder or whiting until you have smooth and fairly stiff pastes.

The two pastes should be applied to the painted surface randomly, building up varying degrees of texture. Don't be too precise about applying the paste and leave some areas of the basecoat showing through. While this is drying, use a thin artist's brush to apply a little well-diluted yellow ochre acrylic paint in small random patches across the surface. When dry, gently pour water over the whole surface, to expose some of the layers beneath.

Sprinkle some whiting or powder over the damp surface, pressing it into the surface and into any mouldings. When almost dry, use a cloth to rub off some of the powder so that the layers underneath show. The finished result should look like the patinated metal it is imitating. When dry, seal with diluted PVA. For a really hard-wearing surface, apply a matt polyurethane varnish. Creating a look of rusted metal can be achieved in a similar way, using brown and red paints.

Verdigris

1 A few small patches of yellow ochre are dabbed across the table's finished paintwork using a thin artist's brush.

2 Gently pour water over the surface of the table to expose some of the under layers of paint.

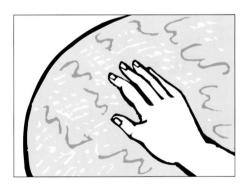

3 Sprinkle whiting powder over the damp surface of the table and press onto the surface and into the mouldings.

4 When almost dry, use an old cloth to rub off some of the whiting powder. When dry, seal with diluted PVA.

Using unusual materials

▲ *Bold and whimsical, these plastic blown-up cushions with their emphatic rows of brightly coloured circles are a throwback to the 1960s but they work surprisingly well in this otherwise deliberately restrained interior. Balance these unusual materials with something more familiar to create maximum impact.*

This section salutes a small but exciting selection of surprising and unlikely materials that can stunningly alter the surface of a piece of furniture. Neither fabric nor paint, there is no collective term that can be used to describe such diverse materials as paper, plastic, jute fibre, wire mesh, glass and ceramic, but used individually or even together they break the boundaries of what is both familiar and predictable in interior furnishing.

Contrast and texture, and the interplay between them, are the keys to using these materials with style and verve. Keep in mind balance and symmetry – a small amount of something unexpected usually goes a long way! Consider hard and soft surfaces together and juxtapose matt opacity with cool glassy light-reflecting surfaces. Imagine, for example, shiny plastic or metal gauze against a smooth rubber or linoleum floor. With

such diversity, it is to be hoped that the days when almost every surface was covered in a floral chintz fabric are dim and distant.

While working with such unusual materials will not be to everyone's taste, it is undoubtedly true that using metal, plastic and paper, for example, as materials for furnishings, will be a challenge to your imagination and perspective. Imagine a glass-topped table draped in a shimmering, gauze-like, finely meshed metal. It would make a wonderful and unusual backdrop for a collection of glass objects. Put a swathe of shot silk beneath the metal and you have a stunning combination. Ribbons or tassels can be tied to sheets of wire mesh for added texture. Metal-framed chairs wound with jute fibre or twisted straw fronds provide fabulous textural contrast.

Mixing and experimenting are the keys to success when using any material with which you are unfamiliar. Some of these, and their applications, are by no means new: mosaic, for example. And although paper is a familiar material, using it as a covering for furniture opens up a new dimension.

We are continually drawing on past styles and themes in attempts to find new ways of decorating surfaces. While few of us have the inclination or ability to re-create the splendid mosaic masterpieces of the ancient Roman artisans, we may well consider and be influenced by their use of pattern and colour in our own more modest creations.

Classic, timeless pieces can be given a twist in new materials. For example, the familiar shape of an upholstered club armchair, with its solid proportions, is retained yet transformed if sculpted from twisted metal or corrugated cardboard.

Wit and a hint of mischief may occasionally take over from practicality – and why not, when wearied by mass-production and safe, 'co-ordinating' schemes? Plastic inflatable cushions for most of us may look best floating on the shimmering surface of a swimming pool, but we are already being introduced to worktops made from plastic waste. So, in pride of place – perhaps on the *chaise longue* so exquisitely crafted from recycled plastic containers – why not a plastic inflatable bolster cushion?

◀ The surprising use of solid glass to make this 'tablecloth' and matching stool, together with the stunning colour, provides a dramatic focal point in the room. The large expanse of glass in the uncurtained window and the equally unusual orange-yellow light fitting over the table contribute to the glass theme.

Paper

Although it is more usually found on the walls of a room, paper is a very exciting medium to use on furniture – whether wood, metal or plastic. In its many forms, it transfers particularly easily to flat, smooth surfaces such as table tops, drawer fronts, cupboard panels and even wooden chairs. Other than glue to paste it to the surface, the only other requirement is a top coat or two of clear varnish, to preserve it from tearing.

Paper can be matt and rough like newsprint, smooth and shiny as on a magazine cover, printed, embossed, plain, silver, thin, transparent, and much more besides. Once you begin to identify the different types available – even those in everyday use – its versatility becomes instantly evident. It offers numerous decorative possibilities, for while it can, of course, be cut with a knife or pair of scissors, torn, folded or scrunched, it can also be stitched and even woven.

Do not assume that paper cannot be a sturdy material. The famous Lloyd Loom chairs are made from twisted paper woven together, resulting in a form that is very strong and hard-wearing. In addition, some types of card – corrugated, for example – are sufficiently rigid to make free-standing pieces, or 'cut-out' cases that may be dropped over or applied to a timber frame – as seating, for example. To achieve a light-hearted decorative element you could also explore the technique of *trompe l'oeil* by painting yourself a magnificent carved wood table or a whimsical chair on a free-standing silhouette of card.

Lay cut or torn pieces of paper on a flat surface under sheets of glass, or perhaps overlay fine black-and-white newsprint with tiny pieces of coloured metallic foil from sweet wrappers in a mosaic pattern. Try weaving strips of multicoloured images from magazine pages between strips of plain coloured paper to create a flat chequered surface which can be laid or pasted, like a mat, on tables or cupboards. Folded strips of newspaper could be woven in the same way – and complemented by brown paper. Such a monotone surface lends itself to cool, clear interiors where natural materials, such as wood, stone or terracotta, feature.

▲ *Painted and decorated paper has been used to cover the structure and drawer fronts of this unusual chest of drawers. This effect is easy to achieve and works particularly well on flat surfaces, as it is easier to manipulate the paper and achieve neat folds and edges. Another advantage is that if you don't like it, you can rip it off and try something else.*

Textured paper

For a smart and sophisticated surface use simple embossed letters or motifs on a beautifully hand-crafted sheet of paper. You can order an embossing press with your own initials or customized image, and the advantage of heavy handmade paper is that it has some texture and thickness. Another simple method of adding texture to paper is to use a sewing machine to punch lines across its surface, but take the thread out of the machine first! The results resemble punched metalwork and can be cut to fit areas such as cupboard door panels.

There are numerous types of specialist handmade paper on the market, many of which have beautiful and unusual textures, while others resemble stone or granite. They are made from recycled paper, often with a scattering of plant pieces, flower petals or onion skins. Some are really lovely, and make wonderful decorative material. Although they appear fragile, they are actually quite strong. For protection on a table surface, however, the sheets will need laying under glass.

Pleating paper

Pleated or folded paper can be used behind glazed cupboard doors as a less-expensive alternative to fabric. Use a crisp, smooth paper or thin card and mark with tiny dots along the top and back edge of the paper. The dots need not be equally spaced but must line up on both edges. Fold on alternate sides, following the marked fold lines. Use a bone letter opener to crease the fold lines. Attach the folded sheets to the timber frame of a glazed door using tacks.   ▷

◀ *Paper is an extremely versatile material available in a huge range of different colours, textures and weights. Here, reproduced antique type-printed paper has been used to cover the lampshade and the wallpaper. Be bold and create unusual effects by experimenting with various different types of paper on different surfaces.*

Paper can be applied directly to a smooth, clean surface using PVA glue, diluted 1:1 with water. A large sheet of newsprint or printed wallpaper could be used across a table top, for example, or if you don't wish to paste directly onto the table, cut a piece of plywood or MDF to the same size and wrap it in the paper. Seal the finished surface with the PVA solution. Alternatively, assemble smaller pieces of plywood, cut to the size of a standard ceramic tile, each covered in a different coloured or printed paper, and lay the paper-covered 'tiles' together on a recessed table top. Protect the surface with a sheet of glass.

Maps are fun to use on or over furniture. Look for old examples in second-hand bookshops, or huge, brand-new, brightly coloured world maps. These are great for children's rooms or more informal, relaxed spaces. Again, use diluted PVA, both to stick down the paper and to seal its surface.

Plain papers can be dyed, painted, stained, marbled or printed on before being used. Children's paintings, pasted onto the sides and base of a simple wooden box and then sealed, would make a fun addition to a playroom. Use acrylic paints on the paper as they will not mix with the glue.

The inside of plain pine chests can be given a lift by using a lining paper inside the lid and in the box itself. Wallpapers with old or contemporary designs are excellent, as the paper is quite tough and the selection of patterns available is wide.

A clever way of brightening up and completely transforming a fairly dull chest of drawers or small seed chest would be to cover all the drawer fronts with paper. Take a pictorial scene – *toile de Jouy* wallpaper would be a good start – and cut the pattern into a grid, one for each drawer. You will need to allow sufficient paper to turn around the sides of each drawer front. Stripes or tartan papers would be equally effective. For a children's room, for example, alternate different bold colours. Remove drawer knobs first. Apply the paper using PVA and make sure the surface is smooth and wrinkle-free. After leaving the paper enough time to dry (and taking care not to tear it), carefully screw the knobs back on again.

Decoupage

This technique is the decoration of surfaces with paper cut-outs. Interesting effects can be achieved by photocopying single images, enlarging or reducing them according to the size of the item you plan to cover, and cutting them out. Almost any printed paper that you can cut and paste can be used: look for old engravings of flowers or fruit, or architectural details for a classical theme, pieces of newspaper, playing cards, old documents, glossy magazine covers, wallpaper borders or elements of more intricate patterns such as old fabric or wallpaper designs. For traditionalists, multicoloured floral designs and fat little cherubs will follow the Victorian style – they used decoupage on just about everything. Also interesting – for a

▲ *This is a delightful and original way to make a feature of a dull hallway or a dreary corner. Every surface is covered with an unusual paper. The toning base colours of the floor, skirting board and wallpaper unite the effect, allowing the printed paper on the table and the pattern on the wallpaper to really stand out.*

kitchen surface perhaps – are hardware catalogues depicting pots, pans and other culinary gadgets. Cupboard handles and mouldings can be photocopied, painted or stained if required, and then pasted into place onto the flat surface of a plain cupboard front. When assembled, the effect is that of a fake dresser or cabinet.

Letters or numbers also make interesting decoration. Use varying styles and sizes cut out from magazines, newspapers or posters, and dot them all over a surface such as a large desk. A background of plain brown parcel paper can be used for contrast. Sheets of different typeface styles also look good when pasted together.

How to decoupage

Use a scalpel to cut out the paper or photocopied images, and a 1:1 dilution of PVA glue and water for pasting and varnishing. Also useful is a decorator's brush for pasting and a smaller artist's brush and diluted emulsion paints (or acrylics) for colouring black-and-white photocopies.

Cut out the images on a hard, flat surface, ideally a cutting board, using the scalpel. Prepare the background: for example, newspaper, brown paper or a painted surface. Coat the paper cut-outs on both sides with the diluted PVA. Position the pasted paper and brush over. When it dries the paper will shrink a little. Paint the image with diluted paint or 'antique' it (see pages 278–279) if this is in keeping with the effect you want.

▲ *Scraps of old letters and music scores have been layered and pasted directly onto the newly painted cream surface of this chest of drawers to provide an unusual but very effective and imaginative look. The overall effect, linked by the neutral colour of the chest's background and the fireplace, creates a harmonious blend.*

Decoupage

1 Select various images from newspapers or magazines and, using a scalpel, carefully cut them out.

2 With a paintbrush, coat both sides of the cut-out shapes with a 1:1 mix of water and PVA.

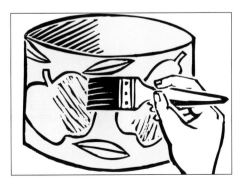

3 Position the pasted cut-outs on the surface you are covering and then brush the shapes over with the mix.

Mosaic

As a decorative art form, mosaic has been around for thousands of years. Little bits of stone, pebble, glass and even shell have been used to embellish walls, floors and other surfaces, both inside and outside, in all sorts of buildings that range from the grandest of cathedrals to the humblest of dwellings. Throughout history, from the time of the ancient Greeks and Romans, mosaics have depicted figurative scenes as detailed as paintings or tapestries. Huge areas were covered in fragments of ceramic, precious or semiprecious stones which had borders of intricate abstract patterns running around the central image. As a purely abstract art form, mosaic ran riot during the Art Nouveau period in Europe, with roofs, courtyards, columns and almost every available surface covered in startlingly bold and detailed designs by skilled practitioners who embraced its versatility and vibrancy.

In contemporary interiors mosaic is being re-employed as a means of decorating surfaces. On furniture it can be used to embellish table tops, mirror frames, bedheadboards or even chairs. The pieces that traditionally formed mosaic are known as

▶ Mosaic is a time-old tradition in most cultures. Here, a lovely pattern has been made from mosaic and set into the top of the round table. The mosaic effect is echoed in the background in the tiles placed around the kitchen area.

Mosaic

1 Break up the pieces for your mosaic into small chips. You may need to cut them again to fit into the edges.

2 Once the pattern has been devised, apply glue to the back of the mosaic pieces and position them.

3 Apply grout across the surface of the mosaic. Spread evenly, filling in the gaps between each piece of mosaic.

4 Before it dries, wipe off any excess grout smeared across the surface of the mosaic with a clean cloth.

tesserae or 'smalti' – small coloured glass or enamel blocks. Tesserae can be bought from specialist suppliers, but it is possible to use a whole variety of materials in mosaic work: interesting effects can be achieved using broken pieces of household ceramic tiles or crockery, glass, perspex or even mirror.

Most surfaces, if prepared correctly, can take mosaic. You may need to score some surfaces, such as metal, in order for glue or cement to take; and wood, plywood or MDF must be sealed first with a 1:1 solution of water to PVA. Hardboard for a table top, for example, can be bought to your specifications from some hardware stores. However, you can apply mosaic directly to the surface of furniture. Keeping the work horizontal until the grout has dried is important. If you have ever tiled a floor or wall, the approach is much the same, but simpler.

Arranging the tiles

Designs, abstract or figurative, may be first mapped out on the base or you can piece the pattern together as you go along, creating a kaleidoscope of colour. For a random design, begin by playing with the segments on the surface of the table or board, moving them around until a pleasing pattern forms. For thicker tiles you may need to score and snap some of the segments that are to edge the board; for thinner tiles and tesserae, use tile nippers to create curves for your pattern.

Crockery or larger tiles can be broken and subsequently cut into more refined shapes. Alternatively, you can use the randomly broken segments in a loose abstract arrangement, but be prepared to use more grout between each bit. Should you wish to embark on more adventurous mosaic projects with harder materials such as marble or smalti, it is worth investing in a hammer and hardie – essentially a small anvil against which the piece is held while a sharp-edged hammer is brought down onto its surface, thus breaking the piece.

Gluing and grouting

Once the pattern has been decided and the pieces cut, apply glue to the back of each piece and stick them down onto your hard-

▲ *This is a wonderful use of mosaic – insetting random and regular patterns within the panelled sections of this wooden bed frame. The decoration is pleasingly restrained and quite beautiful in its simplicity. Small ceramic tiles in tidy rows perfectly balance the irregular pieces of broken tile in the centre.*

board or other surface. Leave to dry. Then mix up the grout, following the instructions, or use ready-mixed grout. Grout can be coloured if desired, using water-based or acrylic paints, which should be added in small amounts to the dry powder type.

Apply the grout across the surface of the mosaic and spread evenly, filling all the gaps between the sections of tile or glass. Before it dries, wipe off the excess with a damp cloth. The piece should be left to dry for at least 24 hours and then the surface cleaned and polished with a clean cloth.

Soft furnishing

Everyone for whom fabrics are a real passion
will find the excitement of handling textiles and
the exploration of their potential – both practical
and decorative – absolutely all-embracing. From
earthy-coloured wool tartans to shimmery, lustrous
silks, the inspiration and fascination are the same.
This has, perhaps, something to do with the tactile
qualities of cloth, with its origins and history, and
with its many and varied forms.

Weave

Both the structure of a weave and the choice of yarn affect the final character of the cloth. Different weave structures used on the same yarn will produce significantly different finished fabrics. Smooth cotton sateen, for example, looks nothing like muslin, although both are made of cotton. This is almost entirely because of the way each is woven.

Plain weave is the simplest and most obvious method of weaving a length of cloth. The weft threads (those travelling widthways across the loom) go under and over alternate warp threads (those travelling lengthways across the loom). On the next row, the warp thread travels over the weft thread where previously it went under, and under it where it went over. Alternating row by row, this pattern repeats itself.

In most woven cloths, the warp threads are assembled on a loom first (in a variety of forms) and then the weft threads are woven through them. In some cloths, however – jacquard cloth, for example – the weave is very much more complex. Indeed, jacquard cloth is produced on its own special loom, from which the cloth takes its name.

Yarn

Different yarns – of cotton, linen, wool or silk – are responsible for giving particular characteristics to fabrics. Yarns may be mixed in one cloth for various reasons: to add more strength or lustre, or for economic reasons.

Cloth may be dyed once woven (piece-dyed) or the yarn may be coloured before the weaving process begins. In addition, an infinite variety of pattern can be achieved by printing on cloth. Complex modern printing methods can achieve stunning effects: computer-generated imagery is used to print holograms onto cloth, for instance, and computers are also used in weaving.

Fabric as a soft furnishing

Applying fabrics to furniture and using them for furnishings are endlessly rewarding; they are so versatile, and full of scope. There are many reasons for wanting to cover a sofa in fabric, for instance: perhaps for mundane practical reasons, or for a change of mood ▷

◀ *Long, seemingly never-ending streams of billowy fabric in gorgeous, jewel-like colours flow down from the ceiling and demonstrate how bold use of fabric can create a stunning effect. Just visible is another light shining through the material, illustrating how fabric, when used in this way, can add dimensions to a room.*

▲ *Combinations of different textures in the blue and white cushions mingle happily together when they are thrown into an attractive heap in the corner of this day-bed. The blues are matched in the stripes of the seat cover, while the intricately woven white cushion covers create a link with the white-painted bedstead.*

or lifestyle; for comfort – replacing some much-loved but worn-out covers that let the itchy stuffing through – or perhaps to follow the ever-changing whims of fashion. Imagine a plain and simple sofa and cover it, in your mind's eye, in pristine white cotton first of all. Then imagine it transformed with a covering of multicoloured kilim. It can become something different again if floral prints are introduced – or tartans or paisleys.

Customizing fabric

New 'fabrics' can be created by mixing and joining old pieces together, rather as you would with patchwork. Borders and edges can be created for fabrics using strips of other cloths, or braids or ribbons – themselves small textiles. Apply paint to create pattern and texture, and mix wallpaper paste into the paint for wonderful textural effects (see pages 296–299) which tend to transform not only the surface but the entire cloth.

Different weights of fabric can be combined: heavy wool can be stitched in strips between narrow lengths of flimsy cotton, for example, and an entirely new fabric will be constructed. The alternating weight creates an interesting movement when it is handled, and this in turn may suggest new, unexpected uses that neither fabric could offer alone.

Fabrics can be embellished with beads, fringes and tassels in varied and glorious ways. Swirling patterns of shiny silk can crisscross a surface of matt cotton and utterly transform it. Braids and cords can be added to fabric edges to give definition, texture and a touch of luxury. The woven detail of some miniature textiles (passementerie) is quite breathtaking, but use them to uplift a plain fabric, for one of the joys of using them is that, until you are close to them, you cannot see the intricate threads and knots and thus they have an inbuilt element of surprise.

Although some types of fabric will lend themselves to particular settings or uses, exciting and unexpected effects can be achieved by shifting them around and trying less predictable applications. A 2.5cm (1in) border of tiny checks of black and cream ribbon running around the edge of a throw of creamy cashmere, for example, draws the

▲ *The combination of fabrics used in patchwork and appliqué throws and cushion covers provides a very effective way of introducing colours and colour combinations into a room. The muted tones in the room above required a splash of vibrancy to add interest and this was amply provided by the various cushion materials.*

eye and enhances the tactile quality of the original fabric. It provides both a quiet definition and a striking note. In other instances, it is a matter of improvisation and surprise. Try, for example, combining a creamy linen with a rough hessian band, or a canary-yellow velvet with a traditional wool tartan. While these two pairings would not sit comfortably with each other, if you change the colour of the velvet to a rich chocolate brown, and the tartan to one featuring earthy reds and ochres, a much more cohesive look appears. It is colour that provides the link and gives you the opportunity to be bold and mix different patterns and styles together. Alternatively, keep to the similar fabric types and use clashing colours. Colour can be fashionable; certain colour groups come in and out of fashion. One minute it may be chic to be all-over neutral but the next everything must be brilliantly bright. New fabric designs are constantly flooding the marketplace,

while retuned old designs continue to surprise and delight. The combination of change and familiarity is what makes using fabrics so exciting, for each new introduction creates an entirely new feel.

When selecting fabrics, do not confine yourself necessarily to traditional furnishing fabric suppliers. Be more inspired and try specialist shops or market stalls; look at stores that sell artist's canvas or Indian saris. It is relatively easy to find antique fabrics too. They do come up at auction, and although they can often be prohibitively expensive or perhaps too fragile or damaged to use for anything major, they can be combined with other cloths or used in a way that does not jeopardize their continued life. It is worth looking at ethnic fabrics too: African barkwork or Native American beadwork, for example, may be used in an exciting way in combination with contemporary machine-made fabrics or against unexpected surfaces.

◀ No attempt has been made to match or co-ordinate any of these clashing fabrics and yet the combinations make for an exciting array of colours and print sizes. Damask mixes with a leopard print which mingles with a floral backdrop – but the uniting factor is the drama provided by each of the bold fabrics.

Directory of furnishing fabrics

Textiles are all woven, even if they have pattern applied later. Non-woven anomalies are included here, as we tend to think of them as fabrics. More unusual textiles, such as felt or suede, often provide a greater number of decorative possibilities.

Appliquéd fabrics are pleasing to use as furnishings. Combined with patchwork, for example, a very personalized cloth can be created. **4**

Crewelwork fabrics, which use stitching to create a surface pattern, often on a ground cloth of thick woven cotton, are wonderfully textural.

Fake fur can be startlingly effective as upholstery fabric too.

Woven and non-woven fabrics

Bouclé
Originally woSuitable for upholstery, characterized by a looped surface.

Brocade
Originally woven from silk, with rich surface pattern and matt background. Gold threads were laid in to highlight.

Broderie anglaise
Cotton fabric, usually white, with embroidered cut-out 'lacy' pattern.

Calico
Cream, plain-woven cotton, originally from India. Can be bleached white.

Cambric
A firm, fine, creamy, plain-woven cotton, often treated to give it a slight sheen. Used for inner covers for pillows and duvets, as its close weave prevents feathers from escaping.

Canvas
Also called duck, a strong, heavy fabric in linen or cotton, it is woven to make it waterproof. Can be dyed or bleached; used for ships' sails and awnings.

Chenille
From the French, meaning caterpillar. Originally made from wool or cotton, it has a thick, soft pile that drapes well.

Corduroy
Traditionally heavy, cotton fabric with evenly spaced, ribbed pile running down the length of the cloth.

Damask
Traditionally woven for fine table-linens. Damask is a fine fabric, with a reversible pattern created by the weaving process. Usually it is one colour throughout.

Dobby cloth
Woven on dobby loom, with simple, small, regularly repeated woven motifs.

Doublecloth
Strong, reversible fabric, comprising two separate but interwoven cloths.

Felt
Made from a mass of wool or hair pulped together until matted and shrunk. Does not fray when cut.

Flannel
A smooth fabric made from wool, traditionally used as suiting but good for upholstery too.

Gauze
Soft, sheer fabric; some warp threads are twisted for a very slight texture.

Gingham
Plain-weave cotton: checked pattern combines white and one other colour.

Hessian
Coarse-fibred jute cloth used for sacking – also upholstery. Firmer, narrow widths are used as webbing tape.

Jacquard
Intricately patterned, reversible fabric; takes name from French loom. **2**

Jute
Fibrous material from plant stems, used as yarn for weaving hessian.

Kelim
Woven like tapestry, made from cotton or wool, and characterized by narrow slits between the areas of pattern. **3**

Lace
Delicate openwork intricately patterned fabric, made by twisting and knotting threads. Traditionally cotton.

Linen
Strong cloth woven from flax. Tends to crease, but this can look attractive.

Madras
Inexpensive, brightly checked and striped, plain-weave Indian cotton.

Moiré
A finely ribbed fabric, usually silk or acetate, with rippling surface pattern.

Muslin
Plain-weave cotton; either very sheer and fine or coarse (like cheesecloth).

Ottoman

Ideal as an upholstery fabric; this is a firm and lustrous, horizontally ribbed, fabric, often made with a silk warp and a cotton weft.

Percale

Very fine, high-quality cotton.

Poplin

Originally made from silk and wool, but nowadays from cotton (Egyptian) and with a slightly silky finish. Poplin has a fine cross-ribbed pattern,

which is formed by using weft threads that are thicker than those of the warp threads.

Satin

A plain, closely woven silk with a smooth and lustrous finish. The wrong side of the fabric has a more matt finish. Satin is resembled by the less-expensive cotton- or wool-based fabric known as sateen.

Silk

Silk is one of the most luxurious of furnishing fabrics but not necessarily the most expensive – especially plain silks and silk mixes. It needs protection from strong sunlight and because it will show water marks it should be dry cleaned only.

Taffeta

A plain woven cloth with subtle surface ribs, traditionally made from silk. Shot-silk taffeta, where the warp and weft threads are in contrasting colours, gives the fabric the appearance of changing colour when light falls on the surface as it moves.

Tapestry

Originally hand embroidered in silk or wool, often depicting a pictorial scene. Nowadays tapestries can be created by jacquard looms.

Ticking

A strong, closely woven twill which forms a herringbone stripe, commonly known as mattress ticking. It is used for pillow cases and mattresses and usually woven with a contrast black, red or blue stripe against an off-white ground.

Tweed

A plain or twill weave from wool, often in two or more colours to create a checked pattern.

Twill

A basic weave with a diagonal grain that can be woven in any fibre.

Velvet

This is a thick, luxurious fabric with a dense pile, which is formed by either lifting the warp threads over wires and then cutting the loop (known as cut pile) or weaving two cloths simultaneously face to face, and then slicing them apart to form two separate velvet piles. Velvet is lustrous and can be woven in silk, linen, mohair and synthetic fibres, with a different finish resulting from each.

Wool

Wool can be used as a furnishing fabric – for example wool tartan (prized for its patterning), chenille, even damask. Worsted, a combed wool gives a strong, smooth finish.

Printed fabrics

Batik

A decorative technique for adding pattern to cloth. A design is drawn on in melted wax. The cloth is dyed, but the dye does not permeate the cloth where the wax is present. The wax is removed, leaving the pattern.

Block print

Printing using carved wooden blocks applied by hand. Major form of printing until the mid-eighteenth century.

Chintz

From the Hindu word *chitta*. Originally a painted or printed cotton cloth from India, this fabric traditionally depicts the tree of life, flowers and foliage, etc. Nowadays, it is used to describe a glazed cloth with floral printed pattern.

Paisley

Stylized curving floral or fruit forms, from patterns originating in India. The pattern can also be woven.

Toile de Jouy

Depicts light-hearted pastoral or pictorial scenes in a single colour on an off-white ground. The style originated in the eighteenth century in the French town of Jouy-en-Josas.

Customizing plain fabrics

Painting

This is an inexpensive way of customizing plain fabrics with your own unique colour schemes and designs. Fabric paints or crayons are easily available from good artist's suppliers or from department stores. Emulsion, acrylic, metallic or spray paints are all equally effective and easy to use. Apply all paints in a well-ventilated area and, if spraying, it is a good idea to wear a face-mask.

To apply the paint, use a decorator's brush in whatever size is most appropriate for the line or shape you are making. Scrunched-up rags can add interesting texture. All the different techniques for applying paint - for example, spattering, stippling and sten-cilling - will result in markedly different effects. If you are using more than one colour, be sure to let each layer dry before the next is added.

Most types of fabrics will accept paint. The flatter the fabric – that is, the less texture it has – the easier it will be to apply the paint. Unbleached calico, canvas or other flattish cottons are perfect. However, silks and velvets provide luxurious backdrops for painting, although they require a little more attention and care. Ironing 'fixes' the paint in place.

Dyeing

There are numerous different dyestuffs and the range of colours, particularly if you mix them yourself, is unlimited. For example, subtle tones can be achieved with the liquid from boiling onion skins or walnut shells. Consult a specific manual if your enthusiasm for natural dyeing so demands.

A clever, and simple, device for giving fabrics a faded look of age is to make an infusion of tea or coffee and dip fabrics into the mixture. Subtle sepia tones can be achieved on plain fabrics, particularly muslin. Relatively inexpensive cotton or linen prints can be transformed by this method, and the technique works exceptionally well on deli-cately printed floral patterns. However, the effect is not permanent and will fade in due course, or with washing.

Dye, like paint, can be fixed by heat when the cloth has dried. At home, an iron pro-vides the most effective method. Proprietary fixers can also be employed.

Dyeing with a wax resist

Hot melted wax can be used to create pat-terns on fabrics. Traditionally, this technique is known as 'batik'. Like paint, wax can be controlled to achieve subtle, detailed texture and pattern or, if you prefer, a looser, more abstract effect. To begin with, hot wax is painted or drawn onto a plain fabric. Use a tjanting, a tool specially designed for dribbling the wax onto the surface. When the wax has cooled down sufficiently the fabric is immersed in dye. Once dry, the wax is removed by applying a hot iron and soaking up the melted wax with a clean cloth. The area where the wax was applied will retain the ground colour.

Dyeing with wallpaper paste

Another technique, similar to dyeing with wax, is dyeing with cold-water wallpaper paste. This gives both texture and stiffness to fabric, and has added bonuses in that the paste is both inexpensive and easy to apply.

The glorious aspect of this technique is that the stiffness of the finished result can easily be altered, as the paste can be repeatedly softened and removed with water.

Spread the clean, dry fabric on a large, flat surface. Mix up the paste, which should be not too thick: roughly the consistency of jam. Using a wide wallpaper-hanging brush, apply the paste and leave it to dry. At this point, immerse the whole piece in a bath of cold-water dye. The colour will be absorbed by the paste. The fabric is slippery at this stage and, before the paste dries again, you can run a dry brush or stick across the surface to make patterns and create texture. The

fabric, still pasted, can be left to dry now, resulting in a fairly stiff, textured cloth. Alternatively, if, after drying, you immerse it again and this time remove all the paste while it is still in the water, the cloth will retain its patterned surface but be softer to the touch.

Calico or lightweight canvas is ideal for dyeing with wallpaper paste. Working with these fabrics is a little like using papier-mâché, in that you can 'sculpt' with the pasted, stiffened cloth. You could try wrapping a side-table (obviously not an antique piece!) in the wet, pasted fabric and folding and draping the fabric to get a snug fit. When the fabric dries, it will retain its shape.▷

◀◀ *Richly coloured fabrics can make a decorative scheme come alive. While the rest of the colours in this conservatory are neutral and understated, the cushions' rainbow hues create a feeling of warmth and informality.*

◀ *Customizing plain fabrics with paint allows a great deal of scope for creativity. The designs embellishing this stone-coloured bed-linen resemble charcoal sketches or plasterwork mouldings, and create an unusual* trompe-l'oeil *effect.*

Printing

To achieve a more controlled pattern on fabric, it is better to print, using a linocut or stamp. Simple borders can be run around the edge of a fabric using this quick and easy method and it can be cleverly utilized for small items like cushion covers.

Obviously, the more professional you want your finish to be, the more likely you are to need proper tools; there are special lino-cutting tools, for example. But whether you use a potato, lino or a sponge, the areas that you cut out will not take up printing ink.

A version of this method uses washing-up sponges – the sort that are rectangular and have a stiff scouring base. Use a felt-tip pen to mark up a grid on the soft side of the sponge. Divide it into squares with 6mm (¼in) gutters between the squares. Cut along the lines and hollow out the channels.

Squeeze acrylic paint onto a plate and thin it with water to the consistency of single cream. Alternatively, use fabric paints. Press the cut face of the sponge into the paint. Do not make it so thin and wet that it drips.

Ensure that your fabric is stretched out flat, either using weights or, preferably, pinning it to a board. Then, carefully and lightly, press the sponge onto the surface of the fabric and you will achieve a kind of mosaic pattern. You may want to test the technique first on a piece of paper to ensure that you have the paint at the correct consistency and so that you can decide how much paint you actually need on the sponge – be careful not to smudge prints you have already made as you print more.

You can make a chequerboard pattern using two sponge 'tiles' and two colours. Print one colour first, filling in the missing squares with the other only when it is dry.

Combining fabrics

This is the fabric equivalent of 'distressed' paint finishes! By breaking down and re-assembling related or contrasting fabrics in one item – a throw or bed-hanging, perhaps – you can create both unexpected and wonderful combinations and a distinctly original 'fabric'. The idea extends and refines the idea of the patchwork quilt. As in all decoration, however, there has to be a balance: the two, three or many more different fabrics that work pleasingly together must result in a piece that is more than just the sum of its parts.

Pile more than half a dozen fabrics together on a table and you will see some kind of link. Maybe it is simply a red line from a tartan which jumps to a silk damask of the same hue, or the creaminess of old bleached linen against a rough jute which in

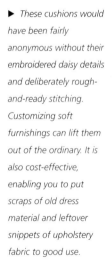

▶ *These cushions would have been fairly anonymous without their embroidered daisy details and deliberately rough-and-ready stitching. Customizing soft furnishings can lift them out of the ordinary. It is also cost-effective, enabling you to put scraps of old dress material and leftover snippets of upholstery fabric to good use.*

Printing fabric

1 Mark a grid with felt pen on the sponge's soft face; cut channels along the lines to make a pad of squares.

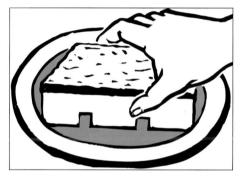

2 Squeeze paint onto plate; dilute with water to single-cream consistency; press cut face of sponge into paint.

3 Test technique on paper to avoid smudging and drips; then press sponge carefully and lightly onto flat fabric.

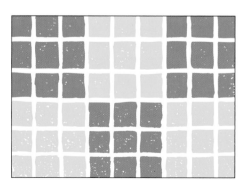

4 Print all the first colour of a chequerboard effect and allow to dry before filling in second-colour squares.

▲ *These fabrics have been painted and resist-dyed in colours of jewel-like intensity. Their inspiration ranges from batik fabrics and Indian saris to the boldly striped walls and furnishings of Regency salons. Simple trimmings can enhance soft-furnishing fabrics still further; here, a gold-braid edging gives the shimmering sapphire-coloured cushion an ornate finish.*

turn lies against a cream and black striped cotton. Occasionally, a cornucopia of pink, lime green, purple and orange, although not to everyone's taste, just simply works.

If the colour links in some way, you can mix your fabrics. Equally, mix different textures – silk, poplin, canvas, damask and velvet, for example.

It is also interesting to use fabrics of varying weights together in one piece: such as thin muslin and velvet, or hessian and silk. You then have a fabric that moves in a different way, and demands to be hung or displayed more cleverly, or suggests new uses.

Stitching small circles of frayed coloured cloth randomly across the surface of another fabric – like mattress tufts – is another exciting method of customizing; as is stitching itself, which can transform fabric by adding colour and texture.

Work out the quantity of fabric you wish to use fairly carefully, allowing extra for hemming, etc. The keys to the success of the final piece are both planning and accurate cutting. Fabrics for piping should be cut on the bias (the cross of the fabric) and therefore more fabric is required. Use faint pencil lines as a cutting guide.

Seating

Seating is all about comfort and style – and balancing the right amount of both. How this is achieved will depend on where in the house, garden or office the seating is to be and, more crucially, the part it is to play. Whether we are working at a desk or flopping down at the end of a busy day, comfort is paramount. A set of chairs able to withstand day-to-day use at family mealtimes will need a more practical design than the more stylish dining-room chairs used only on highdays and holidays.

It does not trouble us if wooden furniture for the garden is allowed to mellow and take on a rough, weathered patina, but we treat an antique mahogany dining chair with tender loving care, polishing it reverently and making sure it receives no damage.

Different rooms and living spaces will, naturally, have varying styles of seating. Individual items are far more likely to make an impact – and be chosen for that purpose – in areas where they can be surrounded by considerable space. For example, an intricately carved old church pew or a tall, elegant wing armchair, whose upholstered sections are each covered in different fabrics, could be viewed as a decorative object when placed individually, and would provide a strong focal point for an interior. Their comfort appeal would be secondary to their looks.

Specific items will undoubtedly influence the addition of others. Selection should, though, be based on what you like and feel good about rather than on trying to 'match' a set of furniture. In areas such as living rooms, where several items of seating often mingle together, overall cohesion is important, although individual items may clash dramatically. This is where balance is essential.

The uses of fabric

Fabric can be used to link or group seating elements together with covers, throws or cushions. By choosing one colour, such as oatmeal, and covering all seating in that colour, whether upholstered armchairs, sofas or dining-chair seats, an interior is created that is instantly calming and uncluttered. However, it would be dramatically livened up if other coloured fabrics or other surfaces – wood, metal, leather, or glass, for example – were allowed in. A riot of different patterns on printed or woven fabrics can coexist provided that there is a strong colour link running through them and given that there are also areas of calm, such as plain walls and floors, to anchor them.

In addition, fabric appeals to our tactile sense, creating a feeling of warmth and comfort. More than any other material, it completely transforms a surface. By introducing a cushion on a painted wooden

◄ *A large kilim anchors the seating area in this wonderfully lively and colourful room. The sofa, upholstered in a plain cream fabric, offsets the riot of colour going on around it. The alcove, with a built-in covered seat, provides a place to escape, while multicoloured cushions occupy every available surface.*

▲ *Furniture has been carefully placed to fill out – but not clutter – this area of a large converted warehouse. The day-bed, sited in the middle of the room rather than predictably hugging a wall, affords dual seating. The position of the lamp next to the sofa and of the large floor rug by the day-bed anchors the furniture.*

window seat or a chunky wool throw over the back of a plain sofa, you can change the style and character of seating surfaces – and the room – with relative ease.

Designing your seating

How seating is arranged in a room or living space is pivotal to the success of the room, from both practical and style viewpoints. In small or awkward spaces such as those under stairs, housing a free-standing piece of seating furniture would be difficult, but a built-in wooden box structure covered with loose cushions would make good use of this kind of space, transforming it into a wonderful 'cubbyhole' seating area for quiet reading. Give the box seat a lid and, of course, you have storage space too!

Long, narrow living rooms need careful planning, with groups of items strategically placed so that the entire room can be used, especially if different activities have to take place in the same space. If the entire living space is one room – whether in a vast warehouse or a more modest abode – an element of flexibility is important. Mix smaller items such as stools and side chairs with larger, more imposing pieces. Combine period-inspired furniture with a modern piece or a simple item found in a junk shop. Don't be intimidated at the thought of larger items, such as sofas or benches, being positioned in the middle of the floor. Set chairs at interesting diagonals to 'break up' space. And if the key to your space is a good desk, a chair and a computer, then put them centre stage!

Basic cushions

Cushions can be roughly divided into two types: those that fit a given space and those that lead a more nomadic existence – the ubiquitous scatter cushion. The former category, usually 'box' cushions, are made to a specific size, dictated by the space between the arms and back of a sofa or chair, or the dimensions of a flat wooden bench top or window seat. The latter group can be of all shapes and sizes and their domain is infinitely varied. These padded, plumped discs and squares of piped, fringed and braided colour can sometimes, surprisingly, be the single element that gives balance and focus to a room or piece of furniture. The eye darts about in a room, settling on pattern, texture and colour, so a small cushion or pile of cushions can attract and become a link between otherwise unrelated items.

Mixing different surfaces, materials and textiles in one space is exciting. For example, adding a pair of square cushions in a fake leopard skin against a cool backdrop of neutral off-white and beige linen inspires a flight of fantasy that could make bringing ornate gilt and black lacquer furniture into the room acceptable, whereas before it might otherwise have been rejected. Against the same backdrop, imagine a pile of cushions made of rich tapestries, old tangled fringes and near-faded silks in a warm mix of red, ochre and terracotta, and you have a completely different atmosphere.

Cushion styles

Basic square, rectangular or round cushion covers have two sides of fabric, stitched together. The opening for the cushion pad can be fastened by simple slip stitches or by way of a zip, buttons or ties (see pages 304–305, 310–313). The two sides need not be of the same fabric – each side could be a combination of fabrics joined before the cushion cover is constructed. Piping or decorative cord can add definition, while braids, fringes and buttons lend texture. Cushion covers can be made so that the stitching line hugs the edge of the pad and is surrounded by a border (like an Oxford pillow case). The border, usually about 5cm (2in) wide, might be in the same fabric as the cushion, or in a contrast.

For a smart tailored look, combine crisp white linen for the main part of the cushion with a fine cotton shirting in a white and coloured stripe for a piping detail, and for the surrounding border use a check of hound's- or dog's-tooth. Use the same three fabrics on other cushions in the same group but switch the focus. Borders can be extended, and for a rectangular cushion, like a bed pillow, a large border at the open end secured by buttons is particularly smart.

For a totally different style, take as your inspiration the rich contrast between a wool blanket and the silky band that borders it

▶ This beautiful wooden bench needs only the simplest of decoration. A box cushion covering the upholstered base offers softer seating, and a row of substantial square cushions in cool, creamy white fabric makes a simple, uncluttered and stylish addition to the piece as well as providing further comfort.

and make a cover that combines smart wool suiting with a surround of brightly coloured silk. Alternatively, mix a multitude of stripes or checks or even different scale floral patterns – printed or woven – but bear in mind that a colour link should bind them. One of the attractive aspects of making cushion covers is that they take only a small amount of fabric and are therefore relatively inexpensive decorative touches.

Making a square cushion cover

To make a plain, square cushion cover without piping, first decide on the finished cushion size. Cut two squares of fabric to the size of the cushion plus a 1.5cm (⅝in) seam allowance all around. With right sides facing and raw edges aligned, pin and tack the two pieces together, then remove the pins. Working a few reverse stitches at each end of the seam, machine stitch around the edge, leaving an opening along one side for turning

---

Making a square cushion

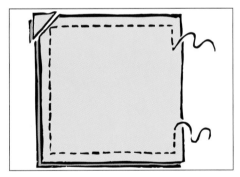

1 With right sides facing, stitch the back and front together, leaving an opening. Trim corners diagonally.

2 Press the seams open. Turn the cover right side out, insert the cushion and slip stitch the opening closed.

and inserting the cushion. Remove the tacking, trim the seam allowances and clip the corners to reduce bulk, leaving a gap of approximately 6mm (¼in) to avoid fraying. Press the seams.

Turn the cover right side out through the opening and push out the corners so that they are sharp. Press the cover and then insert the cushion. Finally, turn under the seam allowances along the opening, pin and slip stitch closed.

Making a round cushion cover

If made without a band between the top and bottom of the cushion, round cushions are just two circular fabric pieces sewn together with or without a line of piping between the two. Cord or a small shallow fringe can be hand sewn around the finished cushion. For variety, cut two halves of different, contrasting fabrics for each side. Join them together and then proceed as if for one piece. ▷

▲ *Layer upon layer of simple cushions provide a comfortable back for the day-bed. A pile of the same cushions, secured with tied tabs around an inner cover concealing the pad, are strategically positioned to form the arms. A mixture of warm terracotta, charcoal and ochre, offset by the occasional black and white stripe, make a bold combination.*

To make a paper pattern for the cushion cover, draw around a suitably sized object such as a large plate, then add a 1.5cm (⅝in) seam allowance all around. Alternatively, cut a paper square with dimensions matching the diameter of the required finished circle plus extra for seam allowances. Fold the square into quarters and lay it on a flat surface. Tie a pencil onto the end of a length of string, then pin the other end of the string to the centre of the folded square so that the string between the pencil and the pin measures the radius of the required circle, plus a 1.5cm (⅝in) seam allowance. Draw a quarter-circle arc on the paper and cut out.

Open out the paper circle and, using this as your pattern, cut out one fabric piece for the front of the cover and one for the back. Pin and tack the two pieces together, with right sides facing and raw edges aligned. Remove the pins. Working a few reverse stitches at each end of the seam, machine stitch around the cover, leaving an opening for turning and for inserting the cushion. Remove the tacking, then trim and notch the seam allowance to reduce bulk. Press the seam open. Turn the cover right side out and press again, turning the seam allowances to the wrong side along the opening. Insert the cushion. Pin and stitch the opening closed.

Tie-on cushions

Square or round cushions that are to be used as seat pads sometimes need anchoring to a wooden or wicker chair or bench so that they don't slip off. Ties looped around the back of the frame are the answer.

Simple covers for seat pads can be made in the same way as a basic cushion cover but with a pair of ties stitched into the back edge of the cushion between the two pieces of fabric. Tie-on cushions may be made square or round, and with or without piping. Alternatively, they can be made as flattish box cushions where the welt or gusset would only be 5cm (2in) or less (see pages 306–307).

The ties can serve a decorative as well as a functional purpose. For example, unyielding wooden chairs, such as old school desk chairs, benefit by tying a cushion onto the seat to add comfort and colour.

▲ *Made to fit the seats of these metal-framed chairs, these round cushions add style as well as comfort. The two on the chair in the foreground both have depth given to them by means of a band or gusset, but the one leaning against the back of the other chair has been made with just two circles of fabric joined together with piping.*

Making a round cushion

1 To make a paper pattern, fold a square of paper into quarters, draw a quarter-circle and cut out.

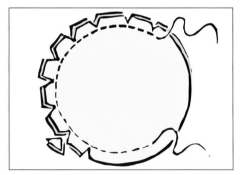

2 Cut two fabric circles. Stitch as for the square cushion (see pages 302–303), but notch the seam allowance.

Making a tie-on cushion cover

To make the ties, cut strips of fabric in either the same or a contrasting fabric (the two fabrics should be the same composition and weight) to a length that will allow for a reasonable knot or bow around the back of the chair frame. The width of the finished tie should be no more than about 3cm (1¼in). Cut the fabric to twice the width of the finished tie, plus a hem allowance of 12mm (½in) on each side and at each short end.

Fold the fabric strip in half lengthways, right sides together, and press. Machine stitch, 12mm (½in) from the raw edge, across one short end and all along the length of the strip. Turn the tube right side out with the aid of a knitting needle or narrow ruler, pushing through from the stitched short end. Alternatively, the tie can be made by top stitching the edges together. To do this, first press the 12mm (½in) seam allowances to the wrong side along both long edges and one short end. Then fold the strip in half lengthways with the wrong sides together, and machine stitch close to the aligned folded edges. Set the finished ties aside.

Next, make a paper pattern to the required finished size and shape of the cushion cover, plus a 1.5cm (⅝in) seam allowance all around. Using this pattern, cut out the top and bottom of the cushion cover. Mark the chair leg (or chair back) positions on the bottom section of the cover, and pin two finished ties to each of the marked positions, with the short raw edges aligned with the raw edges of the cover piece and the ties lying on the centre of the piece. Pin the top of the cushion to the bottom, with right sides together and raw edges aligned. Tack, catching in the ends of the ties in the seam. Remove the pins. Machine stitch around the edge, leaving an opening for turning and for inserting the cushion. Remove the tacking, trim, clip and notch the seam allowance to avoid bulk. Press the seam open. Turn the cover right side out and press. Insert the cushion. Pin and slip stitch the opening closed, as for the square cushion.

Alternative cushion ideas

Cushion covers can be interchanged to suit the mood of the interior. One cover inside another, with the outer one with contrasting ties, is a less formal, more fun approach and great for children's rooms. Big square cushions look good with button fastenings. Choose plain, unfussy buttons for matt fabrics such as cotton tickings, linens or ginghams, delicate little mother-of-pearl buttons for finer fabrics and big, bold, brassy ones for heavy brocades, silks or damasks.

Stitching applied to the surface of plain fabrics lends texture and pattern. Embroidery stitches can be used to great effect. Create spidery latticework, a riot of multicoloured dots or crosses or copy formal motifs. Appliqué stars or other shapes using a bold blanket stitch. Cut out images from printed fabrics, such as farm animals, in bold silhouettes for children's rooms, and stitch them onto plain fabrics.

Try constructing a cushion cover from a knitted square. Use creamy, soft string – the kind you find in a kitchen drawer or that ties parcels. Combine with chunky cotton cord in place of piping and hand sew the opening or use buttons. In bathrooms, or for outside in the summer when all you want is to relax with a pillow beneath your head, use waterproof canvas, and foam instead of feathers, for easy cleaning.

Making a tie-on cushion

1 Make up as for the square cushion (see pages 302–303) but stitch the ties into the seam allowance.

◄ Heavy, comfortable seat cushions on this intriguingly designed sofa and chairs are covered with bright citrus fabrics. Each cover has a row of fabric tabs attached to the cover opening which are tied together, with the knots adding a decorative finish to the back of the cushions.

Box cushions

When a cushion is really a seat and is required to take on a more practical and, consequently, sturdier role, its shape is more like a box than a flat pad. The cover for it, which has a gusset or welt between the upper and lower sections, has six sides, like a box. A box cushion should be fairly solid so that the required shape is kept. It can be filled with feather and down or, for a firmer base, it can be cut from foam with a layer of wadding around it.

Box cushions are most usually seen on the seat of an upholstered armchair, or two or three may be used snugly side by side on the base of a sofa.

An essential part of a Bergère chair, which does not have other upholstered sections, is the box cushion which sits on the flat base. Wooden chairs, where a loose seat pad of some kind is required for comfort, also rely on a sturdy box cushion.

Depending on the design of the chair or sofa, there may also be a box cushion to lean against, made in the same way but positioned roughly at right angles to the base cushion.

Making a box cushion cover

To make your box cushion cover, begin by cutting two pieces of material the same size as the top and bottom of the pad, adding 1.5cm (⅝in) all around for a seam allowance.

The welt is made up of five pieces. Cut one piece to fit the front of the welt, allowing for a seam allowance all around. Then cut two pieces long enough to fit across the back of the welt, plus 5cm (2in) extra at each end so that the back welt will extend around the two back corners, again adding a seam allowance all around each piece. Lastly, cut one welt piece for each side of the cushion to fit between the front and back welts.

Insert the zip between the two back welt pieces (see pages 312–313). With right sides facing, now pin and stitch the gusset pieces together, leaving 1.5cm (⅝in) open at each end of the two front seams. Press the seams open. If you are using piping, stitch it to the top and bottom pieces (see pages 314–315). Next, pin and tack the welt to the bottom piece, with right sides together and front corners matching. Clip the seam allowance

▲ *A simple wooden structure creates a clever seating area and transforms an otherwise featureless window space. Thick, heavy cushions, with their edges rolled rather than piped, align to form a padded, bench-like seat against the three walls. Rather like mattresses, the cushions are buttoned to prevent the covers moving.*

▶ *Piped edgings provide shape and definition to soft furnishings, and here they are used to great effect in highlighting the deliberately overstuffed box cushion seat of this ample Victorian wing chair. Using the same russet and gold damask for the piping as the cover adds a simple touch of refinement.*

Making a box cushion cover

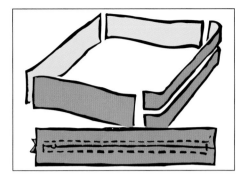

on the welt at each of the two back corners. Remove the pins and stitch into place. Open the zip and attach the welt to the top piece in the same way. Trim the seam allowances and corners and press. Turn right side out through the zip and press.

1 Cut out the top and bottom cover pieces and the five welt pieces. Insert the zip between the back welt pieces.

Decorative effects for box cushions

This type of cushion looks best with piping or cord added along the seams between the top, the base sections and the welt. This emphasizes the distinctive box shape of the cushion, but it can also be a decorative feature, particularly if it is made in a fabric contrasting with the main fabric.

The art of buttoning, although best left to the professional upholsterer, can give the surface of the cushion both texture and a rich, almost quilted look. Secured on either side of the cushion with a linking cord or strong thread pulled right through the cushion, pad and all, buttons or pompoms will cause the top of the cushion to undulate, like a bed mattress. Use fabric-covered buttons or, for a real sense of luxury, small pompons (little tufts of cotton, wool or silk) or small circles or squares of fabric.

To brighten up a rather plain club armchair, choose four different coloured fabrics from the same family: for example, a striped velvet in a peacock blue, a plain dark navy velvet, a deep scarlet and one in tangerine. With the main part of the chair upholstered in a combination of the different fabrics – you might have the tangerine on one arm and the red on the other with the navy blue between – make up the box cushion with each visible facet in a different colour.

2 Stitch the welt strips together, leaving 1.5cm (⅝in) open at each end of the front seams. Check the fit.

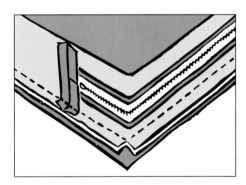

3 Stitch the welt to the bottom of the cover, clipping the welt seam allowance at the two back corners.

Other ideas for box cushions

Long, thin box cushions, essentially with a narrow welt, make the top of a wooden box or bench a comfortable seat. Simply constructed wooden boxes with lids make excellent storage spaces and can double up as seats around an informal kitchen table. Box cushions can also be shaped to fit a window seat. Measure carefully and cut a template from newspaper to ensure that the cushion fits neatly, as sometimes, especially in old houses, the shape may not be symmetrical.

4 Open the zip. Stitch the welt to the top of the cover. Trim the corners diagonally and turn right side out.

Bolster cushions

As their name suggests, bolster cushions offer a means of support for other cushions or pillows. Stuffed with feathers or other fillings, they are long or short rolls that lie along the end or sides of a day-bed or on certain types of sofa. On bench sofas, with one long mattress-type seat cushion, it would not be unusual to see a short bolster at each end.

Open-ended bolster covers

In a room that requires the bed to double up as a sofa by day, an open-ended bolster cover can store rolled bedding quite neatly. A quick knot in the fabric at each end of the cover keeps everything in place. Alternatively, a length of tied cord or a specially made band with a button and buttonhole would do just as well to close the cover, and would add a note of sophistication.

For this type of versatile cover, a long cylinder of fabric is all that is needed. It should be longer than the rolled duvet that will be inside it. The surplus fabric at each end, once tied or secured, can fall attractively over the edges of the bed. The width of the cover should be the same as the circumference of the rolled stuffing. Long fabric ties, sewn to the ends of the cover, secure them.

Closed-end bolster covers

The simplest way to make a bolster cover with closed ends is to sew a tube of fabric and gather each end neatly together so that it meets in the centre of the end like a drawstring bag. On this type of cover, the shape

▲ *Two bolsters lined up across the back of this sofa bring a touch of formality, as does the use of the same fabric for all its elements. However, the use of loose tailored covers and the different finishes made to each end of the bolsters – flat against the inside arms but bunched and tied at the other – create a pleasingly relaxed contrast.*

Making a basic bolster cover

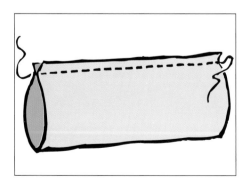

1 Cut the bolster cover piece long enough to exceed the ends and stitch the two long sides together to form a tube.

2 Turn right side out, then turn in the seam allowances at each end. Make a row of gathering stitches along the fold.

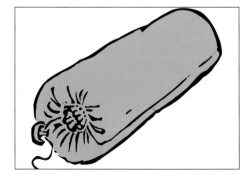

3 Gather the ends of the cover. Stitch a large button or a pompon over each gathered centre.

of the bolster can be defined by adding strips of contrasting fabric to the main fabric at each end which, when the ends of the cover are drawn together, appear as attractive concentric circles. Ribbons can create a similar effect but need to be applied to the fabric – that is, sewn onto the surface like appliqué.

Making a basic bolster cover

To determine the length of the cover piece, add the length of the bolster to the diameter of the end, plus a 2cm (¾in) seam allowance at each end. For the width, add 3cm (1¼in) for the two seam allowances to the circumference of the bolster. Cut a piece of fabric to this size. Fold it in half lengthways, with right sides together and raw edges aligned, and pin. Machine stitch 1.5cm (⅝in) from the raw edge. (If a zip is required, leave a gap in this seam and insert the zip at this stage.) Press the seam open. Turn the cover right side out. Turn 2cm (¾in) to the wrong side at each end and press. Using a strong thread doubled, hand stitch a line of running stitches close to the folded edge at each end. Then insert the bolster into the centre of the fabric tube. Gather the ends of the cover, tying the thread ends together and securing them inside the centre of the gathers.

▲ *Some clever examples of the ways in which bolster covers can be finished off. While a simple, flat end is very functional, a random gathering of surplus fabric at each end of a rolled-up cylinder can be tied into bunches with a band of ribbon. This is one of the simplest and most effective of finishing techniques, requiring no sewing.*

Making a fitted bolster cover

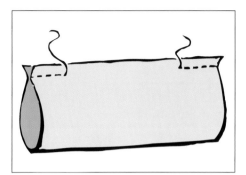

1 Cut the main cover piece and stitch together to form a tube, leaving a gap for the zip. Press the seam open.

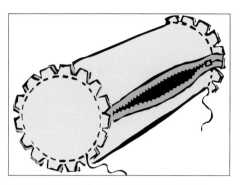

2 Insert the zip. Stitch on the circular ends. Notch the seam allowances and press. Turn right side out.

Adding piping to a bolster cover

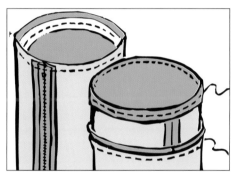

1 Make the main cover piece as for the fitted cover. Stitch the piping to the ends, then add an extra strip of fabric.

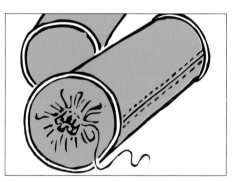

2 Turn right side out and gather the ends. For a fitted cover, simply attach the piping before the circular end.

Fitted bolster covers

For a more tailored look, the bolster end can be a separately inserted circular piece of fabric. The centre of the circle can be further embellished with a whirl of cord, a dangling key tassel, a brass or chrome ring or a button.

Making a fitted bolster cover

Cut the main cover piece as long as the bolster and as wide as the circumference of the bolster plus a 1.5cm (⅝in) seam allowance all around. Fold in half lengthways, with right sides together and raw edges aligned, and pin. Tack and then machine stitch, leaving a gap for the zip. Press the seam open. Turn the cover right side out and insert the zip (see pages 312–313). Open the zip and turn the tube wrong side out. Pin, tack and stitch the circular ends to the tube. Trim and notch the seam allowances. Press the seams open and then turn the cover right side out.

Adding piping to the ends

To attach piping around the circular ends of the bolster, cut and stitch the main cover piece as for a fitted bolster cover. Stitch the piping to the right side of the ends. On a basic bolster cover, add an extra tube of fabric at each end that is long enough to cover the end and turn the cover right side out. Gather the ends as for the basic cover. On a fitted cover, stitch on the circular ends after attaching the piping to the main piece.

Decorative effects for the bolsters

For a more sophisticated bolster, combine fabrics and cord in one cover. For a touch of flamboyance, mix fake leopard skin, dramatic ink-blue silk and a shiny gold cord and key tassel. Hand-stitched braid or other passementerie teams well with all kinds of fabric: a rough hessian looks surprisingly good with an elegantly woven trim, for example.

Directory of fastenings and trimmings

There is a wide range of decorative trimmings available for use on cushion covers, tablecloths, place mats and bed-linen. They can be chosen in a contrasting colour, pattern or texture to add a bold foil to soft furnishings or can be in a plain, matching colour to create a subtle but striking detail.

Fastenings on your cushion covers, loose covers or pillow cases serve a practical purpose but can also be a design focus, as becomes obvious with the use of ties or bold buttons.

Edgings

Bias binding
Bias binding is a strip of fabric, cut on the bias (diagonally across the grain) and used for enclosing piping cord or for covering raw edges – for example, around the edges of place mats.

Bias binding can be handmade from any lightweight fabric, patterned, plain or striped. It can also be bought ready-made in various widths and in a range of solid colours.

Braid
Decorative braid is a narrow, woven strip, often hand-worked, with a raised texture and fancy patterning. It can be applied to fabric to edge cushions, or sewn onto loose or fitted covers to emphasize colour or shape. Often it is used to decorate lampshades.

Two especially effective types of braid are gimp, which is a braided woven trim shaped like a close, continuous 'S', and picot braid, which is a ribbed trimming.

Cords and piping
Cords and piping are used to edge cushions, covers and upholstery and are often positioned to hide seams.

Ready-made decorative cords are usually made from twisted strands of silk, cotton, jute, wool, etc. Cord comes in varying thicknesses and can be single or multicoloured. Some cord comes with a flange for inserting between the fabric layers.

Piping is a fabric-covered cord. It can be bought ready-made or can be handmade by covering a filler cord with a narrow strip of fabric (see pages 314–315). Double-piping is a double row of covered cord (or piping) also used to edge upholstery. **3**

Fringes
Fringe is a loose-hanging trim usually made from wool, silk or cotton. It can be fine or thick, and is often encrusted with knots or beads for added decoration. Bullion fringing is a more elaborate, thick twisted fringe, often containing gold or metallic threads.

Other trims

Rosettes
These small, circular, woven decorations can be stitched to the surface of covers on the front arms of chairs or sofas. They imitate the shape of a rose and can often be quite ornate.

Studs
Metal or brass upholstery studs can be either flat or dome-headed and are nailed into the edges of upholstered chairs, footstools and sofas, particularly Chesterfield sofas, where they form an integral part of the style. They hold the fabric in place, act as a decorative trim or help to conceal raw edges. Some can be quite decorative, with the surfaces 'antiqued' or carved. **4**

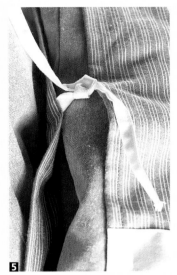

to either side of an opening and then clipped shut to close the opening. They can be used to secure cushions.

Tapestry strips

Firm, narrow woven bands, imitating hand-stitched tapestry, the strips are applied to the edges of covers or cushions or embellish chair and sofa seats. Designs are usually traditional and often echo architectural mouldings.

Tassels

These dangling decorative trims are made of bunched yarn or cord. They are either attached to rope (for example, for looping around sofa ends or holding back curtains) or are joined to small rosettes (key tassels) for attaching to keys on doors or drawers. **1**

Fastenings

Buttons

Available in any number of shapes and sizes and made from brass, glass, bone or mother-of-pearl, to name but a few materials. Buttons and buttonholes are used to fasten all kinds of edges on soft furnishings. Buttons (without buttonholes) can be used to make unusual decorative patterns. **2**

Eyelets

Metal eyelet kits come with a punch and dye to cut holes in fabric and then to secure a brass or chrome ring to hold together the raw edges of the hole. Eyelets are corded or roped together to join two edges of fabric.

Fabric ties and ribbons

Silk, cotton or synthetic ribbons and handmade fabric ties have many uses in furnishings. They can be tied in bows to hold two open edges together or can simply be tied or knotted to edges for decoration. **5**

Press studs

A useful fastening device, but one intended to be hidden, press studs are small metal fasteners that are stitched

Velcro fastening

Much disliked by traditionalists, Velcro (also known as 'touch-and-close' or 'hook and loop' fastening) is a quick and simple method of holding fabric in place. It consists of two pieces of nylon tape, one with a soft, furry, looped surface and the other with a rougher surface which is actually made up of rows of tiny hooks. When the two tapes are pressed together the hooks 'link' with the soft surface and a fairly strong bond results. The tapes are sewn to the edges of the fabric – for example, the underside of the open edges of a duvet cover. Velcro comes in a variety of widths and colours and can be sewn to fabric or stuck to a harder surface.

Zippers

The most practical of fastenings, a zip consists of two fabric tapes edged with metal teeth or a plastic coil. The teeth or coils interlock when the zip head is pulled between the two halves of the zip. Usually hidden from view behind the fabric, zips are inserted in cushion covers and loose covers so that they can be easily removed for cleaning.

Simple fastenings and zips

▲ *Cushions are marvellous furnishing tools – nothing can more easily transform a space than a cushion. They can be made in all shapes and sizes and from various different fabrics. The cushions above are all of different shapes but are linked into a Chinese porcelain theme of blue and white to complement other objects in the room.*

Duvet covers, cushion covers and loose covers that require frequent washing will all require fastenings that are hard-wearing and practical. Velcro, press studs and zips meet these requirements and are the most frequently used fastenings. They are easy to conceal so that they do not detract from the main effect of the furnishing.

Velcro fastenings
Unlike other fastenings for fabrics Velcro fastenings can also be used to attach fabrics to a solid surface. For instance, they could be used to attach removable fabric panels to a room screen or to attach a valance to a wooden bed frame. In these instances and for openings that may be strained, such as duvet covers and box cushions, it is best to attach

strips of Velcro fastening. For smaller openings that do not need to be so hard-wearing, such as small scatter-cushion covers, Velcro spots are more suitable.

Press studs
Straightforward to attach, press studs work well along the inside edge of a cushion or duvet cover opening. They can be bought as single fastenings or already attached to a fabric strip. A strip of press studs is ideal for the opening of a cushion or duvet cover.

Attaching simple fastenings to a cushion cover
To make a cushion cover to be closed with Velcro spot fastenings or press studs, first cut two pieces of fabric as for a basic square

cushion (see pages 302–303), but allow for a hem allowance of 7.5cm (3in) along the opening edge of each piece.

Pin a double hem in place along the opening edge on each piece by turning 2.5cm (1in) to the wrong side twice. Slip stitch or machine stitch the hem and then press. With the right sides facing, machine stitch the two cushion pieces together along the other three sides. Then at each end of the opening edge, stitch 5cm (2in) close to the double hem to strengthen the sides.

Sew Velcro spots, single press studs or even a strip of press studs along each side of the opening on the double hem in corresponding positions. Trim the seam allowances of the cushion and clip the two outside corners diagonally to reduce the bulk.

Turn the cover right side out and press. Insert the cushion pad and fasten the Velcro, studs or strips together. When closed, the fastenings should not be visible.

Simple fastenings

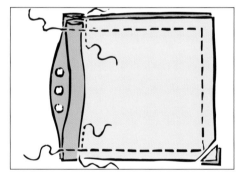

1 *Attach Velcro spots or press studs to the double hems along the opening edge of the cover.*

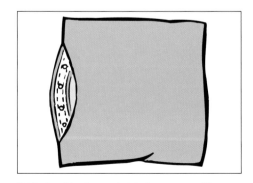

2 *Attach a strip of press studs in the same way. The fastenings will be invisible on the right side.*

Zips

Zips can be bought to an individual size or as one continuous strip of uncut teeth. The latter is used off the reel as required and individually bought zip heads are applied to it. Choose a zip colour that suits the item it is to be attached to.

Zips can be inserted and neatly concealed in the seam of a cushion cover or duvet cover. On a square scatter cushion the zip can either be inserted in the seam at the base of the cushion or in a centre seam on the cover back, as for a round cushion.

Inserting a zip in a cushion's side seam

Cut two pieces of fabric as for a basic square cushion cover (see pages 302–303). With right sides facing, stitch the two pieces together for 5cm (2in) at each end of the opening edge, leaving an opening for the zip. Tack the opening together along the seam line and press the seam open. Pin and tack the zip along the seam line, with the right side of the zip facing the wrong side of the seam. Stitch around the zip (using the zipper foot on the machine) from the right side close to the tacking. Remove the tacking.

Open the zip. Then, with right sides facing, pin, tack and stitch the remaining three sides together. Remove the tacking. Trim the seam allowances, clip the corners diagonally and press the seam open. Turn the cover right side out and press again.

Inserting a zip in a cushion's back

Cut out the front of the cover as for a basic square cushion cover (see pages 302–303). Cut another piece 3cm (1¼in) wider than the first (to allow extra for the zip seam), then cut it in half widthways.

With right sides facing, stitch the two back pieces together for 5cm (2in) at each end of the opening edge, leaving an opening for the zip. Tack the opening together along the seam line and press the seam open. Insert the zip as for the zip in a side seam.

Open the zip and, with right sides together, pin, tack and stitch the back of the cover to the front and complete as for the zip in a side seam.

Inserting a zip in a round cushion

Make a paper pattern as for a basic round cushion cover (see pages 302–305). Cut out the cover front using the pattern. Then cut straight across the paper pattern one third of the way from one edge. Using the two paper pieces, cut out the two pieces for the cover back, adding a seam allowance along each opening edge.

Stitch the two back pieces together as for the square cushion and insert the zip. Then join the back to the front with right sides together. Notch the seam allowance, turn right side out and press.

Cushion side seam

1 Stitch cover pieces together along one edge, leaving an opening for zip. Tack opening together and insert zip.

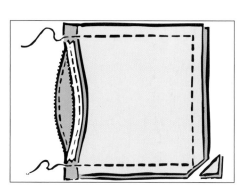

2 Remove tacking. Stitch the other three sides together. Trim and turn the cover right side out through the zip.

Cushion back

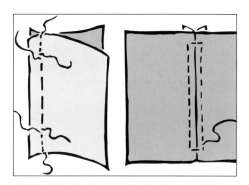

1 Stitch the back pieces together, leaving an opening. Tack opening together, press seam open and insert zip.

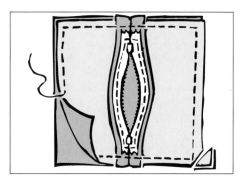

2 Remove tacking. With zip open, stitch the back to the front. Trim and turn the cover right side out.

Round cushion

1 Using a paper pattern, cut one piece for cover front. Cut two pieces for back and insert zip in back seam.

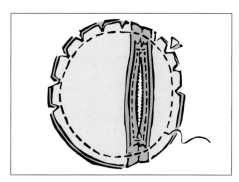

2 Stitch the back to the front and notch the seam allowance. Turn the cover right side out through the zip.

Piping and trims

▶ *Piping can add decoration and definition to a piece of furniture or a cushion. It also serves to strengthen the seams of structured items. Here, a probably unintentional contrast occurs between the formal primness of the cream-upholstered chair and the faded old-gold velvet cover. This contrast is emphasized by the piping.*

Nothing finishes off upholstery and soft furnishings better than edging. Using either piping, fringing, tassels or cord – available in a huge range of materials, colours and textures – creates a very professional touch and adds interest and style.

Piping

Piping is a means of adding decoration and definition to items such as a cushion, an upholstered chair or a duvet cover. It can be made in the same fabric as the main piece to which it is attached (called self-piping) or it can be made from a contrasting fabric to highlight shape or add texture.

Piping is made by enclosing a line of cord in a narrow strip of fabric. The covered cord is then inserted between two layers of fabric and stitched, leaving the piped strip visible along the seam on the right side. The piping filler cord itself is made of twisted strands of (usually) cotton, bleached or unbleached. It

Piping a cushion cover

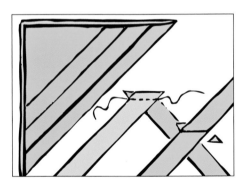

1 Cut the fabric strips to cover the piping on the bias. Join the strips end to end on the straight grain and trim.

2 Stitch the strip around the cord, using a zipper foot. Stitch the piping to the cover front, snipping the corners.

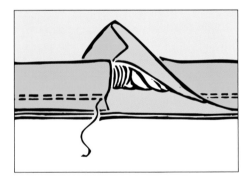

3 Trim the cord so that the ends butt together. Turn in one end of the fabric cover and lap it over the other end.

4 Stitch the cover together along one side, sandwiching the piping between the layers and leaving an opening.

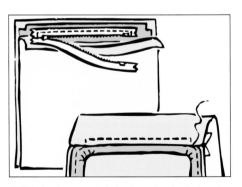

5 With the zip open, stitch the zip to the piped edge, then close it and stitch it from the front to the other edge.

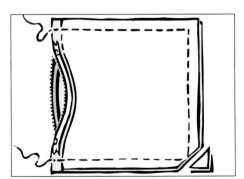

6 Open the zip and stitch the other three sides of the cover together. Trim and turn right side out.

comes in a variety of thicknesses, known by a number: 1, 2, etc. It is best to use pre-shrunk cord for anything that will later be laundered or dry-cleaned.

The strips of fabric used to cover the cord are generally cut on the bias (cross) of the fabric to give it more flexibility for easing around corners and curves. However, this is not essential. It may be that the pattern of the fabric is such that you want to cut across the width or length of the fabric.

Piping a cushion cover

For covering the piping filler cord, measure the amount of piping you think you will need and add about 10cm (4in) to allow for joins. The strips should be about 5cm (2in) wide so that when folded in half lengthways around the cord, the resulting fabric width is 2.5cm (1in).

Find the bias of the fabric by folding diagonally so that the selvedge is parallel with the adjacent edge. Mark strips of the required width parallel to the diagonal fold and cut out the strips. To make one long strip, pin the strips together, end to end with right sides facing, and stitch along the straight grain. Press seams open and trim the seam allowances flush with the strip edge.

Lay the cord along the centre on the wrong side of the strip, then fold the fabric around it so that the raw edges are brought together. Stitch by machine, close to the cord, using a special piping foot or a zipper foot. Trim the seam to 1.5cm (⅝in).

Cut out a front and a back cushion cover piece. Align the raw edges and pin and tack the piping to the right side of the cover front. Snip the piping seam allowance at the corners, leaving a 5cm (2in) overlap where the piping ends meet. Stitch around the cushion. To join the piping ends, pull back the fabric cover and trim both ends of piping filler cord so that they butt together. Trim the fabric so that one end turns under and overlaps the other to give a neat finished edge. Complete the stitching of the seam.

Leaving an opening for the zip and with right sides together, stitch the back of the cover to the front along the opening edge so that the piping is sandwiched between the layers. Press the seam open. Stitch the zip in place one side at a time. Complete the cover as for a cushion cover with a zip in the seam (see pages 312–313).

Cord

Ready-made decorative cords come in all kinds of thicknesses and colours and can be made from cotton, wool, silk or a mixture of fibres. Some cords have gold or other metallic thread running through them that adds sparkle and a touch of luxury. It is also possible to find wonderful antique cords.

Cords designed for inserting as piping come with a flange attached which is usually a piece of cotton webbing. These can be used exactly as you would a length of covered piping. Cords without flanges have to be hand sewn after the cushion cover is made.

Attaching cord to a cushion cover

Leave a small opening in the seam when making the cover. Hand sew the cord over the seam line around the edge of a finished cushion cover. Insert each end into the opening in the seam and secure in place. Alternatively, wrap each end of the cord tightly with a matching thread and butt the ends together neatly where they join. Cord can be looped to make a bow at each cushion corner and stitched into place by oversewing.

Tassels and fringes

Fringes make interesting finishes for cushion covers and these are hand sewn to the completed cushion cover as for cords. Some fringes also come with a flange webbing and can be inserted in a seam line like piping. Tassels add an ornate touch to cushions and bolsters. They are available in a wide range of shapes, sizes and colours, but can also be made by hand.

Attaching a flanged fringe to a cushion cover

Stitch the fringe to the right side of the front of the cover along the seam line, with the fringed edge pointing towards the centre of the cover. Make the cover as for a cover with piping, sandwiching the fringe between the two sides of the cover.

Cord and braid

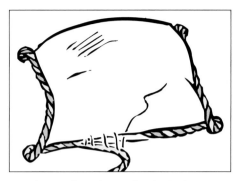

1 Hand sew cord over the seam line, forming loops at each corner if desired. Secure the ends inside the cover.

Fringes and tassels

1 As for a piped cover, stitch the fringe to the right side of the front before joining on the back of the cover.

▲ *The fluffy, colourful fringing perfectly complements the printed Manolo Blahnik shoe drawings on the cushions. Fringing such as that shown here has a flange and can be machine sewn between the two sides of fabric when the cushion is being assembled. Fringes can be specially dyed for particular projects.*

Borders

Both flat borders and ruffles add an extra touch of luxury to what would otherwise be an unexceptional cushion or pillow. They are worth taking extra trouble over, as they help enhance the pillow or cushion fabric.

Flat borders

Flat borders around cushions or pillow cases stand out like a flap. The cushion or pillow is encased within a stitched line and made accessible by a zipped or buttoned opening. A single border can be made either from the same fabric as the rest of the cover or in a contrasting fabric. A double border is essentially two single borders, the under border being slightly larger than the top border.

Making a single border cover

Make a cushion cover as for a cover with a zip across the back (see pages 312–313) but allowing extra fabric on all four sides for the border, as well as the usual seam allowance all around the edge. A standard border or flap is 5cm (2in) deep. Once all the edges of the cover are stitched together, trim the seam allowances and clip the corners diagonally. Press the seam open and turn right side out. Press flat, keeping the seams exactly on the edge and making the corners sharp.

On the back of the cover (zipped side), tack the front and back together along the border line and machine stitch. Alternatively, work satin stitch along the border line and then, if desired, work a second line of satin stitch outside the first. Remove the tacking.

To make a cover with a contrasting single border, cut the cushion cover pieces to the size of a cover without a border and insert the zip in the centre of the back piece (see pages 312–313). Then cut the borders. The size should be a length of fabric to the finished width of the border, plus two seam allowances, by the length of the side, plus two seam allowances. It is a good idea to cut more than you need so that the border strips can be trimmed down later.

Stitch, right sides together, the lengths of border to the cushion fabric, leaving the ends at each corner to trail. Join the border strips at the corner by mitring (see pages 340–341) or butt the ends together, stitching straight across the adjacent border (right sides together), trimming the surplus and pressing the seam flat. By abutting the borders you should finish up with two parallel borders the length of the finished cushion, with the other two set between them. Once the borders are joined to the front and back of the cushion, complete the cover as for a single border.

Single border

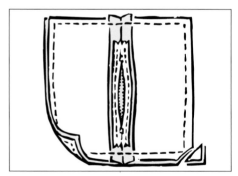

1 Make the cover with a zip across the back, adding extra all around for the border. Trim and press seam open.

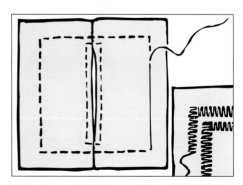

2 Turn the cover right side out and press flat. Stitch along the border line, using straight stitch or satin stitch.

▲ These simple linen cushions use the stripe in the fabric as a border which is set outside the edge of the cushion pad. The stripe is cut and sewn to each side of the central panel before the cushion cover is made up. Each corner is mitred, with the stripe carefully matched for a neat, geometric finish.

Double border

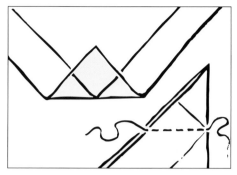

1 Double the depth of the required border all around. Press the border to the wrong side and mitre the corners.

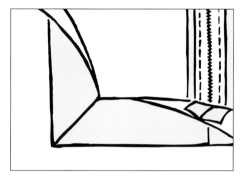

2 Trim the mitre seam allowances and press the seam open. Turn the corners right side out.

3 Determine the final depth of the border. Join the front of the cover to the back and stitch along the border lines.

Ruffles

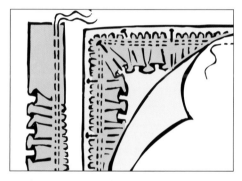

1 Make and gather the ruffle. Pin and tack it to the cushion cover front before stitching on the back.

◄ *Two contrasting finishing techniques combine to make a pleasing effect. The cord piping of the chair is very linear, enhanced still further by the use of striped fabric. Meanwhile, the floral-print cushion cover is finished off with a frivolous, deep-frilled edging.*

Making a double border cover

A cushion cover with a double border is made in the same way as a single border, but double the depth of the required finished border must be added on to the lengths, plus the seam allowances. Make up the back section as for a cover with a zip across the back (see pages 312–313). Fold the borders to the wrong side and press. With right sides together, mitre each corner (see pages 340–341). Trim the mitred corners, turn right side out and press. Lay the two sides together, wrong sides facing, and tack along the border line, catching the raw edge of the border inside the cover. Machine stitch closed.

Ruffles

Ruffles add a softening touch to cushions and other furnishings, and are generally made from light, filmy fabrics or country-cottage prints. But, with imagination and a bold choice of colour, ruffles need not be restricted to the boudoir; they can be used to make a strong impact anywhere.

Attaching a ruffle to a cover

Make a ruffle twice the circumference of the required finished cushion cover. The ruffle can either have a narrow hem or be doubled over so that the raw edges of both layers are aligned. Run a running stitch around the raw edges of the length of the ruffle. Pull the thread to gather the ruffle, then pin and tack it to the right side of the front piece of the cover, aligning the raw edges. Complete the cushion cover in the usual way, catching the ruffle seam allowance in between the front and back sections of the cover.

Covers for seating

The possibilities of covering furniture with fabric are as exciting as they are endless. Do you go for loosely draped, unstructured sheets of cloth that billow like dust covers over an old sofa? Or do you prefer smart, tailored little numbers with tucks and pleats and artfully placed buttons, which might disguise the awfulness of a battered dining chair?

The art of adding fabric to furniture opens up a wealth of decorative possibilities. Small seats can be tightly covered, whereas long, low benches look stunning when loosely dressed; deck-chair frames can be given a new lease of life covered in a different fabric, or natty little folding stools can be sharpened up with new, slung canvas.

Fine detailing adds sophistication to the disguise. Use eyelets, buttons, loops and ties, tassels and trims. Invent new ways of using old materials. However, don't lose sight of the practicalities and the function of the piece, even if your own ingenuity takes over.

Deck and director's chairs

Deck chairs are a simple combination of fabric and wood, a construction that folds neatly away. They have a timeless quality and a modest structure that have endured for many years. However, it is difficult to disassociate them from their exterior environments of beach, garden or on board a ship, although they can look wonderful in a large children's room or bathroom.

A director's chair has much the same feel as a deck chair, but because of its higher seat and more obvious 'chair-like' qualities, it is useful in informal settings in the home. For deck chairs, director's chairs and other folding chairs, the seat and back are made from pieces of fabric slung between two bars, and attaching it to the frame could not be simpler. The method for fitting new fabric depends on the design of the chair and whether the frame needs to be, or can be, taken apart. Where 'sleeves' of fabric can be made, these are ideal for sheathing the bars of the frame for seat and back, but where the design does not allow for this, fabric can be attached by stretching it around the bars on either side of the seat or back, and then stapling it to the outer edges with a heavy-duty staple gun. A

◀ *Traditional striped canvas can provide a whole new lease of life for ancient deck-chair frames. In this instance, mixing the colours of the canvases, which both have the same design, creates a sense of continuity, while also providing a pleasing contrast and more visual interest.*

▲ *While pastel cottons and delicate chintzes make attractive upholstery fabrics, they are difficult to keep clean and are vulnerable to wear and tear. A sensible choice for hard-working kitchen or dining-room chairs is the tough and durable finish shown here, achieved by tightly binding thin rope over a metal chair frame.*

sleeve comprises a loop of fabric, secured down the inner side of each frame bar with a line of machine stitching. If the chair design requires the sleeve to fit over a place where the frame is joined, holes can be punched in the fabric and large eyelet holes secured before reassembling. Choose strong fabrics that are not going to rot or tear. Try unusual material such as tapestry or wool tartan.

Folding stools

Small, low, X-frame stools, made from timber or metal, work well in interior settings. They make useful 'occasional' seating, doubling up as small tables for lightweight items such as books or newspapers. A few of them, dotted around a room filled with other styles of furniture, help to punctuate space. For a more minimalist interior, try a row of them using brightly coloured fabrics against a plain white wall, or mix different patterns on the same theme: for example, children's prints of animals or cowboys to make a perfect ensemble for a young child's bedroom.

The methods for attaching the fabric, whether a sleeve is made or the fabric is stapled, are the same as those for deck chairs.

Drop-in seats

► *These blue and white checked dining-room drop-in seats complement the nineteenth-century Swedish-style table and chairs. The seats provide bursts of colour to contrast against the many different wooden textures of this typically Scandinavian setting.*

The tricky art of fixed upholstery for sofas, chairs and day-beds is often best left to a professional, for when done properly it is worth the investment. However, to re-cover the upholstered seat of a drop-in dining chair is relatively straightforward.

A chair with a drop-in seat is usually a dining chair, and the seat lifts right out. It consists of a simple wooden frame covered in padding (horsehair and wadding) which rests on and is supported by strips of webbing pulled taut across the frame. A calico covering is stretched tightly over the padding and fixed to the underside of the frame by tacks. The top fabric is applied over the calico and fixed in the same way. The underside is finished off with a piece of hessian with its edges turned under for neatness. If the webbing is still good, and the padding is in reasonable condition – it may need some building up – you should not need to strip everything off.

Re-covering a drop-in seat

1 Bring the sides of the new calico to the underside of the frame. Secure with a tack at the centre of each side.

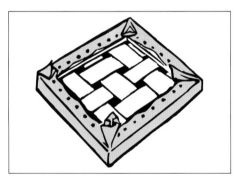

2 Smoothing the calico as you proceed, continue to add tacks along each side of the frame.

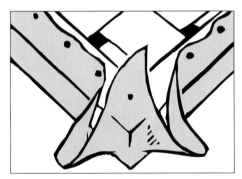

3 Pull the calico taut over the corners and tack. Fold a pleat to each side of the tack and secure.

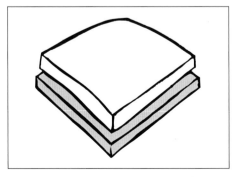

4 Turn the seat over. Lay in place a new piece of wadding the same size as the top of the seat.

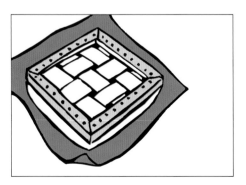

5 Keeping the wadding in place, lay the seat upside down on the new outer covering, centring it carefully.

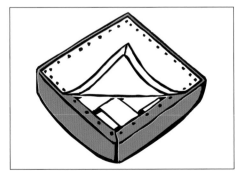

6 Cut out a fresh piece of hessian. Turn under the hem and tack the hessian to the underside of the frame.

For the fabric covering of a drop-in seat, customized fabric is always more challenging than simply using fabric as it comes. Two strongly contrasting colours could be stitched together and the joined fabric could be positioned over the seat so that the seam runs centrally across the chair – front to back or side to side. A pair of chairs with a weathered patina (see pages 280–281) would be a stunning focal point with covered seats in burgundy and indigo silk.

Re-covering a drop-in seat

The only tools you will need are a pair of scissors, a tape measure, a hammer, a mallet and a chisel. The materials needed to cover the padded seat are a sheet of wadding big enough to cover the top of the seat, a piece of calico to fit over the seat, a piece of upholstery fabric for the outer covering of the seat (big enough to go over the top of the seat and the underside of the frame), 1cm (⅜in) fine tacks and black upholstery linen or hessian for finishing the underside of the seat.

With the seat upside down and using the mallet and chisel, remove the tacks securing the old hessian. In the same way remove the tacks that hold the old outer fabric covering in place. Open out the hessian and the old fabric and use them to make paper patterns for the new pieces, making sure that the pattern allows for an extra 5cm (2in) all around for either turning under or stretching over the underside of the frame.

Remove the old top layer of wadding and discard. Beneath this should be a layer of calico, under which is the horsehair. If necessary, remove the old calico, but if it is sufficiently intact, keep it in place. Cut a new piece of calico using the paper pattern made from the old outer cover. Lay the seat upside down on the calico and bring the sides up and over the edge of the frame. Using the hammer, secure the calico with a tack at the centre of each side. Smoothing the calico as you go, add tacks along each side of the frame. Pull the calico taut over the corners and tack. Fold a pleat to each side of the tack and trim away the excess fabric. Turn the seat over. Cut a new piece of wadding to exactly the same size as the top of the seat. This is a

soft layer that prevents the spiky horsehair from coming through the fabric. Lay the wadding on top of the seat.

Using the paper pattern made from the old outer fabric, cut out a piece of fabric large enough to go over the seat to the underside of the frame. Lay the seat (with the wadding on top) upside down on the new outer covering. Tack the fabric to the frame.

Using the paper pattern made from the old hessian, cut out a fresh piece of hessian. Turn under the hem and fasten the hessian to the underside of the frame, tacking at 2.5cm (1in) intervals.

Woven webbing

For a natural, textured look try using upholsterer's webbing tape about 5cm (2in) wide, woven across the frame of a stool or perhaps on a simple dining chair where the seat has gone, leaving an empty frame. A very stylish effect can be achieved by this relatively simple method. You will need enough webbing to be divided equally into short strips that will be fixed side by side across the frame to

create the 'warp' and the same quantity to use as the 'weft', the layer that weaves in and out of the fixed layer. The length of each strip (warp or weft) will be the distance across the top of the frame from edge to edge, plus an amount that can wrap around to the underside of the frame for securing (with tacks or a staple gun) out of sight. If you want the fixing to be a feature, and therefore to be seen, you could use various types of upholsterer's decorative studs.

Cut and fasten the first layer of webbing, making sure each piece is pulled very taut before fixing. The seat will be bound to sag a little as body weight is put on it, so bear this in mind and perhaps allow some excess that can be unrolled for retightening. Weave the second layer of strips between the first, again fixing each end in the same way.

Webbing tape, commonly made of jute, can be dyed so that a colourful, contrasting chequerboard effect can be achieved with relative ease. Alternatively, it is possible to buy coloured webbing of the sort that edges carpets or rugs.

◀ *Webbing can make for an extremely comfortable chair. It is very versatile and can be easily replaced with a different coloured webbing to match any decor. Neutral webbing can be dyed in vibrant, colourful shades and two or more colours can be interwoven to achieve interesting designs.*

Loose covers

▶ *Like 1950s summer dresses out to tea, these linen chair covers in ice-cream colours look spruce and elegant. Against the bleached wood floor, their sharp colours stand out and are perfectly contrasted against the white tablecloth. A row of buttons is a witty addition. Here they are self-covered but they could be just as effective in white or coloured glass – or even brass.*

As their name implies, loose covers are not fixed to the furniture they cover. They might have ties or zips, or even button fastenings, but their essential character is removability. First, there is a practical element governing the choice of fabric for such a cover. Second, the fabric can be used to glorious decorative effect with stitching, folding, pleats, knots – or by simply throwing it over.

Designs for loose covers

The shape of the furniture dictates the look of the loose cover, whether it has a tailored look, where the cover starts to resemble formal upholstery, or a more casual, unstructured effect. The furniture is the mannequin, around which the fabric is pinned, tucked, pleated and stitched, and through experiment the cover will take shape.

Squarish arms on a sofa, for example, can be made more attractive by adding an unexpected kick pleat here and there, and by double pleating the fabric a really textured look can be achieved. Try using a contrasting fabric inside a pleat for further emphasis.

Detail is the all-important thing. Take a leaf from fashion *haute couture* and add exquisite touches that will transform a plain cover, such as punched eyelets along the base of a skirt, or rows of hand-sewn buttons in glorious glassy colours. Fringing and tassels add texture and give a more luxurious feel. To the front of a pleat add a tab of fabric or tape and a bright bold button to fasten. Along the base attach a band of petersham ribbon to a plain fabric for definition and added colour, or hand stitch in thick tapestry wool bold criss-crosses or dots. A row of small pearly buttons down the back of a white linen cover – quite a tailored affair over an upright dining chair – would look very impressive.

Most loose covers have a skirt of some sort which runs around the base and is a separately made piece that extends to the floor. Use double, overlapping layers in the same cloth or one that has a distinctly different texture. Fold wide box pleats around the front edge of a long sofa, and for the two shorter sides, run tiny little pleats or use two-coloured fabrics for a striped effect.

The beauty of making loose, as opposed to fixed, covers is that it allows you to play around with the shape a little more. Take the skirt from the seat height or make a pleat in

Making a loose cover for a dining chair

1 Pin the two back pieces of fabric together wrong side out. Remove from the chair, tack and stitch.

2 Cut out the valance piece and a piece the same size for the lining. Stitch together with right sides facing.

3 Turn the valance right side out and pin it to the chair seat piece with right sides facing. Stitch.

the centre at the back. By taking this idea further you can disguise the shape of a sofa or chair quite considerably.

Making a loose cover for a chair

Measure the front of the chair back from the top of the chair to the seat and then across the width of the back, allowing for the thickness of the frame. Cut out a piece of fabric to these dimensions, plus a 5cm (2in) seam allowance all around. Measure the back of the chair from the top to the floor, then measure the back of the chair across the widest part (usually at the base of the chair), again allowing for the thickness of the frame. Cut out a piece of fabric to these dimensions, plus a 3cm (1¼in) seam allowance.

With the wrong sides facing, pin these two fabric pieces together over the back of the chair, making sure that the cover will slip off easily and keeping the proposed seam lines symmetrical. Remove the cover, tack along the proposed seam line and remove the pins. With the cover still the wrong side out, try it on the chair again and adjust, if necessary, making sure that the tacking stops precisely at the level of the chair seat. Remove, and machine stitch. Trim the seam allowances. Set this piece aside.

Measure from the seat of the chair to the floor and then around the legs of the chair at the base, from one back leg around the front legs and the other back leg. Cut out a piece of fabric to these dimensions, allowing for a 7.5cm (3in) overlap at each side of

the back and adding a 1.5cm (⅝in) seam allowance all around. Cut a lining piece exactly the same size from the same fabric. With right sides together and raw edges aligned, stitch these two pieces together, leaving the edge that will fit around the chair seat opening. Trim the seam allowances and then clip the two corners diagonally. Press the seam open. Turn right sides out and press flat with the seam aligned along the edge. Tack the raw edges together. Set this valance piece aside.

Cut a piece of fabric to fit the chair seat exactly, with a 1.5cm (⅝in) seam allowance all around. Lay this piece wrong side uppermost on the chair seat, then pin the valance to the chair seat with right sides together and raw edges aligned, leaving the extended bit at the back free. Take the pinned pieces off the chair, tack and remove the pins. Stitch and then slip the back section of the cover back onto the chair (still wrong side out). Pin it to the chair seat section where the two sections meet at the back of the seat. Remove, tack and stitch.

Trim the seam allowances around the chair seat. Then cut the two front corners of the chair seat section diagonally and notch the corresponding corners on the valance section. Press the seam open and then towards the centre of the seat.

Cut four lengths of ribbon or make four fabric ties (see pages 342–343). Then cut a piece of fabric to line the back valance drop, including a 1.5cm (⅝in) seam allowance all

around. Put the cover on the chair wrong side out and pin the lining to the back valance drop, with right sides together. Remove and then position the ties along the seam. Tack and stitch, catching the ends of the ties in the seam. Trim the seam allowances and corners and press the seam open.

Remove all the tacking. Turn the whole cover right side out and press. If desired, line the underside of the seat area to enclose the raw edges, slip stitching the lining in place.

Put the cover on the chair right side out. Hand sew ties to the front valance to correspond to the ties at the back.

Covering furniture with throws

Just throwing over a length of fabric and allowing it to fall naturally into folds or gathers is perhaps the simplest way of covering furniture. Blankets, shawls or quilts can be mixed against each other and displayed against a backdrop of bleached white cotton first draped over the furniture. Large pieces of cloth can be handkerchief-knotted on their corners or around the legs of a chair.

To make a very simple throw, sew together two pieces of fabric, as though you were making a cushion, add a layer of wadding or interlining between them and when turned right side out, secure the opening by hand. You will have a lightly padded square or rectangle. Stitch flat buttons or small loops of cord across the surface for decoration and hang the whole thing over the back or arm of a sofa or day-bed.

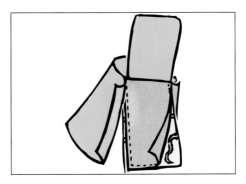

4 Pin the chair seat section to the back cover section along the back of the chair seat and stitch.

5 With the cover wrong side out on the chair, pin a lining to the back valance. Stitch, catching in the ties.

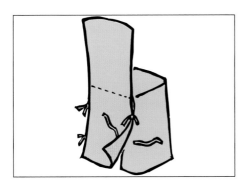

6 Turn right side out. Line the seat if desired. Then stitch ties to the front valance section to match the back ties.

Bedding

From theatrical fantasy to pared-down practicality,
the decoration and covering of your bed will undoubtedly
reflect your personal style. The bedroom is an
intimate environment, whether or not it is shared with
another person. For some, the bedroom is simply
a sleeping space, while for others it may also be an office –
where telephone and other communications to the
outside world must be on hand – or indeed a play area,
with shelving and boxes for toys and children's books.

As well as considering the needs of the bedroom, the requirements of the bed itself may be wildly different – having to double up as a sofa during the day, or perhaps exist as an area of private space as a 'room within a room', curtained and canopied.

Perhaps the most exciting challenge in decorating a bed is that it is three-dimensional. There are both horizontal and vertical planes to consider. This offers considerable scope for the imagination. Whether it is a simple divan, a painted metal bunk or ornately carved wooden four-poster, a bed provides surfaces and shapes to decorate, cover or completely conceal. The whole of the bed, and its immediate surroundings, can become an exciting mix of tactile materials, whether fabric, mosaic, paint or even paper.

Bed-linen

When considering the basic bed-linen, you might choose to look for old, good-quality linen sheets in specialist shops or markets, or decorate newer cotton sheets with a simple stitched motif or a row of buttons. Along the edges of plain sheets or duvet covers, the addition of a striped piping or a border of appliquéd shapes can transform and give character to a neutral surface. Imagine a row of coloured cut-out zoo animals or letters of the alphabet in line across the end of a child's duvet cover.

While basic sheeting may be unpatterned and – typically – white, covers, quilts or valances present a good opportunity to introduce colour and pattern. Imagine striped-cotton quilt covers over white cotton sheets, or linen in faded gentle colours mixed with antique patchwork quilts – or perhaps with a bold contemporary duvet design (provided a colour link is established).

Whether for a tiny baby's cradle or a massive *lit bateau*, warmth should be an immediate consideration. For cold nights, consider chunky warm blankets in bold checks, either as additional throws or in the place of quilts or duvets.

Bed valances – or wonderfully named 'dust ruffles' – can conceal unattractive bed bases or provide curtaining for under-the-

◀ Striped and checked fabrics have been mixed and matched in this bedroom, but limiting the colour scheme to blue and white means the look is crisp and clean rather than jumbled. By day the canopies strung across the beds provide extra shade from the incoming sunlight; by night they create a cosy, cocooning effect.

▲ On entering this bedroom, the eye is drawn to the unusual wrought-iron headboard. Its exaggerated Gothic styling, resembling ornamental railing, is made all the more striking by its juxtaposition with warm colours and soft, highly textured fabrics: the sunny yellow walls and cosy-looking bedspread with its vivid relief design of sunbursts.

bed storage. These are made to fit individual beds, usually with pleats at each corner, and could be made in the same fabric as the main bed cover or in a contrasting material. For added detail, include a border along the base of the skirt in a different fabric or braid. Alternatively, you could box pleat the whole skirt.

Decorating surroundings

As well as layering fabrics on the bed itself, a partial or complete framework of fabric 'walls' can be created over and around the bed from gathered or stretched material. A contemporary metal version of the ornate four-poster provides a structure from which to hang fabrics, simply tied or tabbed at the top. Lightweight muslin can fall airily to the floor; double-layered or heavier cloth can provide warmth and texture. Chunky metal eyelets, punched through the fabric, can be slotted onto a pole, while simple canopies can be supported by a bracket or short pole projecting from the wall above the bed.

Headboards provide support, and can also feature as key elements to cover and decorate. Here, a stamped metal headboard, for example, can provide a contrasting backdrop for pillows in, say, a crisp white and grey stripe. Hang quilted fabrics over a fixed head end; mix stripes and floral patterns, canvas and delicate embroidery, or richly textured tapestries and white piqué to create the style you want.

Pillow cases, valances and throws

The vast range of bedding and bed-linen now available makes the bed the key element in the bedroom's design. How the bed is 'dressed' makes the ultimate design statement.

Pillow cases

Bed pillows should be comfortable and not so numerous that you need to discard most of them in order to sleep! Rectangular or square, on their own or with a long bolster beneath, they are often the focus of the bed.

Their cases are essentially fabric bags like small duvet covers and their construction is much the same. At their most plain they are a top and a base stitched together with a pocket to keep the pillow held inside. They can also have a border all around as on an 'Oxford' pillow case.

Add a line of buttoning, embroidery, lace or a fabric border and a pillow case is instantly transformed. A blanket stitch along the open edge can be a simple detail. For a tailored look, use cases that have a flap around the edge, which can be made from the same fabric as the rest of the case or in a contrast. Layering plain on stripe on check, linking the colour, can be smart and can incorporate a combination of fabrics used elsewhere on other parts of the bed. For an instant monogram try hand stencilling bold letters or motifs, using a permanent dye. These are much cheaper than the embroidered ones that have now become collector's items, although these, if you can find them still in good condition, are very beautiful.

▲ *The key to bed-linen is to keep it simple – but that does not mean it always has to be white. Here, although white is the basic colour, the crisp blue and green ginghams dominate and there are similar colours in the bed cover to provide a harmonious link. The bedstead, with its simple curved iron frame, accentuates the cool, clean overall effect.*

Making a pillow case

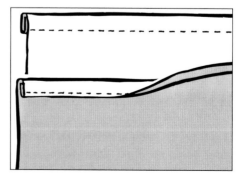

1 Cut out a single piece of fabric for the case and stitch a double hem along each short edge.

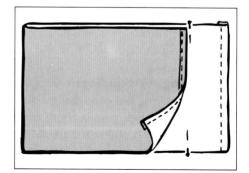

2 Fold the fabric so the right sides are together and the flap extends 15cm (6in) past the end. Pin into position.

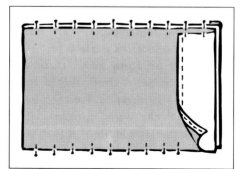

3 Turn the case over and fold the flap back so the folded edge aligns with the hemmed edge. Pin into position.

Old cottons and linens, once thoroughly washed, make beautiful pillow cases. Smart checks and stripes in cool colours can be added as borders, flaps or edgings.

Making a pillow case

Pillow cases should be made from cotton or poplin, or linen. For a pillow with a pocket to hold in the pillow, cut a single piece of fabric twice the length of the pillow plus a total of 20cm (8in) for the inside flap and for the double hem allowances, by the width of the pillow case, plus an extra 3cm (1¼in) for seam allowances.

Along each short side, turn under and stitch a 1cm double (½in) hem (see pages 340–341). Fold the fabric right sides together, the length of the pillow from one end, so that the flap extends 15cm (6in) past the doubled-over pillow case. Pin the raw edges together. Then turn the case over and fold the flap back on the case so that the folded edge aligns with the hemmed edge. Pin the raw edges of the flap to the other layers and tack. Remove the pins and machine stitch through all the layers 1.5cm (⅝in) from the edges. Pink the raw edges or zigzag stitch them and trim. Turn right side out. The flap will now be on the inside of the finished pillow case.

Bed valances (dust ruffles)

These bed dressings form a skirt between the base of the mattress and the floor. The skirt is typically attached to a flat piece of fabric

that sits between the mattress and the bed base. Because it is hidden, this can be made of inexpensive lining. The skirt, in a more interesting fabric, can be flat, with tailored kick pleats at each corner, or, as on beds with a fixed head and foot end, the corner pleats can be split to fall either side of the bed leg.

Box pleats, although taking a considerable amount of fabric – three times that for a flat skirt – are smart and straightforward and, using a contrasting fabric in the pleats, can give a striking effect. For a more sculptural finish, instead of pleats at the corners, simply join the fabric using punched eyelets and tied cord. For a softer effect, gather the skirt into rich folds of crumpled linen, muslin or shot taffeta silk. Whichever style you choose to make, careful measuring and estimating of the amount of fabric required are essential as a valance will not work if there is not enough material in it. As valances tend not be washed as often as covers and pillow cases, a more robust fabric can be used.

Throws

A throw suggests casualness and spontaneity. It is intended to go over all other bedding and provides an extra layer for additional warmth, perhaps used only occasionally and otherwise stored at the end of the bed. Throws can also be a useful device for concealing a mixture of bedding beneath and thus 'tidying' a bed that perhaps by day becomes a sofa.

Throws are generally made from a rectangle of fabric, cut large enough to cover the bed end to end and to fall to the floor on both sides. They are then hemmed and possibly lined as well. Throws can be used with valances, in which case the fabric is cut to fall only part of the way down each side of the bed in order to reveal the valance beneath. Throws may be plain or quilted, with additional borders or edgings that add colour or texture. As the throw is intended to be folded down once the bed is in use, a heavier fabric can be used.

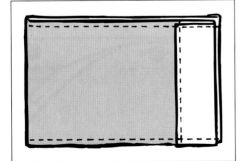

4 Tack and machine stitch through all the layers. Pink the raw edges or zigzag stitch them and turn right side out.

◀ *Cool blue and cream combine to be the dominant theme here. The wonderful midnight-blue backdrop behind the ice-cream swirls of the bed frame is picked up in the checks and stripes and* toile de Jouy *patterns of the various items of bed-linen. The top quilt is reversible, using the three different fabrics to great effect.*

Duvet covers

Making a simple duvet cover

▲ *This is an inspired use of an awkward space – the bed does not attempt to look small. Understated cream and white cotton bed-linen is combined with a minimal use of black and white traditional mattress ticking to create an elegant interior. Subtly stitched motifs criss-cross the duvet cover and a simple line of stitching runs around the edge of it.*

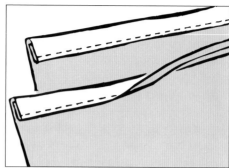

1 *Cut two pieces for the cover. Along the opening edge of each piece, stitch a 3cm (1¼in) double hem.*

2 *Stitch the two pieces together with wrong sides facing, leaving the hemmed edges open. Trim.*

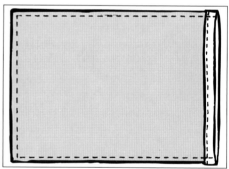

3 *Press the seam open, then turn the cover wrong side out and press flat. Stitch again and turn right side out.*

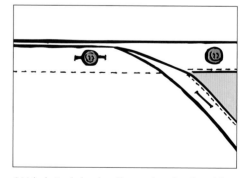

4 *Make buttonholes along the opening edge about 25cm (10in) apart and sew on the buttons to match.*

Duvets have largely replaced sheets and blankets, and their covers are easy both to use and to clean. Essentially two pieces of rectangular fabric joined on three sides, they are a bag for the duvet to fit inside. A large pocket can be made at the open end, to prevent the duvet from slipping out – just like the pocket on a traditional pillow case.

Alternatively, the duvet cover opening can be fastened with ties or buttons. Both these devices can be used to bring contrast and colour, such as checked red and white ties on a plain cover or bold tartan ribbons to fasten one in striped ticking. Buttons can be bold

and eye-catching, while the buttonholes can be made using brightly coloured thread. If you prefer to keep things simple, just use press studs or a zip fastening.

For a more subtle approach, add piping along the seam between the two layers of fabric. On a bed that is covered entirely in white, a piped line of blue and white gingham or multicoloured floral pattern adds just a hint of detail and colour, perhaps picking up another fabric in the room.

For children's bedding, a duvet cover with one fabric on the top and another beneath is fun and can transform a space simply by being reversed. Another way of adding interest is to mimic a patchwork quilt and use large squares to create a chequerboard pattern of two or three bold colours, or a combination of different sizes of stripes.

Cotton is really the only fabric to consider for duvet covers as it is easy to wash and is comfortable to touch. It should not be too heavy. For a double duvet cover, you may not be able to find wide enough fabric, so you will have to join pieces together before cutting out your first pieces to size. Always join with a full width of fabric in the centre, giving you two seam lines.

To make the joins more interesting, add a strip of fabric between the two pieces you are joining together on either side. Press seams towards the insets and then make up as described above.

Making a simple duvet cover

Cut two pieces of fabric, each a little longer than the duvet itself, plus a total of 10cm (4in) for hems and seam allowance, by the width of the duvet, plus 7.5cm (3in) for the seam allowances. Along the opening edge of each piece, machine stitch a double 3cm (1¼in) hem (see pages 340–341).

To join the two pieces together, first pin them together with wrong sides facing and raw edges aligned, leaving the hemmed edges open. Stitch 2cm (¾in) from the edge. Trim the seam allowances to 1.5cm (⅝in) and then clip off the two seam allowance corners diagonally. Press the seam open

and turn the cover wrong side out so that the right sides are together. Press the seam flat, aligning the seam line along the fold. Stitch 2cm (¾in) from the edge. Turn right side out and press.

Making the buttonholes on the cover

Mark the positions for the buttonholes along one edge of the opening about 25cm (10in) apart. Use a button to mark the length of the buttonholes, allowing for the button thickness. If you are making the buttonholes by machine, follow the instructions in your sewing machine manual.

If you are sewing the buttonholes by hand, use a pair of small scissors to cut the buttonhole. Start by oversewing the cut at one end several times. Buttonhole stitch down one side of the slit, oversew the other end, turn the fabric around and buttonhole stitch up the other side. Fasten the thread end into the end of the buttonhole on the wrong side. Sew on the buttons to correspond with the positions of the buttonholes.

Making tie fastenings for the cover

The simple duvet cover can be fastened with ties instead of buttonholes. Use lengths of ribbon with the raw edge slip stitched over, and secure them to each side of the duvet opening in pairs.

Alternatively, ties can be made from strips of fabric, either the same as the cover or in a contrasting pattern. Cut strips about 30cm (12in) long by 6cm (2½in) wide, fold over and press a 1cm (½in) hem on all sides. Fold the strips in half so that the long sides meet, wrong sides together. Top stitch all around and stitch in place as for ribbons.

Making the buttonholes

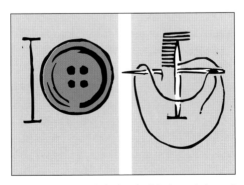

1 Use a button to mark the length of the buttonholes, and buttonhole stitch around the slit, oversewing at each end.

◀ *A blue and white checked gingham duvet cover and buttoned pillows lie comfortably crumpled against the white linen sheet on this simple bed. The interior is cool and understated, with neutral background colours that allow the bed covers to dominate. The gingham is echoed in the frame on the cupboard and helps to unite the theme.*

Bed hangings

▲ *An all-white decorative scheme is often the most striking. Here the choice of bed drapery was influenced by the distressed plaster walls and wooden shutters; the pillows and bedspread, with their unusual leaf-shaped edging, and the swathes of white fabric suspended from a half-corona would not look out of place in a medieval bedchamber.*

Extending the decoration of a bed up into its surrounding space, by hanging fabrics around it or over it, can transform a straightforward bed into something extra-ordinary and magical.

Imagine climbing into a sleeping bunk on a train and closing the curtains to create your own private space, or lying beneath tented canvas, peering out at the stars. These two effects can be easily re-created in your bedroom with a little forethought and planning.

Curtains can become walls, to surround a bed completely, either hung from a frame such as a traditional four-poster, or as a screen, between ceiling and floor. This is effective, for example, in a wide alcove, where a bed might be positioned sideways to the wall.

Fabric hangings to divide or create a space may either hang like curtains, whether from poles or from a support such as a timber canopy or 'pelmet', or be stretched like a screen between a support frame or fixed hooks.

Curtain-style bed hangings

When hung as curtains, if the heading is on show – usually where a tubular frame is fitted above a bed – simple headings such as eyelets, buttons, ties or tabs are most effective.

Tabs made from bands of fabric (see pages 342–343) loop around the pole support. Consider making these in a fabric that contrasts in colour or pattern with the curtains themselves.

For a dramatic effect, use alternate coloured bands of fabric, such as pink and orange velvet atop a teal-coloured velvet curtain. Add brass buttons to the tabs, and to hold the curtains open, heavy rope tie-bands, and you have a wonderfully rich and dramatic bed arrangement.

Eyelets punched through the top of the curtains also provide a stylish method of hanging fabric around a bed, hanging the fabric either on a pole or on hooks from a low ceiling.

The beauty of bed hangings is that they have an inside and an outside, making an ideal opportunity to use two layers of completely contrasting fabrics. Imagine a crisp white linen on the inside and a heavy brocade on the outside, or a wide striped cotton lining a *toile de Jouy*. Obviously, the fullness of the fabric would depend on the effect required, and the type of fabric you were using.

Swathes of gathered fabric can be hung from traditional wooden pelmets as part of a four-poster, half-tester or corona. Usually these headings, which are not really seen except from inside the bed, are gathered with tape, like curtain headings.

Screen-style bed hangings

A flatter, screen-like effect can be achieved by sewing a sleeve at the top and base of a piece of fabric – a strong canvas works well, for instance – and by stretching it between a tubular frame. A side and an end, with a bed positioned sideways on to the wall, create a simple enclosure for a child's bunk bed, for example. Sew pockets onto the side of the fabric that faces the bed, for pyjamas or teddy bears.

The premise of using stretched fabric can be further extended to make a complete pitched roof for a bed. Try using sewn sleeves to slot over three horizontal poles, two parallel either side of the bed, and one higher up, centred over the middle section of the bed.

A flap, hanging part way down each side, can cleverly mimic a tent. For added detail, shape the edges or hang small key tassels. Similarly, a pole hanging above and across each end of the bed can support a length of fabric which, at the head end, can fall behind the pillows, thus creating a backdrop.

If you also cut the fabric long at the foot end, and attach strips of fabric or ribbon to either side, it will allow the fabric to be rolled up and tied to the poles like a rolled-up tent flap.

▶ *This sleeping area, little more than an alcove, could have had a rather claustrophobic atmosphere. Instead, a suspended canopy draws the eye up and across the ceiling, exaggerating the tiny space. A candle sconce and painted wall design provide interesting Gothic detail.*

Screens

Free-standing screens were once the interior item no discerning household was without, mainly because they acted as excellent draught excluders, protecting seating areas from the vastness of the room beyond. They have been much neglected of late, which is difficult to understand as they can be very decorative and act as clever room dividers. They are, in essence, a transportable wall.

Usually made in three or more hinged sections, which allows them to stand freely, screens can be constructed using timber or metal frames covered with canvas or fabric.

Free-standing screens make useful window coverings where a more familiar curtain or blind is perhaps difficult to install. And, in a low-ceilinged room where floor-to-ceiling windows have been designed to frame a view

beyond and a permanent covering would be a hindrance, screens come into their own, folding away when not required. If a screen is to move from place to place make sure that it is not too heavy.

Decorating a screen

Each side of a screen is on show to different sections of a room, so they can be decorated to display a different design style. The frames are more than just supports and form an integral part of the overall design. Timber frames can be stained, painted or polished, shaped across the top like a wooden pelmet or straight. You could commission a wrought-iron frame with splendid curved legs to support the fabric screen off the floor, and with decorative flourishes atop the

uprights. Artist's canvas stretched over a simple wooden frame can be painted directly with abstract or figurative designs.

All kinds of fabric can be used when making a screen; it all depends what kind of style you wish to create and the decorative or functional use the screen may have. Consider a sheer fabric that diffuses light, such as gauze or muslin, or perhaps a rough-textured linen or hessian. Fabric can be quilted or appliquéd or you could combine different fabrics (see pages 298–299).

To explore further the idea of a screen that allows light to penetrate, consider stretching chicken wire across a rough timber screen. Other metal sheeting can be substituted, from punched brass to galvanized steel. A solid wood screen covered in felt, with ribbons criss-crossing over it and secured with drawing pins, provides the perfect means for displaying cards, notes and other small pictures. Adapted for a children's room (remove the pins and use stitching instead) it can double up as a room divider and pin-board. Brown parcel paper is surprisingly elegant, and finished off with wonderful dome-headed pins around the edges of the frame makes a handsome screen, sufficiently neutral for all kinds of interiors.

Decoupage (see pages 286–287) can be exploited to wonderful effect on a flat screen. To use pasted paper to decorate a screen, a solid panel has to be attached to the frame. Use a thin plywood to keep the weight low if the entire panel is to be covered with paper. Alternatively, if the background to the cut-outs is to be painted, use stretched artist's canvas, primed and painted first.

Making a fabric-covered panel screen

Panel screens are made in sections from wood. The panels, once finished, are hinged together, so that each section can be at an angle to the next, thus allowing the whole screen to stand unaided.

Determine the height of the screen required and the width of each panel. As a guide, allow 180–200cm (72–78in) high by 50–60cm (20–24in) wide. You will need lengths of 5 x 2.5cm (2 x 1in) timber, wood

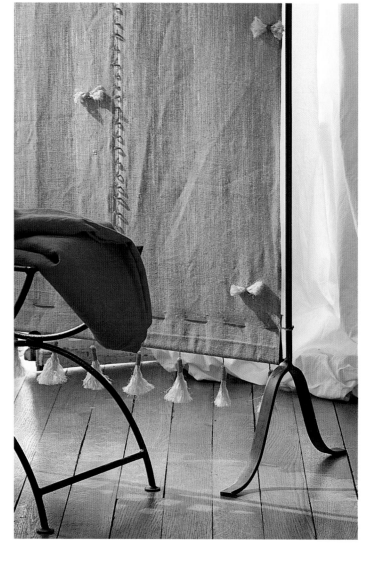

▶ *Two narrow strips of rough linen are suspended between each other and the metal frame of the screen by hand-stitched red cord. The cord adds a clever decorative element which is carried though onto the little tassels made from twine. It is a clever but simple combination, offset by the sturdy black metal frame.*

Making a fabric-covered panel screen

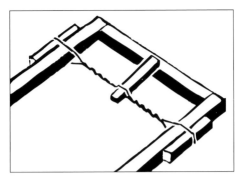

1 Secure the frame in place while the glue dries, using string and tourniquets to tighten the string.

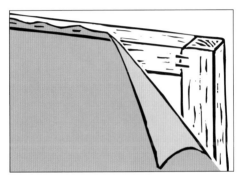

2 Keeping the fabric taut, staple one of the fabric pieces over the frame along the narrow outer edge of the frame.

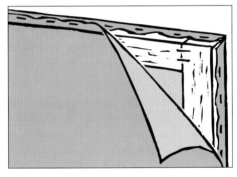

3 Attach the other fabric piece in the same way, stapling it in place along the narrow frame edge over the first piece.

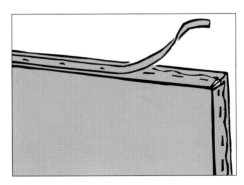

4 Tack the braid around the outer edge with upholstery nails or decorative studs. Hinge the panels together.

◄ *Screens make clever backdrops and add colour and texture to areas with few features, as shown here. A subtle cream-on-cream colourwash has been applied to the natural wooden frame, giving a beautiful finish to this simple screen constructed from five hinged panels. The hand-painted textured finish mimics the natural roughness of the stool.*

glue, a staple gun, a metal square (for ensuring that the corners are true right angles), long woodworking clamps, and three hinges between each panel plus the fixing screws.

For each panel, cut two lengths of timber to the height of the screen, and two short pieces which will fit between the long ones. Make a rectangular frame, using wood glue to join each piece and staples to secure each join on both sides of the frame. Use the metal square to ensure that the corners are absolutely true, and clamp the frame in place while the glue dries, or alternatively tie it together with string using bits of wood as tourniquets to tighten.

Sometimes it may be necessary to have a cross-piece of timber positioned halfway down each panel to brace the frame and prevent it 'twisting'.

To cover the screen you will need fabric, interlining (if required), a staple gun or studs or upholstery tacks, and ribbon or braid for covering the joins, if desired. Cut the fabric pieces, sufficient to cover each panel plus allowances in the width and length to go around the side of the timber. When using braid or ribbon to finish off, leave the edges of the fabric raw. (If studs or upholstery nails are to be used, secure a folded fabric edge.) Keeping the fabric taut and straight, staple (or tack) one of the fabric pieces over the frame. The staples go into the outer narrow edge of the frame. When one piece is secured, attach the other piece. Tack the braid or ribbon in place with upholstery nails or studs.

When each panel is finished, screw hinges between each of the panels at the same height across the screen.

Tableware

How you choose to decorate a table will depend on a number of factors: the table's style, its shape, the material from which it is made, its setting and its particular role. Tables may, for example, be covered by day to protect their surfaces and only uncovered in the evening for meals. Conversely, a large wooden refectory table in a kitchen is highly functional, serving as both a dining table and a work surface, so covering it with a cloth would be impractical.

◄ *An attractive striped tablecloth in a heavy woven fabric is contrasted with the whisper-thin table napkins, which have matching brown tassels.*

▲ *A massive, unjoined long table such as the one above shouldn't be hidden underneath a tablecloth. Instead, the points of colour are provided by the ceramic plates.*

Tables that are not particularly attractive to look at, such as functional trestles or basic chipboard models, may require a permanent disguise, such as a casually draped cream dust sheet or a pair of old velvet curtains, while a beautiful table that is reserved for special dinner parties might be used at other times as a display area for decorative objects such as pots or vases of flowers, arrangements of shells and driftwood, or ornaments and curios.

Tablecloths

Tablecloths can be used purely for decoration or they can have a practical role – protecting a polished top, for instance, or covering up a less-than-attractive surface. They are easy to make. For the simplest of cloths, take a square of fabric – perhaps with country-style checks or deck-chair stripes – and simply machine sew a hem around the edges. Jazz up a plain cloth by sewing on a central panel of fabric, adding a wide border and mitring the corners. Punched eyelets in the corners of a cloth add detail and have an added bonus in that they can be anchored to the ground with pegs if you want to use the cloth for alfresco meals or picnics.

Although there is probably nothing to beat a fine white linen tablecloth for formal settings, a less expensive version in white mattress ticking with a fine herringbone weave can be just as effective – especially if it is starched. A rough-textured linen cloth in beige or taupe is equally attractive and creates a good neutral backdrop for colourful table settings. Many fabrics can be painted with relative ease. Stick to simple stencilled shapes, applied sparingly across the cloth, such as large, bold letters or images in keeping with a particular theme, be it Hallowe'en, Easter or Christmas. Keep the design uncomplicated and don't use too many colours or the finished result will look muddled and messy.

A combination of cloths in different sizes, placed one over the other, is both attractive and practical. Choose fabrics in contrasting textures (white linen over grey wool suiting or tweed) or contrasting colours (shiny silks in deep orange and purple). On a round table a square cloth draped over a circular one provides more visual interest than a single, large area of fabric. Always let the fabric trail on the ground a little. Heavier fabrics, such as chenille (a traditional covering for protecting polished dining tables when they are not in use) in a dark, rich crimson or moss green, can be trimmed with a rope fringe or edged with shimmering taffeta for elegant, candlelit settings. For long, oblong tables, a fitted cloth with pleated corners that falls to the floor (see pages 336–337) is particularly effective.

A temporary cover, such as a sheet of thick plywood, can help enlarge and make a table more sturdy. A plywood sheet can also be placed over a run of small trestles to make a large enough table for a dinner party.

Every sit-down meal requires a table setting. Even the most informal, impromptu snack calls for plates, cutlery and glasses, arranged in some kind of order. For sophisticated dinner parties, Sunday brunches or children's tea parties, the table can be set and decorated to create a particular atmosphere or theme. Start with a colour scheme before adding decorative details in the form of flowers, berries, fruit, shells or ribbons. Take care, however, not to overload the table with too many objects. It may be better to provide a focus in the form of a single, striking flower arrangement or a co-ordinated set of coloured glassware.

Starched white linen napkins, the bigger the better, are hard to beat. Look for them on antique stalls or flea markets – they don't have to match. Roll them into napkin rings (antique silver ones if you're fortunate enough to own them) or secure them with wide satin ribbons tied into rough knots. Ribbons edged with wire can be twisted into marvellous ornamental bows. To reflect a particular celebration or anniversary, ribbons with printed motifs can be found. Similarly, try to find napkin rings to suit the occasion. For instance, for a glamorous dinner party, pierce small squares of brightly coloured silk with pieces of wire and twist the wire around plain white napkins. Plain wooden napkin rings can be brightly painted, while inexpensive Perspex ones are available for those who favour the minimalist look.

Candles provide the best light for evening suppers or dinner parties. Use chunky church candles of different heights or tiny night lights, one for each table setting. Home-made candles in small glass jars are attractive, or, for an alfresco table setting on a metal or wooden garden table, substitute terracotta holders or containers: look out for old miniature flower pots and group them together for maximum effect. Spiky metal candlesticks of varying shapes look good grouped together, and cast atmospheric shadows on the walls.

Table-linen

▲ *A plain wooden table tucked away in a corner of a room can all too easily fade into the background. Lit by incoming sunlight, this snugly fitted blue and white gingham cloth has a fresh, country-style appeal that makes the table a real focus of the room, as well as complementing the chequered china and soft furnishings.*

Circular tablecloths are usually decorative, often found covering an occasional table in the corner or at either side of a bed. Because of this they do not have to fulfil a very practical function so you can have fun with choosing different fabrics for the cloths.

Circular tablecloths

As circular tablecloths are very wide, especially those that drape right down to the floor, it is unlikely that you will find a large enough piece of fabric to cut the circle in one piece, so several widths may well need to be joined. They should never be joined down the middle as this would look unsightly on the table, but a full width of fabric should be centred and the extra widths should be added on either side of this central panel.

Making a circular tablecloth

To calculate the amount of fabric required, first measure the table's diameter and height. The basic width (diameter) of the finished cloth will equal twice the height of the table, plus the diameter of the table top. To this add 5–10cm (2–4in) to give some draping on the ground, plus an extra 3cm (1¼in) for the seam allowance around the circular edge. (Adjust if you want a shorter drop.) This gives the final width and length of fabric needed.

Circular tablecloth

1 *Join the fabric pieces, positioning a full width in the centre. Join lining pieces in same way. Press seams open.*

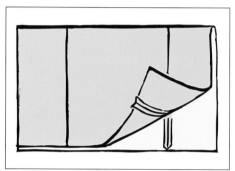

2 *Fold the fabric in half, aligning the seams. The width along the fold measures the full diameter of the circle.*

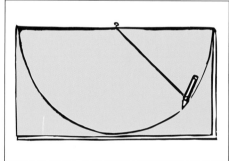

3 *Mark a half-circle on folded fabric, using a pencil and a length of string. Cut lining to same shape.*

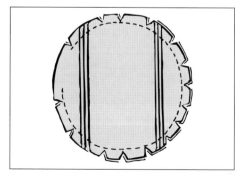

4 *Pin lining to fabric and stitch, leaving an opening for turning. Trim, notch and turn right side out.*

The lining will be the same size. Join the main fabric pieces into a square wide enough to make up the required diameter of the tablecloth, positioning a full fabric width in the centre and remembering to allow extra for seams. Press the seams open. Next, fold the fabric in half, lining up the seams. Mark the centre point along the folded edge with a pin. Tie a pencil onto the end of a length of string. Measure the length of the required radius (half the diameter) from the pencil along the string and pin the string at this point to the marked centre point. Mark out the circumference of half the circle. Cut along this half-circle through the two layers. Unfold the fabric and use it to cut a lining of the same size. (Cut an interlining if required.)

If using interlining, attach this first to the wrong side of the fabric, using large loose stitches (see pages 342–343). With right sides together, pin the circle of fabric to the lining circle. Machine stitch 1.5cm (⅝in) from the edge, leaving an opening of about 25cm (10in) to turn the cloth right side out. Trim and notch the seam allowances and press the seam open. Turn right side out. Press under the seam allowances along the opening and slip stitch closed. Press.

Rectangular tablecloths

Straightforward rectangular tablecloths are the most versatile and are very easy to make. For an interesting variation, two covers can be made for one table – one that sits across the table widthways only and the other over the top of it lengthways only, with each cloth falling to the floor. Use contrasting colours or patterns for maximum effect – two sizes of blue check, for example.

Determining the size of a simple rectangular tablecloth couldn't be easier. All you have to do is measure the length and width of the table, and the required drop. The length of cloth required is the length of the table plus two times the drop, plus hem allowances. The width of cloth required is calculated in the same way. For neatness, hems can be hand sewn, but this can obviously be quite time-consuming and machine stitching is more practical.

Rectangular tablecloths with skirts
'Fitted' tablecloths can be made by adding a skirt or valance in much the same way that a fitted bedspread is made.

Before embarking on purchasing fabric for this type of tablecloth, you should carefully consider how the skirt will be constructed. The height of the table (that is, the drop of the skirt) is likely to be less than the standard width of fabric. Therefore if you are using plain fabric or a pattern that can be used either horizontally or vertically, you can do what is termed 'railroading' – using the width of the fabric as the drop. However, if you are using a stripe or other vertical pattern, you may have to join fabric widths in order to achieve the total length that goes around the table. Plan where your seams will be and adjust the quantity of fabric required accordingly to avoid asymmetrically placed seams.

One way to hide any necessary seams in the skirt is to position them inside the box pleats at the corners. A pleat can also be added in the centre of each long side for this purpose. An interesting detail is achieved if the pleats are cut separately and made from a contrasting fabric. If you are attempting this, be sure to position the joining seams just inside the pleat so they to do not show on the pleat folds. ▷

▲ With each colour given equal weight, fresh citrus yellow and white marry perfectly in this kitchen. Because of the large size of the table, the yellow drape used on its own would have appeared too overpowering, upsetting the colour balance. Breaking up the mass of yellow with a smaller, white rectangular cloth restored a sense of harmony.

▲ *A combination of tablecloths can be practical as well as decorative. This fringed green and white pinstriped throw is thick and hard-wearing, making it ideal for daytime use. For formal evening meals or entertaining, this protective layer can be removed to reveal the fine white linen tablecloth beneath.*

Making a rectangular tablecloth with a skirt

To calculate the amount of fabric needed, first measure the flat surface area of the table top and add a 1.5cm (⅝in) seam allowance all round. These are the dimensions for the top piece. For the skirt (which will have a kick pleat in each corner), measure each side of the table. At each corner add 20cm (8in) extra for folding into the box pleat. The total length of all the sides plus the pleat allowances and any necessary seam allowances is the required length of the skirt piece (or pieces) for both fabric and lining. For the width of the skirt piece, measure the drop of the skirt from the edge of the table top to the floor and add 5–10cm (2–4in) to drape on the ground, plus seam allowance at both sides.

You will need enough main fabric for the top piece and the skirt and the same amount of lining fabric. Cut the table-top piece and the skirt piece (or pieces) from the main fabric and from the lining. Begin by making up the skirt. If you have several pieces of fabric for the skirt, pin and stitch them right sides together to make a large cylinder of fabric. Press the seams open. Do the same for the lining. With the right sides together, pin and stitch the lining to the fabric along one long edge. Press the seam open, then turn right side out. Press, aligning the seam along the fold. Pin the raw edges together (with wrong sides facing).

Next, pin and tack the pleats in place. The pleats must be placed precisely so that when the skirt is attached to the top of the cloth they fall exactly at each corner (and in the middle of a long side if additional pleats were made). Pin and tack the skirt to the top panel, right sides together. Machine stitch all around, making sure the pleats do not lose their position. Trim the seam allowance. Clip the seam allowance corners of the top panel piece diagonally, and notch the skirt section corners. Press the seam open and then towards the centre of the top.

Turn the seam allowance of the top panel lining to the wrong side and press. Pin the folded edge along the seam line where the skirt joins the top panel and hand sew it in place, using slip stitch. Turn the cloth right side out and press.

Rectangular tablecloth with skirt

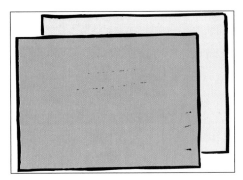

1 Cut one piece of main fabric and one piece of lining to size of table top plus seam allowance all around.

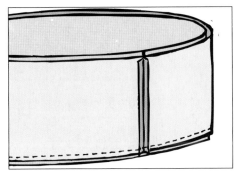

2 Cut the skirt piece (or pieces) and join into a cylinder. Make the skirt lining and join to the skirt along one edge.

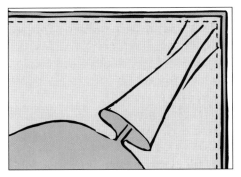

3 Turn the skirt right side out. Pin and tack the pleats at the corner positions and stitch the skirt to the top panel.

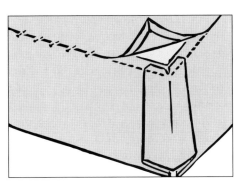

4 Press under the seam allowance on the top panel lining. Slip stitch the lining to the wrong side of the tablecloth.

Decorative square tablecloths

Arranged so that their points hang over the sides of a rectangular or square table, square tablecloths make effective drapes. They are made in the same way as simple rectangular cloths, but to determine the size you want, you will have to measure the fabric in a slightly different way. Start by deciding how far down each side of the table you wish the top cover cloth to fall. From this point, which will be the corner of the cloth, to the top of the table, doubled, is the length of each side of the cloth.

There are many simple ways to embellish a square cloth. The hem around the cover can be made with two rows of parallel stitching to add more detail. Using contrasting sewing thread will give the cloth more definition. To embellish the corners of the top cloth, if desired, attach small key tassels.

Other decorative details that can liven up plain cloths, such as fringe or braid, should be attached to the edges of the cloth by hand after the cloth is made up. A fringe should always overlap the base edge of the cloth by most of its length, allowing a few centimetres to trail on the ground. A braid applied to the edge of the cloth should line up with the finished edge. Flat braids or ribbons can also run across a square or rectangular cloth, parallel to the sides, set in about 10cm (4in) or so, and crossing at the corners to create a small square at each corner.

◄ Napkins, place mats and flower arrangements are the finer details that can give a meal a real sense of occasion. A classic scheme of delicate white chinaware on a white linen tablecloth has been given a twist with the addition of roughly stitched, bold scarlet napkins tied with raffia coils.

Sewing guide

Machine stitched seams

Basic flat seam

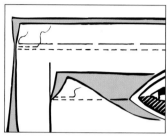

Place the two pieces of fabric together with raw edges aligned and right sides facing. Pin and tack along the edges. Remove the pins. Stitch 1.5cm (⅝in) in from the edges, working a few stitches in reverse at both ends to secure the thread. Remove the tacking and then press the seam open.

French seam

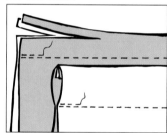

A self-neatening seam suitable for joining lightweight fabrics and for joining straight edges, French seams are ideal for items where both sides are to be visible, as no additional line of stitching will be seen. To make a French seam, place the two pieces of fabric with wrong sides together, and machine stitch a single seam 6mm (¼in) from the edge. Trim the seam allowances to 3mm (⅛in) and press the seam. Turn the fabric so that the right sides are together and press along the seam line. Next, tack a line of stitching close to the folded edge and sew a second seam 1cm (⅜in) from the folded edge. When completed, turn the fabric right sides out and finally press the seam allowance flat to one side of the finished seam.

Flat fell seam

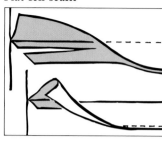

This self-neatening seam is extremely useful where strength is the essential element. With right sides together, sew 1.5cm (⅝in) from the aligned raw edges. Press the seam open. Trim one seam allowance to 6mm (¼in), fold the wide allowance over the narrow allowance and press. Fold under the edge of the wide allowance to enclose both raw edges, and top stitch close to the fold through all the layers. Press. The additional line of stitching will be visible on both sides of the fabric.

Neatening curves and corners

Clipping straight seam allowances

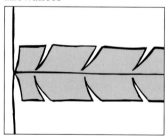

To ease tight selvedges, cut into the seam allowance at approximately 5cm (2in) intervals, diagonally to the seam line and pointing downwards.

Trimming corners

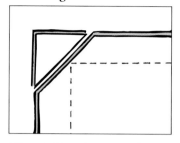

After stitching the seam, trim any corners on the diagonal, making sure you leave approximately 6mm (¼in) of the seam allowance to avoid any subsequent fraying of the fabric.

Clipping and notching curves

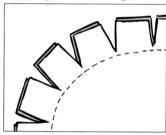

To enable curved seams to lie flat when pressed open, the seam allowances need to be clipped or notched. On inward curves, make straight clips at intervals to allow the seam allowance to open out. On outward curves, cut out tiny wedges (called 'notches') at short intervals to remove the excess bulk of the fabric.

Neatening raw edges

Pinking

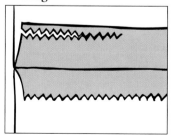

The simplest and quickest way to neaten raw edges is to use a pair of pinking shears, although it is not the most hard-wearing of methods.

Machine zigzag stitching

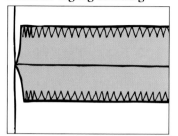

Using the zigzag setting on your machine, make a line of stitching as close to the raw edge as possible.

Self-binding (overlocking) seam

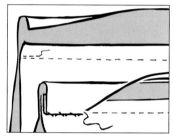

Useful where there is extra bulk – when attaching a gathered edge to a flat edge, for example. Make a seam allowance of about 3cm (1¼in) and trim one edge to 6mm (¼in). Folding the wide edge over the narrow edge, tuck the raw edge underneath. Pin and then slip stitch along the fold.

Bias binding

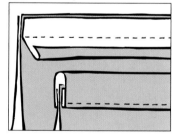

Align one unfolded edge of the bias binding along the edge of the fabric and pin, tack and machine stitch along the fold of the binding. Fold the binding over the edge to the other side of the fabric, and either machine sew through all layers or slip stitch the binding in place along the stitching line. This is also a way of neatening the raw edges of fabric – the edges of tablecloths, napkins, or place mats, for example – in which case, the seam is made with wrong sides facing. If you do not want the stitches to show, slip stitch along the folded edge instead, as for a self-bound (overlocked) seam.

Oversewing by hand

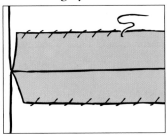

Oversewing is the best way to neaten raw edges by hand to prevent fraying. Take equal-spaced, equal-length diagonal stitches over the raw edge(s), working against the grain of the fabric.

Hems and mitring

Hems

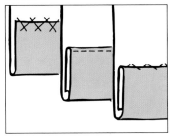

Single hems: For thick, heavy fabric, turn under the required amount of hem and press. Using herringbone stitch, sew along the edge so as to attach it to the back of the main fabric.

Double hem: A double hem secures a firm edge and is particularly suitable for sheer fabrics. Simply fold over half the hem allowance and then fold over again along the hem line. Pin, tack and finally slip stitch the hem in place.

Slip stitched hem: This hem uses less fabric than the double hem and is useful for medium-weight fabric. Turn 6mm (¼in) to the wrong side along

the raw edge and press. Fold the hem allowance to the wrong side along the hem line. Pin and tack. Finish off by slip stitching the hem into place.

Mitred corners

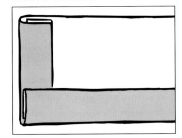

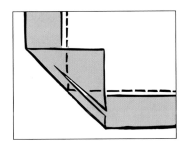

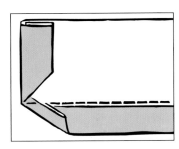

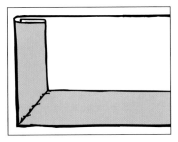

Mitred corners are used where neat corners are required. They can be made on single or double hems, and those of equal or varying widths. For single hems of equal width, turn up both side and bottom hems and press. Open out the hems, then fold in the corner of the fabric at the point where the two pressed lines cross. Check that the pressed lines on the triangle align

with those on the fabric. Turn in the hems again to form a neat join, then slip stitch the diagonal join and herringbone stitch the hems in place. For double hems of equal width, simply turn up both hems twice, unfold once, then turn in the triangle and continue as before. Both the diagonal join and the hems can be slip stitched.

When side and bottom hems are of different widths, turn in single hems and press them. Unfold the hems, but mark the limit of the turns with pins on the edge. Fold up a corner through the point where the pressed lines meet and the points marked with pins. Refold the bottom and side hems to form a neat mitre; stitch as before. For double hems of this kind, simply turn in double hems, unfold to single and mark the limit of the double turns.

Hand stitches

Running stitch

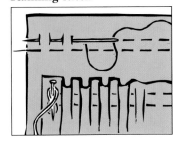

This stitch is used for simple sewing and gathering. It is worked from right to left and consists of small stitches of equal length. To gather fabric, begin on the right side of the fabric and sew two parallel lines of large running stitch. Finish each line off by winding the thread end around a pin. Pull both threads by applying even pressure to both ends of the line of sewing.

Back-stitch

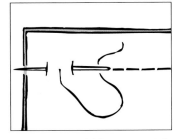

Back-stitch is useful for seams or tight corners where it is awkward to use a machine. Working from right to left, bring the needle out of the fabric and insert it a little way behind where the thread came out, then bring the needle forward the same distance in front of that point. The forward stitch will be double the length of the backward stitch. Continue in this way, making sure that you always insert the needle into the end of the last stitch so there are no gaps in the stitched line.

Ladder stitch (slip tacking)

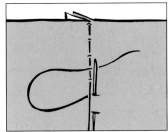

Ladder stitch, also known as slip tacking, is useful for matching patterned fabric exactly and is worked on the right side of the fabric. Press the seam allowance onto the wrong side of one piece of fabric, then with right sides upwards, place this over the unfolded seam allowance of the second piece. Pin firmly in place. With a knotted thread starting under the fold, stitch up through the fabric and across the join into the bottom piece. Next, take the needle under the fabric for a little way, then back up and across the join into the folded edge again, between the two layers of fabric. Repeat these small stitches across the join for the length of the fabric.

Slip stitch

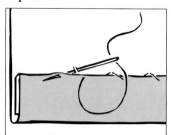

Slip stitch is used to stitch down a folded edge, such as a hem, or to join two folded edges, as in a mitred corner. In one continuous movement, working from right to left, take a tiny stitch in the main fabric, close to the previous stitch; insert the needle into the fold – about 6mm (¼in) to the left – and bring it out to the front. Continue, alternately making a tiny stitch in the main fabric and a larger stitch inside the folded edge.

Lock stitch

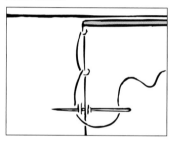

This loose stitch secures layers of fabric together – for example, holding lining and interlining in place. With wrong sides together, place the lining over the main fabric. Pin down the complete length of the fabric in the centre. Fold the fabric back against the pins.

Using matching thread, make a horizontal stitch through the folded edge and the main fabric, picking up only one or two threads of the fabric. Work at 5cm (2in) intervals down the fabric, keeping the thread very loose between the stitches. Work additional rows of lock stitch as instructed.

Herringbone stitch

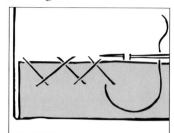

This firm stitch, worked from left to right, is used for hemming heavyweight fabric over a single hem. Bring the thread up through the hem. Move diagonally down to the right, then take a small straight stitch just above the hem edge. Move diagonally up to the right, and take a small stitch from the hem again. Continue making crossed stitches along the length of the hem.

Blanket stitch

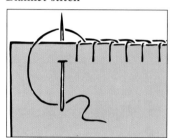

Blanket stitch can be used to neaten the edge of the fabric or as a decorative stitch when worked in a contrasting colour. Insert the needle down through the fabric at the required distance from the edge. Holding the thread under the needle point, pull the needle through at the edge, forming a loop along the edge of the fabric. Closely packed blanket stitch is used for making buttonholes.

Prick stitch

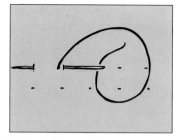

Prick stitch is used for inserting zips and for occasions where the sewing must be unobtrusive. It is sewn in the same way as backstitch, but the top stitches are smaller and should appear as pricks in the fabric. Working on the right side, take the needle back a couple of threads behind where the thread came out and then take a stitch a little way in front of that point.

Ruffles and pleats

Ruffles

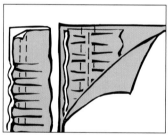

Single ruffles: Calculate the dimensions of the ruffle and add a hem and seam allowance. Cut the strip. Turn up the hem and stitch. Stitch two parallel rows of long, straight machine stitch and gather to the required length. Pin and tack to the main fabric with right sides together. Remove the pins. Machine stitch in place along the seam line and remove the tacking. Neaten the edges using machine zigzag and press upwards.

Double ruffles: To produce a full ruffle, cut double the depth of the fabric and allow twice the required top seam allowance. Fold the material in half lengthways and gather the top, as for a single ruffle.

Pleats

For each pleat allow three times the required width and remember to cut parallel to the cross grain of the fabric to ensure that the pleats hang straight.

Knife pleats

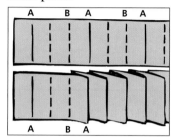

Having decided upon the required pleat width, calculate the number of pleats by measuring the edge to which the pleats will be attached and dividing by the width of the pleat. Multiply this number by three to calculate the width of fabric needed and add the seam allowances. Calculate the depth required and add seam allowances. Flat fell the seams to join the widths together and pin and stitch the hems. Mark the pleats on the fabric at right angles to the edge of the fabric. Mark the pleat line (A) and then measure twice the pleat width and mark on the placement line (B). Alternate (A) and (B) markings and measurements along the fabric. Fold the fabric on the first pleat line (A) and bring to line (B); repeat to the end of the fabric. Tack along the top of the fabric and press. Stitch in place as for ruffles.

Box pleats

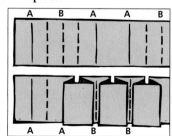

Box pleats consist of two pleats folded in such a way as to turn towards each other. Begin in the same way as for knife pleats. Mark pleat line (A), measure twice the width and mark placement line (B). Then measure twice the pleat width again, to mark the next pleat line (A), then twice the width again, to the beginning of the next sequence, pleat line (A). To pleat the fabric, simply fold the two pleat lines (A) outwards to meet over the placement line. Inverted box pleats are assembled in the same way except that the pleat lines are folded inwards to meet over the placement lines.

Trimming

Piping

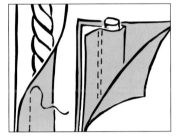

Join bias strips until they are the same length as the required length of piping cord. Place the cord on the wrong side of the strip, fold the strip over, align the edges, and first tack and then machine stitch along, close to the cord, using a zipper foot attachment. Pin the piping to the edge of the main fabric along the previous stitching line. Tack and stitch in place.

Fastenings

Buttons, hooks and studs

Buttons: Mark the position for the button and secure the thread. Slide the button over the needle and place a matchstick over the top of the button. Work stitches through the holes of the button and over the matchstick. Remove the matchstick and pull the button up, so the slack thread is behind the button. Finish by winding the working thread around the slack to make a shank, securing the thread end inside the shank.

Hooks and eyes: Fix the eye part of the fastener every 5–10cm (2–4in) along the fabric by sewing a few stitches through each hoop. Ensure that the hooks are correctly aligned, then fix to the other side of the fabric by stitching over the neck.

Press studs: Mark the positions of the press studs by measuring every 5–10cm (2–4in) along the fabric and 6mm (¼in) from the edge. Mark the positions with pins. Sew the socket part on the seam underlap by working a few stitches through each hole. Place the ball half on the overlapping fabric and check its alignment with the socket half before securing it in place.

Fastening tapes

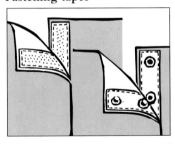

Press stud tape: This is a length of tape which has press studs fixed at set intervals along the tape. It is available in several widths.

To fix press studs, simply separate the two layers and sew the socket layer to the underneath of the fabric and the ball part to the top layer of the fabric. Stitch down the long edges of the strips, using a machine zipper foot.

Velcro: This consists of two strips of fabric, one of which has tiny hooks and the other, tiny loops. These strips stick together when pressed. Separate the two layers and stitch in place down the long edges.

Zips

Useful for cushions and chair covers, zips are available with either metal or nylon teeth and in a full range of colours, lengths and weights.

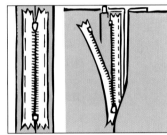

Centred zip: Stitch the seam up to the zip opening. Then tack the seam along the opening and press it open. Lay the zip downwards onto the wrong side of the fabric, exactly along the seam line, then pin and tack it in place. Turn the fabric right side up and sew the zip in place, just inside the tacking lines, using a zipper foot attachment. Fasten the threads and remove the tacking from the opening.

Zip inserted in a piped seam: Open the zip and lay one side, right side down, on the right side of the piped seam with the zip tape in the seam allowance and the zip teeth aligned with the piping. Tack and then sew in place 3mm (⅛in) from the teeth using a zipper foot attachment. Close the zip and fold back the seam allowances of both edges. Laying the plain edge on the zip, line up with the piping, pin, tack and sew in place.

Fabric ties

Flat fabric ties make a wonderful alternative to other fastenings and are useful for bed-linen and cushions. Rouleau strips – tubes made from bias strips – can be mounted as loops and used as an alternative to buttonholes.

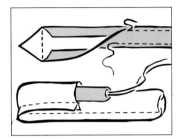

Flat ties: Cut a piece of fabric to the desired length and twice the width, adding 1cm (⅜in) all around. Folding the edges of the length to the wrong side by 1cm (⅜in), press and cut the corners at a diagonal before folding and pressing the width ends down to the wrong side. Fold the fabric in half lengthways and stitch all the sides, 3mm (⅛in) from the edge.

Rouleau ties: Fold the desired length of bias of a width of 2.5–3cm (1–1¼in) in half and sew the long edges together, 6mm (¼in) from the edge. Push a blunt-ended needle threaded with strong thread through the tube, having first secured it to one end, working along the length until it pulls through the other end. Pull the thread and the rouleau will be turned right side out. Finish by tucking the ends into the tube and then oversewing.

Stockists and suppliers

Architectural mouldings

Stevensons of Norwich, Roundtree Way, Norwich, Norfolk NR7 8SQ

The Newson Group, 491 Battersea Park Road, London SW11 4NH

Curtain and blind accessories

Arthur Beale, 194 Shaftesbury Avenue, London WC2H 8JP
Ropes, rings and eyelets.

The Kite Store Ltd, 48 Neal Street, London WC2H 9PA
Parachute nylon, eyelets and cord.

Fabrics

Baumann Fabrics, 41 Berners Street, London W1P 3AA

Colefax and Fowler
(*See* Wallpapers.)

Designers Guild
(*See* Wallpapers.)

Ian Mankin Ltd., 109 Regents Park Road, Primrose Hill, London NW1 8UR

MacCulloch & Wallis Ltd., 25–26 Dering Street, London W1A 3AX
Mail order service available.

Osborne & Little,
Co-ordinated fabric and wallpaper collections.
(*See* Wallpapers.)

Paine & Co., 47–51 Barnsbury Street, London N1 1TP

Pierre Frey, 253 Fulham Road London SW3 6HY

Pongees, 28–30 Hoxton Square, London N1 6NN
Especially silks.

Sandersons, Arthur & Sons Ltd.
(*Also see* Wallpapers *and* Paints, stains and varnishes.)

Timney Fowler, 388 Kings Road, London SW3 5UZ

VV Rouleaux, 10 Symons Street, Sloane Square, London SW3 2TJ
Ribbons, tassels and braids.

Zoffany, 63 South Audley Street, London W1Y 5BF
(*Also see* Wallpapers.)

Flooring

Flexible flooring

The Amtico Company Ltd., Kingfield Road, Coventry CV6 5PL

First Floor, 174 Wandsworth Bridge Road, London SW6 2UQ

Forbo-Nairn, PO Box 1, Kirkcaldy, Fife KY1 2SB

Sinclair Till, 791-793 Wandsworth Road, London SW8 3JQ

Wicanders, Amorium House, Star Road, Partridge Green, Horsham, West Sussex RH13 8RA
Natural wood and cork.

Decorative wood flooring

Campbell Marson, 573 Kings Road, London SW6 2EB

Campbell & Young Hardwood Flooring, 16 Lettice Street, Fulham, London SW6 4EH

Wallis Wood Floors, Bush House, 294 Ongar Road, Writtle, Chelmsford, Essex CM1 3NZ

Hard flooring
(*also see* Tiles)

Burlington Slate Ltd., Cavendish House, Kirkby-in-Furness, Cumbria LA17 7UN

Fired Earth plc.
(*See* Tiles.)

Gooding Aluminium, British Wharf, Landemann Way, London SE14 5RS

Naturestone, Crossways, Silwood Road, Ascot, Berkshire SL5 0PZ
Limestone, marble, sandstone and slate.

Paris Ceramics Ltd.
Limestone and terrazzo.
(*See* Tiles.)

Soft flooring

The Alternative Flooring Company, 14 Anton Trading Estate, Andover, Hampshire SP10 2NJ
Natural floor-coverings.

Crucial Trading Ltd., The Market Hall, Craven Arms, Shropshire SY7 9NY
Natural floor-coverings.

Resista Carpets, 255 New King's Road, London SW6 4RB

Paints, stains and varnishes

Bollom, J W, 13 Theobolds Road, London WC1X 8FN

Brodie and Middleton, 68 Drury Lane, London WC2
Fabric paints, pigments and canvas.

Cole & Son
Own range, with historic colours a speciality.
(*See* Wallpapers.)

Cornelissen & Son Ltd., 105 Great Russell Street, London WC1B 3RY
Vast selection of artists' pigments. Also brushes and gilding materials.

Craig and Rose, 172 Leith Walk,
Edinburgh EH6 5EB

Crown Berger Europe, PO Box 37,
Crown House, Darwen, Lancs BB3 0BG
With a paint advisory service.

Dulux, ICI Paints, Wexham Road, Slough,
Berkshire SL2 5DS

Dylon International Ltd,
Worsley Bridge Road, Lower Sydenham,
London SE26 5HD
Dyes.

Farrow & Ball Ltd., Uddens Trading Estate,
Wimborne, Dorset BH21 7NL

Foxell and James, 57 Farringdon Road,
London EC1M 3JB.

J H Ratcliffe and Co (Paints Ltd.),
135A Linaker Street, Southport PR8 5DF

John Oliver wallpapers and paints,
33 Pembridge Road, London W11 3HG
(*Also see* Wallpapers.)

Nutshell Natural Paints (*Mail Order*),
Newtake, Staverton, Devon TQ9 6PE
A range of natural earth and mineral pigments.

Paint Magic, 116 Sheen Road,
Richmond TW9 1VR

Papers & Paints, 4 Park Walk,
London SW10 0AD

Potmolen Paint, 27 Woodcock Industrial
Estate, Warminster, Wiltshire BA12 9DX

Russell & Chapple, 23 Monmouth Street,
Shaftesbury Avenue, London WC2H 9DE
Canvas. Gilding materials.

Sanderson, Arthur & Sons Ltd., 112–120
Brompton Road, London SW3 1JJ
(*Also see* Wallpapers *and* Fabrics.)

The Stencil Store, 91 Lower Sloane Street,
London SW1W 8DA

For mail order:
PO Box 30, Rickmansworth,
Hertfordshire WD3 5LG

Tiles

British Ceramic Tile Council,
Federation House, Station Road,
Stoke-on-Trent ST4 2RT

Fired Earth plc., Twyford Mill, Oxford
Road, Adderbury, Oxfordshire OX17 3HP
(*Also see* Hard flooring.)

Paris Ceramics Ltd., 583 King's Road,
London SW6 2EH
Include terracotta and mosaic.

Pilkington Tiles Ltd., PO Box 4,
Clifton Junction, Swinton,
Manchester M27 8LP

World's End Tiles, Silverthorne Road,
Off Queenstown Road, Battersea,
London SW8 3HE

Wallpapers

Arthur Sanderson & Sons Ltd.
(*See* Paints.)

Cole & Son, 142–144 Offord Road,
London N1 1NS
Selection of hand-blocked wallpapers.
(*Also see* Paints, stains and varnishes.)

Colefax and Fowler, 39 Brook Street,
London W1
Traditional English-style wallpapers.
(*Also see* Fabrics.)

Designers Guild, 271 and 277 King's Road,
London SW3 5EN
(*Also see* Fabrics.)

John Oliver wallpapers and paints
From traditional-style papers to glitzy metallics.
(*See* Paints, stains and varnishes.)

Osborne & Little, 304–308 Kings Road,
London SW3 2HP

Co-ordinated wallpaper and fabric collections.
(*Also see* Fabrics.)

Watts & Co., 7 Tufton Street,
London SW1P 3QE

Zoffany
(*Also see* Fabrics.)

Australia and New Zealand

Paints, stains and varnishes

Levene & Co, 68 Harris Road,
East Tamaki, Auckland

Dulux Australia, McNaughton Road,
Clayton, Victoria 3168

Taubmans, 425-427 Riversdale Road,
Hawthorn East, Victoria 2123

Wattyl, 82 Levanswall Road, Moorabbin,
Victoria 3189

Wattyl, 4 Steet Street, Blacktown,
New South Wales 2148

Hardware Stores

Mitre, 10 Princes Highway, Hallam
Victoria 3803

Home Hardware, 414 Lower Dandenong
Road, Braeside, Victoria 3195

McEwans, 387-403 Bourke Street,
Melbourne, Victoria 3000

BBC Hardware, 192 Gaffney Street,
Coburg West, Victoria 3058

South Africa

Dulux Paint 'n' Paper, Head Office,
34 King's Road, PO Box 788, Pinetown
And at branches nationwide.

Plascon Paint City, 1b Walkers Lane,
Greyville, Durban

Index

Acknowledgments

1 Ray Main; 2 Hans Zeegers/Ariadne; 4–5 Richard Waite (Designer: Louise Cotier)/Arcaid; 6 Hotze Eisma/In Huis; 8–9 Todd Eberle; 10 Hotze Eisma; 11–12 Mads Mogensen; 13 James Merrell/Options/Robert Harding Syndication; 14–15 Todd Eberle (Designer: Michael Formika); 16 Verne Fotografie; 17 *above* Richard Glover; 17 *below* Eduard Hueber (Whitney Powers); 18–19 Rob van Uchelen/Ariadne; 19 John Hall; 20 Eduard Hueber (Dean Wolf); 20–1 Jerome Darblay; 21 Fritz von der Schulenburg (Architect: Nico Rensch)/The Interior Archive; 22 Polly Wreford/Homes & Gardens/Robert Harding Syndication; 24 Paul Ryan/International Interiors; 25 Jerome Darblay; 26 *left* Henry Bourne/World of Interiors; 26 *right* David Phelps; 27 *above* Richard Felber; 27 *below* Chris Drake/Country Homes & Interiors/Robert Harding Syndication; 28 Ray Main; 29 *above* Paul Ryan/International Interiors; 29 *below* Antoine Rozes; 30 *above* Jean Pierre Godeaut (Yuri Kuper); 30 *below* Verne Fotografie; 31 *above* Dominique Vorillion (Arch: B. Urquietta)/Stock Image Production; 31 *below* A. Bailhache (Stylist: M.Gibert)/Marie Claire Maison; 32 Eduard Hueber (Dean Wolf); 33 Fritz von der Schulenburg (Paula Navone)/The Interior Archive; 34 *above* Hotze Eisma (Ron Jagger); 34 *below* Scott Frances/Esto; 34–5 Peter Cook; 36 *above* John Hall; 36 *below* Todd Eberle (Designer:Michael Formika); 37 *above* Scott Frances/Esto; 37 *below* Marie-Pierre Morel (Stylist: C. Peuch)/Marie Claire Maison; 38 Todd Eberle; 39 Fritz von der Schulenburg (Adelheid Gowrie)/The Interior Archive; 40 *above* Simon Brown (Justin Meath Baker); 40 *below* Christopher Drake/Options/Robert Harding Syndication; 41 Fritz von der Schulenburg/Country Homes & Interiors/Robert Harding Syndication; 42 Francis Hammond; 42–3 Jean-Francois Jaussaud; 43 Antoine Bootz; 44 *above* John Hall; 44 *below* Christian Sarramon; 45 *above* Henry Wilson (Mazzuchi)/The Interior Archive; 45 *below* Francis Hammond; 46 Simon McBride; 46–7 Verne Fotografie; 47 Jerome Darblay; 48–9 Fritz von der Schulenburg (Richard Mudditt)/The Interior Archive; 50 Simon Kenny/Belle Magazine; 51 *above* Earl Carter/Belle Magazine; 51 *below* Simon Kenny/Belle Magazine; 52 Schoner Wohnen/Camera Press; 53 Verne Fotografie; 54 *above* Hannah Lewis (Sue Parker)/Elle Decoration; 54 *below* Pascal Chevalier (Michel Klein)/Agence Top; 54–55 Paul Ryan/International Interiors; 55 *above* Christopher Drake/Homes & Gardens/Robert Harding Syndication; 55 *below* Paul Ryan/International Interiors; 56 Henry Wilson (Ian Dew)/The Interior Archive; 58 David Churchill/Arcaid; 61 Christophe Dugied/Marie Claire Maison; 62 Henry Wilson (Celia Lyttleton)/The Interior Archive; 63 *left* Henry Wilson (Celia Lyttleton)/The Interior Archive; 63 *right* Jacqui Hurst; 64 Jean-Pierre Godeaut (Designer: Manuel Mestre); 66 Huntley Hedworth/Elizabeth Whiting & Associates; 66–7 Simon Brown/The Interior Archive; 67 Simon Brown/The Interior Archive; 68 Henry Wilson (Giola Rossi)/The Interior Archive; 69 Crown Paints; 70–1 Mads Mogensen; 72 English Stamp Company; 73 Alberto Piovano (Architect: Mariano Boggia)/Arcaid; 74 Schoner Wohnen/Camera Press; 75 Simon McBride; 76 Tim Beddow/The Interior Archive; 77 Jacques Dirand; 78 Henry Bourne (Melissa North)/Elle Decoration; 78–9 *above* Anaglypta Wallcoverings; 78–9 *below* Cole & Son/Michael Dyer Associates; 79 *above* Anna French; 79 *below* David Barrett/Homes & Gardens/Robert Harding Syndication; 80 Christopher Drake/Country Homes & Interiors/Robert Harding Syndication; 82 Sanderson Design Archive; 83 Ray Main; 86 *above* Ari Ashley/Interior Archive; 86 *below* Hotze Eisma; 89 *above & below* Ian Parry/Abode; 90 Schoner Wohnen/Camera Press; 91 Christopher Drake/Homes & Gardens/Robert Harding Syndication; 92 Paul Ryan/International Interiors; 92 *below* James Merrell/Country Homes & Interiors/Robert Harding Syndication; 94 Jerome Darblay; 95 Laura Ashley; 96 Dolf Straatemeier/V.T. Wonen; 98 Christopher Simon Sykes/The Interior Archive; 99 Mike Parsons; 100 Scott Frances/Esto; 100–1 Homes & Gardens/Robert Harding Syndication; 101 *above* Muraspec Wallcoverings; 101 *below* Henry Wilson (Christopher Davies)/The Interior Archive; 102 Nadia Mackenzie; 103 Lucinda Symons/Country Homes & Interiors/Robert Harding Syndication; 104 Simon Brown; 105 *above* Henry Wilson (Ian Dew)/The Interior Archive; 105 *below* Dominque Vorillon; 106 *left & right* Richard Glover; 106 *below* Paul Warchol; 106–7 Fritz von der Schulenburg (Mimmi O'Connell)/The Interior Archive; 107 Hotze Eisma/V.T. Wonen; 108 Trevor Mein/Belle Magazine; 109 Fritz von der Schulenburg (Paula Navone)/The Interior Archive; 110 Ray Main; 111 Eric Morin; 112 Ray Main; 113 Ross Honeysett (Architect: Ian Moore); 114 Mark Darley/Esto; 115 David Simmonds/Elle Decoration; 116 Simon Kenny/Belle Magazine; 118 James Merrell/Options/Robert Harding Syndication; 120 John Hall; 121 Dominque Vorillon; 122–3 Verne Fotografie; 124 *above* Ray Main; 124 *below* Sølvi Dos Santos; 125 *left & right* Ray Main; 126 Ken Adlard; 127 *above* Eduard Hueber (Whitney Powers); 127 *below* Antoine Rozes; 128 *above* Scott Frances/Esto; 128 *below* Andreas von Einsiedel/Country Homes & Interiors/Robert Harding Syndication; 129 Hotze Eisma (Karen Butler); 130 *above* Jean-Pierre Godeaut (J.Prisca); 130–1 *above* David Phelps; 130–1 *below* James Mortimer/The Interior Archive; 131 *above right* Ingalill Snitt; 131 *below right* Fritz von der Schulenburg (Architect: Nico Rensch)/The Interior Archive; 132 John Miller; 133 Ianthe Ruthven; 134 Peter Cook (Sergison Bates); 135 Gilles de Chabaneix (Stylist: Fasoli)/Marie Claire Maison; 136 John Hall; 137 Eric Morin; 138 *above* Simon McBride; 138 *below* Rodney Hyett/Elizabeth Whiting & Associates; 139 Richard Waite; 140 David Cripps/Elizabeth Whiting & Associates; 142 T. Jeanson (Maison McCoy)/Stock Image Production; 143 Nina Ewald/Abode; 144 Thomas Lane; 146 Michel Claus; 147 Fritz von der Schulenburg (Dot Spikings)/The Interior Archive; 148 Scott Frances/Esto; 149 Tim Street-Porter (Designer: Barbara Barry); 150 Fritz von der Schulenburg (Architect: Nico Rensch)/The Interior Archive; 150–1 Peter Cook (Jonathon Woolf)/Hilary Coe; 151–2 Verne Fotografie; 154 Otto Baitz/Esto; 155 Michel Claus; 156 Deidi von Schaewen; 158 Hotze Eisma; 159 *above* John Heseltine; 159 *below* Christopher Simon Sykes/The Interior Archive; 160 *above* Neil Lorimer/Elizabeth Whiting & Associates; 160 *below* Nadia Mackenzie; 160–1 Paul Warchol; 161 *above* David Parmiter; 161 *below* Jean Pierre Godeaut (Dimitri Xanthdolis); 162 *above* Mads Mogensen; 162 *below* Jean Pierre Godeaut; 164 *left* Michael Freeman; 164 *right* Fritz von der Schulenburg/The Interior Archive; 166 Ray Main; 167 Paul Warchol; 168–9 Michel Claus; 168 *above* Georgia Glynn-Smith; 168 *below* Verne Fotografie; 169 Tim Street-Porter (Daniel Sachs); 170 Richard Felber; 172 David Phelps; 173 Ari Ashley/Interior Archive; 174 *above* John Hall (Faulkner); 174 *below* John Hall; 176 Todd Eberle; 177 Alexander van Berge/V.T. Wonen; 178 Hotze Eisma; 178–9 John Hall; 179 *above left* Eduard Hueber (M. Burger); 179 *above right* Sinclair Till; 179 *below* Deidi von Schaewen; 180 Neil Lorimer/Elizabeth Whiting & Associates; 182 John Hall (Michael Carter & Elizabeth O'Donnell); 183 Fritz von der Schulenburg (Adelheid Gowrie)/The Interior Archive; 184 Sinclair Till; 184–5 Paul Warchol; 185 *above left & right & below* Sinclair Till; 187 Fritz von der Schulenburg (Mimmi O'Connell)/The Interior Archive; 188 James Merrell/Woman's Journal/Robert Harding Syndication; 190 Alexander van Berge; 191 Fritz von der Schulenburg/The World of Interiors; 192 *left* Nina Ewald/Abode; 192 *above right* Vaughan; 192 *below right* Jean-Paul Bonhommet/Elizabeth Whiting &

Associates; **193** *left* Simon Brown (John Stefanidis)/The Interior Archive; **193** Simon McBride; **194** Henry Wilson (Sophie Saren)/The Interior Archive; **195** Ken Adlard; **196–7** John Hall; **198** Jan Baldwin (Andrew Mortada); **198–9** Simon McBride; **199** *above* Sølvi Dos Santos; **199** *below* Simon McBride; **200** Paul Ryan/International Interiors; **200–1** Albert Roosenburg/V.T. Wonen; **201** Nicolas Tosi (Stylist: C. Ardouin)/Marie Claire Maison; **202** John Miller; **203** Hotze Eisma; **204** Albert Roosenburg; **205** Hotze Eisma; **206** Polly Wreford/Homes & Gardens/Robert Harding Syndication; **206–7** Trevor Richards/Homes & Gardens/Robert Harding Syndication; **208** Francis Hammond; **209** Michael Mundy (Wilkinson); **210** Fritz von der Schulenburg/(Adelheid Gowrie) The Interior Archive; **211** Hotze Eisma; **212** Richard Felber; **213** John Hall; **214** Henry Wilson (Celia Lyttleton)/The Interior Archive; **215** Richard Bryant/Arcaid; **216** Albert Roosenburg; **217** Jean Pierre Godeaut (Lisa Lovatt Smith); **218–9** David Phelps; **219** Dominque Vorillon; **220** *above* Simon Brown (Justin Meath Baker); **220** *below* Eric Morin; **221** Fritz von der Schulenburg/The Interior Archive; **222** John Hall; **223** Henry Wilson (Ian Dew)/ The Interior Archive; **224** John Miller; **225** Albert Roosenburg/V.T. Wonen; **226** *above* Gilles de Chabaneix (Stylist: M.Kalt)/Marie Claire Maison; **226** *below* Alexander van Berge; **226–7** Peter Woloszynski/The Interior Archive; **227** *above* Fritz von der Schulenburg/The Interior Archive; **227** *below* Marie-Pierre Morel (Stylist: J. Borgeaud)/Marie Claire Maison; **228** Marie-Pierre Morel (Stylist: C. Peuch)/Marie Claire Maison; **229** Ray Main; **230** *above* Henry Wilson (Ian Dew)/The Interior Archive; **230** *below* Nicolas Tosi (Stylist: J.Borgeaud)/ Marie Claire Maison; **231** Polly Wreford/ Homes & Gardens/Robert Harding Syndication; **232** *above* James Merrell/Homes & Gardens/Robert Harding Syndication; **232** *below* Henry Wilson (Ashley Hicks)/The

Interior Archive; **232–3** Gavin Kingcome/ Homes & Gardens/Robert Harding Syndication; **233** *above* Nicolas Tosi (Stylist: J. Borgeaud)/Marie Claire Maison; **233** *below* Ray Main; **234** Tim Clinch/The Interior Archive; **235** Polly Wreford/Country Homes & Interiors/Robert Harding Syndication; **236** *above* Marie-Pierre Morel (Stylist: C. Peuch)/Marie Claire Maison; **236** *below* Jacques Dirand/Maison & Jardin; **236–7** Trevor Richards/Homes & Gardens/Robert Harding Syndication; **237** *above* Sanderson; **237** *below* Henry Wilson (Stephan Ryan)/The Interior Archive; **238** Fritz von der Schulenburg (David Bennett)/The Interior Archive; **238–9** *above* Christopher Drake/Country Homes & Interiors/Robert Harding Syndication; **238–9** *below* Jacques Dirand/Maison & Jardin; **239** Trevor Richards/Homes & Gardens/ Robert Harding Syndication; **240** Paul Warchol; **241** *above* Jan Baldwin/Options/ Robert Harding Syndication; **241** *below* Todd Eberle; **242** Jacques Dirand/Maison & Jardin; **243** Andreas von Einsiedel/Homes & Gardens/Robert Harding Syndication; **244** Christopher Drake/Homes & Gardens/ Robert Harding Syndication; **245** Jacques Dirand/Maison & Jardin; **246** Christopher Drake/Country Homes & Interiors/Robert Harding Syndication; **247** Brigitte/Camera Press; **248** Fritz von der Schulenburg (Paula Navone)/The Interior Archive; **248–9** Debi Treloar/Homes & Gardens/Robert Harding Syndication; **250** Tom Leighton/Elizabeth Whiting & Associates; **251** Fritz von der Schulenburg (Mimmi O'Connell)/The Interior Archive; **252** Ray Main; **253** Jacques Dirand/ Maison & Jardin; **254** Christopher Drake/ Homes & Gardens/Robert Harding Syndication; **255** Hotze Eisma; **256** A. Gelberger/ Maison Francaise/Agence Top; **257** John Hall; **258** Otto Baitz/Esto; **259** *above* Fritz von der Schulenburg (Architect: Nico Rensch)/The Interior Archive; **259** *below* Christian Sarramon; **260** Laura Ashley; **261** Peter Woloszynski (A.Parlance)/ The Interior

Archive; **262** John Hall; **263** Henry Bourne/ World of Interiors; **264** James Mortimer/The Interior Archive; **265** Christophe Dugied (Stylist: M.Bayle)/Marie Claire Maison; **267** Dominique Vorillon; **268** Henry Wilson (Christopher Davies)/The Interior Archive; **269** *above* Jean-Francois Jaussaud; **269** *below* Trevor Richards/Homes & Gardens/Robert Harding Syndication; **270** Fritz von der Schulenburg (Mimmi O'Connell/Painter: Juliette Mole)/The Interior Archive; **272** Ray Main; **273** *above* Henry Bourne/The World of Interiors; **273** *below* Scott Frances/Esto; **274** Trevor Richards (Kerry Skinner, Dawna Walter) /Abode; **275** Mark Luscombe- Whyte/Elizabeth Whiting & Associates; **276** Mads Mogensen; **277** Fritz von der Schulenburg/The Interior Archive; **278** Mads Mogensen; **279** Hotze Eisma; **280** Fritz von der Schulenburg (Dot Spikings)/The Interior Archive; **281** Marie-Pierre Morel (Stylist: G. Le Signe)/Marie Claire Maison; **282–3** Gilles de Chabaneix (Stylist: D. Rozensztroch)/Marie Claire Maison; **284** Trevor Richards (Kerry Skinner)/Country Homes & Interiors/Robert Harding Syndication; **285** Pierre Hussenot (Roy-Comte)/ Marie Claire Maison; **286** Hugh Johnson/ Homes & Gardens/Robert Harding Syndication; **287** David Parmiter; **288** Geoffrey Frosh/ Homes & Gardens/Robert Harding Syndication; **289** Marie-Pierre Morel (Stylist: C. Puech/G.Le Signe)/Marie Claire Maison; **290** Marie-Pierre Morel (Stylist: J. Postic)/ Marie Claire Maison; **291** Dominic Blackmore/ Ideal Home / Robert Harding Syndication; **292** James Merrell/Options/ Robert Harding Syndication; **293** Jan Baldwin/Options/ Robert Harding Syndication; **294** *above* Nadia Mackenzie; **294** *below* Trevor Richards/Homes & Gardens/Robert Harding Syndication; **294–5** Solvi Dos Santos; **295** *above* Nadia Mackenzie; **295** *below* Designers Guild; **296** Gilles de Chabaneix (Stylist: C de Chabaneix/ V. Mery)/Marie Claire Idees; **297** Christophe Dugied/Marine Archang; **298** Sandra Lane/ Homes & Gardens/Robert

Harding Syndication; **299** Francis Hammond (Ashley Studio); **300** Spike Powell/Elizabeth Whiting & Associates; **301** Hotze Eisma; **302** Paul Ryan/International Interiors; **303** Tim Beddow (Kelly Hoppen)/The Interior Archive; **304** Simon Brown; **305** Todd Eberle; **306** Fritz von der Schulenburg (Architect: Nico Rensch) The Interior Archive; **306–7** Kiloran Howard/ Homes & Gardens/Robert Harding Syndication; **308** Jerome Darblay; **309** Christophe Dugied (Stylist: J. Postic)/Marie Claire Maison; **310** *left* Paul Ryan/International Interiors; **310** *right* Paul Warchol; **310** *below* Ariadne; **311** *left* Nadia Mackenzie; **311** *right* Ariadne; **312** Ianthe Ruthven; **314** John Hall; **315** Todd Eberle; **316** Simon Brown/Homes & Gardens/ Robert Harding Syndication; **317** Hotze Eisma; **318–9** Christophe Dugied (Stylist: J.Postic)/Marie Claire Maison; **319** James Merrell/Country Homes & Interiors/Robert Harding Syndication; **320** Alexander van Berge; **321** MariePierre Morel (Stylist: C. Puech)/Marie Claire Maison; **322** Laura Ashley; **324** Tom Leighton/Wedding & Home/Robert Harding Syndication; **325** Henry Wilson (Ian Dew)/The Interior Archive; **326** Tom Leighton/Wedding & Home/Robert Harding Syndication; **327** Hotze Eisma; **328** Tim Beddow (Kelly Hoppen)/The Interior Archive; **329** Hotze Eisma/V.T. Wonen; **330–1** Marie-Pierre Morel (Stylist: M. Bayle)/Marie Claire Maison; **332** Christophe Dugied (Stylist: J. Postic)/ Marie Claire Maison; **333** Louis Gaillard (Stylist: C. Puech)/Marie Claire Maison; **334** Christophe Dugied (Stylist: J.Postic)/ Marie Claire Maison; **335** Simon McBride; **336** Simon Brown; **337** Simon Upton/ Options/Robert Harding Syndication; **338** Hotze Eisma; **339** Sandra Lane/Homes & Gardens/Robert Harding Syndication.

Authors' acknowledgments

Anoop Parikh

Many of the ideas in the Design and Detailing chapter were unashamedly stolen from the homes show-cased in magazines such as *Elle Decoration* (UK and USA editions), *Marie Claire Maison* (France) and *Martha Stewart Living* (USA). My greatest thanks therefore go to the many designers and home-owners featured during 1995 and 1996, and to the editors for producing such consistently inspiring titles.

Several books were also invaluable sources of practical information on materials and construction. These were Terence Conran's *The Essential House Book*, Albert Jackson and David Day's *How to Store Just About Anything*, and *The Reader's Digest Complete Guide to DIY* – my thanks to them all. The shops and manufacturers mentioned in the list of suppliers were a mine of useful product and technical information, but I am particularly grateful to The Newson Group, and to the Department of the Environment's Energy Efficiency Office for their useful leaflets on energy-saving lighting.

Debora Robertson

At *Homes & Ideas*, I would like to thank my colleagues Virginia Hiller and Amanda Cochrane for their support, advice and good humour. And without the highly professional team at Conran Octopus, producing this chapter would have been far less enjoyable than it was. In particular I would like to thank Catriona Woodburn, whose calm demeanour, persistence and attention to detail are truly awe inspiring.

Thomas Lane

With thanks to all the individuals and companies who gave me their help while I was researching the finer points of flooring, and in particular to Adrian Smart for his advice on tiling. With thanks to Joanna for her patience and support, and all the staff at Conran Octopus.

Elizabeth Hilliard

I would like to thank: Felicity Bryan and Michele Topham, Georgina Cardew, Karen Hill, William Selka, Jan Walker, and Deborah Walter.

Melanie Paine

Heartfelt thanks to my colleague Joanne Outram for all her hard work and for holding the fort so admirably whilst I was working on the book.